# 1314: The Year of Bannockburn

# 1314: The Year of Bannockburn

### Callum Watson

Pen & Sword
**MILITARY**
AN IMPRINT OF PEN & SWORD BOOKS LTD.
YORKSHIRE – PHILADELPHIA

First published in Great Britain in 2024 by
Pen & Sword Military
An imprint of
Pen & Sword Books Ltd
Yorkshire - Philadelphia

Copyright © Callum Watson, 2024

ISBN 978 1 39903 518 7

The right of Callum Watson to be identified as the Author of this work has been asserted by him in accordance with the Copyright, Designs and Patents Act 1988.

A CIP catalogue record for this book is available from the British Library.

All rights reserved. No part of this book may be reproduced or transmitted in any form or by any means, electronic or mechanical, including photocopying, recording or by any information storage and retrieval system, without permission from the Publisher in writing.

Typeset in INDIA by IMPEC eSolutions
Printed and bound in England by CPI (UK) Ltd.

Pen & Sword Books Ltd. incorporates the Imprints of Pen & Sword Archaeology, Atlas, Aviation, Battleground, Discovery, Family History, History, Maritime, Military, Naval, Politics, Railways, Select, Transport, True Crime, Fiction, Frontline Books, Leo Cooper, Praetorian Press, Seaforth Publishing, Wharncliffe and White Owl.

For a complete list of Pen & Sword titles please contact

PEN & SWORD BOOKS LIMITED
47 Church Street, Barnsley, South Yorkshire, S70 2AS, England
E-mail: enquiries@pen-and-sword.co.uk
Website: www.pen-and-sword.co.uk

or

PEN AND SWORD BOOKS
1950 Lawrence Rd, Havertown, PA 19083, USA
E-mail: uspen-and-sword@casematepublishers.com
Website: www.penandswordbooks.com

# Contents

*Acknowledgments* — vii
*Abbreviations* — viii
*Introduction: The Road to Bannockburn* — 1

**Chapter 1**  'They Pray the King for Redress' — 14
First Steps on the Road to War, October to December 1313.

**Chapter 2**  Starting Slow is Still a Start — 28
Scottish Reaction and English Preparations, December 1313 to February 1314

**Chapter 3**  Building Momentum
Mounting English Preparations and Continuing Scottish Disruption, February to March 1314 — 53

**Chapter 4**  On the Road
Edward Travels North and the Scots Counterattack, April to May 1314 — 80

**Chapter 5**  'To Reskew Strevillyne with Bataill' — 97
The Deal with the Stirling Garrison, Scottish Preparations, and the Final March to Bannockburn, May to June 1314

**Chapter 6**  'Let the Retaliation of Scotland Depend on Her Foot-Soldiers': — 135
The Battle of Bannockburn, 23 to 24 June 1314

**Chapter 7**  'Eftre the Gret Journé' — 164
The Aftermath of Bannockburn, June to October 1314

**Chapter 8**  'King Robert Now Wes Wele at Hycht' — 185
The Benefits of Bannockburn, October to November 1314

*Appendix: Image Descriptions* — 203
*Bibliography* — 207
*Notes* — 217
*Index* — 255

In memory of Dennis Aubrey

# Acknowledgments

My greatest academic debt is undoubtedly to Professor Steve Boardman of the University of Edinburgh. His passion, enthusiasm, and humour were what first drew me into studying Scottish medieval history way back in my first year at university, and his insight and understanding were invaluable as a PhD supervisor. I would also like to extend my thanks to Professor Judith Green, whose encouragement played a huge role in my decision to pursue the PhD.

It would be remiss of me not to acknowledge my colleagues at the Battle of Bannockburn Visitor Centre. In particular, I owe a great debt of gratitude to Scott McMaster for giving me the opportunity to work there in the first place. I would also like to extend special thanks to Gillian Fraser, the best work bestie I could ask for. And perhaps most importantly, I wish to thank the many visitors whose inventive and frequently surprising questions have helped refine many of the ideas and arguments explored in this book.

In a personal context, I could not fail to show my gratitude to Doctor Lauren Chochinov for all of our adventures over the years. Many thanks too to Doctor Danielle Howarth and Bianca Maggs for their unflinching faith in my ability to complete this project on time. I am deeply indebted to Alistair, Kirsten, Paul, and Sammy, who made sure I still had a social life alongside the writing process. Much gratitude is also due to Tom and Allie for trusting me with their special day and giving me something to look forward to once the writing was over. I wish to extend my most profound gratitude to my parents, Denise and Trevor, for the moral and financial support they have provided to me. Their encouragement and indulgence of my passion for history has been absolutely integral to the development of this book. Last but most assuredly not least, I wish to thank my late grandfather Dennis for first inspiring my love of history with the stories he told me as a child. This book is dedicated to him.

# Abbreviations

*Anglo-Scottish Relations*
Stones, E. L. G. (ed) *Anglo-Scottish Relations, 1174–1328: Some Selected Documents* (London, 1965).

*Ann. Connacht*
Freeman, A. M. (ed) *The Annals of Connacht* (Dublin, 1944).

*Ann. Inisfallen*
Airt, S. Mac. (ed) *The Annals of Inisfallen* (Dublin, 1951).

*Ann. Londoniensis*
Stubbs, W. (ed) *Chronicles of the Reigns of Edward I and Edward II*, Rolls Series, vol. 76:1 (London, 1882).

*Cal. Chancery Warrants*
*Calendar of Chancery Warrants. Vol. I, Hen. III–Edw. II.* (London: HMSO, 1920).

*Cal. Close Rolls*
Maxwell-Lyte, H. C. (ed) *Calendar of Close Rolls, Edward II: Volume 2, 1313–1318* (London: HMSO, 1893).

*Cal. Inq. P.M.*
*Calendar of Inquisitions Post-mortem and Other Analogous Documents Preserved in the Public Records Office, Edward I*, vol. 4. (London: HMSO, 1912).

*Cal. Patent Rolls*
*Calendar of Patent Rolls, Edward II*, 5 vols. (London: HMSO, 1894–1904).

*CDS*
Bain, J. (ed) *Calendar of Documents Relating to Scotland*, 5 vols. (Edinburgh, 1881–1888).

*Chron. Baker*
Preest, D. (ed and trans) *The Chronicle of Geoffrey Le Baker of Swinbrook* (Woodbridge: Boydell, 2012).

*Chron. Boece*
Boece, H., *The Chronicles of Scotland*, ed. R. Chambers and E. Batho (Edinburgh: Scottish Text Society, 1938–1941).

*Chron. Bower*
Bower, W. *Scotichronicon*, ed. D. E. R. Watt, et al., 9 vols. (Aberdeen, 1987–1999).

*Chron. Guisborough*
Rothwell, H. (ed) *Chronicle of Walter of Guisborough* (Camden Society: London, 1989).

*Chron. Fordun*
Skene, W. F. (ed) *Johannis de Fordun, Chronica Gentis Scotorum*, 2 vols. (Edinburgh, 1871–1872).

*Chron. Lanercost*
Maxwell, H. (ed) *The Chronicle of Lanercost, 1272–1346* (Glasgow, 1913).

*Chron. Le Bel*
Bryant, N. (trans) *The True Chronicles of Jean Le Bel, 1290–1360* (Woodbridge: Boydell & Brewer, 2015).

*Chron. Rishanger*
Riley, H. T. (ed) *William of Rishanger, Chronica et Annales*, Rolls Series (London, 1865).

*Chron. Trivet (Cont.)*
Trivet, N., *Nicolai Triveti Annalium Continuatio* (Oxonii: E Theatro Sheldoniano, 1722).

*Chron, Trokelowe*
Riley, H. T. (ed) *Johannes de Trokelowe and Henrici de Blandeford, Chronica et Annales*, Rolls Series (London: 1866).

*Chron. Wyntoun*
Amours, F. (ed) Andrew of Wyntoun, *The Original Chronicle of Andrew of Wyntoun*, 6 vols. (Edinburgh: Scottish Text Society, 1903–1914).

ER
Stuart, J., et al. (eds) *The Exchequer Rolls of Scotland*, 23 vols. (Edinburgh, 1878–1908).

*Foedera*
Rymer, T. (ed) *Foedera, Conventiones, Litterae et Cuiuscunque Generis Acta Publica*, 20 vols. (London, 1704–1735).

*Historia Anglicana*
Riley, H. T. (ed) *Thomae Walsingham, quondam monachi S. Albani, Historia Anglicana*, vol. 1, (London, 1863).

*Historiae Dunelmensis*
Raine, J. (ed) *Historiae Dunelmensis Scriptores Tres* (London, 1839).

*Instrumenta Publica*
Thomson, T. (ed) *Instrumenta publica, sive processus super fidelitatibus et homagiis Scotorum domino regi Angliae factis, A.D. MCCXCI–MCCXCVI* (Edinburgh: Bannatyne Club, 1768–1852).

*Itinerary*
Hallam, E., *The Itinerary of Edward II and his Household, 1307–1328* (London, 1984).

*Menteith*
Fraser, W., *The Red Book of Menteith*, 2 vols. (Edinburgh, 1880).

*MRH: Scotland*
Cowan, I. B. & Easson, D. E. *Medieval Religious Houses: Scotland*, 2nd ed. (London, 1976).

*Northern Registers*
Raine, J. *Historical Papers and Letters from the Northern Register* (London, 1873).

*ODNB*
*Oxford Dictionary of National Biography*, www.oxforddnb.com.

*Paisley Registrum*
Innes, C. (ed) *Registrum Monasterii de Passalet* (Glasgow: Maitland Club, 1832).

Palgrave, *Docs.*
Palgrave, F. (ed) *Documents and Records illustrating the History of Scotland* (London, 1837).

*Parl. Writs*
Palgrave, F. (ed) *Parliamentary Writs and Writs of Military Summons*, 2 vols. (London, 1827–1834).

*PROME*
Given-Wilson, C., et al. (eds) *Parliament Rolls of Medieval England* (Woodbridge, 2005), *British History Online*, www.british-history.ac.uk/no-series/parliament-rolls-medieval.

*RMS*
Thomson, J. M. & Paul, J. B. (eds) *Registrum Magni Sigilii Regum Scotorum*, 11 vols. (Edinburgh, 1882–1914).

*Rot. Scot.*
Macpherson, D. (ed) *Rotuli Scotiae in Turri Londinensi et in Domo Capitulari Westmonasteriensi Asservati*, 2 vols. (London, 1814–1819).

*RPD*
Hardy, T. D. (ed) *Registrum Palatinum Dunelmense: The register of Richard de Kellawe, lord palatine and bishop of Durham, 1311–16, Volume 1* (London, 1873).

*RPS*
Brown, K. M., et al. (eds) *The Records of the Parliaments of Scotland to 1707* (St Andrews, 2008), www.rps.ac.uk.

*RRS*
Duncan, A. A. M. (ed) *Regesta Regum Scottorum, v: The Acts of Robert I, 1306–29* (Edinburgh, 1986).

*Scalacronica*
King, A. (ed) *Sir Thomas Gray: Scalacronica (1272–1363)* (Surtees Society, 209: 2005).

Stevenson, *Docs.*
Stevenson, J. (ed), *Documents Illustrative of the History of Scotland*, 2 vols. (Edinburgh, 1870).

xii   1314: The Year of Bannockburn

Map 1. Key places referenced in the text.

*Introduction*

# The Road to Bannockburn

The Battle of Bannockburn has long been celebrated as one of the most influential moments in Scottish history. The fighting that took place on 23 and 24 June 1314 has been explored in a number of works, both scholarly and popular.[1] It is frequently presented as a stirring tale of how a small but committed and well-organized militia army can overcome a larger, better-resourced foe; it is also described as a crucial early turning point in the long, bitter, and destructive conflicts between Scotland and in England in the late medieval and early modern period. Modern scholarship has tended to offer a more restrained interpretation of events, casting doubt on how truly decisive the event was while still acknowledging the role that the Scots' discipline, superior tactics, and shrewd leadership played in securing a favourable outcome. The reigns of Robert I of Scotland and Edward II of England, the two kings who led the opposing armies into battle in 1314, have also been subject to repeated examination.[2] The former has been cast variously as patriotic hero, talented statesman, and ambitious (and often unscrupulous) opportunist. The latter's reputation has often been dismissed as an incompetent ruler and an inept war leader, with even sympathetic writers highlighting his domestic difficulties when seeking to explain the events of 1314.

However, the immediate context of the battle has received only cursory attention, even in otherwise in-depth studies of the event. This book seeks to redress this omission by looking in detail at the preparations that both sides undertook in the months leading up to the battle, and the reactions of the two sides in the months that followed. It will offer a detailed study of the immediate context of the battle, seeking to explain why the English chose 1314 to invade, how both sides prepared, and why King Robert ultimately chose to modify his preferred guerrilla strategy to sanction open confrontation with the invading army. By presenting a chronological exploration of the events of 1314, this book will seek to explain how the outlooks, aims, and perspectives of the two sides developed over the course of the year, where previous analyses have either taken for granted that the Scots were seeking open battle from the outset or else made the decision to fight on the spur of the moment in June 1314. The book will also consider the possible ill health of King Robert in late 1313 and early 1314 and the impact this may have had on the activities of both the Scots and the English. The possibility that the king suffered a bout of illness during this period has been noted in passing in other works but never adequately factored into how this likely influenced the events of 1314. Yet the state of the king's health in the months leading up to the battle would have had an enormous impact on the leadership of the Scots during this crucial period, shaping the Scottish response to the threatened invasion. It thus sheds fresh light on how events unfolded.

The work will begin by considering the state of affairs in Scotland in October and November 1313 and how this influenced Edward II's decision to invade Scotland in 1314. It will also attempt to reconstruct the initial Scottish response to this threat. This will draw on evidence not only from Edward's earlier invasion of Scotland in 1310–11 and the activities of the Scots in the early months of 1314, but also on general Scottish military practice during the reign of Robert I. The preparations made by the English crown for the proposed campaign will receive detailed examination and will be considered alongside Scottish military activities in the months leading up to the battle in an effort to understand how these interacted. Detailed consideration will be given to what we know about the siege of Stirling itself and the resultant deal made between the Scots and the garrison there. This will serve to highlight how this development fundamentally altered the expectations of both sides and placed them inexorably on the path to direct confrontation at Bannockburn. The battle itself will receive close examination, taking into account how Bruce's preparations in the weeks before the event and his inventive use of the landscape secured victory for the Scots. The book will conclude by exploring the immediate fallout of the battle during the remainder of 1314. This will cover efforts by the English crown to consolidate the defences of northern England against renewed Scottish raiding, the experience of relatives of Englishmen killed or captured at the battle, and the cautious attempts at diplomacy – including arrangements made for the exchange of prisoners – undertaken in the months that followed. Finally, the work will examine the benefits of Bannockburn from a Scottish perspective and the limitations of Bruce's achievement. In particular, we will consider how King Robert's parliament at Cambuskenneth Abbey in November 1314 and the gradual redistribution of lands that this facilitated shaped the history of Scotland for the remainder of the fourteenth century.

Before focusing in on the events of the year in question, however, some context for the events of the battle will be valuable. By November 1313, the war between Scotland and England had dragged on intermittently for more than seventeen years, so an in-depth examination of the whole conflict is impractical. Instead, a summary of the experience of the two kings whose activities will be the primary focus of this study will serve to clarify their respective outlooks and attitudes in the months leading up to the battle.

Ostensibly, the origins of the war can be traced to the succession crisis precipitated by the sudden, untimely death of King Alexander III of Scotland in March 1286. However, the Scottish political community as a whole responded swiftly and decisively to the initial crisis, appointing a council of six (perhaps originally seven) guardians to govern the kingdom in the absence of an adult monarch.[3] The guardians also arranged for Margaret, Alexander's granddaughter and only surviving descendant, to be dispatched from Norway, recruiting the assistance of the late king's brother-in-law King Edward I of England to facilitate the process. A further attempt at stabilizing the situation was made with the betrothal of Margaret to Edward I's son and namesake, the boy who as a man would lead the English to defeat at Bannockburn in 1314.[4] Far from simply being a case of general dynastic uncertainty then, the 'crisis' that gripped Scotland in late thirteenth century was, to a significant extent, caused by the ambitions of the Bruces.

Lords of Annandale since the twelfth century and earls of Carrick since the marriage of the future King Robert's father to Marjory c.1271, the Bruces had been a formidable – though hardly dominant – force in Scottish politics during Alexander's reign. Their lands in south-western Scotland were situated on the boundary between the predominantly Gaelic-speaking west coast and the rest of Scotland, where French remained the primary language of the nobility, Latin was the chief administrative language, and 'Inglis' (i.e., Older Scots) was emerging as the vernacular. As a result, the future King Robert would have grown up in a multi-lingual and multi-cultural environment. This would equip him with a remarkable ability to appeal to individuals across various cultural divides, an ability that would serve him particularly well during his troubled kingship, as we shall see. The Bruces also boasted a scattered collection of lands in England and connections to the English crown through service in war and diplomacy. The phrasing of the so-called 'Turnberry Band', ratified in September 1286 barely six months after Alexander's death, subtly hints that even then the family nursed hopes of making a future bid for the kingship in the wake of King Alexander's death.[5] Margaret's death in 1290, before she had managed to set foot on Scottish soil, enflamed these ambitions further.

The Bruces certainly had a strong claim to the kingship through Robert I's great-grandfather Robert (IV), lord of Annandale, who had married Isabella, second daughter of David, earl of Huntingdon (d.1219), brother of King William 'the Lion' (r.1165–1214). This claim was not however as strong as that of John Balliol, lord of Barnard Castle in England and heir to the lordship of Galloway in Scotland, whose grandfather had married Earl David's *eldest* daughter Margaret. The unwillingness of the Bruces to accept this threatened what stability the guardians had been able to establish and provided a pretext for English involvement in mediating the dispute – the 'Great Cause of 1291–2'. This in turn would be exploited by the English crown to interfere in Scottish affairs in the years that followed, ultimately leading to the outbreak of war.

It is in the failure of the Bruce cause in the 'Great Cause' that the future King Robert first made his mark on events. As the legal proceedings wound down and it became clear that the Bruces' increasingly desperate arguments were not having the desired effect, the future king's grandfather Robert (V) 'the Competitor' resigned his claim to the kingship onto his son, Robert (VI), who in turn resigned the earldom of Carrick in favour of 'our' Robert (VII). This seemingly obtuse bit of horse-trading was intended to ensure that the person in whom the Bruce claim to the throne was invested – Robert (VI) – would not have to pay homage to Balliol for any lands in Scotland. Even in defeat the Bruces still hoped to again press their claim to the kingship within King Robert's father's lifetime. But more importantly in the long term, possession of Carrick gave the future king his earliest known experience of managing extensive landed interests and political networks. It also gave him a greater degree of flexibility and independence of action in the years that followed.

This is not to say that the future king immediately distinguished himself in 'patriotic' service. In fact, when the English invaded in 1296, he likely supported them alongside his father, apparently hoping that Edward I would now replace King John with a Bruce candidate. When this failed to materialize, however, and popular unrest against the administration imposed by the English began in

1297, the younger Bruce was to be found among the Scottish lords offering open resistance to the new regime. It has been suggested that this was the cause of some dissension among the Bruce kindred, with Bruce's father (and probably his brothers as well) remaining in English allegiance during this time.[6] Of course, service in defence of the realm furthered Bruce's royal ambitions, since it promised the opportunity to convince the wider political community of his suitably for the kingship. But Dr Michael Penman has reasonably suggested that the future king's decision may also have reflected a genuine sense of patriotism influenced by a closeness with Bishop Robert Wishart of Glasgow, who was certainly one of the most vociferous proponents of Scottish independence in the early stages of the conflict and does seem to have enjoyed close and positive relations with Bruce.[7]

It was in the company of Bishop Wishart and another magnate from the south-west coast, James the Steward, that Bruce made a brief but very public demonstration against the English administration at Irvine in July 1297. The trio was soon forced into a rather embarrassing climbdown by an English armed force jointly led by northern barons Robert Clifford, who would later be present at Bannockburn, and Henry Percy. This capitulation was no doubt motivated in part by memories of the overwhelming military might demonstrated by the English in the previous year, but also perhaps by a recognition that the three men lacked widespread support among the Scottish political community at this point. Nevertheless, the victory of William Wallace and Andrew Murray at Stirling Bridge in September 1297 – an event in which Bruce played no part – demonstrated that resistance to the English was not futile after all, while Wallace's defeat at Falkirk in July 1298 – from which Bruce was again absent – cleared the way for Bruce to make his presence felt at the heart of Scottish politics.

After Falkirk, Bruce was appointed joint-guardian alongside John Comyn, lord of Badenoch. This gave him his earliest experience at government and, theoretically at least, provided an opportunity to demonstrate his administrative capacities to the wider community. However, the experience was no doubt soured by his relationship with his co-guardian. Comyn was John Balliol's nephew and, since his uncle had been taken prisoner in 1296, the *de facto* leader of the Balliol faction in Scotland. Their joint appointment had likely been intended to balance the interests of the competing factions and thus lessen tensions between them, but it had the opposite effect. There is no single better illustration of this point than during an assembly at Peebles in August 1299 which ended in a brawl between the two guardians![8] Bruce's tenure as guardian may have actually undermined his reputation with certain sections of the community, and by 1300 he had been replaced in the office.

It was around this time that the future King Edward II had his earliest impact on events in Scotland. Roughly ten years Bruce's junior, Edward 'of Caernarfon', as he was frequently styled, was an athletic young man, though he may have been discouraged from participating in typical knightly pursuits like tourneying due to fears over the impact his injury or death in such an activity might mean for the future of the English royal dynasty.[9] Nevertheless, he gained his first experience of campaigning in Scotland in 1301, when he was given responsibility for breaking Scottish military power in the south-west, which his father hoped would ensure he received 'the chief honour of taming the pride of the Scots'.[10] Though he was unsuccessful in this aim, his military activities in 1301 did play a significant role in encouraging Robert Bruce's submission to the English in the following year.

The future King Robert's 'defection' from the 'patriotic' cause in 1302 was motivated by a number of factors. On a basic, material level, one of the few tangible successes of Prince Edward's campaign through the south-west in 1301 had been the capture of Turnberry Castle, the *caput* (i.e., administrative centre) of Bruce's earldom of Carrick. Thus, an accommodation with the English crown would be necessary if Bruce was to enjoy continued physical possession of his most lucrative estates. Moreover, the cooling climate at the end of the thirteenth and the beginning of the fourteenth centuries may have made access to supplies through English-held towns in southern Scotland too tempting to resist.[11] Submission to the English crown also brought with it marriage to Elizabeth de Burgh, daughter of Edward I's chief Irish ally Richard de Burgh, earl of Ulster, which also expanded Bruce's political connections across the Irish Sea. Most importantly of all, by early 1302 Bruce was, somewhat ironically, at risk of becoming a victim of the Scots' success. While the English remained unable to neutralize Scottish military capacity, both the Papacy and King Philippe IV of France were growing increasingly receptive to Scottish requests for support in their ongoing struggle against their southern neighbour. At the time of Bruce's submission, rumours were apparently circulating that King Philippe might soon return Balliol – who had been in effective French custody since late 1301 – to Scotland through direct French military intervention. Such an outcome would decisively end Bruce's hopes of securing the kingship for himself. In those circumstances, securing his interests as a private lord would take priority while he watched and waited for a more promising situation to arise. As always, Bruce's actions make the most sense when viewed through the lens of his ambition to be recognized as king.

Bruce's subsequent faithful but unremarkable service to the English crown over the following two years can hardly be said to have contributed to creating the conditions in which he could make his next bid for power. Rather, Edward I, freed from French diplomatic pressure following the unexpected defeat of a French royal host by a Flemish militia army at Courtrai in July 1302, led an astonishingly effective sustained campaign into Scotland over the course of 1303 to 1304. Accompanied throughout by his son Edward of Caernarfon, the English king oversaw the piecemeal reoccupation of key areas of the kingdom, extracting submissions from leading members of the community as he went. The campaign culminated in the siege of Stirling Castle in July 1304, at which not only Edward of Caernarfon but also Robert Bruce, earl of Carrick, was present. Stirling would remain in English hands until these two men fought for it again, this time on opposite sides, in June 1314.

The seemingly final collapse of Scottish resistance in 1304 was, when viewed from Bruce's perspective, simply the collapse of the Balliol faction as natural leaders of the community. It merely cleared a space for him to reassert himself as an alternate focus of authority within the kingdom. This was particularly true as it became clear that the English had learned the lessons of 1296 to 1297, when they had sought to insert English personnel into key positions in the Scottish government. After 1304, the English crown instead sought to assimilate Comyn and his allies into the new regime.[12] Had it been given time to fully embed and consolidate its position, this might have given the administration a veneer of legitimacy that the earlier one had lacked.[13] It simultaneously muscled Bruce and his allies out of the most influential offices in the day-to-day government of the realm while increasingly associating his rivals among the Balliol-Comyn Scots with the English crown.

Bruce may now have found himself rapidly accruing new allies. The Scottish clergy had been the chief ideologues of independence since the death of Alexander III, largely to protect the Scottish Church's status as a 'special daughter' of Rome. Scotland's leading churchmen were unlikely to see much appeal in Comyn's approach, which appears to have been to wait out Edward I – who was aged and increasingly unwell by this point – and hope to reassert his uncle's rights at some future juncture. By comparison, Bruce, ambitious and willing to bend legal and social convention in his quest for power, may have begun to present a more promising figure, even in spite of his previous vacillation. Thus, on 11 June 1304, even as Stirling was encircled, Robert Bruce and William Lamberton, bishop of St Andrews, met at nearby Cambuskenneth Abbey to ratify a bond of mutual friendship.[14] Though carefully worded to avoid any obviously treasonous implications, it is apparent that this pact was intended to secure the bishop's tacit support for Bruce's pursuit of his kingly ambitions in the future. It is likely that over the next two years, comparable arrangements were made with other influential members of the community, both clerical and secular, in an effort to establish political networks that would help him to consolidate his position when he made his bid for power.

By early 1306, Bruce was apparently ready to approach Comyn about the preparations he had been making. Much ink has been spilled on the infamous meeting between the two men at Greyfriars Kirk in Dumfries on 10 February 1306, but debate persists on almost every element of the incident.[15] Yet the notion that Bruce may have taken this opportunity to disclose at least a sense of his plans to his rival and offer him the chance to play a part in them is suggested by the claims of early Scottish writers that an 'indenture' of some kind existed between the two men, which Comyn broke, leading to their deadly confrontation.[16] Of course, if Bruce did make such an offer to Comyn and Comyn refused to comply – which, given their history, he almost certainly would – then Bruce could not let him leave Greyfriars alive. He would after all have tipped his hand to his hated rival, who would surely then use this knowledge to shatter Bruce's already shaky relationship with the English crown. Even sympathetic writers like John Barbour, Archdeacon of Aberdeen, admit that Bruce 'mysdyd' in killing his rival in a church.[17] But there can be little doubt that that the removal of his most influential and experienced domestic rival facilitated the rise of King Robert in the long run.

Indeed, in the months that immediately followed the killing of Comyn, Bruce's prospects looked remarkably promising. Bishop Wishart absolved him of any sin committed – lessening the domestic impact of the sentence of excommunication passed against him by Pope Clement V – in return for assurances that the interests of the Scottish clergy would be well represented in Bruce's government. The community of the realm split along largely predictable lines based on their previous association with the long-standing Comyn and Bruce factions. Bruce was even able to lure Isabella, wife of the Comyn earl of Buchan, to fulfil her family's traditional role in placing a circlet of gold on the new king's head at his inauguration at Scone on 25 March.[18] The new king's men also set to work carving out a zone of territorial control from Perthshire across to the south-west, apparently to provide Bruce with an escape route into friendly territory in the event of sustained English military intervention.[19] Overall, the impression given was that he was ready to, as a contemporary English commentator put it, 'defend himself with the longest stick that he had.'[20]

It was King Robert's defeat at the Battle of Methven at the hands of the soon-to-be earl of Pembroke, Aymer de Valence, in June, followed by the scattering of his remaining forces by John Macdougall of Argyll at Tyndrum some weeks later, that turned his first year as king into a shocking disaster. Further troubles were heaped on the king when his brother (and perhaps also his nearest male relative) Neil was captured by Kildrummy Castle and subsequently executed. Moreover, his queen, Elizabeth; daughter from his first marriage, Marjory; sisters Christian and Mary; and ally, Isabella, countess of Buchan, were overtaken and captured at Tain in Ross and sent to indefinite imprisonment in England. The royal women were most likely on their way to take shelter with another of the king's sisters, Isabella, in Norway, but their capture created a serious sense of dynastic uncertainty for the Bruce regime that would continue to haunt it even in the build-up to Bannockburn. Military defeat and personal catastrophe thus reduced Bruce to the status of an outlaw in his own kingdom within six months of his inauguration.

Far from hiding in caves or communing with spiders, however, Bruce most likely spent the winter of 1306 to 1307 travelling around the western Highlands and Hebrides appealing to his allies in the region for assistance in rebuilding his position as king. His familiarity with the culture of the *Gàidhealtachd*, gained during his youth in Carrick, would have been crucial to his success in this. Bruce was able to exploit local rivalries to muster newfound support for his kingship, and in early 1307 he returned to the mainland – possibly via the Isle of Arran, according to Barbour – at the head of a mostly Gaelic-speaking armed force augmented by his erstwhile tenants in the region. This period was not without further setbacks, with two more of his brothers – Alexander and Thomas – being captured and executed while attempting a separate landing in Galloway. Early attempts to secure military gains against local English forces initially proved difficult, but in May, Bruce finally succeeded in driving off an armed force led by Valence near Loudoun Hill in Ayrshire. Though little more than a minor tactical victory, Loudoun Hill was the first time in more than a decade of intermittent conflict in which a king of Scots had taken to the battlefield and emerged victorious. This singled Bruce out as a different prospect to previous Scottish leaders, both to the Scottish political community and to his English opponents.[21]

The Bruce received another boost on 7 July 1307 when Edward I died at Burgh-on-Sands on the Cumbrian coast. The English king had been on his way into Scotland with an army intended to crush this latest challenge to English authority. Whether or not the fledgling Bruce regime could have endured direct royal intervention in Scotland at this early stage, King Robert was no doubt grateful at never having to find out. Edward of Caernarfon inherited both the kingdom and the war as Edward II, but he initially showed little enthusiasm for the latter, continuing the campaign only as far as Dumfries before returning southward. This indifference was in part reinforced by the attitude of the English political community, which had grown increasingly frustrated with the financial burden and administrative disruptions of a seemingly never-ending conflict. As early as January 1308, when Edward married Isabella, daughter of Philippe IV of France, at Boulogne, a group of his leading subjects secretly agreed to pressure the king to enact a package of reforms for the governance of the realm. Among those who ratified the Boulogne agreement were future Bannockburn veterans, such as Aymer de Valence, earl of Pembroke, and Humphrey de Bohun, earl of Hereford.

Demands for reform would only grow stronger in the years that followed. While some of this stemmed from wider problems relating to war and the royal finances with origins in his father's reign, King Edward did not help matters by displaying favouritism to his close familiars. Favouritism was a cardinal sin for a medieval king, whose primary public function was to see that patronage was fairly distributed among his subjects. One of Edward's favourites in particular, Piers Gaveston, was a source of considerable controversy. Gaveston compounded Edward's problems by personally aggravating a great many English magnates, and he found himself driven into exile three times between 1307 (before Edward even became king) and 1311.

In the meantime, Edward's disinterest in Scottish affairs gave Bruce space to concentrate on his domestic opponents. He first focussed his attention on the north, where direct English intervention was more difficult anyway. During late

1307, Bruce conducted a devastating campaign through the region, beginning by targeting the interests of William, earl of Ross – who had been responsible for the capture of the royal women in 1306 – in the north-west before moving eastwards, reducing castles as he went. This strategy of seizing the castles and strong places of the kingdom and 'slighting' them so that they could not be held against him again would become standard policy during his reign and would play a crucial role in the build-up to Bannockburn, as we will see in the chapters that follow. In the winter of 1307 to 1308, King Robert also suffered the first of several bouts of what appears to have been the same illness that would eventually kill him in 1329, another theme that we will revisit throughout this study.

By the spring of 1308, Bruce had recovered sufficiently to resume his military activities in the north. At Inverurie, King Robert defeated the remaining leaders of the Comyn faction and forced them to flee Scotland. The resulting 'herschip' ('harrying') of Buchan by King Robert and his followers was still remembered bitterly by the locals as late as the 1370s.[22] Sometime afterwards, the king also defeated the Macdougalls in the Pass of Brander in Argyll, not far from where they had ambushed and defeated him in 1306. By March 1309, King Robert felt confident enough to hold a parliament at St Andrews. This was a striking demonstration of the king's confidence in his ability to effectively administer the realm. Bruce also used the occasion to launch a diplomatic offensive intended to ingratiate himself with the king of France and the pope, with whom he had been formally reconciled in 1308.[23] The surviving documents from the parliament also indicate that Bruce had made speculative grants of lordships in the south to his more formidable war leaders, such as his brother Edward Bruce, now lord of Galloway, and his nephew Thomas Randolph, now lord of Nithsdale. These grants were no doubt intended to encourage these men to seek to pacify these regions on behalf of their king.

A combination of Bruce's newfound confidence, the collapse of 'native' resistance to King Robert, and a desire to extricate himself from his own domestic problems, led Edward II to mount an invasion of Scotland in 1310. His army did not advance far north, however, and confined its activities to areas still under English control. However, Edward remained at Berwick until the following July, trying to maintain what pressure he could on the Bruce Scots. King Robert, on the other hand, eschewed open confrontation, preferring instead to conserve his military strength and harass the English forces as and when opportunities presented themselves. This proved to be remarkably effective, and no doubt influenced King Robert's attitude concerning best practice for dealing with subsequent English invasions, as we will examine in detail.

On returning to England, King Edward was presented with the Ordinances, no fewer than forty-one recommendations for reform drawn up by a council of disgruntled lords in his absence. These reflected the heavy financial burdens placed on the English nobility by the continuing war in Scotland but also singled out Gaveston for exile 'as the evident enemy of the king and of his people'.[24] In the circumstances, Edward had no choice but to accept the Ordinances, but he quickly turned to the pope to help him annul them as an affront to his sovereignty. By January 1312, Gaveston was back in England, provoking a stern response from the Ordainers.[25] The earls of Pembroke and Surrey, both of whom were moderate figures within the baronial opposition to King Edward, were dispatched to apprehend Gaveston.

According to one of Edward's own courtiers, the English king was so desperate to protect his familiar that he offered to recognize Bruce's rights as king in return for him sheltering Gaveston, though King Robert apparently rebuked him.[26] The aim of this writer may simply have been to highlight the Scottish king's intransigence, since it seems unlikely that Bruce would have dismissed the opportunity to fulfil his primary goal out of hand. The fact that Edward and Gaveston spent the crisis period in northern England, and the fact that northern barons Clifford and Percy – the same men who had confronted Bruce at Irvine in 1297 – were mobilized to prevent King Edward from communicating with Scotland may also lend credence to the suggestion that the desperate English king at least contemplated extending such an offer to Bruce.

In the event, Gaveston found himself besieged at Scarborough Castle in May 1312 and surrendered himself into Pembroke's custody. However, on 10 June, as he was being transported south, Gaveston was seized by Guy Beauchamp, earl of Warwick, at Deddington in Oxfordshire. Nine days later, he was summarily executed on Blacklow Hill in Warwickshire, with the approval of a party of barons headed by King Edward's own cousin – and chief political opponent – Thomas, earl of Lancaster. This shocking act, while undoubtedly personally upsetting for Edward, ironically served to galvanize support for the crown, perhaps more so than had been the case since Edward acceded to the throne. While few among the political community of England had any affection for Gaveston, many felt deeply uncomfortable with the extrajudicial manner of his death. This led to a marked swing of moderate opinion away from the baronial rebels in favour of King Edward.[27] The circumstances of Gaveston's death also created deep-seated personal enmity between the king and those responsible, but even his most committed domestic opponents were pressured into publicly making their peace with the king over the course of 1313. Edward's confidence was no doubt also boosted by the birth of his first son, the future Edward III, in November 1312.

King Robert's fortunes too had gone from strength to strength since weathering the English invasion of 1310 to 1311. In October 1312, he had concluded a treaty with representatives of King Håkon V of Norway at Inverness. Though it imposed significant financial commitments on the Bruce regime, the treaty represented the earliest formal recognition by a foreign ruler that King Robert was the figure to negotiate with if one had dealings in the Scottish realm. This kind of acknowledgement was probably worth the financial concessions, and his willingness to make this kind of trade-off is illustrative of Bruce's aptitude for statesmanship. Bruce's military successes continued apace as well. Following an unsuccessful attempt to seize Berwick-upon-Tweed in December 1312, Bruce moved his forces swiftly north to capture Perth in January 1313. The king himself is credited with personally leading the assault on the town in this case.[28] The fall of Dumfries in February extended Bruce control further into the south-west, while in the summer King Robert personally took possession of the Isle of Man. Man occupied a strategically significant position in the Irish Sea that meant it might be used as a base from which to trouble English shipping in the Irish Sea and even strike at coastal targets in the west.

Thus, by the end of 1313, both kings had reason to consider themselves to be in the strongest position of their respective reigns. This confidence no doubt contributed to their approach to the war in 1314. For Edward, the seeming pacification of his domestic enemies likely influenced his decision to propose an invasion of Scotland which, if it led to a successful confrontation with Bruce, could consolidate the gains he had made in the wake of Gaveston's death. The expansion of Bruce's control over his kingdom had not been so great that it had convinced him to abandon his previous strategy of avoiding direct confrontation and frustrating English activities on a small scale. However, a general sense that the momentum of the war was moving in his direction may have inclined King Robert to be more aggressive than usual when the opportunity to give battle presented itself.

*Chapter 1*

# 'They Pray the King for Redress'

# First Steps on the Road to War, October to December 1313

## Security, Succession, and 'Seknes': The Situation in Scotland, October 1313

In October 1313, King Robert was to be found in Dundee, while King Edward was ensconced at Westminster. From these places, the two kings began down separate paths that would lead them both to their fateful confrontation at Bannockburn the following June. Yet, for the former at least, such a possibility would have been unthinkable at the time.

Bruce's priority in late 1313 seems to have been the consolidation of his domestic position. No doubt the recent conclusion of a truce until midsummer had encouraged him to turn his attention towards internal affairs.[1] The king's extant acts from October 1313 show that he was accompanied at Dundee by William Lamberton, bishop of St Andrews; Henry Cheyne, bishop of Aberdeen; David, bishop of Moray; John of Kininmund, bishop of Brechin; the king's brother, Edward Bruce; his nephews, Thomas Randolph, earl of Moray, and David Strathbogie, earl of Atholl (the latter now also lord constable of Scotland); his long-standing ally Malcolm, earl of Lennox; the hereditary marischal Sir Robert Keith; and 'lesser' lords Sir Gilbert Hay, Sir John Menteith of Arran, Sir Henry Sinclair, and Sir Alexander Menzies.[2] This was more than the king's usual entourage and suggests a large, formal gathering of a substantial part of the community of the realm, if not perhaps a full parliament.

Though the surviving *acta* from the Dundee assembly are hardly of national importance – being a grant of free alms to the Blackfriars of Inverness and another to the Blackfriars of Elgin, and a grant of the Forest of Stocket to the burghal community of Aberdeen – the main business of the meeting is hinted at in the witness lists. For in March 1313, when witnessing his brother's inspection of charters of William 'the Lion' and Alexander II, Edward Bruce was styled 'lord of Galloway'.[3] On 21 October, the younger Bruce brother was styled for the first time 'earl of Carrick'. This new title was almost certainly conferred in an effort to formally identify the king's younger brother as his *de facto* heir.

The earldom of Carrick had come into the possession of the Bruces through Robert and Edward's formidable mother, Marjory. Being one of the 'ancient' earldoms of Scotland, it immediately became the family's most valuable holding. Its value was not only in the status it conferred, though it did indeed raise them to the highest rank in the Scottish nobility. After the war broke out, Carrick had also provided the Bruces with a firm landed base from which to operate even in times of extreme difficulty, and a loyal tenantry, who by 1313 would be counted among some of the most experienced soldiers in the kingdom. Throughout the fourteenth and fifteenth centuries, the title 'earl of Carrick' would also become synonymous with the Scottish heir. Later in the reign, Bruce would confer the title on his own son David, would who in turn use the title to designate John Stewart of Kyle as his heir after 1368.[4] A charter granting the earldom to Edward Bruce survives, and although the grant merely offers the conventional justification for the gift as being 'for his [i.e., Edward's] homage and service', it likely represents the earliest instance in which Carrick was used as a means of identifying the king's prospective heir.[5] The grant is, frustratingly, undated, but it may have been made during the assembly at Dundee in 1313. Conferring the earldom on the king's brother on such a public, formal occasion would serve both to advertise the king's preferred succession arrangement to the wider political community and – by extension – to secure the consent of the community for this succession plan. Dr Roland Tanner has convincingly argued that one of Robert I's great strengths as king was his ability to use public assemblies such as great councils and parliaments to give his decisions a veneer of communal approval.[6]

The clarification of the line of succession would prove to be a recurrent theme throughout King Robert's reign. Within a year of his victory at Bannockburn, Bruce would draw up an entail concerning the succession, establishing in law the principle that Edward Bruce should become king if Bruce died without male progeny of his own.[7] This was done in the context of another assembly, this time at Ayr, once more adding legitimacy to the king's preferred succession plan. Then again in December 1318, in response to Edward Bruce's death in October of that year, Bruce drew up yet another entail for the succession, this time at a full parliament at Scone.[8] Even after he had a legitimate son of his own, and with the 1315 and 1318 entails still technically in effect, Bruce still felt inclined to make his intentions for the succession explicit. Thus, a third entail – now sadly lost – was drawn up at a parliament at Cambuskenneth Abbey in July 1326.

If the grant of the earldom of Carrick to Edward Bruce in 1313 was intended to single him out as the king's preferred heir, then it in essence proposed the same arrangement that the 1315 entail made legal. In 1315, 1318, and 1326, the kingship was entailed in the male line, meaning that Bruce's male relatives were to be favoured over his female relatives regardless of how closely related to Robert these women might be. In 1315, at least, this significantly improved the likelihood of King Robert being succeeded by an adult, male, and above all, experienced war leader. Recognition of Edward Bruce as heir in 1313 would, in practice, have the same effect. But with Bruce's daughter, Marjory – his legal heir – indefinitely imprisoned in England, the legal side of things had to be fudged somewhat. When the 1315 entail was drawn up, Marjory had to consent to the arrangement, since it was her rights that were being circumvented, and her seal appears on the document ahead of everyone save her father Robert and her uncle Edward. Recently, Borthwick and MacQueen have argued for a highly developed legal consciousness on the part of the Scottish political community of the fourteenth and fifteenth centuries.[9] It is therefore reasonable to suppose that even a king as adept at securing recognition for his will in parliament as Bruce could not convince the estates to condone an outright breach of legal niceties while Marjory was still alive and thus theoretically able to claim her legal rights. In Marjory's absence, the grant of Carrick at least singled out Edward Bruce as the natural recipient of his brother's former titles. In doing so, it in turn served to identify him as the next in line for the kingship, by extension if not in strict legal terms, at a point when the Scottish royal administration was unable to make a binding legal acknowledgement of this arrangement.

The concern on the part of the king – and indeed the wider community – to clarify the question of succession is understandable in light of the initial cause of the war. It was the dynastic uncertainty caused by the deaths of King Alexander III in 1286 and his granddaughter Margaret in 1290 that had created the conditions which had led to the outbreak of open conflict between England and Scotland in 1286. The destruction and dislocation of nearly two decades of war were thus traceable to the lack of a clearly established line of succession. On a more cynical level, no one was better placed to comprehend how such a situation could be exploited by a shrewd and ambitious lord to overturn the established order than Robert Bruce. It was his willingness to do precisely this that had delivered him into power in the first place, as explored in the introduction. Clarity over the succession thus served to consolidate the Bruce dynasty, which in turn reassured the community of the realm of the stability of the Bruce regime.

Bruce may have had another, more urgent reason to name an heir in late 1313 – his health may once again have been in question. Bruce had suffered his first serious bout of ill-health in the winter of 1307 to 1308. The late-fourteenth-century Scottish poet John Barbour attributes the king's 'seknes' to 'his cald lying / Quhen in his gret myscheiff wes he', i.e., the harsh conditions he endured campaigning in all weathers early in the reign.[10] He is described as being so weak he was unable even to stand, and both the English and the Scots doubted at the time that he would not recover.[11] A third flare-up in late 1319 is possible, since the king was noticeably absent from the military actions that took place at that time. His son-in-law Walter Stewart led the defence of Berwick-upon-Tweed in that year, while the devastating raid into northern England that ultimately forced Edward II to lift the siege was led by Thomas Randolph, earl of Moray, and Sir James Douglas.[12] Then from around 1327 onwards, Bruce's health began to deteriorate significantly and never fully recovered. He was once again left physically weakened by his illness and is described by one hostile eyewitness to his visit to Ulster in 1327 as being 'so feeble and so weak that he will not last much longer from this time, with the help of God, because he cannot move anything except his tongue'.[13] Other similarly hostile sources claim that King Robert was leprous in his final years, but we should be cautious of accepting this uncritically.[14] He remained not only active but also available to his subjects until the very end of his life, which does not suggest he was suffering from something especially infectious.[15] The king's bouts of ill health seem to have primarily occurred in the autumn and winter months before receding in the spring and summer, at least until his final years, perhaps confirming Barbour's prognosis of a viral illness aggravated by cold conditions.

The king's illness in late 1313 was thus most likely another bout of the recurring illness that he first contracted in the winter of 1307 to 1308 and which would eventually kill him in 1329. The idea that Bruce was unwell in early 1314 was first speculated by Duncan.[16] There is no direct evidence in the surviving documents produced at Dundee in October 1313 to point to the king's ill-health. However, the events of early 1314, and in particular Bruce's conspicuous absence from them, certainly hint at another period of poor health, as will be explored in more detail. If Bruce was unwell, perhaps once again fearful that he would never recover, then the appointment of a successor would be vital to ensure the smooth transition of power in the event of the king's death. Moreover, the chosen heir might even be expected to assume some degree of responsibility for the governance of the realm if, as in 1307 to 1308, Bruce's illness left him physically infirm. In the circumstances, his younger brother was the obvious choice to run things. The possibility is at least worth bearing in mind as we explore the months leading up to Bannockburn.

Another matter remains unmentioned in the surviving documentation of October 1313 but has been inferred by subsequent historians as a major item of business undertaken at the Dundee assembly. The source of this inference originates, obliquely, in Barbour's *Bruce*, a long narrative poem written by John Barbour, Archdeacon of Aberdeen, in the 1370s. According to Barbour, in the wake of his victory at Bannockburn, King Robert – on the advice of his privy council – issued an ultimatum to the effect:

> 'That quha-sa clemyt till haf rycht
> To hald in Scotland land or fe,
> That in thai twelf moneth suld he
> Cum and clam yt and tharfor do
> To the king that pertenyt tharto,
> And giff thai come nocht in that yer
> Than suld thai wit withoutyn wer
> That hard thareftre nane suld be.'[17]

A sentence of forfeiture along these lines was indeed passed at a parliament at Cambuskenneth Abbey (tellingly within sight of the battlefield at Bannockburn) on 6 November 1314.[18] Of course, if those affected by it had been given 'twelf moneth' to make their submissions, then the ultimatum cannot have been issued after Bannockburn, barely four months earlier. October 1313 would just about fit the bill, and thus it has been conjectured that it was at the Dundee assembly that Bruce made his threat to forfeit those who remained outwith his allegiance.[19]

Dr Michael Penman has even suggested that news of this ultimatum influenced Edward II's decision to launch his invasion of Scotland in 1314.[20]

The obvious problem with this interpretation is that there is no direct evidence from the Dundee assembly of such a declaration being made. This is not necessarily a fatal problem, since the records are far from complete. Yet neither is there any mention of an ultimatum in any of the surviving documents relating to the early English preparations for the campaign in 1314. This includes the petition made to the English crown in November 1313 that led to King Edward's initial announcement of the campaign, a document which will be explored in detail. Though the petition survives only in a summary, if a concern that Bruce intended to forfeit Edward's remaining Scottish allies was really a key motivation behind the decision to invade, we would surely expect it to feature prominently among the list of reasons for direct English intervention at this moment.

This issue is compounded by the fact that the sentence of forfeiture produced at Cambuskenneth in November 1314 also makes no mention of a year-long period having been extended to Scotland's landowners in which to submit to King Robert. Instead, the document simply states that those being forfeited 'had been often summoned and lawfully expected' (*'licet sepius vocati et legitime expectati'*) and yet still had not made their peace with the king.[21] The term 'often' (*'sepius'*) may hold the key to unpicking this problem. It seems likely that, far from issuing an unusual proclamation of his intent to forfeit his domestic opponents at Dundee, Bruce had made similar pronouncements whenever he presided over a gathering of the community. At least two such meetings had occurred before 1313. The submission of William, earl of Ross, had been taken, along with 'many other nobles, clerics and laymen' at Auldearn in Moray towards the end of October 1308.[22] King Robert then held a full parliament at St Andrews in March 1309.[23] Penman has identified a further four occasions on which Bruce may have held other assemblies between the St Andrews parliament and 1313, which would make the Dundee gathering his seventh in total.[24]

A threat of forfeiture was likely promulgated at each of these earlier assemblies, and so another *was* probably issued at Dundee in 1313. This would probably have been viewed as another empty threat to those who stood to lose out if it was acted upon, and it is unlikely to have caused much concern for the English king or encouraged him to contemplate a renewed invasion. What changed in the year between the Dundee assembly and the Cambuskenneth parliament was that victory at Bannockburn empowered Bruce to carry out his ultimatum. Instead, there were far less lofty, but much more urgent, concerns that would bring about Edward II's announcement of his invasion of Scotland at the end of 1313.

## A Cry for Help: Origins of the English Invasion, November to December 1313

While Bruce was holding his assembly at Dundee, there were already hints that Edward II was growing increasingly concerned with matters in Scotland. As early as 30 September, amid other payments for the maintenance of various Scottish prisoners, exchequer officers ordered 200 marks to be paid to William Fiennes, the Gascon captain of the English garrison at Roxburgh, for 'arrears of pay and loss of horses'.[25] Located on an island in the River Teviot close to the Anglo-Scottish border, Roxburgh Castle was a formidable fortress and had been one of the major centres of royal power in Scotland before the war began.[26] It had a garrison of nearly 160 men in 1311 – fifty men-at-arms, eighteen crossbowmen, sixty-one archers, and twenty-nine lightly armed horsemen known as hobelars – though this number had almost certainly diminished by 1314.[27] Then, early in October, Ralph Fitzwilliam, a senior northern judicial officer, wrote to Walter Reynolds, archbishop of Canterbury, that Berwick was 'grievously menaced with treason' but reassured him that the garrison remained loyal and would continue to defend it against the king of Scots and the king of France until relieved. Critically, Fitzwilliam wrote that he 'hopes to be comforted by news of this', suggesting a degree of anticipation of direct royal intervention in Scotland among the crown's northern officers at this time.[28]

The earliest evidence suggestive that King Edward himself was contemplating a military expedition into Scotland comes in the form of a letter produced on 12 October at Westminster. The letter was addressed to Andronikos II, styled by Edward 'emperor of Constantinople', and concerned the release of Sir Giles d'Argentan.[29] Sir Giles was a renowned crusader and would later be celebrated as 'the thrid best knycht perfay/That men wyst lyvand in his day'.[30] In October 1313, Sir Giles was imprisoned at Salonika, having been 'captured by men of the emperor's power whilst on a voyage to the island of Rhodes' according to King Edward's letter. Thus, Edward wrote to Andronikos asking the emperor to arrange for Sir Giles's swift release. On the same day, Edward also wrote to Andronikos's son and heir, Michael (also styled 'emperor of Constantinople'); Andronikos's wife, Irene; their son Theodore I, marquis of Montferrat; King Frederick II of Sicily; and several other notables, requesting that they use their influence with the emperor to help Edward secure Sir Giles's freedom. The connection between King Edward's concerns for Sir Giles and his plans for a Scottish campaign might not at first seem obvious. However, Sir Giles is credited by the later English chronicler Sir Thomas Gray as having 'the king's rein' on 24 June, meaning he had personal responsibility for King Edward's safety on the battlefield.[31] The timing of Edward's entreaties to Emperor Andronikos strongly suggests that they were made specifically so that the fearsome and renowned Sir Giles could serve as King Edward's bodyguard on the upcoming campaign.

On 24 October, detailed instructions for the payment of the garrison at Lochmaben Castle were issued.[32] Sir Roger Kirkpatrick, another unnamed knight in Kirkpatrick's service, and four squires were to share £4, 16s. between them for twelve days of service. Sir William Herries and his squire were to share 36s. for the same period, as was Sir Thomas de Torthorwald and his squire. Valets Alan de Donewithy and Walter de Bosco were to receive 12s. each, while a hobelar – a lightly armoured horseman – named Matthew de Eye was to receive 6s. Furthermore, wages for the infantry at Lochmaben were also laid out. Their constable Jordan de Kendale and the sixty-five archers were to receive £8, 12s. 8d. between them. The crossbowmen stationed in the pele – the fenced-off area surrounding the castle – were to receive £4, 15s. 8d. This payment included the wages of their corporal Robert de Larkedaunce and nineteen other crossbowmen. The five crossbowmen within the castle shared 30s. 4d. between them while Henry of Carlisle – who seems to have been some kind of engineer since he is described as an 'attilliator' – received 6s. The chaplain, identified only as 'Sir Robert', was to be given 7s. and a watchman named Gilbert was to receive 3s. 6d. Overall, this amounted to the impressive sum of £25, 7s., 2d. Not only does this record offer a valuable insight into the makeup and personnel of the English garrison, it also demonstrates a substantial material investment in the defences of south-west Scotland. Given that Edward's soon-to-be announced invasion of Scotland was to begin in the east, this might reasonably be seen as an early attempt to reinforce the English administration in the west against possible Scottish reprisals once preparations for the campaign were underway.

A little over two weeks later, on 8 November, Edward II issued letters praising several Scottish lairds – Adam Gordon, Edward Letham, Robert Colville, John Landale, Alexander Stewart of Bonkyl, William Soules, and Thomas Somerville – for their loyalty, and in particular for their continued contribution to the defence of Roxburgh against the English king's 'enemies and rebels' (*'inimicorum et rebellium'*). On the same day, King Edward installed Fitzwilliam as guardian (*custos*) of Berwick-upon-Tweed.[33] It seems reasonable to suppose that by now Archbishop Reynolds had communicated the content of Fitzwilliam's missive to King Edward, and so his appointment may have been in response to Fitzwilliam's profession of fidelity. In the coming months, with Berwick serving as the primary mustering point for the English army, custodianship of the town would be an extremely privileged position and would require a trustworthy royal servant. In this context, the timing of Fitzwilliam's nomination suggests that Edward was already drawing together plans for the 1314 campaign.

These incidents are useful for getting a sense of Edward's growing interest in Scottish affairs towards the end of 1313. But the most significant event that contributed to his decision to invade in 1314 was the presentation of a petition to the English king on behalf of his dwindling Scottish allies.[34] The dating of the petition is difficult to pin down since it does not survive in its original form but only as a summary. King Edward made his response to the petition on 28 November, and thus it has generally been presumed that it was presented to him within a month or so of that date. The detail that it mentions – a truce due to run out on Martinmas (11 November) – further suggests that it was produced earlier than that date. The fact that one of the petitioners – Adam Gordon – was one of those thanked for his service by Edward on 8 November may indicate that the king was already aware of the petition and its contents by then.

The petition itself was presented in the name of the wider Scottish political community. However, it was brought to Westminster by a pair of Scottish envoys – Patrick Dunbar, earl of March, and Sir Adam Gordon. Both were lords with lands in the south-east and thus had a material interest in maintaining friendly relations with the English king, since their property was both vulnerable to attack and relatively easy for the English crown to confiscate. March also had personal reasons for opposing Bruce, since his mother was Marjory Comyn, a daughter of the late Alexander Comyn, earl of Buchan. He and his father had consistently remained in English allegiance since the outbreak of war in 1296, though this had accomplished little beyond securing their interests in the south-east. It had certainly not brought any obvious improvement to their overall status in either kingdom. Gordon had also been a reliable supporter of the English crown during the conflict and had played a more active role in the war effort. He had for instance served as warden of the East March and justiciar of Lothian on behalf of the English royal administration. He was present in the English army for Bruce's defeat at Methven in June 1306 and was afterwards given custody of Bruce's nephew Thomas Randolph following the latter's capture at that battle. Thus, by sending the petition to Westminster in the hands of March and Gordon, King Edward's remaining Scottish allies were ensuring that their representations were being made by a pair of trusted and long-standing crown servants and thus more likely to be received favourably.

The complaints March and Gordon brought to Edward in late 1313 were several and grievous. First and foremost, they alleged that since the king had returned from his previous campaign into Scotland in August 1311, they had incurred losses of no less than £20,000 in the form of blackmail and other depredations by the Bruce Scots. The most recent truce had apparently cost them 1,000 quarters of corn and they remained under pressure. Tellingly, the complainants dreaded the king's own garrisons at Berwick and Roxburgh as much as the Bruce Scots. Gilbert de Middleton and Thomas of Pencaitland and their followers from the Berwick garrison appear to have enacted a particularly harsh retribution in response to the recent truce, which received special mention in the November petition. Presumably the truce had been arranged without the garrison's consent and thus may have been seen as a betrayal by the likes of Middleton and Pencaitland, who may also have felt that a private truce between the locals and the Bruce Scots left the town even more vulnerable to attack. On another occasion, when the locals had purchased a truce from King Robert for fifteen days around midsummer, the Berwick garrison had seized thirty local men 'in their beds' and held them to ransom, along with 300 'fat beasts', 4,000 sheep, some horses, and other slaughtered animals. On another, the Berwick garrison had confiscated eight tuns of wine belonging to the bishop of St Andrews, leaving the bishop too afraid to report to the English king.[35] Pencaitland and his men had once seized local hostages and gone so far as to kill those who could not afford the ransom, throwing the bodies into the Tweed, the petitioners claimed.

The garrison at Roxburgh and its Gascon captain, William Fiennes, also came in for considerable criticism in the petition. During the midsummer truce, Fiennes and his men had detained a group of local men who had to be ransomed at the cost of eighty marks. To add insult to injury, the Bruce Scots then extorted a further 160 marks from the locals, having apparently deemed the violent actions of the garrison to have been in breach of the truce. The petitioners complained that the Roxburgh garrison routinely 'plunder and imprison the merchants who come there'. Moreover, the king's chamberlain for Scotland, John of Weston, was accused of supporting the garrison against the wronged locals. The petitioners claimed that when the civic dignitaries of Roxburgh had complained to Weston of the garrison's behaviour, he had conspired to lure Gordon into meeting him and then imprisoned him to the astonishment of 'all his good people of Scotland'.

These were undoubtedly outrageous accusations and provided plenty of justification for dissatisfaction among Edward's diminishing pool of Scottish allies. Not only were the king's officers failing to protect his Scottish subjects from attack by the Scots, they were also inflicting even more pain and penury on them than the supposed enemy. This struck at the very heart of Edward's claim to govern in Scotland. One of the core purposes of the Bruce Scots' raiding efforts was to undermine the confidence of the local populace in the English king's ability to protect their interests and thus to lure them back into Bruce's allegiance.[36] Based on the complaints laid out in the petition, it appeared that Edward's own servants were doing the Bruce Scots' work for them. It was absolutely vital that Edward address this issue and bring his unruly garrisons under control. Happily for the king, in light of the reaction of the bulk of the English political community to the brutal treatment of Gaveston and the recent submissions of Edward's leading domestic opponents, he found himself in an unusually strong position from which to react.

It is for this reason that it seems likely that the appointment of Fitzwilliam as *custos* of Berwick occurred after Edward had seen the petition, and indeed had been done in direct response to it. The intrusion of a trusted royal servant, one who had so recently been in contact to emphasize his fidelity and commitment to the preservation of the crown's interests in Scotland, seems likely to have been part of a deliberate effort to address the complaints directed towards the Berwick garrison in the petition. Fitzwilliam's experience of royal service had been mostly judicial in nature, and moreover his recent service had been undertaken in the north-west. He had for instance been made *custos* of Cumberland earlier in the year.[37] He was thus untainted by prior association with the troublemakers in the garrisons of south-eastern Scotland and might prove to be just the man to keep the likes of Middleton and Pencaitland in check. The earlier payments to the garrison at Lochmaben Castle may also be interpreted as a response to the grievances set out in the petition, suggesting that it had been presented to King Edward in October. With the situation clearly already out-of-hand in the south-east, the English royal administration may have felt compelled to hurriedly invest in what remained of their holdings in the south-west to avoid the problem spreading any further.

King Edward's main response to the complaint came on 28 November.[38] On this date, he issued a missive addressed to the 'bishops, abbots, priors, and beloved and faithful ones, earls, barons, knights, free persons, and all others in the land of Scotland'. In it, he committed himself to appear with an army at Berwick by 24 June the following year.[39] In the meantime, Edward enjoined his Scottish allies to remain faithful to him and to continue their 'gratuitous works' (*'gratis operibus'*) on his behalf. He promised to provide a 'suitable remedy' (*'remedium competenas'*) to the complaints presented to him by March and Gordon, who are conventionally described as 'beloved and faithful' (*'dilectis et fidelibus'*), who he also sent north to provide further reassurances of the king's concern for his subjects' welfare. Two days earlier – on 26 November – King Edward had summoned a parliament to meet at Westminster on 21 April, which he likely hoped would be a forum for the upcoming invasion to be discussed and at which support for this endeavour could be raised.[40]

Edward's response to March and Gordon's complaint on 28 November was the first public announcement of the campaign that would ultimately lead to Bannockburn. No specific plan of action was laid out yet, other than a vague promise 'to advance against our enemies and rebels in those parts'.[41] However, from this we can infer that the broad approach would be largely the same as that taken in 1310 to 1311, which was, after all, already standard English war policy in regard to Scotland.[42] The English king would raise as large an army as he could, intended to emphasize the might and majesty of the English crown, and then seek to lure the Scots into an open confrontation. In the event of such a confrontation, it was expected that the English could overwhelm the Scots with sheer weight of numbers – much as had happened at Falkirk in 1298 – and decisively smash

Scotland's military capacity. Following this, it was expected that territory could be reoccupied with relative ease, as had happened after the Battle of Dunbar in 1296, and the Scottish political community could be compelled to make its peace with the English royal administration, as had occurred in 1304. Though this strategy had enjoyed some qualified success in the past, by 1314 it had repeatedly failed to deliver lasting gains for the English in Scotland. It was particularly ill-suited to counter Bruce's ruthless and practiced guerrilla strategy. These flaws will become strikingly apparent in the following chapters.

For now, however, Edward II turned his attention to stabilizing his financial position ahead of the proposed campaign. Thus, on 12 December the English king was to be found at Boulogne to meet with his French counterpart Philippe IV. Here, Philippe gave his approval to a deal between King Edward and Pope Clement V whereby the pope loaned Edward money directly as well as giving him access to the crusading 'tenth' to be collected from within the English king's dominions – including those areas of southern Scotland still under Edward's control.[43] The pope could reclaim the loan from the revenues of the duchy of Aquitaine, hence why the arrangement required Philippe's approval as Edward's feudal superior from his lands in south-west France. Naturally, these funds were not explicitly granted for the coming war in Scotland. However, the Bannockburn campaign would undoubtedly be Edward's largest expenditure in 1314 and, following the announcement of the campaign at the end of November, the English royal administration at least would already have anticipated this even if Philippe and Clement did not.

On the one hand, Phillipe's involvement in facilitating the financial side of the Bannockburn campaign might be seen as hardly a comradely move towards the Bruce Scots by the French king. A generous interpretation might view Phillipe's actions as being mitigated by the involvement of the pope. Although he had lifted Bruce's sentence of excommunication in 1308, Pope Clement might reasonably be expected to prioritize placing a financial obligation on the English crown over any concerns about what it would mean for the Scots. Once the pope had committed to the loan, Philippe could hardly withhold his approval without risking his own relations with the papacy. Yet a more realistic interpretation might see the entire affair as an illustration of how peripheral Anglo-Scottish affairs were to Philippe or Clement at this time. The Bruce regime may have viewed the French crown and the papacy as being the twin pillars of its diplomatic policy, but it had not yet convinced either of them to weigh its needs against the opportunity for material and diplomatic gains with England.

By the end of 1313, Edward II had committed himself to a large-scale invasion of Scotland in the coming summer. He enjoyed greater domestic support than he had done for most of the reign, had at least superficially pacified his leading domestic opponents, established a firm financial position from which to make his preparations, and limited the likelihood of major opposition to his ambitions from the Continent. Bruce too was in the best domestic position of his reign and had clarified – as best he could – what the future should hold for his fledgling dynasty. Yet he now faced another concerted threat from his more populous and powerful southern neighbour, probably the most serious material threat his royal administration had yet faced. Moreover, King Robert may have been physically infirm, meaning he might have to delegate direct leadership of his response to his – albeit experienced and energetic – subordinates. On balance, as 1313 came to a close, the English crown may have had more reason for optimism than its Scottish counterpart.

*Chapter 2*

# Starting Slow is Still a Start

## Scottish Reaction and English Preparations, December 1313 to February 1314

On 18 December 1313, King Robert was at Ayr. Here, he granted lands at nearby Cumnock, formerly belonging to John of Seton, to Roger, son of Finlay. John had, along with his son and brother, stolen horses belonging to Roger and so Bruce made the grant to compensate Roger.[1] Although it is only a snapshot of Robert's activities around this time, this rather mundane business does not give the impression of a king feverishly preparing for the upcoming English invasion of Scotland. His presence at Ayr in December suggests he may have spent his last Christmas before Bannockburn at his late mother's castle at Turnberry down the coast from Ayr, or at least nearby.[2] If Bruce was already aware of Edward II's plans to campaign into Scotland in 1314, he was not showing any obvious concern about it. News of the coming English invasion must surely have reached him, since it had been announced almost three weeks earlier. But Bruce was probably planning to simply stay out of Edward's way while the English army passed through Scotland, wait for Edward's patience and money to run out, and then resume terrorizing the remaining English garrisons and Edward's dwindling Scottish allies after Edward had returned home. This strategy had served Bruce well the last time Edward invaded, in 1310, and he had no obvious reason to abandon this winning formula yet.

### Robert Bruce Stood Afar Off, That He Might See the End: The Example of 1310 to 1311

To understand the initial Scottish response to Edward II's second threatened invasion of Scotland, it is worth considering their experience of Edward's first invasion in 1310 to 1311.[3] As in 1313, Edward's decision to invade in 1310 was ostensibly a response to a petition by his Scottish allies. On 16 June 1310, Edward had been in conference with Sir Alexander Abernethy, Sir Ingram Umfraville, and father and son Alexander and John Macdougall of Argyll, who warned him he risked the loss of 'both the land [of Scotland] and those who still remain faithful to him by reason of default and laxity'.[4] The timing of this incursion probably also reflected King Edward's concerns over Bruce holding his first full parliament at St Andrews in March 1309. This was a momentous occasion for King Robert, reflecting as it did the extent to which he had constructed a stable administration capable of presiding over a meeting of the community of the realm, or at least the growing portion of the community willing to accept his authority as king. English anxiety over this assembly was no doubt exacerbated by the fact it was attended by William Lamberton, bishop of St Andrews, who had essentially absconded from English custody.[5] The 1309 parliament thus served as a potent illustration of Edward's diminishing authority north of the border. Yet perhaps Edward's most pressing, if unspoken at the time, motivation for invading Scotland in 1310 was a desire to remove himself from the situation with the Ordainers.[6] The Ordainers were a council of twenty-one prelates, earls, and barons elected in March 1310 to develop a far-reaching programme of reform for the English government in light of long-standing and increasingly acute tensions between King Edward and the wider political community.[7] Unwilling to remain in the vicinity of the Ordainers while they deliberated, and even less willing to assist them in their task, Edward seems to have viewed a campaign in Scotland as a means to remove himself physically from this latest politically awkward position in which he found himself. Moreover, if he could inflict a defeat on his Scottish enemies – perhaps capture or kill one or both of the surviving Bruce brothers – he might generate the kind of political capital to soften the attitude of the Ordainers.

King Edward was immediately faced with serious difficulties in recruitment. The earls of Lancaster, Hereford, Warwick, and Pembroke excused themselves from serving since they had been appointed as Ordainers, although all four likely viewed this simply as a convenient justification for their lack of cooperation. Meanwhile, Henry de Lacy, earl of Lincoln, had been appointed to serve as *custos regni* to govern the realm in Edward's absence, and so also sent only the minimum number of troops he was required to provide. In the end, the king's nephew Gilbert de Clare, earl of Gloucester; John of Brittany, earl of Richmond; John de Warenne, earl of Surrey; and Edward's infamous familiar Piers Gaveston, earl of

Cornwall; were the only magnates to appear in person on the campaign in 1310.[8] The *Vita Edwardi Secundi* ('Life of Edward II', written by an anonymous English chronicler in the mid-1320s) makes explicit the king's worries about Gaveston's fate if he remained behind with those disgruntled nobles who had not responded to the summons in person.[9] When it set off from Berwick-upon-Tweed in mid-September, Edward's army numbered roughly 1,700 cavalry and 3,000 infantry, meagre compared to most of the English armies that served in Scotland in the late thirteenth and early fourteenth centuries, including that raised in 1314.[10] Efforts had been made to raise a further 500 men-at-arms, 300 hobelars, and 2,000 cavalry from Ireland, but were ultimately abandoned due to bad weather.[11] Edward advanced smartly from Berwick to Roxburgh, then on to Selkirk, Biggar, Renfrew, Glasgow, Linlithgow, Edinburgh, and back to Berwick by November, remaining there until August 1311.[12] McNamee has noted that Edward's progress cautiously circumvented Ettrick Forest, apparently in recognition of the danger of approaching this long-standing focus of Scottish guerrilla activity.[13] We have evidence for the resupplying of garrisons at Roxburgh and Linlithgow undertaken in September and October by Edward's forces.[14] We then find wages being paid to Sir Walter Fitz Gilbert at Bothwell Castle in October and Sir Philip Mowbray at Kirkintilloch Castle in November.[15]

The Scottish response to Edward's progress through southern Scotland was a resolute refusal to engage in all but a few isolated harrying actions. As the *Vita* puts it, 'not a rebel was found to lay a hand upon him [i.e., King Edward] or his men, except that a few from the army, out foraging or on a plundering raid, were cut off'.[16] Bruce's precise movements are difficult to reconstruct, but it would appear he remained on the move throughout the incursion. For at least some of the time, King Robert may have shadowed the movements of the English army, deliberately remaining just beyond his enemy's reach while retaining the ability to easily monitor their advance. Prof. Davuit Broun has argued that a letter from Bruce to Edward, which survives in a later English transcript, belongs to this period. The missive, dated 1 October and produced at Kildrum (now part of Cumbernauld), implores the English king 'to cease from the persecution of us and the disturbance of the people of our kingdom in order that devastation and the spilling of Christian blood may henceforth stop'. In return, Bruce extended an offer of peace talks and at least the hint of material remuneration for the damage done in the destructive border warfare conducted in recent years.[17] The earnest, at times almost obsequious, amiability in the tone of the letter contrasts sharply with the inability of the English army to physically threaten the Scottish king, a bitter irony that may have been deliberate on Bruce's part.

If the letter was dispatched from Kildrum on 1 October 1310, it would have found King Edward at Biggar, a little under thirty-five miles away. On 6 October, while still at Biggar, Edward was informed that Bruce was 'with his forces on a moor near Stirling'.[18] This reinforces the impression that Bruce remained mobile while his southern counterpart was present in Scotland and was, understandably, unwilling to stay close to the English army for too long. It also implies that King Robert kept an armed following of some description in the field during the English incursion, possibly even a substantial portion of his overall military capacity at this time. This also seems to have been his response during Edward's fourth and final invasion of Scotland in 1322, when he is described as having 'gaderyt his men bath fer and ner' at Culross to wait out this latest incursion.[19] The impression that Bruce gathered a significant armed force in response to the English invasion in 1310 is further reinforced by the Lanercost chronicler's report that, around the time that Edward returned to Berwick in November, Bruce 'invaded Lothian and inflicted much damage upon those who were in the king of England's peace'.[20] The Scots may even have contemplated counter-raids against other English possessions while Edward was away in Scotland. This was a strategy they would employ to devastating effect during Edward II's third campaign in 1319.[21] On Christmas Day in 1310, English officials in Cheshire, Lancashire, Cumbria, and Westmoreland were put on alert due to reports of a planned Scottish assault on the Isle of Man.[22]

The Scots remained cautiously open to negotiation in the midst of this military activity. Thus, according to an anonymous contemporary letter, Sir Robert Clifford and Sir Robert Fitzpayne apparently had the king's permission to travel to Selkirk 'eight days before Christmas, to speak with Robert Bruce'. The same letter reports that after this, Gloucester and Cornwall were due to negotiate with Bruce near Melrose, but apparently the Scottish king did not keep this appointment due to concerns that this was a ruse to capture him.[23] These abortive talks suggest that military action and diplomatic activity were being undertaken, or at least contemplated, simultaneously throughout the 1310 invasion. Bruce was apparently open to using any and all means open to him to achieve his aims, even while under direct threat from Edward and his army. There may even have been secret talks conducted during this period concerning the possible provision of sanctuary by the Bruce Scots for Edward's favourite Piers Gaveston in return for Edward's recognition of Bruce's rights as king.[24]

Desultory English operations resumed in early 1311. Further forays as far north as Perth were led by the earls of Cornwall, Gloucester, and Surrey, but Edward stayed at Berwick.[25] An anonymous report of April 1311 dourly observes that Edward remained 'in no mood yet for a parliament' – reinforcing the impression that the English king saw the ongoing Scottish campaign as a way to escape his domestic woes – and adds that 'it was said that Robert Bruce meant to fight [Piers Gaveston] the Earl of Cornwall; but he did not believe he was able to meet the King's forces in a plain field'.[26] This confirms that, having apparently exhausted his hopes of making diplomatic headway, King Robert had returned to resolutely refusing to offer the English any hope of the kind of large-scale military engagement that might have salvaged this debacle for King Edward. As the author of the *Vita* puts it:

> 'But Robert Bruce stood afar off, that he might see the end, for there seemed no safe place for him in such a neighbourhood, but always as the [English] army approached he kept to the trackless boggy mountain places, into which such an army could not easily penetrate. And indeed even if the king of England were to lay siege to Scotland for seven years, being shorthanded as he was, he would never commit Robert Bruce to his prison.'[27]

Once Edward had admitted defeat and made his reluctant journey south to face the judgment of the Ordainers in July, however, Scottish activity suddenly intensified again. On 12 August 1311, 'Thursday before the feast of the Assumption of the Glorious Virgin' as the Lanercost chronicler puts it, Bruce spent eight days raiding Gilsland, Haltwhistle, and Tynedale, 'taking with him a very large booty in cattle'. Then again in September, Bruce returned to Northumberland for fifteen days of raiding, 'laying waste those parts which he had previously spared'. The community of Northumberland was extorted for the sum of £2,000 to secure their safety until the following February, while Edward's Scottish allies in the south-east also apparently bought a truce as well.[28]

The overall impression we are left with when examining Bruce's response to the threat of invasion in 1310 is of a cautious but highly adaptive war policy. King Robert appears to have mustered some, if not all, of his forces but refused to commit them to a single course of action. Instead, they remained highly mobile and responsive to the changing situation. His primary concern was the avoidance of a pitched battle, but remained alert to any opportunities to make gains as and where he could. Bruce sought to shape events to his benefit – for instance with his letter to Edward in October, his tentative efforts at diplomacy during the winter, and his opportunistic raids into Lothian and northern England – but above all he was willing to adapt his plans depending on how events developed. This strategy did not simply preserve the Bruce administration against English military intervention. It also had a deleterious effect on the moral of the English military elite, which would continue to have an impact on subsequent English incursions into Scotland – including that undertaken in 1314.[29] Memories of the frustrations of the 1310 campaign would have undermined the confidence of Edward's subjects in his ability to intervene effectively north of the border. Additionally, recollections of the humiliation he had suffered on returning to confront the Ordainers would have resonated with King Edward and likely prayed on his mind as he made his decisions in 1314. These are all vital points to bear in mind when considering the initial Scottish reaction to Edward's announcement of his invasion plans towards the end of 1313.

## 'Umquile with Strenth and Quhile with Slycht': Chivalry and War Policy in Bruce's Scotland

This much we can tell about the general Scottish approach to the anticipated invasion of 1314, but what about the ways in which they justified and legitimized it? It is clear from their condemnatory tone that English authors like the Lanercost chronicler and the author of the *Vita* found Scottish war policy to be underhand and cowardly. But what of the Scots themselves? Did they see this cautious, pragmatic approach to warfare as a shameful activity, something that they must reluctantly practice out of necessity with no moral value beyond this? As is so often the case when dealing with attitudes in late medieval Scotland, our study is hampered somewhat by the fragmentary nature of the sources that survive to us.

But it is possible to at least begin to get a sense of how, even in Bruce's own time, his calculating approach to warfare was assimilated into wider ideas of chivalry and 'proper' knightly behaviour by those who practiced it.

Bruce was a literate king who seems to have encouraged quite a vibrant literary culture at his court. His contemporary Jean le Bel was aware of a 'history commissioned by King Robert himself' apparently recounting Bruce's life and adventures, while the later English chronicler Sir Thomas Gray, writing in the 1350s, references 'chronicles of his [i.e., Bruce's] deeds' (*'croniclis de sez gestis'*) seemingly produced during Bruce's lifetime.[30] A document produced for parliament circa 1364 reports that:

> 'Sir Robert Bruce, our king of Scotland, whose soul God rest, used continually to read, or have read in his presence, the histories of ancient kings and princes, and how they conducted themselves in their times, *both in wartime and in peacetime*; from these he derived information about many aspects of his own rule.'[31]

This confirms Bruce's love of reading, and reading history in particular, and perhaps most significantly for our purposes, explicitly associates his literary pursuits with his martial activities. Frustratingly, none of the literature commissioned by King Robert during his lifetime survives in complete form. However, fragments are preserved in the *Scotichronicon*, produced by Walter Bower, abbot of Inchcolm, in the 1440s. Bower includes portions of no fewer than three separate works, a fact that becomes most apparent when recounting the birth of the future David II in 1324, at which point he presents all three of them together. One Bower attributes to Bernard, abbot of Arbroath (Bruce's chancellor for all but a few months of the reign), another to 'a certain monk of Arbroath', and one left entirely anonymous.[32] One fragment in particular is instructive as to how literature was used to cultivate an appreciation for calculating, prudent warfare at King Robert's court:

> 'Let the retaliation of Scotland depend on her foot-soldiers, her mountains, her mosses, her countryside; let woods, bow and spear serve as secure walls.

Let her warbands threaten among the narrow places, and let her plains be so kindled with fires that they are abandoned by the enemy.

Let her sentinels be watchful, crying out by night.

Thus thrown into disorder the enemy will retire, put to flight by the sword of hunger; it is a certainty, so King Robert assures us.'[33]

The author of these lines is difficult to discern, since Bower does not identify them, but given their seemingly personal reference to Bruce, we might tentatively conclude that this was Bernard's work. The use of the present tense when writing about King Robert suggests not only a personal familiarity with the king, but also that the text was produced during Bruce's own lifetime. Whoever the author was, they promote the use of guerrilla warfare but present it as a noble and honourable endeavour to make it more appealing to their audience. The passage serves to reinforce Bruce's war policy while simultaneously giving it a sheen of respectability. The glorification of unconventional warfare, the emphasis on the exploitation of the landscape, and the expectation of victory through attrition rather than direct confrontation, resonate strongly with Bruce's war policy throughout his reign. The high likelihood that these verses were composed for recitation at Bruce's own court, indeed to be listened to by the individuals responsible for prosecuting the war in service of King Robert, implies that a Scottish chivalric tradition focused more on personal discipline than fantastical adventure was actively cultivated by the king himself in order to forge a cadre of faithful lieutenants committed to prosecuting his style of warfare.

While this passage hints at the origins of the association of military prudence and chivalry in Scottish literature, the trend finds its most full-throated endorsement in the long narrative poem known as *The Bruce*. Admittedly this means jumping ahead in time beyond the end of Bruce's reign, but this is an unfortunate reflection of the gaps in the surviving literature. *The Bruce* was written in the 1370s, probably for Bruce's grandson Robert II (r. 1371–1390) or Archibald Douglas 'the Grim', lord of Galloway. Robert II and Archibald are the only uncontestably contemporary figures mentioned in the text, making them the poet's most likely patrons.[34] The author John Barbour was archdeacon of

Aberdeen from 1356 until his death in 1395 and was closely associated with the Scottish royal administration in the reign of Robert II.[35] His stated aim in the opening lines of his poem is to bring pleasure to his audience by recounting how Robert Bruce and Sir James Douglas 'Wan gret price off chevalry', for which they were 'In ser landis renownyt'.[36] Consequently, *The Bruce* offers a valuable and fascinating insight into the expectations and perceptions of Barbour's late-fourteenth-century aristocratic audience concerning idealized knighthood.

Barbour's thoughts on this subject are particularly interesting because Barbour was writing at a time when, although a truce was technically in effect, tensions were mounting between Scotland and England over lands that had been annexed by England in 1357. In fact, the 'informal' process of the recovering these lands – sometimes through violent means – had already begun by the time *The Bruce* was being composed.[37] As in the 1310s and 1320s, crucial to the Scottish strategy in this period was the avoidance of large-scale English retaliation in response to the Scots' recovery of the disputed lands. Like the author of the verses preserved in Bower's *Scotichronicon*, Barbour was writing for a mostly aristocratic audience who were leading the efforts at reclamation of the annexed lands and who would serve as Scotland's main war leaders in the event of open conflict. Moreover, most of these would have been sons and grandsons of the man who had been responsible for the prosecution of the war during the First War of Scottish Independence.[38] While removed in time from Robert I's reign by some fifty years, the interests and concerns of Barbour's audience were sufficiently similar to those of Bruce's lieutenants to make it useful to consider the poet's attitudes here. Moreover, the fact that Bower, a further seventy years after Barbour was writing, was familiar with the literature from King Robert's own reign as examined above means we cannot discount the possibility that Barbour too had been influenced by these now lost works.

Barbour is explicit in making a sense of military prudence into a full-blown chivalric virtue. This is most clearly expressed in his commentary on 'worschip' (that is, 'worthiness') that follows a somewhat fanciful episode in which King Robert defends a ford alone against 200 men while on the run in the early part of the poem.[39] For Barbour, 'worschip' is a combination of 'hardyment' ('boldness') and 'wyt' ('intelligence'). It can be expressed in attack or defence and requires self-discipline to achieve:

> 'And may na man haiff worthyhed
> Bot he haiff wyt to ster his deid
> And se quhat ys to leve or ta.'[40]

'Worschip', says Barbour, has two extremes – 'fule-hardyment' ('foolhardiness') and 'cowartys' ('cowardice'). The former seeks to achieve any goal no matter the difficulty or risk, while the latter refuses to undertake any action at all. 'Worschip' is the 'mene betuix tha twa', doing whatever can be done in pursuit of a goal, avoiding anything too hazardous to attempt, and using one's 'wyt' to determine what is the best course of action to take.

Barbour also encourages his readers to embrace the use of 'slycht' in warfare. In its broadest sense, the term means simply 'craft' or 'skill'. For instance, the wrights employed to construct a manor house for Sir James Douglas at Lintalee circa 1317 are described by Barbour as 'sley'.[41] However, in a military context, 'slycht' should be more accurately understood to mean 'cunning', and it is repeatedly used in this sense throughout *The Bruce*.[42] When Barbour's heroes cannot overcome their enemies by strength alone, as is usually the case when facing superior English numbers, they invariably resolve to proceed with 'slycht' instead. For example, when Douglas sees he cannot overcome the English forces in his father's lordship of Douglas with 'mycht', he instead resolves to 'wyrk with slycht':

> 'Sua did it her, bot he wes wys
> And saw he mycht on nakyn wys
> Werray his fa with evyn mycht
> Tharfor he thocht to *wyrk with slycht*.'[43]

This leads directly to one of the most infamous passages in the poem, the so-called 'Douglas Lardner', for which Barbour reserves no criticism. Douglas is also said by Barbour to have regained control of Ettrick Forest from the English through a combination of 'hardiment and slycht'.[44] This use of 'slycht' to temper Douglas's natural 'hardiment' here draws a strong connection to Barbour's commentary on 'worschip'. Barbour reports that Bruce employs 'slycht' in his efforts to capture Perth in 1313:

> 'Bot the gud king that all wytty
> Wes in his dedis everilkane
> Saw the wallis sa styth off stane
> And saw defens that thai gan ma
> And how the toun wes hard to ta
> With opyn sawt strenth or mycht.
> Tharfor he thocht to *wyrk with slycht*,
> And in all tyme that he thar lay
> He spyit and slely gert assay
> Quhar at the dyk schaldest was,
> Till at the last he fand a place
> That men mycht till thar schuldris wad.'[45]

In this case, Barbour explicitly connects Bruce's 'wytty' leadership and his ability to apply 'slycht' to a situation to improve his chances of success. Earlier in his poem, Barbour attributes these words, which again sum up the author's thoughts on prudence, to Bruce himself:

> 'Tharfor men that werrayand war
> Suld set thar etlyng ever-mar
> To stand agayne thar fayis mycht
> Umquile with strenth and quhile with slycht
> And aye think to cum to purpos.'[46]

The notion that 'slycht' is a chivalric characteristic that Barbour's knights can compete with one another over in order to increase their 'worschip' is reinforced by the poet's observation that Thomas Randolph's capture of Edinburgh Castle was inspired by tales of Douglas's earlier capture of Roxburgh Castle by ruse:

> 'Bot fra he hard how Roxburgh was
> Tane with a trayne, all his purchas
> And wyt and besines Ik hycht
> He set for to *purches sum slycht*
> How he mycht halp him throu body
> Mellyt with hey chevalry

> To wyn the wall off the castell
> Throu sumkyn slycht, for he wyst weill
> That na strenth mycht it playnly get
> Quhill thai within had men and met.[47]

There are a number of other minor examples of this preference for a cautious, calculating style of warfare in *The Bruce*. For instance, Barbour recounts Douglas's record of wins versus losses while operating out of Ettrick Forest to illustrate the value of being willing to flee if it means fighting in a more advantageous position later on:

> 'For in his tyme as men said me
> Thretten tymys vencusyt wes he
> And had victouris sevin and fyfty.
> Hym semyt nocht lang ydill to ly,
> Be his travaill he had na will,
> *Me think men suld him love with skill.*[48]

When the Scots and the English engage in a standoff in Weardale in 1327, Barbour claims that the English feared Douglas as much for 'his playis' (i.e., his tricks) as for any of his other ample chivalric virtues.[49] Towards the end of the poem, when a horribly scarred but highly esteemed English knight first meets Douglas at the court of King Alfonso XI of Castile, he is surprised to find that the Scottish knight has never been wounded on his face. Barbour has Douglas answer the Englishman by somewhat cryptically stating that he always had 'Handis my hed for to wer [i.e., protect]', and then claims that whoever would keep to that answer would know its meaning.[50] While on the surface this would seem to be highlighting Douglas's physical prowess, in the context of Barbour's general praise of prudence the case might be made that the poet is once again alluding to Douglas' use of careful planning to avoid serious harm, emphasizing the benefits of a cautious approach to warfare while at the same time demonstrating that this could enhance the reputation of a knight.

This is not without precedent in chivalric literature of the late medieval period. Prof. Craig Taylor has offered a detailed analysis of how several chivalric writers in fourteenth- and fifteenth-century France drew distinctions between courage, cowardice, and rashness in order to inculcate a sense of prudence in their knightly audience.[51] The French knight and courtier Sir Geoffrey de Charny, writing in the 1350s, admonishes his readers who 'do not consider the benefit or advantage to their friends or the harm done to their enemies' when engaging in feats of arms, echoing Barbour's commentary on 'worschip'.[52] Honoré Bonet, writing no more than a decade after Barbour, encourages his readers to flee if they can no longer prevent the loss of a battle but can at least save themselves without injuring their fellows.[53] Bonet's comment is particularly striking as he was writing in the wake of a period of Anglo-French conflict in which the French crown had – like the Bruce Scots in the early fourteenth century or Barbour's contemporary audience – been forced to resort to cautious, calculating warfare in an effort to reoccupy lost territory and regain the upper hand in an armed struggle that had previously gone against them.[54] The notion that a sense of military prudence should direct the actions of those responsible for the Scottish war effort resonates strongly with Scottish experience throughout the reign of Robert I, particularly during the invasions of 1310 to 1311, 1319, and 1322. As we explore the events of 1314 in greater detail, we will find repeated examples of these principles put into practice by the leading Scottish war leaders in the build-up to Bannockburn, and during the battle itself.

## 'To Repress their Rebellion and Iniquity Manfully and Powerfully': Edward's Earliest Preparations, December 1313 to February 1314

If Bruce spent Christmas 1313 planning a return to the kind of warfare that he had practiced in 1310 to 1311, Edward II too was taking largely the same approach he had taken three years earlier. The English king seems to have been anticipating a larger turnout than in his first invasion of Scotland, a reflection of the political settlement that he had been able to achieve since Gaveston's death. Thus, on 23 December, Edward was at Westminster, where he issued orders for no fewer than ninety-two named men – eight earls and eighty-five barons of various standings – to assemble at Berwick-upon-Tweed by 'the Monday nearest the Feast of St Barnabus the Apostle next to come...with horses and arms and all service due to us'.[55] The Monday in question would have been 10 June 1314. Those who had been summoned were to be ready to make war 'manfully and powerfully' ('*viriliter et potenter*') on the Scots, described by Edward as 'our enemies and rebels' ('*imimici et rebelles nostri*'). Edward complained that Bruce and his 'accomplices' had 'invaded and seized both our towns, our forts, villages, and territory in our land of Scotland and our other adjoining lands, committing murders, robberies, arson, sacrileges, and innumerable other crimes'.[56] On the same day, Edward also issued a general summons of the feudal host, including archbishops, bishops, abbots, priors, 'widows and other women' ('*viduas et alias mulieres*'), in response to the 'malice and treacherous rebellion' ('*malitiam & rebellionem perfidam*') of the Scots.[57] The summons was to be proclaimed publicly and failure to respond was punishable by loss of life, land, and property. On previous campaigns, magnates such as those named in the December summons would not have served for a wage and would instead have paid their followers from their own resources.[58] The timing of the early muster orders may therefore have been designed to give these men time to get their affairs in order in time for the proposed beginning of the campaign. The essential conservatism of Edward's military organisation in 1313 to 1314 has already been noted by Powicke.[59] Nonetheless, King Edward was attempting to mobilize the entire English military community for this latest incursion into Scotland. The countdown to Bannockburn had officially begun.

Even at this early stage, there were some issues with this ambitious undertaking. Of the eight earls summoned, only two – his nephew Gilbert de Clare, earl of Gloucester, and Aymer de Valence, earl of Pembroke – could be counted upon to support the king actively and enthusiastically. Of the rest, one – the king's half-brother Thomas of Brotherton, earl of Norfolk – was underage, while four others had recent and often bitter histories of opposing the king. Edward's cousin Thomas, earl of Lancaster, would prove to be his fiercest political opponent throughout the reign and his kinship with Edward served to make him a potent focus for dissent against the king's will.[60] Guy Beauchamp, earl of Warwick; Edmund Fitzalan, earl of Arundel; and Humphrey de Bohun, earl of Hereford; all had joined Lancaster in pursuing Gaveston in 1312 and had collectively approved his execution.[61] Arundel also had domestic distractions in 1314, as he sought to annul his marriage to Joan of Bar. Joan was Edward's niece, so his efforts cannot have endeared him to his monarch either.[62] Arundel's brother-in-law John de Warenne, earl of Surrey, also took part in the pursuit of Gaveston, though he had – like Valence – given assurances for Gaveston's safety on his surrender and afterwards swiftly submitted to the king.[63] Sure enough, Lancaster, Warwick, Arundel, and Surrey declined to serve in person in 1314 and sent only the minimum number of troops according to their legal obligations, which has been suggested to be as few as sixty men in total.[64] None of these four stood to gain anything from helping Edward to achieve a military breakthrough in Scotland, and they likely hoped that another pointless northern sojourn might weaken the king's position sufficiently for them to regain the upper hand in their domestic disputes with the crown. None of them could, however, have anticipated the sheer scale of the disaster that was to befall this latest campaign into Scotland.

Another possible indication of Edward II's anxieties amid the early preparations for the campaign of 1314 may be seen in his attempt, on 1 January 1314, to prohibit an upcoming unlicenced tournament at Blyth. The sheriff of Nottingham was instructed to publicly proclaim that no earl, baron, knight, or any other man-at-arms could participate in a tournament or 'presume to exercise some other deeds of arms' ('*aliqua alia facta armorum excercere praesumat*') anywhere in the kingdom without Edward's special permission.[65] Tournaments had often been a source of unease for medieval monarchs during times of political tension, when these gatherings could become opportunities to foment dissent against the crown.[66] Edward in particular seems to have generally shown at best disinterest and at worst open hostility towards the activity for most of his reign.[67] In this case, Edward was perhaps as concerned about the likelihood of participants sustaining injuries that would drain the fighting strength of his army than he was about any politicking that might go on there. Yet the timing is also indicative of the confidence – or lack thereof – that the English king had in his subjects to respond enthusiastically to his proposed campaign.

There was some cause for hope identifiable among the king's business in January 1314, however. It seems at least one Scottish lord had taken the opportunity presented by Edward's direct intervention in Scotland to renew his connections to the English crown. Thus, on 6 January, while Edward was at Windsor, he sent a private letter to Roger Mowbray, licencing him 'to send his brother Alexander with men-at-arms and footmen to help David, earl of Atholl, against Edward Bruce, on account of the dissension between them.'[68] David Strathbogie, earl of Atholl, was King Robert's nephew. Atholl's mother, Marjory, had been the sister of Bruce's first wife, Isabella.[69] His father John Strathbogie, earl of Atholl, had been executed in 1306 for supporting Bruce's bid for the throne (in)famously being hanged higher than his compatriots due to the fact his great-great grandfather had been King John of England.[70] However, David was married to Joan Comyn, daughter of the John Comyn, lord of Badenoch, who Bruce had killed at Greyfriars Kirk in Dumfries in February 1306. Joan would have been relatively young and was probably living in England with their son David at the time the letter was produced.[71] Yet their relationship gave Atholl more capacity than most to negotiate shifts in allegiance between the Bruce and Balliol camps. In May 1307 he had submitted to the English crown and in return was permitted to purchase his father's earldom back from Ralph Monthermer, then earl of Gloucester in right of his wife Joan of Acre (Edward's elder sister), for 10,000 marks, with half paid by the English crown.[72] Strathbogie played an active role in the warfare and diplomacy against the Bruce Scots, even hunting King Robert through the Aberdeenshire countryside in the winter of 1307 with the help of Roger and Alexander's father, John Mowbray.[73]

By 1312, however, Bruce had gained sufficient control over northern and central Scotland to threaten Strathbogie's possession the earldom of Atholl. Earl David thus found himself facing the prospect of paying the English crown for property that they could not secure possession of for him, although he had apparently not paid a penny of the 5,000 marks he owed for the recovery of his earldom before March 1311 anyway.[74] Hoping to retain his Scottish estates, and probably also keen to escape his substantial debts in England, Strathbogie submitted to King Robert by October 1312, when he witnessed Bruce's treaty with King Håkon V of Norway.[75] His 'defection' was apparently not immediately noticed by the English crown – or else he sought for a time to play both sides, as it were – because as late as 4 December 1312 (almost three months after witnessing the Scoto-Norwegian treaty) a prest (i.e., a formal way of issuing an advanced payment, usually for wages) worth 100s. was issued in his favour by the English exchequer for his attendance at a parliament 'on the affairs of Scotland' earlier in the year. Strathbogie was rewarded for his change of allegiance by his uncle King Robert with his appointment as lord constable of Scotland at the expense of Sir Gilbert Hay, a long-standing Bruce ally.[76] Gray attributes the capture of Perth in January 1313 to Atholl's leadership, a believable claim given the influence the earl would likely have over the fighting men of the local area.[77] Bruce may even have sought to integrate his nephew into his dynastic plans by arranging the betrothal, perhaps even the actual marriage, of the earl's sister Isabella to the king's younger brother Edward.[78]

According to Barbour, this was ultimately the source of the 'dissension' between Strathbogie and his would-be brother-in-law. Having gotten Isabella pregnant (Barbour tells us), Edward Bruce promptly abandoned her in favour of another Isabella, the daughter of William, earl of Ross.[79] There may be at least a grain of truth to Barbour's accusation. Isabella Strathbogie certainly had a son with Edward Bruce, though she appears to have remained with the Bruce Scots after 1314, even being recognized as countess of Atholl in place of her brother.[80] Her son, Alexander, also seems to have been well-favoured by Bruce and was granted his father's earldom of Carrick, possibly indicating that King Robert at least considered him to have a legitimate place in the line of succession.[81] Dissension between Atholl and Carrick may have been exacerbated during this period if, as we have explored above, King Robert's health was again in question and Carrick was perceived as being close to assuming the kingship. In this case, Edward Bruce's abandonment of Isabella would deny Strathbogie's nephew of his own claim to someday be king. The fact that the letter of 1314 specifically mentions tensions between Strathbogie and Edward Bruce would suggest that the earl himself sought to justify his decision in terms of a personal dispute with King Robert's younger brother. But the subsequent goodwill between the Scottish crown and Strathbogie's sister and nephew suggests that there was more to Atholl's defection than Barbour or even the earl himself would have us believe.

In reality, Strathbogie's decision to switch sides in 1314 was more likely motivated by the squeezing of his interests in northern Scotland, particularly by another of King Robert's nephews – Thomas Randolph. Around the time of Strathbogie's defection in 1312, Bruce had revived the earldom of Moray for Randolph, described – as he frequently was – as 'our beloved nephew', adding to its territorial boundaries and also appointing him 'lieutenant from Forth to Orkney'.[82] On the one hand, Bruce's intrusion of Randolph into Highland politics as a check to Strathbogie influence in the region was no different than his policy of balancing grants of land in the Marches between his relatives like Randolph or Edward Bruce and 'newcomers' like James Douglas, or his promotion of Stewart and Campbell lords as a counter to Macdonald influence in the west.[83] Nevertheless, Strathbogie may have perceived Randolph's dominance as a usurpation of his rightful position the most important magnate in the north, to which he may well have felt entitled given his status as a nephew of the king. This seems a far more likely source of Atholl's disaffection with the Bruce cause than any melodrama that might have been unfolding between Isabella Strathbogie and Edward Bruce. Either way, it is striking that Edward's letter commissioning the Mowbrays to assist Strathbogie in January 1314 confirms that Strathbogie had already resumed communications with the English crown *before* the 1314 campaign had begun, and indeed before anyone knew a battle would be fought at Bannockburn in the summer. Dissent among the Scottish aristocracy would surely be a source of considerable hope for Edward II ahead of this latest military undertaking, especially if it meant securing an ally with recent access to the heart of the Bruce royal administration.

King Edward could, however, still not avoid trying to deal with the practical difficulties that had necessitated his promise of military intervention in Scotland. Thus, on 4 February, letters were issued from the exchequer to the mayor and bailiffs of Newcastle and the customs officers at Hartlepool, instructing them to raise £100 (Newcastle) and £315 (Hartlepool), all of which was to be spent on for munitions. These sums were to be paid to Sir William de Fiennes, the Gascon constable at Roxburgh Castle, and were apparently already long overdue.[84] The exchequer's apparent anxiety to resupply the garrison at Roxburgh was clearly tied into the complaints made by Edward's Scottish allies in November. While raising an army was naturally a slow process, re-establishing lines of supply for a stronghold as close to the border as Roxburgh was – in theory, at least – something that could be accomplished relatively easily before Edward's forces even set off. Yet the strained tone of the missives produced in February suggest that this was not progressing at the pace the crown wanted.

So long as the flow of wages and other supplies into Roxburgh remained unreliable, the garrison's morale and discipline would continue to suffer. As the complaints of November 1313 dramatically illustrate, this had a deleterious effect on the relationship between the garrison and the local populace, which in turn undermined the confidence of the locals in the ability of the English royal administration to protect them. In early 1314, the situation at Roxburgh seems to have drawn the particular attention of a certain young and ambitious figure from among the Bruce Scots. Though Bruce's natural inclination was probably still to avoid battle as he had done the last time Edward had come north in 1310, if the king was ill – as examined in chapter 1 – his ability to direct the day-to-day activities of his most active war leaders would naturally be diminished. No matter how much King Robert had sought to instil a sense of unity and discipline in his subordinates, if the king's survival from this latest bout of poor health was uncertain, then there would have been a certain amount of pressure for those whose recent careers had relied on faithful service to King Robert to demonstrate their continued usefulness to his successors. One such figure was James Douglas, who had already proven himself to be a fearsome war leader in service of the Bruce cause but whose landed interests at this time remained confined to a relatively small and still contested area in Lanarkshire.[85] Moreover, the fact that the English army was not due to set off until June gave the Scots time to disrupt English lordship in the south-east as much as possible before the invasion began. The demoralized and undisciplined Roxburgh garrison thus presented an inventive and opportunistic warlord like Douglas with a tempting target, as we will see in more detail.

## Unburdening the Soul: Piety and Pilgrimage

By mid-February 1314, both kings were seeking saintly intercession, although perhaps for different reasons. On 16 February, King Robert was at Scotlandwell near Kinross. Here, he granted the lands of Cairnie and 'Dalcorachy' in Perthshire to Inchaffray Abbey 'for [the] salvation of his soul and for the salvation of the souls of his predecessors and successors, the kings of Scotland'.[86] As with his grant to Roger, son of Finlay, in December, this does not seem particularly indicative of a king in the midst of frantic preparations for an approaching battle. Bruce's generosity to Inchaffray Abbey is also not unusual. As one of the leading devotional sites for the cult of St Fillan, a saint who Bruce believed had protected him during the difficult and dangerous first year of his reign, the abbey held a special place in the king's heart. Moreover, Maurice, abbot of Inchaffray, had probably been present at Bruce's inauguration as king in 1306 and the king had likely taken shelter at the abbey following his disastrous defeat at the Battle of Methven later that year.[87] The relics of St Fillan, which may have been carried with the Scottish army at Bannockburn, were kept at Inchaffray Abbey, and Bower claims that Abbot Maurice personally addressed the troops ahead of the fighting on 24 June.[88] Inchaffray Abbey continued to be the beneficiary of royal acts later in the reign.[89]

Yet the emphasis on the state of Bruce's immortal soul, the concern with his successors, and his presence at Scotlandwell in particular may indicate that this visit was motivated as much by concerns about the king's physical health as for his spiritual wellbeing. We have already explored the possibility that King Robert may have been suffering another bout of the debilitating illness that would eventually kill him in 1329. Scotlandwell takes its name from a spring associated with curative miracles.[90] Moreover, the hospice there was also dedicated to St Thomas Becket and a priory dedicated to St Serf was situated on an island in Loch Leven, just west of the village.[91] Bruce was a pious devotee of the cults of both St Thomas and St Serf, suggesting the king was going all-out in his search of a miraculous recovery.[92] The king's illness also helps to explain one of the most striking and perplexing features of the build-up to Bannockburn. The months leading up to the battle were a time of considerable activity for the Scots, as we shall see in the coming chapters. Yet King Robert was noticeably absent from events in the early months of the year. Indeed, his visit to Scotlandwell in February is the last time we have direct evidence for what the Scottish king was up to until we find him, in June, awaiting the English on the first day of the battle. This is all the more remarkable given how active King Robert typically was in the Scots' military affairs, both before and after 1314, as well as how prominent he would be on the battlefield in June.

With the king unwell, and without any guarantee that he would recover, the Scottish response to the planned English invasion would now be shaped by other individuals within the community. We have already mentioned how the up-and-coming James Douglas may already have viewed the deteriorating state of the English garrison at Roxburgh as an inviting opportunity to demonstrate his martial abilities to the royal administration. Similarly, the king's nephew Thomas Randolph would be eager to maintain his status as the chief royal agent in the north of Scotland if his uncle did not survive his latest period of ill-health. And, of course, Edward Bruce himself, as the only realistic successor to his brother, must have been keen to reassure the community that he could provide the type of forceful kingship they expected and maintain Robert's record of military success against the English. As winter drew to a close, the political situation in Scotland may have been more fluid than has generally been accepted by historians, and indeed more fluid than at any other time since Bruce began to reassert his control over the kingdom in 1307.

King Edward too had apparently turned his thoughts to spiritual matters around this time. On 17 February, the day after Bruce's grant to Inchaffray Abbey, the English king was to be found at Canterbury in Kent. Like Bruce at Scotlandwell, he does not seem to have been overly concerned with the upcoming invasion of Scotland. His only known act on 17 February was the provision of a letter in favour of one Richard Lovel. Lovel was apparently being sued by a John Covert over the manor of 'Storghton' (probably Stoughton in West Sussex) but had failed to appear before the judges appointed to answer the charge against him. Edward's letter assured the judges that he had failed to appear simply because he 'was engaged in the king's service' and instructed them not to hold that against him in reaching their verdict.[93] However, Edward's presence at Canterbury in February 1314 strongly suggests that he undertook a pilgrimage to the shrine of St Thomas Becket, hoping to secure the saint's intercession ahead of the planned invasion. Becket had been a twelfth-century archbishop of Canterbury who had quarrelled with Edward's great-great grandfather Henry II over church rights and was killed in 1170 by four knights associated with the king.[94] Becket's tomb quickly became a focus of a popular cult and by 1173 he had been officially acknowledged as a saint by Pope Alexander III. Henry, eager to reconcile himself with the church and absolve himself of the blame for Becket's death, publicly supported the cult and assisted in its early growth.[95] Henry's grandson and namesake Henry III (Edward's grandfather) was an even more enthusiastic sponsor of the Becket cult and over the course of the thirteenth century Canterbury became one of the main centres of royal devotion in England.[96] By visiting Canterbury in early 1314, Edward II likely intended to secure the support of one of the English crown's chief saintly patrons against a bitter and intractable enemy.

The irony, of course, was that Robert Bruce was also a fervent devotee of Becket's cult and almost certainly actively sought the saint's intercession in 1314 as well. Becket had gained considerable popularity in Scotland after 1178, when King William 'the Lion' dedicated his newly founded abbey at Arbroath to Becket following a disastrous attack on northern England.[97] The Bruce family's devotion to the Becket cult before the Wars of Independence may have been primarily a reflection of their ambitions as English lords seeking to associate themselves with a cult patronized by the English crown.[98] One of Robert's younger brothers was named Thomas, almost certainly in honour of the saint.[99] Bruce's association with the cult of St Thomas came to the fore at several crucial junctures in his life. In the early years of the war, Bruce had been required to swear an oath of allegiance to the English crown while touching one of the swords that had martyred Becket.[100] Around the time of his marriage to his second wife Elizabeth de Burgh (c. 1302) Bruce paid to have two rings placed upon the high altar at Canterbury Cathedral, apparently in the hope of gaining the saint's blessing for the union.[101] King Robert is even claimed to have invoked St Thomas by name ahead of the Battle of Bannockburn itself.[102] It is up to the reader to decide whether either king received the intercession they prayed for from Becket in 1314, but even as King Edward was making his representations at Canterbury, his interests in Scotland were about to receive a significant blow.

## 'Thai Wend the Douglas and His Men/Had Bene Oxin': The Fall of Roxburgh, 19 to 20 February 1314

On the evening of 19 to 20 February 1314, James Douglas launched a daring assault on Roxburgh Castle under cover of darkness. This was the first armed confrontation on the road to Bannockburn and proved to be a shocking reversal for the English and a striking success for the Bruce Scots. Douglas was the eldest of three surviving sons born to Sir Walter Douglas 'the Hardy', a minor Lanarkshire baron. Sir Walter had been a thuggish character who had gained prominence in the first year of the war, fighting for a time alongside William Wallace.[103] His estates had been confiscated by Edward I and regranted to Robert Clifford, a Yorkshire baron whose service in war had been tremendously useful to the English crown.[104] According to Barbour, the young James spent three years ('thre yer') immediately after his father's forfeiture in Paris but returned to Scotland and sought employment in the household of William Lamberton, bishop of St Andrews, eager to recover his inheritance.[105] Douglas initially looked to the English crown to restore his rights, but by 1307 (if not before) he had come to see Bruce as being best able to guarantee his interests.[106] Douglas quickly emerged as one of the Bruce Scots' most fearsome and effective war leaders, terrorizing the English garrisons of southern Scotland from the relative safety of Ettrick and Selkirk Forests.[107] As we have seen, the garrison at Roxburgh had gone without wages or provisions from the English crown for some time and had been growing increasingly demoralized and undisciplined because of this, making them particularly vulnerable to Douglas's cunning and unpredictable style of warfare.

Our most detailed account of the capture of Roxburgh is found in *The Bruce*, although earlier English accounts survive in the Lanercost Chronicle, the *Vita Edwardi Secundi*, and Sir Thomas Gray's *Scalacronica*. Barbour, though writing in the 1370s, obliquely claims to have based his narrative on earlier, apparently now-lost sources.[108] Regardless of how far we trust the poet's testimony in this regard, the level of detail he provides offers potentially valuable insights into the Scottish preparations that we would not expect English writers to know. For instance, he mentions that before undertaking the attack, Douglas set 'a crafty man' named Syme or Simon Ledhouse (probably one of his followers from Clydesdale) to work constructing rope ladders to enable the Scots to scale the walls:

> 'Till he gert Syme off the Leidhous
> A crafty man and a curious
> Off hempyn rapis leddris ma
> With treyn steppis bundyn sua
> That brek wald nocht on nakyn wis.
> A cruk thai maid at thair divis
> Off irne that wes styth and squar
> That fra it in a kyrneill war
> And the ledder tharfra straitly
> Strekit, it suld stand sekyrly.'[109]

These are described in more detail by the Lanercost chronicle, albeit it in the context of an earlier, unsuccessful attack on Berwick-upon-Tweed:

> 'They were of wonderful construction, as I myself, who write these lines, saw with my own eyes. For the Scots had made two strong ropes as long as the height of the wall, making a knot at one end of each cord. They had made a wooden board also, about two and half feet long and six inches broad, strong enough to carry a man, and in the extremities of the board they made two holes through which the two ropes could be passed; then the cords, having been passed through as far as the knots, they had made two other knots in the ropes eighteen inches higher,

and above these they placed another board and so on to the end of the ropes...They had also made an iron hook...and this was to lie over the wall...Two men lifted the ropes and boards with a spear, and placed the iron hook, which was not a round one, over the wall.'[110]

Barbour says that when the rope ladders were completed, Douglas and sixty ('Thre scor') of his men approached the castle under cover of darkness.[111] That the attack occurred at night is confirmed by all three English accounts of the incident.[112] They wore black cloaks ('blak frogis') to conceal their armour and crawled commando-style up to the castle walls.[113] Barbour adds a colourful passage, no doubt designed to entertain his contemporary audience, in which a pair of guards assigned to keep watch notices the dark shapes moving towards the castle but mistake them for stray cattle belonging to a nearby careless farmer. One even jokes 'It is na dout/He sall mak mery tonycht thocht thai/Be with the Douglas led away'. The irony, of course, is that Barbour has Douglas listening quietly in the darkness, and the poet assures us that his hero 'rycht gud tent has tane/Till thar spek'.[114]

On reaching the castle, the Scots laid their ladders against the wall and swiftly climbed them, with Ledhouse reaching the top first and killing a guard who spotted him.[115] The attack took place, according to Gray and Barbour, on Shrove Tuesday ('fasteryngis evyn'), the last day before medieval Christians were expected to begin their forty-day Lenten fast in preparation for Easter.[116] The Scots thus apparently found the bulk of the garrison feasting in the great hall and, to the sound of their infamous battle-cry, 'Douglas!', they fell amongst the revellers, killing some, capturing others, and – Barbour claims – provoking some to leap over the castle walls in their desperation to escape.[117] The Gascon captain of the garrison, William de Fiennes, whose 'gret valour' Barbour magnanimously praises, took refuge in one of the towers with a few others, but by the morning of 20 February this was the only part of the castle not overrun by the Scots. Douglas's men made 'ane assalt' (i.e., an assault) on the tower the following day, during which Fiennes was wounded in the face by an arrow. Fearing for his life (rightly, since he died of his injuries soon after), Fiennes negotiated the surrender of the tower in return for he and his men being allowed to return safely to England.[118]

With Roxburgh now back in Scottish hands, Barbour claims that Ledhouse was dispatched to inform King Robert of this development. Though Bruce may not have sanctioned the attack, Barbour insists that the king gave Ledhouse 'full gud rewarding' for the service he had provided in facilitating the castle's downfall.[119] It was, however, the king's brother Edward Bruce, earl of Carrick, who was then dispatched with a 'gret cumpany' to demolish the castle and bring the rest of Teviotdale into Bruce's allegiance.[120] As noted in the introductory chapter, it had been standard Scottish policy to slight captured castles and thus deny the use of them to the English since 1307.[121] The fact that Carrick, not the king himself, came to slight the castle and accept local submissions lends further weight to the notion that King Robert was unwell in the early months of 1314. Even if Bruce was sick, however, the fall of Roxburgh – and its subsequent destruction – was a major blow to Edward's aspirations in Scotland for the year. The start date for his campaign was four months away, but the situation for the English administration in Scotland was *still* growing increasingly desperate. It also marked a notable departure from the precedent set in 1310, with the Scots adopting a more aggressive war policy than the last time King Edward had come north. This change again likely reflects the disruptions in the leadership of the Bruce Scots caused by the king's illness. As the English preparations for the invasion of Scotland were ramping up, it appeared that the pressure was mounting more seriously on the English, rather than the Scots. Even so, there was as yet no evidence that the Scots were planning to engage the English in battle once the campaign was under way.

*Chapter 3*

# Building Momentum
# Mounting English Preparations and Continuing Scottish Disruption, February to March 1314

## Business as Usual: The English 'Response' to Roxburgh

It is not entirely clear at what point Edward II was made aware of the disaster at Roxburgh. On 20 February, while his garrison at Roxburgh Castle were engaged in their desperate last stand against Douglas and his men, he was still at Canterbury. He did at least show a continued interest in Scottish affairs, however, as he was overseeing the partition of lands belonging to the late Robert de Ros of Wark.[1] Described by Edward as 'a Scottish rebel of the late king [i.e., Edward I]', Ros had interests either side of the border, but when war broke out in 1296, he sided with the Scots. His reason for doing so, according to the contemporary chronicler Walter of Guisborough, is that he was in love with a Scottish woman, though the chronicler naturally condemns him for his decision.[2] Ros was forfeited by the English crown and died soon after, leaving behind two daughters – Margaret and Isabella. Margaret and Isabella were minors at the time of their father's death (they were 15 and 12 years old in 1307, so would have been born around 1292 and 1295, respectively), and so were unable to appeal his forfeiture or assume control of their inheritance.[3]

The (admittedly tangential) relevance to Bannockburn becomes clear when we consider that Edward I had granted Ros's estates to John Comyn, lord of Badenoch, who had famously been killed by Bruce in front of the high altar at Greyfriars Kirk in Dumfries in 1306. Comyn's son – also John – had been taken into the care of the English crown and was still considered the rightful owner of the Ros estates even though he had apparently not been able to take physical possession.[4] However, Margaret and Isabella had grown up and by 1314 were both married – Margaret to John Salvayn and Isabella to John de Knoches. They had already had formal recognition of their rights from Edward II as early as 1312 (by which time they had married), having proven their ages to Edward's chancellor of Scotland, William de Bevercotes.[5] Then, on 20 February 1314, Edward wrote specifically to John de Evre, escheator (a royal officer for dealing with inheritances) beyond the Trent, instructing him on how the Ros inheritance was to be divided. As the elder daughter, Margaret and her husband were entitled to the larger share and were now to immediately receive their portion of her father's estates, while the English crown would retain possession of Isabella's inheritance for the time being.

This business is further connected to the preparations for Bannockburn because the Ros inheritance included the barony of Wark, centred around the castle of Wark-on-Tweed. Indeed, it was this portion of the patrimony that the young John Comyn had struggled to take possession of in 1311.[6] Wark would be one of two muster points Edward had assigned for the army he was gathering for his planned invasion of Scotland in June. It may be then that the advancing preparations for the coming campaign had focused Edward's attention on the long-standing uncertainty over this border lordship. Clarifying the possession of these lands might also have encouraged Salvayn and Knoches to serve in Edward's army and to persuade their newfound tenants to do so as well. On the same day as Edward saw to the Ros sisters' inheritance claims, Edward also arranged the payment of £200 to the Genoese merchant Antonio Pessagno.[7] Pessagno was routinely described as 'the king's merchant' and had been acting as Edward's chief financial 'fixer' since 1312.[8] Pessagno would continue in his crucial role as royal financier during the Bannockburn campaign. King Edward had thus not forgotten about the upcoming invasion of Scotland and may now have been turning his attention to how to pay for it.

Four days later, on 24 February, Edward was still in Canterbury, though this was probably his last day there before moving on. Before leaving, he appointed three justices 'at the insistence of Henry de Beaumont' to track down and punish the 'evil-doers' who had attacked Joanna Comyn at Faxfleet in Yorkshire and carried off £500 in goods. A later document produced on 5 July identifies Joanna as the 'widow of Alexander Comyn of Buchan', which would mean she was Beaumont's mother-in-law and had been born Joanna Latimer.[9] While again this act may not seem immediately relevant to the build-up to Bannockburn, Beaumont's eagerness to protect the interests of his Comyn kin was closely bound up with his ambitions in Scotland. Beaumont was a distant relative of Edward II's mother, Eleanor of Castile, and had risen to prominence as a knight in the English royal household since 1297.[10] He was married to Joanna's daughter Alice, whose uncle John Comyn, earl of Buchan, had died soon after being driven out of Scotland by Bruce in 1308; Alice's subsequent marriage to Beaumont circa 1310 may have been designed to ensure the support of a leading knight in the English royal household so the Comyn claim to Buchan would be vigorously maintained.[11] Beaumont could not, after all, enjoy practical possession of his wife's inheritance so long as Robert Bruce was king of Scots. Joanna's *terce* of her husband's Scottish estates was valued at £500 annually in 1311, and this was only part of what Beaumont stood to gain through his marriage to Joanna's daughter.[12] If that had been the aim of the union, then it certainly paid off. Beaumont would personally play a prominent role in the fighting at Bannockburn on 23 June – which we will explore in more detail in a later chapter – and he would continue to promote an aggressive English war policy right up until his death in 1340.[13]

By 26 February, Edward had moved north to Hadleigh in East Anglia, where he would remain for at least a week. Building, perhaps, on his payments to Pessagno earlier in the week, the king once more turned his attention to the matter of supplying his army for the upcoming campaign. Describing himself as being 'determined on the voyage in Scotland soon after Easter for the redressing of his business', Edward claimed to have 'great need of victuals' but professed to being uncertain that appropriate arrangements were being made to deliver the necessary goods. Consequently, he issued a mandate that supplies should be gathered in the same speedy manner as had been the custom in the reign of his father Edward I. He also appointed members of his own household (unfortunately unnamed in the surviving document) to supervise those royal officers responsible for gathering the supplies.[14] Two important points are raised by this mandate. First, even this early in the preparations for the campaign, Edward was apparently already anxious about the speed with which crown officials were responding to the material requirements that leading an army into Scotland entailed. This is, in turn, suggestive of difficulties in generating widespread enthusiasm for the campaign.

Second, the expectation that the regional administrators should perform their duties 'as in the time of the king's father' offers a hint at King Edward's personal perspective on the purpose of the 1314. It was, of course, not uncommon for documents such as this to refer back to previous practice.[15] But this takes on added meaning in the context of Edward's experience as king in the early years of his reign. Edward had, after all, mounted an unsuccessful and grossly undersubscribed campaign into Scotland in 1310. He had launched that from a position of weakness, in the midst of mounting domestic pressure from the Ordainers, as discussed in the previous chapter. In 1314, by contrast, Edward was acting from a position of strength – relative at least to 1310 – and must have hoped that a better-attended and more successful campaign might wipe out memories of his earlier humiliation for both his allies and his enemies.

The king could not escape the fear that the military community of his realm were unwilling to show the required level of engagement with the proposed undertaking. On 1 March, while still at Hadleigh, he wrote to every sheriff in England, ordering them to arrest anyone found to have travelled overseas to compete in tournaments 'contrary to the prohibition which we recently made'.[16] The penalty for those found guilty of having done so was indefinite imprisonment and the forfeiture of their property. As on 1 January, when Edward issued his instruction to the sheriff of Nottingham to prevent a tournament taking place at Blyth, Edward did not explicitly associate this prohibition to his planned invasion of Scotland. However, the timing would seem to indicate that Edward did not want to risk men who might otherwise serve on the coming campaign seeking to enhance their chivalric reputations abroad when they could otherwise be putting their martial skills to use in war with the Scots. Again, it is difficult not to interpret this as an acknowledgement of the fact that Edward still lacked confidence in the fighting men of England to readily answer his summons to war, but his efforts to force their participation were about to intensify.

## Castling Queenside: Specific Muster Orders and New Arrangements for Elizabeth

On 9 March, now back at Westminster, King Edward issued the most detailed muster orders yet for the army he was planning to lead north into Scotland in the summer. To begin with, he was concerned with recruiting archers ('*sagittariis*') and he looked to the northern and midland counties of England to supply them. He thus summoned 2,000 archers from Yorkshire, 1,000 from Northumberland, 1,000 collectively from Nottinghamshire and Derbyshire, and a further 500 from Lincolnshire.[17] This comes to a grand total of 4,500 men; a substantial number, though not the largest proportion of the overall force that would set off in June. Over the course of the fourteenth and into the fifteenth century, archery would become absolutely integral to English military success.[18] In 1314, however, the English were still only beginning to experiment with the use of large numbers of archers in their armies. It is true that at the Battle of Falkirk in 1297 the role of Edward I's missile troops in disrupting the tightly packed Scottish infantry formations had been absolutely crucial in ensuring victory.[19] Yet this may not have been immediately apparent to the English military community, who may have viewed the contribution of the archers at Falkirk as merely a divisionary tactic designed to give them time to mount fresh horses and launch their second, successful cavalry charge (which ultimately drove the Scots from the field). The archers at Falkirk had been pushed forward only as an afterthought when the cavalry had failed to break through the Scottish spearmen. The English thus had yet to determine how best to deploy them on the battlefield to be fully effective, as would be brutally demonstrated at Bannockburn. It was not until the reign of Edward's son Edward III that the English crown would work out how to fully exploit the effectiveness of their bowmen on the battlefield, a lesson largely learned through the defeats inflicted on it by Robert Bruce in the 1310s and 1320s.[20]

That same day, Edward wrote to the sheriff of Northumberland, who likely had responsibility for recruiting the 1,000 archers from that county, instructing him to 'pay 50 marks to the king's yeoman Master Walter le Ferour [i.e., 'the farrier'], whom the king is sending to the parts of Corbrigg' [i.e., Corbridge] to provide horse-shoes ('*ferris*') and horse-nails for the war in Scotland'.[21] Corbridge was 'the centre of Tyneside ironware trade' in the medieval period according to C. M. Fraser, so it is understandable that the king would send his personal farrier there for supplies ahead of the campaign.[22] However, it's reputation for iron-working also made the village a tempting target for the Scots, who required iron for making their arms and armour and shoeing their horses too. Bruce had burned Corbridge in 1312 and then used the ruins as a base from which to attack nearby Durham on market day.[23] In the months after Bannockburn, Corbridge was one of several Tynedale villages that contributed to the sum of £20 15s. which the Scots demanded to spare them from further harassment.[24] A fortified stone tower in the centre of the village – known locally as the 'Vicar's Peel' – may have been constructed during this period to provide additional protection against Scottish attacks.[25]

The following day, Edward commissioned Alexander le Convers (described elsewhere as the 'king's clerk') and Thomas 'de Eggefeld' (probably Edgefield in Norfolk) to begin gathering supplies from Norfolk and to make preparations for delivering them to the army ahead of the planned campaign. Alexander and William 'de Thunneyk' were given the same responsibility for Yorkshire; Alexander and John 'de Torryng' for Lincolnshire; Alexander and William of Stowford for Essex and Suffolk; and Stephen 'Blound' for Northumberland and the Bishopric of Durham. Some of these men may have been employed for their experience as sailors, since another document produced on the same day indicates that the supplies were to be primarily transported by sea.[26] As an interesting – if largely coincidental – aside, 'Blound' was probably the Sir Stephen Blount, who would later be chosen to escort Bruce's queen Elizabeth de Burgh on her release from captivity after the Battle of Bannockburn, and then was appointed as deputy-chamberlain of Scotland in June 1315.[27] He was probably a Scot, related to the William Blount who in 1325 was granted lands in Angus by King Robert.[28] The appointment of these individuals to oversee the requestioning of goods might be interpreted as a follow-up on the concerns about the speed with which supplies were being sent to his army that the king had expressed at Hadleigh on 26 February. It certainly demonstrates that, whatever anxieties he may still have harboured about the community's attitude towards his latest military endeavour, King Edward intended to proceed on the expectation that the required provisions would be supplied on time.

On the same day, Edward also wrote to the 'abbots, priors, sheriffs, bailiffs, and other faithful' ('*abbattibus prioribus vicecomitibus ballivis et aliis fidelibus*') of the kingdom instructing them to comply with the efforts of Nicholas of Tickhill ('de Tykehull') in 'purchasing and procuring' ('*emendis et arrestandis*') horses for the expedition into Scotland.[29] Those intending to fight as cavalry would likely provide their own horses, so Edward was probably purchasing these animals for use in transporting supplies on campaign. This was an immense undertaking, nonetheless. While the author of the *Vita*'s claim that the English baggage train measured twenty leagues (almost seventy miles) in length is surely hyperbolic, it is not unreasonable to suppose hundreds, perhaps even thousands of horses would be required to keep Edward's army on the move. Assuming that a man-at-arms on campaign required a minimum of three horses – one to ride into battle, one to travel on, and (at least) one to carry his equipment, and given that estimates for the English cavalry at Bannockburn have run anywhere between 2,500 and 3,000, this would mean anywhere between 6,000 and 9,000 horses were needed just to service this small portion of the army.[30] Again, the crown would not have to buy all or even most of these animals, but it is fair to suppose that Nicholas was encouraged to overestimate rather than underestimate in his preparations.

As well as the general needs of his army as a whole, Edward was also concerned with the preparations of some of his individual subordinates. To that end, he issued letters of protection for Nicholas Somerset, Thomas Folquardby, John and Warin 'le Ferur', and 'Novellus Lumbard', all of whom were being dispatched north by Gilbert de Clare, earl of Gloucester, 'to make provision there against his advent to the parts of Scotland'.[31] The surname 'le Ferur' would suggest that, like the aforementioned Walter who had been sent to Corbridge by King Edward on 9 March, John and Warin were farriers, and Warin and Novellus (whose surname suggests he came from northern Italy – i.e., 'Lombard') are specifically mentioned in the letters as having responsibility for the earl's 'horses and harness [i.e., his armour]'. Gloucester was King Edward's nephew and he had enjoyed considerable prominence in the English royal administration during his uncle's reign. Though he had served as an Ordainer in 1310 to 1311 and consented to the final, ultimately fatal pursuit of Gaveston in 1312, Gloucester had retained his uncle's trust in matters of war, diplomacy, and governance.[32] He had, for instance, served as 'guardian of the realm' ('*custos regni*') of England while Edward was conducting diplomatic business on the Continent in 1313.[33] He had also been militarily active in Scotland and the northern Marches for brief periods earlier in the reign, but the distractions of domestic politics had prevented the earl from having much impact on the conflict so far.[34] Although he was King Robert's brother-in-law according to contemporary canon law – since the earl was married to Mathilda de Burgh, sister of Queen Elizabeth – Gloucester appears to have viewed the war in Scotland as a perfect opportunity to develop a respectable martial reputation.[35] He had assumed the role of mediator in the long-running and frequently bitter disputes between King Edward and his magnates, apparently hoping that stability at home would allow Edward to focus on matters in Scotland.[36] Gloucester was only 22 years old when his uncle announced his intention to invade Scotland in November 1313, being born circa 10 May 1291.[37] The combination of his relative youth and his frustrations over the lack of opportunities to demonstrate his military prowess in Scotland likely help to explain Gloucester's apparent eagerness to get his own preparations underway in 1314. As we will see in later chapters, his enthusiasm would not be rewarded.

Two days later on 12 March, Edward appointed John Sturmy and Peter Bard as 'admirals' ('*admiralli*') of a fleet apparently intended to accompany the English army up the east coast as it passed into Scotland in the summer. He also laid out how crews for the ships should be chosen, and issued further instructions for the collection of provisions, arms, and armour for the upcoming campaign.[38] Edward was also occupied with another matter, less immediately integral to the prosecution of the war, but significant nonetheless. He now turned his attention to what to do with his most valuable captive, Elizabeth de Burgh. Elizabeth was the daughter of Richard de Burgh, earl of Ulster, an important ally of the English crown in Ireland.[39] In 1302, she had married Robert Bruce, then earl of Carrick, partly to consolidate Bruce's political networks across the Irish Sea, but also probably in part to reinforce Bruce's recent reconciliation with Edward I's royal administration after four years of resisting English ambitions in Scotland.[40] Elizabeth had been inaugurated as queen of Scots alongside Robert in March 1306, though one English chronicler suggests she was not overly convinced by her husband's ambitions as she glumly observed, 'I appreciate that you are the summer king; perhaps you will not be [in] winter'.[41] If so, Elizabeth was almost proven correct, as within months she had been captured at Tain in Ross, probably while fleeing north to seek shelter with her sister-in-law Isabella Bruce in Norway, and sent to England as a prisoner.[42] Initially, Elizabeth was imprisoned in a manor house at Burstwick in Yorkshire, where she was allowed only two attendants who, by order of the English crown no less, were to be 'elderly and not at all gay'.[43] In an undated letter to Edward II, Elizabeth complained that at Burstwick she was allowed only three changes of clothing a year, no headgear, and no bedding, while even her attendants received only one robe each in a year.[44]

By October 1310, she was living at Bisham ('Bistelesham') in Berkshire; in early 1312, she was transferred to the Tower of London with a brief stay at Windsor Castle between the two. By now, she had acquired a more substantial household consisting of two young women, two squires, and two yeomen and was even receiving 40s. a week to pay for them.[45] By February 1313, Elizabeth had been moved again, this time to the nunnery at Shaftsbury in Dorset. Her household had dwindled to four – Elena Edgar, John Claydon, Samuel Lynford, and William Preston – and her weekly expenses had reduced by half.[46] She may have resided at Shaftsbury for as little as twelve weeks before being moved to Barking Abbey, just outside London, but amid the preparations for the campaign of 1314, King Edward decided to move Elizabeth again. This time, he ordered that Elizabeth – styled 'wife of Robert Bruce' ('*uxorem Roberti de Brus*') rather than 'queen of Scots' – should be taken from Barking Abbey to Rochester Castle in Kent. Here, the constable Henry Cobham was to provide her with a 'sufficient chamber with the said castle' ('*cameram infra dictum castrum competentem*') and 20s. per week. Elizabeth was also allowed to take exercise within the castle grounds and the grounds of nearby St Andrews Priory 'at suitable times, under sure guard' ('*oportunis temporibus spatiari sub salva custodia*').[47]

The reasoning behind this move is not made explicit in the document but likely reflects a desire to increase the security arrangements around Elizabeth as preparations for the summer campaign intensified. Rochester Castle was certainly a stronger prison than Barking Abbey, but given the enormous distance between Barking and the border, it seems unlikely that the Scots could attempt – let alone pull off – a rescue, regardless of how the approaching campaign played out. Perhaps Edward simply felt it was better to be safe than sorry. Possession of the Bruce women – not only Elizabeth, but also her stepdaughter Marjory and her sister-in-law Christian Bruce – represented Edward's greatest advantage over Bruce at this time.[48] With Elizabeth in English custody, Bruce was unable to father more successors. The loss of his daughter and sister(s) limited his ability to extend his personal political networks through the strategic marriages of his female relatives. All of this added to the dynastic uncertainty that plagued the Bruce regime at this time, as we saw in the first chapter. The transfer of Elizabeth from Barking to Rochester may also reflect a wider sense of unease on the part of the English royal administration. Edward would by now surely have been aware of the recent fall of Roxburgh Castle, and he may also have known that Edinburgh too was under threat from the Scots. Far from cowing the Scots into submission, the threat of renewed invasion seemed to have provoked a period of frenzied activity from the Scots and placed the ailing English administration in Scotland under even more pressure than before. By moving Elizabeth to Rochester then, Edward have hoped to reassure himself of the advantages he had left.

## 'For the Crag Wes Hey and Hidwous': The Fall of Edinburgh, 14 March 1314

While Edward did his best to hasten preparations for his summer campaign and sought to strengthen his domestic position, the situation in Scotland continued to deteriorate. There was in truth little King Edward could do about this until his army was on the move. Although they had avoided condemnation alongside the garrisons at Roxburgh and Berwick in the petition presented to Edward in November 1313, discipline does seem to have been an issue among the Edinburgh garrison as well. The main source of contention in this case appears to have been the local sheriff and keeper of the castle, Piers Lebaud. Like Fiennes at Roxburgh, Lebaud was a Gascon by birth and had served as sheriff of Edinburgh and Linlithgow since at least 1310.[49] However, his loyalty is called into question by many of the most useful accounts of the events surrounding Edinburgh's capture in 1314. The author of the *Vita*, who describes Lebaud as Gaveston's cousin, claims that he betrayed the castle to the Scots.[50] Barbour too claims that Lebaud 'spokyn had with the king', although he adds that the garrison learned of this and imprisoned Lebaud before he could betray them to the Scots.[51] Gray suggests that Lebaud remained faithful to Edward until the castle was overrun but afterwards 'became Scottish' ('*deueint Escotoys*').[52] Lebaud's loyalties remained in doubt even in Scottish service, however, and by March 1316, he had been executed by Bruce for an unspecified 'betrayal' ('*prodicio*') of the king.[53]

The precise chronology of events surrounding the fall of Edinburgh Castle on 14 March 1314 is complicated by the early historiography of the incident. Unlike at Roxburgh, the assault on Edinburgh was probably not a surprise attack. According to Barbour, Edinburgh was already under siege before James Douglas had captured Roxburgh Castle on 19 February.[54] The lack of any reference to events at Edinburgh in surviving contemporary documents produced by the English crown until after it had fallen to the Scots would tend to suggest that Barbour is wrong to assert that the castle had been under siege for over a month. Alternatively, the armed force that Barbour informs us Edward Bruce, earl of Carrick, led south to slight Roxburgh Castle after Douglas had seized that fortress in February may have then been diverted directly to Edinburgh once the defences at Roxburgh had been neutralized. Barbour though makes no reference to Edward Bruce at Edinburgh, instead placing command of the besieging army in the hands of Thomas Randolph, earl of Moray, a claim echoed by Gray and the late-fourteenth-century Scottish chronicler John of Fordun.[55] As we have noted elsewhere, King Robert is once again conspicuous by his absence, as he was from all of the Scottish activities in the early months of 1314. This again serves to reinforce the impression that the king's health may have been suffering during this period, a fact that placed leadership of the Scottish war effort in the hands of his senior lieutenants.

Randolph was probably the son of an elder half-sister of Bruce, being regularly described by the king as 'our dearest/beloved nephew' ('*dilecto nepoti nostro*'), and was treated throughout the reign as Bruce's most favoured kinsman.[56] Randolph had come out in support of his uncle when he became king in 1306, but he was captured at the Battle of Methven and thereafter served the English crown.[57] Possibly this shift of allegiance was made under duress, and after being recaptured by the Scots in 1309 he was quickly reconciled with the king.[58] Barbour has Randolph rebuke the king in the immediate aftermath of his recapture, accusing his uncle of 'cowardy' for his reluctance to confront the English in open battle. This exchange is likely Barbour's invention however, designed to give him another opportunity to reinforce to his contemporary audience the value of caution and calculated in warfare (a central theme of Barbour's work) in the form of King Robert's reply to Randolph's outburst. That Randolph was chosen by Barbour to fill this role is part of a wider pattern within the poem of using Randolph as a contrast to the 'greater' heroes of his work like King Robert and Sir James Douglas, a trend which is itself was bound up with the politics of southern Scotland in Barbour's own time.[59] There is certainly no trace of any hostility between the king and his nephew in the numerous generous grants of lands and rights that the former bestowed upon the latter throughout the reign. In 1312, King Robert revived the extinct earldom of Moray for Randolph, giving him wide-ranging powers to act as the chief royal agent north of the Forth, and granted him the strategically important southern lordships of Nithsdale and Annandale (the latter a former possession of the Bruces) as well.[60]

Barbour asserts that it was on hearing of the unorthodox manner in which Douglas and his men had gained access to Roxburgh that Randolph was inspired to seek a similarly unconventional means of entry into Edinburgh.[61] We must once again be cautious about accepting this uncritically, given Barbour's tendency to undersell Randolph's achievements particularly in contrast to Douglas. But the notion that Randolph was inspired by news of Douglas's accomplishment is believable in the context of early 1314. As previously discussed, if the king was sick – and perhaps appeared to be terminally ill – we might expect the leading figures among the Bruce Scots to compete with one another to demonstrate their value to King Robert's successor. Given his exalted position within the royal administration under his uncle Robert, Randolph had particularly pressing reasons to ensure that he enjoyed a similarly prominent place in the Scottish government if his uncle Edward was soon to accede as king.[62] This is in addition to the influence the spirit of friendly chivalric competition that the poet intended to evoke, which was also a powerful motivator of knightly behaviour in this period.

The plan that Randolph adopted to capture Edinburgh was suggested to him, again according to Barbour, by a local man named William Francis. A William 'le Fraunceys' appears in the so-called Ragman Rolls of 1296 and is described as belonging to the county of Edinburgh.[63] This individual may in fact have been Francis's father, who Barbour states had previously served as 'keeper' of Edinburgh Castle.[64] As a young man, Francis had thus lived in the castle and claims that because he 'lovyt a wench her in the toun' he discovered a secret, precipitous route in and out of the castle via the north face of Castle Rock so that he could visit her without anyone knowing. Francis offers to show Randolph this hidden route and so they secretly ascend to the foot of the castle walls accompanied by 'thretty [thirty] men wycht and hardy' according to Barbour.[65]

Barbour insists that Randolph and his men achieved this feat under cover of darkness – 'in a myrk nycht' as the poet puts it.[66] The contemporary Lanercost chronicler broadly agrees with this, stating that the Scottish attack occurred 'in the evening'. The Lanercost chronicler adds the detail that the rest of the Scottish force conducted a diversionary assault on the southern side of the castle, where the approach was less steep, to distract the garrison.[67] This may even explain why Randolph was the one to lead his followers in their perilous climb up the north face of Castle Rock. Edward Bruce, as the senior figure present in the besieging army, may have led the diversionary assault while his nephew scaled the cliffs with a smaller force and took the garrison by surprise. Whatever the case, once Randolph and company were at the summit, they scaled the walls (presumably on rope ladders like those employed by Douglas at Roxburgh) and quickly overwhelmed the unprepared and beleaguered garrison. Gray, while mentioning neither Francis nor the diversionary attack, broadly confirms the accounts of the Lanercost chronicler and Barbour in observing that the Scots 'took it [i.e., Edinburgh Castle] at the highest part of the Rock', which the garrison 'had not been concerned about'.[68]

Ever the dramatist, Barbour adds a number of suspenseful but highly dubious details in his narrative of the events of 14 March. Echoing the earlier incident in which Douglas and his men were mistaken for stray cattle by the hapless lookouts at Roxburgh, the poet claims that, as Randolph approached the walls at Edinburgh, a member of the garrison happened to hurl a stone down the cliff and speculatively yelled 'Away, I se you weile' into the darkness. Randolph and his followers of course hold their nerve and remain still until the guards move on, at which point they resume their progress.[69] Even less plausibly, Barbour includes a digression on a supposed prophecy of St Margaret concerning the event. According to the poet, there was a painting of a man climbing a ladder into a castle on the wall of St Margaret's Chapel within the confines of the castle. The words 'Gardys vous de Francais' had been written above it, apparently by the saint herself in the eleventh century 'as auld men sais'. This had been misinterpreted, says Barbour, as a warning that the castle would one day be captured by the French, when in fact it was a prophecy concerning William Francis instead.[70]

As had happened at Roxburgh – and indeed most castles and strongholds taken by the Scots during Bruce's reign – once Edinburgh was back under their control the Scots slighted it – 'myne doun [i.e., undermined] all halily/Bath tour [tower] and wall rycht to the grond' as Barbour puts it. Interestingly, Barbour claims that King Robert himself oversaw the demolition of the castle's defences in this instance and afterwards toured the local area, bringing it 'till his pes', perhaps suggesting some kind of ayre even.[71] This would certainly challenge the notion that King Robert was in uncertain health at this time. However, this is probably merely wishful thinking on the part of the poet. Certainly, there can have been little scope for a royal progress around Lothian as Barbour seems to suggest. As we shall see in more detail in later chapters, even without a garrison at Edinburgh, King Edward remained confident enough in his control of this region to march his army through it and reside for a time at Edinburgh itself in the summer.

Nevertheless, the fall of Edinburgh was yet another frustrating setback for King Edward. It strikingly demonstrates the shocking weakness of the English administration in Scotland after seven years of sustained, methodical, and ruthlessly effective pressure from the Bruce Scots. Even in spite of all of the preparations King Edward had undertaken thus far, as of the first three months of 1314, the English had actually lost two castles since the announcement of the upcoming campaign. The threat of a renewed English invasion had clearly not deterred the Bruce Scots from their opportunistic assaults on vulnerable targets north of the border. The situation for Edward's allies in Scotland was getting worse, not better, even as the date set for Edward's advance drew near. Most seriously of all, the fall of Edinburgh opened a yawning gap of nearly seventy miles in the English supply line between the most northerly English-held castle at Stirling and the nearest friendly stronghold at Dunbar. The garrison at Stirling must have received news of events at Roxburgh and Edinburgh with mounting dread, expecting that they too would be targeted before Edward's army set off in June. They cannot yet have known, however, that their response to this threat would bring King Robert and King Edward head-to-head on the battlefield at Bannockburn.

## Getting into Gear: Continuing English Preparations and Further Specific Muster Orders

No business concerning Scotland is known to have been conducted by Edward II on 14 March, although the exchequer issued a prest of 10 marks for the expenses of Andrew, bishop of Argyll.[72] Two days after the castle had fallen, at which point he may not yet have known about the situation in Edinburgh, King Edward excused one Walter Fauconberg from appearing before the king's justices to answer for 'certain trespasses' committed by him against two minor Yorkshire lords – Sir Miles Stapleton and Sir Marmaduke Tweng. Walter had been performing undisclosed 'service' to the king and was therefore unable to attend. Edward would excuse Fauconberg from appearing yet again on 29 April, by which point the king would have moved northwards to Kirkstead in Lincolnshire on his way to the muster at Berwick.[73]

The precise nature of these 'trespasses' is unclear, but Fauconberg and Tweng were cousins, and this may offer some clue as to the nature of these disputes. The former's father, also Walter, had married Agnes Bruce, eldest sister and primary heir of Peter Bruce of Skelton, who had died in 1268 with no offspring and so his estates were divided between his four sisters. Agnes and her husband received the barony of Skelton; her younger sister Lucy – Tweng's mother –

received Brotton near Yarm; the next youngest sister, Margaret, married Robert de Ros of Wark and received Kendal; and the youngest sister, Laderina, received Kentmere and Carlton. By 1290, Laderina's daughter Sybil had married Stapleton, meaning all three men involved in the suits mentioned above were related to one another either by blood or by marriage.[74] It is tempting to suggest that Fauconberg's 'trespasses' related in some way to their various claims to the lands of the Bruces of Skelton, though this is necessarily speculative. The Bruces of Skelton were distant cousins of King Robert and were technically the senior branch of the kindred, though since they had separated in the twelfth century, the Annandale branch (to which the king belonged) had become more significant both in terms of their political importance and the value of their lands.[75] By the fourteenth century, the two branches were largely estranged and so we would not expect King Robert to have had any interest in these matters. Yet a residual recognition of the Skelton Bruce offspring as part of his wider kindred would influence Bruce's actions in the immediate aftermath of Bannockburn, as we will see in a later chapter.

Related though they may have been, Fauconberg, Stapleton, and Tweng had very different experiences of, and attitudes towards, the English royal administration. As the documents of March 1314 indicate, Fauconberg was 'engaged in the king's service' and performing duties that Edward at least felt were sufficiently important to justify delaying the legal challenges being made against him. Stapleton too had once been a close servant of King Edward, having served in Edward's household during his time as prince of Wales. He also had the keeping of the manor of Burstwick-in-Holderness, where Bruce's wife Elizabeth was held prisoner following her capture in 1306. When Edward became king in 1307, he made Stapleton the steward of the royal household, but their relationship soured in 1308 when Edward's favourite, Piers Gaveston, began to encroach on Stapleton's interests.[76] Stapleton's growing frustration with Gaveston's rise seems to have driven him closer to Edward's cousin and rival Thomas, earl of Lancaster. Also among Lancaster's regular followers was Tweng.[77] Unlike Stapleton, Tweng had not enjoyed close connections to the royal administration, but both men had extensive military experience in the war with Scotland. Association with Lancaster meant that both Stapleton and Tweng were implicated in the killing of Gaveston in 1312, an act that Edward would not forgive despite his public reconciliation with those responsible in 1313.[78]

In this context, Edward's actions of 16 March 1314 take on a new light. Far from innocently postponing a pair of (possibly related) legal cases to ensure the smooth running of the royal government, Edward was likely deliberately obstructing two individuals in their pursuit of their rights because he held them in suspicion. This is an example of the partiality that generated such fierce antagonism from the wider English political community throughout Edward's reign.[79] It is particularly interesting for our purposes, because all three men involved in the legal proceedings – Fauconberg, Stapleton, and Tweng – served in the English army that invaded Scotland in the summer of 1314, and thus all of them fought at Bannockburn in June. Edward's interference in Stapleton and Tweng's legal affairs therefore not only offers an insight into the general frustrations felt by Edward's subjects at this time but also serves as a powerful illustration of the specific divisions within Edward's army in 1314. King Edward might well be able to call on more troops than Bruce. But with his subordinates often in dispute with one another, and their king exacerbating these tensions in order to settle personal scores, Edward's army lacked cohesion. This would contribute to the defeat by King Robert in June, with particularly dire personal consequences for the trio mentioned above. Fauconberg and Stapleton were both killed fighting at Bannockburn, while Tweng was captured.

On 18 March, Edward returned to the matter of finance and supplies, issuing instructions to Antonio Pessagno, a Genoese merchant (*mercatori Januensi*) and the king's chief financier, to secure provisions for the army and have it 'carted' ('*cariari*') to Berwick.[80] Born circa 1280 in the wealthy and well-connected trading city of Genoa in northern Italy, Pessagno had first come to England around 1306 or 1307 with the intention of exporting English wool to the Continent.[81] However, his fortunes took a dramatic upturn in 1311 when the Frescobaldis of Florence, on whom Edward II had previously relied for financial support, went bankrupt after being exiled from England by the Ordainers.[82] Pessagno, who had already been loaning small amounts of money to the king, quickly stepped in to fill the gap in Edward's finances, and Edward soon came to rely on him to keep the English royal administration solvent. Between March and the beginning of the Bannockburn campaign in June, Pessagno would provide the English crown with over £21,000 in cash to fund the invasion of Scotland.[83]

It is noteworthy that in March 1314, the period Pessagno was given in which to provide the requested supplies was 'until the Feast of the Nativity of St John the Baptist next to come', i.e., 24 June 1314.[84] This would suggest that Edward still did not expect his army to be setting off until 24 June, and the absence of any mention of Stirling strongly indicates that the castle was not perceived as being directly under threat from the Scots. Though the Scottish siege of Edinburgh Castle was now over, the siege of Stirling Castle must not yet have begun, and the deal for its relief was not yet in effect.

If news of the fall of Edinburgh had not reached Westminster before 18 March, Edward surely must have been aware of it by 21 March, by which point an entire week had passed. Yet even at this juncture there is no particular sign of great haste on the king's part to hasten preparations for the campaign. Instead, he issued an exemption for his younger half-brother Thomas of Brotherton, earl of Norfolk, excusing him from serving on the upcoming campaign into Scotland.[85] Edward's decision to leave his brother behind in 1314 is not entirely surprising. Thomas was only 13 years old at the time the exemption was issued and would celebrate his fourteenth birthday on 1 June 1314, a mere nine days before he and his fellow magnates had been summoned to appear at Berwick-upon-Tweed.[86] It was not unknown for teenagers as young as Thomas to appear on battlefields, often in supporting roles such as protecting their lords in combat and providing them with fresh weapons if theirs broke. Moreover, King Robert's son David II nominally led his earliest raid into northern England as early as 1341, when he was only 17 years old, while Henry 'Hotspur' is credited with playing a significant role in the recovery of Berwick in 1378 despite being only 14 years old at the time.[87]

There were, however, political considerations that likely deterred Edward from bringing his half-brother on campaign in 1314. Thomas was, at this point, second in line to the throne. Indeed, he had been first in line until the birth of Edward's son, the future Edward III, in November 1312.[88] The birth of a son and direct heir had strengthened Edward's position as king, a fact that may have influenced the timing of his planned invasion of Scotland, but not so much so that he felt confident in putting both himself *and* a potential heir in harm's way on campaign. Thus, Edward wrote, as 'a special favour to our beloved brother, Thomas of Brotherton, earl of Norfolk, we have remitted and pardoned him his service which he is bound to do for us.'

Although Thomas thus avoided accompanying the English army to defeat at Bannockburn in 1314, he would be actively involved in his half-brother's Scottish policies later in the reign. When Edward Balliol, son of Bruce's deposed rival

John Balliol, returned to England in 1318, providing Edward II with potential political leverage against Bruce, he was sheltered in Thomas of Brotherton's household.[89] In 1319, Norfolk accompanied his brother's third campaign into Scotland, which began and ended with an unsuccessful siege of Berwick-upon-Tweed.[90] He was charged, as marshal of England, with transporting Scottish prisoners to the Tower of London in 1321.[91] Despite the apparent brotherly affection expressed by King Edward in 1314, when Queen Isabella set out to depose her husband in 1326, Earl Thomas was one of the first magnates to join her.[92] His service to the English crown continued into the Second War of Scottish Independence, however, where he fought for his nephew Edward III at the bloody Battle of Halidon Hill – celebrated by contemporary English writers as a reversal of Bannockburn – and in 1337, the year before his death, he served as keeper of Perth for Edward III.[93]

The day after he had excused his half-brother from service on the summer campaign, Edward undertook several items of royal business related – directly or indirectly – to the upcoming Bannockburn campaign. First, he summoned ships from various ports across the south coast of England to serve in a fleet being assembled in the Irish Sea.[94] The ultimate purpose of this fleet was likely to disrupt any activity by the Bruce Scots in the Irish Sea over the summer and perhaps to mount a naval assault on Bruce's western possessions while Edward terrorized the Scots by land. As we examined earlier, in response to rumours of a planned Scottish attack on Man in April 1311, Edward prepared to send a fleet to land on the Argyll coast commanded by the same John Macdougall of Argyll who would be in charge of the fleet in 1314. Edward had predicted – incorrectly as it would turn out – that this manoeuvre would be 'one of the greatest movements of the war'.[95] Man had fallen to the Scots in the summer of 1313, meaning that it could now be used as a base from which the Scots could launch counter-raids against the coasts of eastern Ireland, northern Wales, and even western England. Edward would have hoped to prevent this, as it would serve to further undermine his subjects' confidence in his ability to protect them.

The fleet may thus have been intended to assault or retake Man and forestall any Scottish activity in the Irish Sea, or perhaps to land on the west coast of Scotland, as in 1311. The requested ships were to assemble at Aberconwy in north-west Wales by 'the Feast of Pentecost next to come' ('*festo Pentecostes proximo futurum*'), i.e., 26 May. In any event, this fleet never seems to have put to sea and certainly does not seem to have set sail at all in 1314. In all likelihood, the operation was hastily switched from an offensive to a defensive stance following the news of the English defeat at Bannockburn, amid fears that the Scots might exploit their victory and launch seaborne attacks of their own. Considerable investment would be directed into this fleet in the coming months, however, and, as will be discussed, the nature of that investment offers further clues as to its purpose.

Also, Edward made formal assurances to the widow Isabella de Vescy that her property at Tickhill ('Tukehale') in Yorkshire would be free from interference by the king's ministers while William de Vescy was away on campaign in Scotland. The document states that William had specifically requested this protection for Isabella.[96] Isabella was the wife of William's late father, but she was not William's mother. William was illegitimate, but his father had ensured that he had still inherited the bulk of the Vescy estates. Isabella must have been a good age in 1314, since she was already a widow when she married William's father, and her first husband had died in 1265.[97] It is striking that William still felt some responsibility to protect her interests despite not being directly related to her; this is suggestive of a degree of genuine affection between William and Isabella. According to the document, William would be serving in the following of Aymer de Valence, earl of Pembroke, in the upcoming campaign. As already discussed, Pembroke had a somewhat ambiguous relationship with the English crown in the early years of Edward's reign, but since Gaveston's death in 1312, Pembroke was so horrified by the actions of the king's opponents that he became a fierce supporter of the king. As a result, Pembroke played a leading role in the preparations for Bannockburn and likely remained close to King Edward on the battlefield. Closeness to the king was not enough to save poor William, however, who was killed in the fighting at Bannockburn.

Edward's most important business of 22 March concerned the recruitment of soldiers from Ireland to serve in the planned invasion of Scotland. Edward issued summonses to twenty-five 'native' (i.e., *Gaeilge*-speaking) Irish lords (by name), seventeen Irish prelates, the baillies of twelve Irish towns, and twenty Anglo-Irish lords (again by name).[98] We have no way of telling how well these orders were heeded, but at least Richard de Burgh, earl of Ulster, would be with Edward at Newminster in Northumberland by late May.[99] Ulster is named as 'captain' ('*capitaneum*') of the Irish contingent in the March document, suggesting he would have turned up at Newminster with as many Irish troops as he could muster.[100] The presence of 'the Red Earl', as he was known, would perhaps have seemed particularly galling for King Robert, since Ulster was also the father of Elizabeth de Burgh and thus was the Scottish king's father-in-law. That King Robert held a grudge over this might be inferred from the fact that Ulster would arguably suffer more than any other Anglo-Irish lord during the Bruce invasion of Ireland in 1315. One Irish annalist reports that, as a result of Bruce attacks on his property in 1315, 'Richard de Burgh, earl of Ulster, was a wanderer up and down Ireland all this year, with no power or lordship'.[101]

Some of the 'native' Irish lords summoned by Edward were later associated with the Bruces. Whether or not this meant they were willing to serve in the English army at Bannockburn remains uncertain. 'Doneval O Neel, duci Hibernicorum de Tyrowyn' is surely the same Domnall Ó Néill, king of Tyrone, who would be the Bruces' most faithful and active supporter among the 'native' Irish nobility during the Scottish invasion of Ireland from 1315 to 1318.[102] The 'Remonstrance of the Irish Princes', a letter to Pope John XXII written in 1317 and expressing support for Edward Bruce's claim to be king of Ireland, was even given in Ó Néill's name.[103] 'Dermod O Kahan, duci Hibernicorum de Fernetrewe' may be one of the O'Cathains who the *Annals of Inisfallen* claim aided the Bruces in 1315, though their decision to do so may have been made after the Scots arrived in Ireland.[104] Similarly, 'Eth' Offlyn, duci Hibernicorum de Turtery [Tuitre in Antrim]' may be one of the O'Flains also accused of assisting the Scots after 1315. 'Donethuth O Bien, duci Hibernicorum de Tothmund [Thomond]' is almost certainly the Donnchad O'Brien who approached the Scots with an offer of support in 1317, though developments in Thomond itself prevented O'Brien from ever rendering any assistance to them.[105]

Other names on the list appear to have had a more ambiguous relationship with the Scots, though again this does not necessarily mean they answered Edward's call to join his army in 1314. 'Felyn O Honoghur, duci Hibernicorum de Connach' is perhaps the same Feidlim Ó Conchobair, king of Connacht, who helped the earl of Ulster pursue the Scots from Dundalk to Carlingford in autumn 1315 but then abandoned the earl when he learned that his cousin Cathal had usurped his authority in Connacht – leaving Ulster to be defeated by the Scots in battle at Connor.[106] 'Neel O Hanlan, duci Hibernicorum de Erthere' likely represented the Ó hAnluain of Armagh, who raided English-held lands around Dundalk in 1316, although whether this was in support of the Scots or not is unclear.[107] 'Fyn O Dymsy' shares at least his surname with the 'Yrsche king', who Barbour claims tried to drown the Scottish army in Ireland by flooding part of his own estates where he had invited them to make camp.[108] For all Edward seems to have made a wide-ranging attempt to recruit the fighting potential of medieval Ireland for his Scottish campaign, it seems likely that fewer than were summoned actually joined his army.

On 24 March, King Edward cancelled the parliament he had previously summoned to meet at Westminster in April, claiming that Scottish affairs now took precedence, and simultaneously reiterated his instructions to twenty-two lords – chief among them the recalcitrant earl of Lancaster – that they should present themselves, ready to make war on the Scots, this time at Newcastle-upon-Tyne by 1 June.[109] He also issued further detailed muster orders. The bulk of the soldiers are described as infantry (*peditibus*), though some would also serve as archers (*sagittariis*). 2,000 archers were summoned from Yorkshire, 1,000 from Northumberland, 1,000 from Shropshire and Staffordshire, 1,000 from Nottinghamshire and Derbyshire, 500 from Cheshire, and 100 from the Forest of Dean. Furthermore, 100 crossbowmen (*balistariis*) were ordered to come from Bristol, although Edward was apparently willing to accept any sort of archer from them if crossbows could not be procured. A further 1,900 infantry were summoned from Wales under the command of Edward's nephew Gilbert de Clare, earl of Gloucester, Humphrey de Bohun, earl of Hereford, and several other Marcher lords.[110] All of these soldiers were to present themselves at Newcastle-upon-Tyne within three weeks (*tres septimanas*) of Easter (which would have been 7 April in 1314), ready to serve in Scotland. This is significantly earlier than the previous summonses, which had emphasized June as the beginning of the campaign, but these muster orders were explicitly tied to the planned invasion of Scotland. Possibly, Edward merely anticipated a degree of difficulty in encouraging his common subjects to serve and felt that an ambitious start date could be more easily expected to give his regional officials additional time to gather sufficient numbers. Alternatively, he may simply have felt that once he had these troops physically present in the north, he could more easily induce them to remain with him beyond the time he had requested.

As in the case of the Irish lords summoned on 22 March, we cannot be certain how many of those summoned actually turned out. As we will see in a later chapter, there is good reason to suppose that Edward was disappointed with the response, since he had to reiterate his muster orders again in May. Desertion was also common in armies held together primarily by bonds of feudal obligation, meaning that the number of troops that left England with King Edward may not have been the same as the number that arrived at Bannockburn.[111] Although punishments for desertions could range from anything from a hefty fine to execution, the practical limitations of the medieval state to keep close track of its subjects made slipping away – especially after one had made a token appearance at the muster point – relatively easy. The reasons for desertion were varied. For a soldier who lived primarily as a tenant farmer, they might feel pressured to return home in time to see to the harvest, or to take care of whatever family they had left behind. Doubts about the capabilities of the army's leaders might also encourage soldiers to remove themselves from the army before they were led to disaster. And while English soldiers in this period received a wage for their service, the longer a campaign went on the more likely it was that wages would go unpaid. We have seen already the difficulties that Edward had endured trying to keep his garrisons in Scotland paid. The Scottish crown did not pay its soldiers a wage in the early fourteenth century, but this naturally created a separate set of issues in terms of encouraging men to serve.[112] Of course, all medieval armies suffered from this problem, not just Edward's. Nevertheless, the muster orders produced on 24 March – combined with those sent out in May – give the impression that Edward intended to advance into Scotland at the head of an impressive host. Its purpose was to demonstrate the sheer power of the English crown, to intimidate those who encountered it, and to overwhelm any opposition it found. The downside was that it was difficult for such a force to advance quickly or to pass through wooded, hilly, or marshy places, where Bruce's highly mobile guerrilla forces could hide until Edward returned home, as King Edward had experienced even with a smaller army during his first invasion of Scotland.

As well as this general muster, King Edward also appointed Aymer de Valence, earl of Pembroke, as 'guardian of the land of Scotland'.[113] Pembroke had originally been appointed to this office by Edward's father, Edward I, in response to Bruce's killing of John Comyn, Pembroke's brother-in-law, in 1306.[114] He had defeated Bruce at the Battle of Methven that June but then fled from Bruce at the Battle of Loudoun Hill and was afterwards replaced as guardian.[115] The reversal of Pembroke's attitude towards King Edward since the death of Gaveston in 1312 once again explains the trust he placed in the earl in 1314. The earl was given 'full power to make arrangements regarding the state of the aforesaid land, as he thinks should be done for our honour and the salvation of the aforesaid land' until Edward arrived. His primary responsibility in this instance would be to oversee preparations for the coming invasion. The timing of his appointment may have been influenced in part by developments in Scotland since Edward announced his intention to invade in November 1313, most notably the fall of Roxburgh and Edinburgh. With the Scots showing no intention of curtailing their military activities ahead of the invasion, and the English administration in Scotland still unravelling, Pembroke's appointment was likely designed to reassure the king's Scottish subjects that the English crown was taking the issue seriously and that preparations were still advancing.

The following day, King Edward empowered Pembroke to receive into the king's peace any Scots who wished to join him.[116] The earl had been similarly empowered during his tenure as lieutenant in 1306.[117] While the recent military successes of the Bruce Scots in the early months of 1314 might make it seem like there would be few takers for such an offer, the gains made by Douglas and Randolph in the south-east could not be consolidated before the English army was due to set off in June. Those Scots who anticipated that Edward's army might pass through their lands might therefore be expected to make timely submissions to the English king's authority on the understanding that this would spare their property from damage.

The other royal business of 25 March was also concerned with Edward's Scottish allies, potential or otherwise. King Edward appointed John Macdougall of Argyll as 'admiral of the western fleet' (*'admirallus flotae occidentalis'*).[118] As noted above, Edward had previously issued orders for ships from a variety of southern English ports to gather at Aberconwy in north-west Wales by Pentecost. This is surely what Edward meant by 'the western fleet' and Macdougall's appointment reinforces the impression that it was intended to put pressure on the Isle of Man and perhaps even directly threaten Scotland's western seaboard while King Edward led his army into Scotland by land. Precedent for such a plan had been set in 1311, and in February 1315 English forces led by Macdougall would recover Man from the Scots and afterwards take twenty-three prisoners 'on the sea coast of Scotland' before withdrawing again to Man.[119] Macdougall's mother had been a close relative of the John Comyn, lord of Badenoch, who Bruce had killed at Greyfriars Kirk in Dumfries in 1306, an act that instantly made

Macdougall one of Bruce's most implacable enemies.[120] He had ambushed and defeated Bruce near Tyndrum on the borders of Argyll within months of Bruce's inauguration but was defeated in turn by Bruce at the Pass of Brander beneath Ben Cruachan in 1308.[121] In the wake of this defeat and the subsequent capture of his castle at Dunstaffnage on the Argyll coast, Macdougall fled Scotland but continued to resist the Bruce Scots as a servant of the English crown.

Macdougall had considerable influence in Argyll and the western Highlands more generally, which could be potentially useful to Edward in draining support away from Bruce in that region. To that end, King Edward empowered him to receive 'the men of the Isles and of Argyll' ('*Insulares et homines de Argayl*') into Edward's peace. A sample of how useful Macdougall's influence could be to the English crown is found in the fact that at the same time as he was made admiral and given authority to accept submissions, four other Scots were formally accepted into Edward's peace – Donald 'of Islay' ('*de Insula*') and his brother 'Gotherus', John Macnakild, and Patrick Graham.[122] John has been suggested as Donald's brother, and their names certainly indicate that they belonged to the *Gàidhealtachd* (that is, Gaelic-speaking Scotland).[123] Graham, meanwhile, was Macdougall's son-in-law and would ultimately prove to be a less-committed opponent of King Robert than his father-in-law had been.[124] By 1320, Graham had 'defected' to the Scots again and would be one of the Scottish lords named in the Declaration of Arbroath.[125] The Bruce administration clearly still had its suspicions about Graham, and he was tried (and acquitted) for treason when a plot against the King Robert was discovered later that year.[126]

Most intriguing of all for our purposes, King Edward also commissioned one Thomas Sanser (or Sancer) to procure supplies for the garrison at Stirling. The document in question mentions the garrison commander, Sir Philip Mowbray, by name.[127] Like Macdougall, Mowbray was a Scot whose Comyn connections made him unwilling to accept a Bruce kingship.[128] More Scots – Roger and Geoffrey Mowbray (Philip's kinsmen), Alexander Abernethy, and David Graham – were mentioned as being assigned to assist Sanser in delivering the requested supplies. However, the date set for the delivery of the supplies was 'the Feast of St Michael next to come' ('*festum Sancti Michaelis proximo futurum*'). Michaelmas was not until 29 September, a little over six months after Edward issued his instructions to Sanser. This would seem indicate that the Scots had not yet begun their siege of Stirling Castle, and indeed that the castle was not yet believed to be in imminent danger of falling to the Scots. Certainly, the deal between the Stirling garrison and the Bruce Scots, which brought the two armies to battle at Bannockburn, cannot have been in effect if Edward believed he could wait until September to resupply his troops there.

On 27 March, King Edward issued a summons for 'masons, carpenters, and smiths' (*'cementariis, carpentariis, et fabris'*) from every English county to accompany his army into Scotland.[129] This serves to illustrate the point that Edward's mission in 1314 was not only to seek battle, but also to prop up the ailing English administration in Scotland. This would necessarily include the physical repair of their remaining strongholds and defences. Again, the timing of Edward's summons was surely influenced by the recent loss of the castles at Roxburgh and Edinburgh. When it eventually set off, the English army stopped at Edinburgh for around two days on the way to Bannockburn, so they may have used this time to have these craftsmen assess the damage done to the fortifications there and make plans for their eventual reconstruction.

Edward also instructed the sheriff of Norfolk and Suffolk to divert supplies originally scheduled to be delivered to Westminster to instead be sent to Berwick-upon-Tweed, from where Edward was due to set off for Scotland on or about 10 June. These supplies included 'forty lasts of herring, ten thousands of mulvel [cod], eight thousands of 'stokfissh' [dried but unsalted fish], and twenty barrels of sturgeon'.[130] This rather fishy delivery was to be received by one of the king's clerks, William de Northwell. It is possible that the supplies were to be used to feed the king's army, but it seems more likely that they were meant to be enjoyed by the royal household while they resided at Berwick ahead of the campaign.

King Edward also spent some time on 27 March addressing the wider issue of Scottish piracy in the North Sea. He instructed the civic authorities at Scarborough in North Yorkshire to seize goods belonging to Flemish merchants in the town to the value of £170 18s. 4d. This was in response to the complaints of two English merchants – Richard de Fimmer and Richard de Slengesby – who had loaded a ship belonging to a Fleming named Peter Bellard of Sleperdam with £127 18s. 4¼d. in wool, wool-fells (i.e., fleeces) and other goods and then sailed from Kingston-upon-Hull, intending to sell it all in Antwerp. However, the ship was captured by Flemish pirates led by one John le Seger, who assaulted the two Richards and then dropped them off at Aberdeen as hostages of the Scottish crown before sailing back to Flanders with their ship and merchandise. Since

Count Robert of Flanders had apparently ignored Edward's request for him to bring the perpetrators to justice, the English king therefore gave the go-ahead to the seizure of the other Flemings' goods.[131]

The reason for the £43 difference between the sum taken and the sum to be recovered from the hapless Flemish merchants in Scarborough is not entirely clear and may have been a genuine scribal error. This conclusion is supported by Edward's ruling in a similar case on the same day. Warin le Draper, Thomas de Scalby, and Richard de Sneton, merchants from Scarborough, had loaded nine sacks, two pockets (*poketos*), and three stone of wool, and other merchandise to the value of £172 2s. 8d, onto a ship at Kingston-upon-Hull and also sailed for Antwerp. On their way, the same John le Seger and 'other malefactors of Flanders' had seized them and their ship, deposited them as prisoners at Aberdeen, and then sailed back to Flanders with their ship and goods. This time Edward ordered the mayor and bailiffs of Hartlepool to seize £86 1s. 4d. worth of goods from the Flemings within their jurisdiction, while another £86 1s. 4d. was to be recovered by the bailiffs of Whitby. Since this would recover precisely the amount the wronged merchants had lost, we can reasonably infer that this had been the intended outcome in the case of Fimmer and Slengesby as well. Whatever the case, these rulings present a striking impression of the disruptions the war was causing to North Sea trade.

Finally, on 28 March, Edward issued the last of his instructions concerning the upcoming campaign before setting off from Westminster on his slow progress northward to Berwick-upon-Tweed (though further matters would be dealt with on the journey). Edward was now putting the finishing touches to arrangements concerning the western fleet he had been gathering as well as preparing transport and provisions for the Irish contingent in his army. In particular, King Edward sought to recruit 'infantry, archers, and others' ('*peditibus, sagittariis, et aliis*') from Ireland in order to serve in the fleet. He also took this opportunity to arrange transport for the Irish troops he was expecting to serve in the army that would eventually fight at Bannockburn in June. It was barely a week since Edward had issued his initial summonses to various Irish potentates. The king now sought to ensure they had sufficient ships with which to transport themselves across the Irish Sea as well as supplies to keep them going on the coming campaign. The supplies King Edward requested included 2,000 quarters of corn (*frumenti*), of which 1,000 were to be milled into flour and stored in barrels (*doliis*), 2,000 quarters of oats (*avene*), 200 quarters of salt (*salis*), 2,000 fish (*piscis*), and 500 barrels of wine (*vini*). All of this was to be delivered to the king's officers Alexander le Convers and Richard le Chasteleyn at Skinburness in Cumbria.[132] The hefty quantities King Edward required to provision even a small portion of his army offers a striking impression of how enormous the baggage train that accompanied the English army to Bannockburn would have been. The logistical issues that went along with this placed severe restraints on what the army could and could not do, and how quickly they could do it. King Robert would later exploit these limitations when formulating his plan to defeat the English army at Bannockburn. Yet as King Edward set out northward in the last days of March 1314, he must surely have felt that the preparations he had made over the previous fortnight boded well for a campaign that would erase the bitter memory of 1310 to 1311 and secure for him the military victory he badly needed.

*Chapter 4*

# On the Road
# Edward Travels North and the Scots Counterattack, April to May 1314

## 'Making Progress Toward the Parts of Scotland': Edward's Journey North Begins

In the closing days of March 1314, King Edward II of England set out northwards on the journey that would eventually bring him to Berwick-upon-Tweed ready to campaign into Scotland. It would take him the best part of two months to reach his destination, but his slow progress, while reflective of the campaign's lack of focus, did not necessarily betoken an unwillingness to get the planned invasion of Scotland underway.

Edward's first port of call was St Albans Cathedral, not far from where he had grown up at King's Langley in Hertfordshire.[1] Here, on 30 March, King Edward made a gift of a gold cross decorated with precious stones to the shrine where St Alban's body was reputedly buried and commended himself and his affairs to the protection of the saint.[2] St Alban was a third- or fourth-century Christian martyr, the first martyr recorded in Britain.[3] Edward's gesture of piety at St Albans was surely connected to his upcoming campaign into Scotland and was the first of several similar acts that contrast sharply with the contemporary Lanercost chronicler's claim that Edward 'said things to the prejudice and injury of the saints' ahead of the Battle of Bannockburn.[4] It may be that this was merely an attempt by a moralizing chronicler to justify the defeat at Bannockburn in terms of the English king's supposed impiety. In the case of the notoriously anti-Scottish Lanercost chronicler in particular, there may have been a desire to place the blame on Edward's personal shortcomings rather than Scottish tactical superiority. However, the Lanercost chronicler may also have been referring to another incident relating to St Alban that would occur at Ely the following week.

On 1 April, while still at St Albans, Edward resumed the business of supplying his army and oversaw further preparations for the western fleet, as well as trying to settle some of his financial arrangements. First, King Edward empowered his *vallettus* Adam Couper to acquire provisions for the king's animals (*animalibus*) on his upcoming campaign into Scotland.[5] As a valet, Couper would probably have been a squire, possibly as young as 14 years old. The animals in question would of course have been the king's horses, not merely the war horse he would ride onto the battlefield but also at least one horse for travelling to the battlefield (most likely a palfrey), as well as horses to carry the king's gear or pull wagons with his equipment in them.[6] This would include weapons, armour, clothing, tents, tableware, even perhaps some furniture, so Couper may have had to acquire supplies for a substantial number of animals ahead of the campaign.

The victualling of the army also continued apace, with the king now ordering specific quantities of goods for his army from five south-western counties. From Somerset and Dorset, Edward requested 500 quarters of corn, 500 quarters of malt, 300 quarters of beans and peas, 1,000 quarters of oats, 200 quarters of salt, 300 sides of bacon, and 100 barrels of wine. From Gloucestershire, Edward ordered 500 quarters of corn, 500 quarters of malt, 300 quarters of beans and peas, 1,000 quarters of oats, 300 sides of bacon, and 100 barrels of wine. From Devonshire, he ordered 1,000 quarters of oats, 500,000 salted fish, and 100 barrels of wine, while from Cornwall he called for 1,000 quarters of oats, 500,000 salted fish, and 100 barrels of wine.[7] The aforementioned efforts of Antonio Pessagno to raise funds for the 1314 campaign may have limited the need for Edward to rely on prise (i.e., the right to seize foodstuff for royal use without payment) and purveyance (i.e., the right of the monarch to fix prices for provisions), both of which had been highly controversial practices during Edward's reign so far.[8] There is no indication in the surviving documents produced on 1 April concerning how the goods would be paid for, however, which may indicate that King Edward still intended to exploit his royal prerogatives to the maximum in 1314.

Simultaneously, the king showed concern for settling some of his outstanding debts. He thus wrote to his treasurer and the lords of the exchequer instructing them to make account with the burgesses of Great Yarmouth 'for diverse sums of money paid by them in wages of mariners going to Scotland for the war there, and for the repair of certain of the king's ships'. The king's financial officers were told to 'make them [i.e., the burgesses] allowance for what the king owes them', which may indicate that rather than straightforwardly repaying the cash owed, the burgesses would instead be allowed to recoup their losses by paying less to the crown in customs and other royal concessions until the king's debts had been cleared.[9] Even with his finances beginning to stabilize somewhat under Pessagno's talented management, Edward fiscal priorities remained focused on advancing his personal ambitions rather than repaying his previous backers.

Finally, King Edward wrote to the 'barons, baillies, and good men of the port of Dover' requesting six ships – the *De Hastinges*, the *Hethe*, the *Romehale*, the *Winchelsea*, the *Sandwyco*, and the *De la Rye* – to be sent to Skinburness on the Solway Firth 'on the feast of St John the Baptist next' in the expectation that they would proceed against the Scots.[10] As noted in the previous chapter, Skinburness was the port through which supplies and soldiers from Ireland were expected to arrive for the approaching campaign. These vessels may therefore have been intended to help ferry these supplies across the Irish Sea. They may however also have been expected to join the fleet commanded by John Macdougall of Argyll, muster orders for which had been going out for almost two weeks now.

King Edward moved from St Albans to Ely, where he celebrated Easter at Ely Cathedral on 7 April.[11] During his stay at the cathedral, a rather awkward exchange is reported to have taken place between the king and the local monks. As noted above, towards the end of March, King Edward had arrived at St Albans, during which time he had visited the shrine reputedly containing the body of St Alban. However, the monks at Ely Cathedral also had a reliquary associated with the saint. The chronicler Thomas Walsingham – a monk of St Albans, albeit after Edward's death – reports that when the king heard this he asked the monks at Ely if he could examine the reliquary:

> '"You know", he said, "that my brothers of St Albans believe that they possess the body of the same martyr. In this place the monks say that they have the body of the same saint. By God's soul, I want to see in which place I ought chiefly to pay reverence to the remains of that holy body."'

The monks proceeded to open the reliquary for him, only to reveal that it contained the blood-spattered robe that the saint had been wearing at the time of his martyrdom.[12] However, the incident also resonates with the contemporary Lanercost chronicler's claim that the king indulged in actions 'to the prejudice and injury of the saints' while on his way to Bannockburn.[13] As noted above, this comment may simply be an attempt by a critical writer to explain the subsequent English defeat on the king's supposed lack of appropriate piety. The king's embarrassing interrogation of the monks at Ely would be unlikely to endear him to a clerical audience, which may have influenced the Lanercost chronicler's observation about Edward's relationship with the saints.

Even among the Easter festivities, Edward remained active in preparing for the coming invasion of Scotland. For instance, he made further provisions for feeding his horses while on campaign.[14] He also instructed his tax collectors in North Yorkshire to pay 200 marks to Ralph Fitzwilliam, keeper of Berwick-upon-Tweed, 'for the maintenance of himself and the men in his company garrisoning that town'. Additionally, Edward reiterated his instructions to Pessagno to send 'corn, meat, oats, and victuals' to Berwick 'with all speed'.[15] It was of course from Berwick that Edward was planning to set off into Scotland in June. The document addressed to the Yorkshire tax collectors implies that the Berwick garrison had been waiting some time for this payment to arrive. This problem was compounded by the fact that indiscipline among the Berwick garrison - which would only be exacerbated by the non-payment of wages - was one of the key complaints from Edward's Scottish allies in 1313. Edward must therefore have been eager to impress upon the royal officials responsible for its payment of the need to expeditiously fulfil their duties so that he would not face too many awkward questions about the money from Fitzwilliam and his men when he arrived at Berwick. Finally, King Edward wrote to 'the master-mariners of the ships setting out for Scotland, now lying in the Thames and elsewhere on the sea', forbidding them 'under penalty of life and limbs' from taking provisions without paying for them, from forcing men into serving on their ships against their will, and from taking bribes from those who wanted to avoid service altogether.[16] The kind of sharp practice described in the document can only have served to make generating enthusiasm for Edward's latest military endeavour more difficult, and thus it is understandable that Edward wished to stamp it out.

By 13 April, Edward was at Peterborough. Here, he reiterated his demands for military service from leading English clergymen as well as his sheriffs.[17] He had travelled to Peterborough via Ramsey in Cambridgeshire, where on 11 and 12 April he had dealt with minor issues not related to the coming campaign, for example paying the king's huntsman for looking after his hunting dogs and arranging supplies for his son's household.[18] This serves to demonstrate that even as he made his way towards Berwick, Edward remained deeply involved in the mundane day-to-day business of domestic governance as well as continuing preparations for war. From Peterborough, the king enjoined 'the mayor and sheriffs of the city of London to be conservators of the peace for the city, as the king is about to depart for Scotland with his army, and is the more anxious that the peace should be duly observed'.[19] One of the major differences between the kingdoms of England and Scotland in the fourteenth century was that England had a far more centralized royal administration centred around London (and Westminster in particular). This had allowed for a fairly sophisticated bureaucracy to develop, which was able to extend royal authority into the localities without the king having to physically visit the more remote regions in order to make his presence felt. It is no wonder then that King Edward was eager for the civic authorities in London to maintain law and order there in his absence, to ensure the stability of the royal administration while the king was on campaign in Scotland.

Scottish governance was much more decentralized by comparison and Scottish kings remained itinerant well into the fifteenth century. In other words, rather than having a fixed bureaucracy in one specific place, the machinery of the royal administration tended to go wherever the king himself went and could move location depending on the preferences of an individual monarch. The potential downside of this was that Scottish kings had to periodically tour the more remote regions of their kingdom to administer justice and personally reinforce royal authority. If a king was unable – or unwilling – to do so, it could alienate powerful regional lords and encourage them to ignore the royal will and act entirely in their own interests.[20] However, during the Wars of Independence, the itinerant nature of Scottish kinship proved to be a major advantage, especially to King Robert himself. It effectively meant that there was no one town or region that the English could occupy that would enable them to definitively seize control of the Scottish royal administration. So long as there were Scots at large who were willing to recognize an individual as king of Scots, the English would be unable to bring the war to a truly decisive conclusion. It was for precisely this reason that Bruce's response to Edward II's invasion of Scotland in 1310 to 1311 had been to avoid battle by keeping to the wooded, hilly, and marshy places of the kingdom, and why he probably intended to do the same in 1314. By removing himself – and by extension the apparatus of Scottish government – to the more remote and inaccessible regions of his kingdom until time and financial constraints forced Edward to withdraw, King Robert could ensure the survival of his regime indefinitely. The event that would lead Bruce to modify his strategy and face the English head-on – the eventual deal between his younger brother and the garrison at Stirling – was getting closer, but still some time away. Nevertheless, the Scots remained militarily active in April 1314, as was about to be painfully illustrated to the communities of northern England.

## 'The Scots Are Exceedingly Bold and Fearsome': The Scottish Raid of April 1314

On 16 April – 'Tuesday after the octave of Easter' as the Lanercost chronicler put it – Edward Bruce, earl of Carrick, led a raid into north-west England.[21] According to the anonymous monk at Lanercost Priory, Carrick's actions were 'contrary to agreement', although the same chronicler later admits that the raid was motivated by a failure on the part of the local community to pay for a truce they had previously negotiated with the Scots.[22] As early as September 1307 we find wardens being appointed on the West March with a specific remit 'for the better preservation of those parts from incursions of the king's enemies'.[23] Around the same time, Thomas de Multon was instructed by the English crown to do more to combat what were called 'the thievish incursions of Robert Bruce', a strangely whimsical phrase that belies an undoubtedly brutal reality.[24] In October 1309, no fewer than fifty-five Cumbrian landowners were warned to make their estates ready to withstand an attack from the Scots, illustrating a concerted effort to shore up the defences along the Solway.[25] Almost as soon as Edward had left Berwick in early August 1311, Bruce launched a series of deadly raids into Northumberland, targeting the former Bruce estates at Haltwhistle in August and then devastating the lands of the pro-Balliol Umfraville earls of Angus at Prudhoe in September. As a result of these assaults, the community of Northumberland bought a truce to last until the following February.[26] By immediately undertaking his most far-reaching and destructive raids yet, Bruce was seeking to hammer home the point that Edward had failed so badly that things were going to get worse, not better, for the communities of northern England.

King Robert attacked northern England again in early in the summer of 1312, capitalizing on the explosion of political turmoil surrounding Gaveston, this time targeting the southern parts of Northumberland as well as County Durham. Having burned Hexham and Corbridge, the Scots then descended on Durham itself on market day, where they 'carried off all that was found in the town and gave a great part of it to the flames, cruelly killing all who opposed them but scarcely attacking the castle and priory' in the words of the Lanercost chronicler.[27] In response, a delegation headed by Richard Kellaw, bishop of Durham, met with Bruce at Hexham and agreed to pay the massive sum of 2,000 marks, the first instalment of which was due to be paid at Holm Cultram Abbey (where Bruce's father was buried) in Cumbria on 29 September. Tellingly, in the text of the agreement Bruce is styled 'the noble prince Sir Robert, by grace of God King of Scots'.[28] Bruce had no doubt demanded that the northern communities acknowledge him by his preferred title if they wished to cut a deal with him. The readiness of Bishop Kellaw and those he represented to accept this demand serves as a powerful illustration of the willingness of the northern communities to ignore English royal policy if they felt the English crown was failing in its responsibility to protect them from Scottish depredations.

The history of Scottish raiding from 1307 to 1314 is particularly useful for illustrating an important development in Scottish strategy during Bruce's reign. The Scots raided northern England as early as 1296, but previously these efforts had been largely unruly affairs designed to cause indiscriminate destruction and generally undermine English morale.[29] Bruce's efforts, by comparison, were targeted, systematic, and highly disciplined. Property and produce were frequently destroyed, but by and large the Scots only killed those who put up resistance. Even the hostile Lanercost chronicler admits that the Scots 'killed few men apart from those who wished to defend themselves by resistance'.[30] In 1315, the inhabitants of Hartlepool seem to have been allowed to flee into their fishing boats before the Scots descended on the town, which they looted but did not burn.[31] Of course, since the Scots intended to repeat their depredations as regularly as possible, it was in their interest to ensure that the northern counties remained populous so that they could be raided again at a later date. While hardly a moral endorsement of the behaviour of the Scots, this aspect of Scottish raiding in the 1310s and 1320s further underlines the discipline of Bruce's men. Fielding disciplined and increasingly experienced troops enabled Bruce to make his raids unpredictable, which in turn made it more difficult for his opponents to second-guess where the Scots might strike next, adding to the effectiveness of his overall strategy. Discipline also helped the Scots remain responsive to rapidly changing situations. The timing of the April raid may serve to highlight this. 16 April – the day Carrick crossed the border – was the earliest day we know for sure that King Edward's lieutenant Aymer de Valence, earl of Pembroke, was at Berwick to oversee the ongoing mustering efforts.[32] The decision to lead a raid into England's western March while Edward II's army was mustering in the east may well suggest the Scots were seeking to disrupt the smooth operation of northern English society while minimizing the risk of direct armed conflict with English forces in the region.

While they certainly had a deleterious effect on morale in the northern counties, the primary aim of these raids was invariably the extortion of payments from the local populace, usually in the form of 'the three C's': cattle, cash, and corn – all in short supply in Scotland at the time. Cattle should, hopefully, be self-explanatory. Cash was generally to be made either through blackmail – that is, screwing payments out of the locals to save their property from attack – or seizing prisoners and ransoming them back to their families. If a prisoner was important enough, the English crown might even contribute to their ransom, as we will see in the concluding chapters. Discipline was particularly vital for the purposes of blackmail since, as Dr Colm McNamee puts it, 'English communities would not pay over large sums to the Scots if they thought that they were going to be robbed in any case'.[33] 'Corn' in this context means grain, rather than the maize that modern readers may be familiar with, which of course was originally native to the Americas. The need for this particular resource was exacerbated by repeated famines both north and south of the border during the early fourteenth century.[34] Where crops had not yet been reaped, the Scots were inclined to burn them, but when they could easily transport the grain they found, the Scots certainly seem to have treated it as one of their core priorities.[35] Additionally, the Lanercost chronicler observes that 'Scotland is not rich in iron', a vital resource used in making steel for arms and armour, and the chronicler claims that the bountiful haul of iron the Scots seized at Furness in 1316 was seen as a significant boon by Bruce's forces.[36] McNamee has speculated that this may explain why Corbridge, something of an ironware emporium in early-fourteenth-century Tynedale, was so frequently targeted by the Scots in the period.[37] By 1314, this system was already highly organized and ruthlessly efficient, representing a major innovation on the part of King Robert and making a significant contribution to his growing success in contrast to his predecessors and to the English administration.

As well as these general observations on Scottish war policy during Robert I's reign, we can also reconstruct a reasonable impression of the appearance of early-fourteenth-century Scottish raiding parties, thanks to the testimony of the chronicler Jean le Bel.[38] Le Bel had first-hand experience of campaigning against a similar Scottish force, albeit in 1327, and provides considerable detail about Scottish raiding practices.[39] Though his account was written towards the end of the war, there is little reason to suppose that his observations would not still be broadly true when applied to 1314. The Scots were, in Le Bel's opinion, 'exceedingly bold and fearsome fighters' with 'much experience of waging war' and 'very little fear of the English', at least during King Robert's reign. He claims that the Scots were able to 'cover 20 or 32 leagues [roughly 60 to 96 miles] at a stretch, by day or night, at which people can be greatly astonished if they don't know their custom'. He reports that the Scottish troops would all travel on horseback, with the wealthier soldiers riding 'good strong rounceys (*ronchins*) and coursers (*coursiers*)' and the poorer soldiers 'on little hackneys (*haguenées*)'. By 1327, the fighting men would be accompanied by a 'rabble' (*ribaudaille*), who followed behind on foot. These were not part of the army as such but would pick through the devastation the troops left behind and loot any remaining valuables. This feature was perhaps something that had developed in the years since 1314, or at least had gotten worse as the Scots had begun to enjoy even greater success over the English border communities.

Le Bel marvelled at the Scots' 'abstinence' ('*sobrieté*') when on campaign, claiming that they brought with them no baggage but instead subsisted on 'half-cooked flesh, without bread, and good river water, without wine'. What meat the Scots ate came, Le Bel insists, from the cattle they would rustle on their passage through English territory. Occasionally, the Scots apparently supplemented this diet with oatcakes (*ung petit tourtel*) to settle their stomachs. These they would cook themselves on the large flat stones they carried beneath their saddles, using bags of flour they carried behind them as they rode. The Scots would dismount to fight, but – to Le Bel's amazement – would not tether their horses, instead just letting them graze freely while their owners were engaged elsewhere. Le Bel's account offers a potentially valuable insight into the nature of the armed force that Carrick likely led into north-west England in April 1314. It almost certainly would have been a highly mobile, highly reactive fighting force, capable of moving swiftly through enemy territory and responding quickly and unpredictably to any challenges it faced. Significantly, the fact that Le Bel treats these tactics as a novelty, something with which his Continental readers would not be familiar, reinforces the impression that these tactics were a specific development of the Bruce administration.

According to the Lanercost chronicler, Carrick and his men entered England 'by way of Carlisle' and occupied the bishop of Carlisle's manor house at Rose near Dalston. Carrick apparently remained at Rose for three days, using it as a base from which to raid southwards and westwards. The Lanercost chronicler tells us:

> 'They burnt many towns and two churches, taking men and women prisoners, and collected a great number of cattle in Inglewood Forest and elsewhere, driving them off with them on the Friday.'

This is broadly in keeping with what we know about the Scottish raiding practices examined above. The Lanercost chronicler adds that the Scots 'killed few men except those who made a determined resistance', and again this is reflective of wider practice. The Lanercost chronicler also notes that Carrick led an unsuccessful assault on Carlisle 'because of the knights and country people who were assembled there'.[40] In this case, the aim was presumably to capture these 'knights and country people' in the hopes of extorting further ransom from their relatives.

What is again arguably most striking about the April raid of 1314 is the fact that Edward Bruce, not Robert, was leading it. There are a number of ways that Carrick's prominence can be interpreted. On the one hand, perhaps the Scots recognized the inherent danger in potentially putting their king in harm's way while the English were preparing a full-scale invasion of Scotland for the summer. King Robert was, after all, approaching 40 years old and had only one legitimate child – Marjory, who was a prisoner in England and thus effectively neutralized as a potential heir. In this context, the Scots may have felt understandably hesitant to risk their leader's life during such a tense and dangerous time. It was certainly not unheard of, either before 1314 or after, for Scottish war leaders other than the king to carry out cross-border raiding. Carrick had, without a doubt, been one of the most active of the Bruce Scots in the early months of 1314, and was a natural alternate focus for military leadership. However, the precariousness of his dynasty had not stopped King Robert from being actively involved in leading the war effort on numerous earlier occasions. Neither would it stop him from being in the thick of things at Bannockburn in June. Indeed, when Edward II invaded Scotland again in 1322, King Robert – now pushing 50 years old and still having no legitimate, adult, male heir – not only seems to have led the Scottish preparations to resist this but even marched an army into England once the invasion was over.[41] Rather, King Robert's absence surely serves as further evidence that he was currently incapacitated and thus unable to directly participate in events in person.

This of course would have given considerable influence over Scottish war policy to Carrick, who stood to become king himself if his elder brother did not recover his health. Barbour's later presentation of Edward Bruce as the less-measured copy of King Robert is primarily a rhetorical device employed by the poet to reinforce the value of prudence in warfare to his late-fourteenth-century audience.[42] Yet the frantic activities of the Scots in the early months of 1314 certainly contrast with the more cautious responses to the threat of invasion in 1310, 1319, and 1322. This may at least indicate a more aggressive approach on the part of the king's brother. At an uncertain point after his return to Scotland on Friday 19 April, Carrick would lay siege to Stirling Castle. It may be the case that Carrick already harboured ambitions to strike at the increasingly isolated garrison at Stirling even as he descended into Cumbria on 16 April. On balance, a date in May for the beginning of the siege seems more likely. Whatever the case, it would be the siege of Stirling that completely revolutionized the Scottish situation in 1314, a point that we will unpack in detail now.

## 'If Only They Had Had the Lord as an Ally': Edward's Journey North Continues

As the Scots trooped back across the border on 19 April, King Edward was to be found at Kirkstead in Lincolnshire, once again dealing with fairly minor local business not connected to the war in Scotland.[43] The following day, however, Edward had moved to Lincoln, where he issued orders for additional infantry 'beyond the numbers previously commissioned' from various English counties to serve in the army he was planning to lead into Scotland in June. These troops were to arrive at Berwick by 19 May.[44] Though there is reason to suppose that King

Edward experienced recruitment difficulties for the Bannockburn campaign, the phrasing of the document produced on 20 April gives the impression that this was not a response to these problems. Rather, it appears to have been an attempt to muster even more foot soldiers than Edward had initially requested. This in turn suggests that the king appreciated the important role that infantry might play in any pitched battle against the Scots. On the one hand, this may imply that he understood that at the Battle of Falkirk in 1298 – the last time an English royal army had confronted a Scottish army in open battle – it had been an intervention of his father's infantry against the tightly packed Scottish spear formations that had turned the tide of the battle in England's favour. Equally, it may simply reflect the fact that Edward expected to be hunting for King Robert in the wooded, marshy, and hilly places of the kingdom, where infantry would be more effective than heavy cavalry. Either way, Edward's sudden concern with expanding the numbers of his army – and in particular with soldiers better suited for hunting the Scots across rough ground – might be interpreted as a reaction to the news of Edward Bruce's recent raid through north-west England.

On 23 April, Edward was at Torskey in Lincolnshire, where he turned his attention once again to his most valuable hostage – Elizabeth de Burgh, queen of Scots. He issued additional instructions to Henry Cobham, keeper of Rochester Castle – to which he had transferred Elizabeth in March – to allow Elena Edgar, John de Claydon, Samuel de Lynford, and William Preston access to the castle as Elizabeth's retinue. Strangely, the surviving summary of Edward's instruction to Cobham misnames Elizabeth 'Isabella', perhaps a later scribal error.[45] This document is primarily interesting as it provides us with the names of Elizabeth's attendants during this period of her captivity. The four individuals are otherwise obscure, although Preston may have belonged to a noble family of the same name who came from Preston in East Lothian. The Prestons would emerge as influential figures at the court of Elizabeth's son David II, but in the early fourteenth century they were a fairly minor family.[46]

By 27 April, King Edward had reached Beverley in Yorkshire. Here, he gave Robert de Harwedon, one of the king's clerks, authority to act as the keeper of the royal forest south of the Trent while Hugh Despenser 'the Elder' was away on campaign in Scotland.[47] Despenser had been one of the king's familiars even before the beginning of the reign. He had first been appointed keeper of the royal forest south of the Trent by Edward's father Edward I in 1297, an appointment that Edward II had renewed in 1308 and made lifelong in 1309.[48] Despenser and his son – another Hugh – would apparently remain close to King Edward during the Bannockburn campaign. According to the contemporary Lanercost chronicler, the younger Despenser 'after Piers Gaveston, was as his [i.e., King Edward's] right eye'.[49] During the 1320s, the closeness of the Despensers to the king enabled them to emerge as the most prominent members of the royal court, which brought generous royal patronage in terms of land, titles, and rights. However, this soured the relationship between Edward and his queen Isabella, who found herself unable to fulfil her traditional queenly function as intercessor to her husband due to the interference of the Despensers. Thus, when Isabella turned against her husband in 1326, the Despensers were high on her list for recriminations. The elder Hugh surrendered at Bristol in late October and, having been hastily tried for treason, was hanged, drawn, and quartered.[50]

Edward's presence at Beverley suggests that the king paid a visit to the shrine of St John of Beverley at Beverley Minster on or about this day too, and possibly even collected a banner associated with the saint to be borne in the army he was planning to lead into Scotland.[51] John of Beverley was an eighth-century cleric who had served as bishop of Hexham and bishop of York during his lifetime. He was known personally to the Venerable Bede, who recounted a number of miraculous tales associated with the saint.[52] His tomb at Beverley quickly became the focus of a flourishing cult dedicated to him. Though not, strictly speaking, a saint associated with the English royal crown, John of Beverley had by the early fourteenth century come to be associated with military success against the Scots. His banner had been present when Archbishop Thurstan of York had defeated the Scots at the Battle of Northallerton in 1138, was taken on campaign into Scotland by Edward I, and would later be taken into Scotland by Edward III and Henry IV. Edward I had even founded a chantry in Beverley Minster in honour of the saint.[53] In this context, it would seem remarkable if Edward had not collected St John's banner at Beverley. Further pious preparations for the approaching invasion were made at York on 2 May, when he granted the monks at St Albans 100 marks – to be raised by the tax collectors of Hertfordshire – to fix the cathedral's choir stalls.[54] Edward had apparently been made aware that his father had promised to assist the monks with refurbishing their choir while visiting St Albans Cathedral at the end of March, hence the later gift of money. Both his appearances at Beverley and his contribution to the renovations surely reflect an eagerness to secure the intercession of St John of Beverley and St Alban ahead of his latest campaign into Scotland. As we have seen repeatedly in this chapter, this casts some doubt on the contemporary Lanercost chronicler's accusation that Edward had failed to observe the proper spiritual practices ahead of his campaign in 1314.[55]

On 3 May, still at York, King Edward ordered lands belonging to the late Dionisia, wife of Hugh de Veer, to be handed over to Aymer de Valence, earl of Pembroke, as her nearest heir.[56] This does not, of course, directly relate to the preparations for Bannockburn. Yet the timing suggests that it should be understood as another small act of patronage in favour of a man who was already playing a crucial role in the build-up to the campaign and may have provided an important service to the king on the battlefield as well. On 24 March, Edward had appointed Valence 'guardian of our land [i.e., Scotland], and our tenant in the same place until our arrival at that quarter'. Since at least 16 April, possibly sooner, Valence had been at Berwick-upon-Tweed personally overseeing the preparations for the campaign in anticipation of King Edward's arrival. The king's confirmation of his rights as Dionisia's heir in May reflected Valence's continuing importance to King Edward during this critical period in the build-up to the battle.

Over the next two-and-a-half weeks, Edward's journey north continued gradually and without much incident. On 10 May, at Easingwold in North Yorkshire, the king issued letters of credence for two substantial delegations of men who were to report to the archbishops of Canterbury and York on various matters, including 'the war in Scotland'.[57] By 13 May he had covered the roughly eleven miles to Thirsk, and on 16 May he arrived at Durham, where he remained for about a week.[58] 19 May was the deadline that King Edward II of England had set for the roughly 20,000 soldiers he had summoned from across England and Wales on 24 March and 20 April to arrive at Berwick-upon-Tweed. We cannot be certain how many of those summoned actually turned up, but the fact that two separate summonses had been promulgated strongly suggests that Edward had concerns about recruitment. While the April muster order makes it clear that these troops were to be gathered *in addition to* those summoned in March, the king's repeated demands for more soldiers may indicate a growing concern that the desired numbers were not initially forthcoming. There was precedent for this. King Edward had issued a second, additional feudal summons during his preparations for his first campaign into Scotland in 1310.[59] In 1314, Edward would issue yet another order for additional troops on 27 May. Although, by the time the third summons was issued, he was aware of the deal the Scots had struck with the garrison at Stirling, these multiple requests for troops may reflect continued struggles to gather the required numbers.

Edward's visit to Durham almost certainly involved a visit to the magnificent cathedral there. Here, he would have venerated the tomb of St Cuthbert and he may also have collected St Cuthbert's banner to accompany his army on his upcoming campaign into Scotland. St Cuthbert was a seventh-century clergyman who began his religious career as a monk at Melrose Abbey in southern Scotland. Coincidentally, Melrose is where Robert Bruce's heart would later be buried following his death in 1329.[60] Cuthbert helped Abbot Eata of Melrose establish a new monastery at Ripon in North Yorkshire but returned to Melrose after a dispute with King Aldfrith of Northumbria. At an uncertain date, Cuthbert moved to Lindisfarne – an island off the Northumbrian coast that was home to a priory founded by an earlier abbot of Melrose, St Aidan, and he lived for several years as a hermit on the island of Inner Farne. During this time, according to later hagiographies (i.e., saintly biographies), he received miraculous help from the local animals in order to survive. St Cuthbert was briefly lured out of his life as a hermit to serve as bishop of Lindisfarne in 685, but he had returned to the solitude of Inner Farne by the time of his death in 687.[61]

Cuthbert was initially buried at Lindisfarne and his saintly status was apparently confirmed when his body was found to have not decayed eleven years after his death. The traditional explanation for why his body was eventually moved to Durham is that the monks of Lindisfarne fled there with the saint's remains following a Viking attack on Lindisfarne in 793. However, more recent research has suggested that there may have been more cynical reasons for the move, not least the growing importance of Durham in relation to Lindisfarne.[62] At Durham, the cult of St Cuthbert came to be particularly associated with the right of sanctuary. In the medieval period, criminals fleeing justice had the right to claim sanctuary for thirty-seven days at Durham Cathedral, during which time they would be sheltered by the monks under the notional protection of the saint himself. After this, they would either have to submit themselves for judgment by the authorities or else accept exile from the kingdom altogether.

St Cuthbert, and in particular a banner associated with the saint held at Durham Cathedral, also became closely associated with warfare – and, more importantly, victory – against the Scots. Edward's father Edward I had, for example, taken the banner on campaign into Scotland in 1298 and subsequently defeated Sir William Wallace at the Battle of Falkirk.[63] The saint was also invoked by the victorious English army at the Battle of Neville's Cross in 1346, at which Bruce's son David II was wounded and captured, and was still being carried by English armies in battle against the Scots as late as 1513.[64] It seems highly likely therefore that Edward II venerated St Cuthbert and perhaps collected the banner in 1314, though there is no direct evidence of this. There is similarly no evidence that Bruce engaged in any veneration of St Cuthbert ahead of the battle. Yet Cuthbert was likely born in Lothian and had lived for a time at Melrose Abbey, and the cult of St Cuthbert was fairly popular in parts of southern Scotland. It is thus at least possible that some of those in Bruce's army, and even perhaps the king himself, also turned to the saint for his intercession and protection here in 1314.[65]

By 23 May, King Edward had moved on to Newcastle-upon-Tyne, less than seventy miles south of where his army was mustering at Berwick. Here, the king issued letters under the Great Seal in favour of Sir Edmund Mauley, steward of the royal household, concerning the manor of Uvedale ('Ulvedale') near Keswick. The manor had been forfeited by one Alexander Stewart, possibly Alexander Stewart of Bonkyl, a Berwickshire knight.[66] Stewart's father had been killed leading the Scottish archers at the Battle of Falkirk in 1298, so it may be that the forfeiture had taken place around this time.[67] He had not initially accepted Bruce as king in 1306, however, and had apparently refused to submit even after being captured by the Bruce Scots at the Water of Lyne in 1308, preferring instead to be ransomed.[68] This reference to Stewart's 'rebellion' in 1314 indicates that he switched sides before Bruce's victory at Bannockburn, perhaps even in response to the fall of Roxburgh or Edinburgh. Either way, the timing of King Edward's grant to Mauley should probably be interpreted as patronage related to Mauley's service on the coming campaign into Scotland: a way of reinforcing Mauley's loyalty to the crown by reassuring him that Edward would protect and promote his personal interests. Mauley would not fare well on the battlefield at Bannockburn, however, as we will see in the following chapter.

Meanwhile, at Abingdon in Berkshire also on 23 May, Richard, abbot of Abingdon, promised to pay the English treasurer a fine for the three knights' service he owed 'in the army against the Scots', so long as the fine did not exceed sixty marks.[69] Arrangements such as these had grown out of an earlier practice known as 'scutage' (from the Latin word *scutum*, meaning 'shield'). In principle, this furnished the crown with ready cash, which could be used to employ more soldiers or to supply the army with victuals. For landowners like Abbot Richard, it was a means of converting the physical burden of maintaining tenants who could serve in the royal host if called upon to do so into a more manageable financial obligation. As with much crown business in Edward's reign, particularly that relating to the royal finances, the practice was not without controversy. Within a year of Bannockburn, at a parliament at Westminster in April 1315, Edward received a petition complaining that scutage was being levied on the basis of outdated agreements of military service, meaning that the king's subjects were being asked to pay more knights' fees than they actually owed.[70] Abbot Richard's careful clarification of the maximum sum he was willing to pay is likely reflective of ongoing frustration of the king's sharp practice in this regard.

King Edward was still at Newcastle three days later on 26 May, when he approved the payment of £20 for the repair of two mills, two bakehouses, and a prison at Penrith in Cumbria, all of which had been 'burnt and wholly destroyed by the Scottish rebels lately invading that county'.[71] This was surely a reference to the *chevauchée* (i.e., 'horse charge') Carrick had made through north-west England the previous month. Over the course of the following century, the town of Penrith would develop an unfortunate tit-for-tat relationship with Dumfries on the opposite side of the border, with the local lords tending to respond to the burning of one by burning the other in retaliation.[72] In 1314, the promise of the major summer campaign into Scotland no doubt superseded any local desire for direct revenge. Nevertheless, the repairs funded by Edward offer a valuable insight into the extent of the damage caused by the April raid.

For all that the king's activities in late April and early May were clearly of considerable concern for him and his subjects, they were nevertheless fairly prosaic in the grand scheme of the preparations for the upcoming invasion of Scotland. Little of the royal business conducted in these weeks can have realistically been expected to have a decisive impact on the outcome of the proposed campaign. Events were about to unfold in Scotland however – and indeed may already have been underway by the time Edward was making his grant to Mauley and Abbot Richard was drawing the line with the treasurer – that would dramatically alter the situation for both sides and propel the two armies towards their fateful clash at Bannockburn.

*Chapter 5*

# 'To Reskew Strevillyne with Bataill'

## The Deal with the Stirling Garrison, Scottish Preparations, and the Final March to Bannockburn, May to June 1314

### The Return of the King: The Deal with the Stirling Garrison, May 1314

At an uncertain date in May 1314, Edward Bruce, earl of Carrick and King Robert's younger brother, made a deal with Sir Philip Mowbray, commander of the garrison at Stirling, for the relief of Stirling Castle. Though not necessarily sanctioned by King Robert himself, this deal would prove to be the pivotal moment that led Bruce to give battle against Edward II at Bannockburn. When we last saw the earl, he was leading the Scots in a devastating *chevauchée* through Cumbria at the end of April. It is unclear when precisely after this he placed Stirling Castle under siege. Neither the fall of Roxburgh nor Edinburgh had been preceded by lengthy sieges. In the case of Roxburgh, the castle had fallen to a surprise assault. The garrison at Edinburgh appears to have been surprised too, but whether there had been a period during which the Scots had openly surrounded the castle before this is unclear. If they did, it is unlikely to have been for an extended period, since there is no evidence that the English royal administration knew the castle was under threat in the build-up to its capture. Similarly, the lack of any specific concern from the English crown about the situation at Stirling Castle until 27 May implies that the castle was not under siege for long before this. It seems equally unlikely that there was much time between the siege beginning and the deal being struck between the besiegers and the garrison, given that there is no evidence of anything similar to the attacks on Roxburgh and Edinburgh being attempted before the agreement was reached.

The precise terms of the deal, sadly, do not survive. However, the *Scalacronica* may preserve a close approximation of the terms offered in May 1314. Gray might have had access to an accurate record of the deal during his captivity at Edinburgh Castle in the 1350s, perhaps even in one of the *croniclis* apparently commissioned by King Robert that Gray mentions. Alternatively, it may be that he was simply drawing on his own extensive military experience to postulate a believable reconstruction of the terms. According to Gray:

> 'Philip Mowbray, knight, who had the ward of the castle for the King of England, had made terms with Robert Bruce to surrender the castle when it was besieged, if he was not relieved; unless the English army came nearer than three leagues from the castle, within eight days of St John's [the Baptist] day in the summer next to come, he would surrender the castle.'[1]

In return, the Scots would be expected to let the English garrison return home unharmed in the event that no army arrived and the castle was duly surrendered. The garrison at Roxburgh had also been allowed to return to England unscaled following their surrender in February.[2] A league was roughly three miles, meaning that Edward's army would have technically fulfilled their end of the deal once they were within nine miles of Stirling (around Larbert). Furthermore, a deadline within eight days (inclusive of the feast itself) of St John the Baptist's feast day (24 June) meant the English army would have until 1 July to reach their destination.

Though it may seem alien to modern eyes, deals such as the one made in 1314 were not uncommon in late medieval warfare. The Scottish garrison at Berwick in 1333 negotiated a comparable deal with Edward II's son Edward III in 1333, leading to the disastrous Scottish defeat at Halidon Hill.[3] Similarly, in 1424, a beleaguered French force at Ivry-sur-Seine agreed to surrender itself to a besieging English army if not relieved by 15 August, an arrangement that led to another battle with heavy Scottish casualties at Verneuil-sur-Avre.[4] Deals such as these offered both the besieged and the besiegers an opportunity to limit the potential dangers involved in a long, protracted siege. It should, however, be obvious that the deal struck in 1314 dramatically favoured the English over the Scots. Edward II had after all been planning to raise an army for a summer campaign into Scotland since November 1313. He had been issuing muster orders since March; already by April the formidable Aymer de Valence, earl of Pembroke, had arrived at Berwick-upon-Tweed to oversee those portions of the army that had already arrived. Even accounting for Edward's difficulties in recruitment, it was virtually impossible for him to miss the deadline of 24 June (let alone 1 July). Indeed, the relatively short timeframe that the English were given to respond to the arrangement (precisely five weeks to the day after King Edward apparently first heard about the deal) may be a concession on the part of the garrison in recognition of the fact that it otherwise put the Scots at a significant disadvantage.

This raises a very serious question: why did Edward Bruce accept or propose the deal in the first place? One possible interpretation is that by 1314 the Bruce Scots felt confident enough to finally challenge Edward II in open battle and that the deal was a way for the Scots to arrange for this to happen on their own terms. Dr Michael Penman, in his excellent scholarly biography of King Robert, has argued that from as early as October 1313 the Bruce Scots had been looking for an opportunity to fight and win the kind of large-scale pitched battle that might provide sufficient diplomatic leverage to revolutionize the Scottish situation diplomatically; therefore, King Robert likely endorsed the decision to cut a deal with the Stirling garrison ahead of time.[5] On the other hand, while the Scots had certainly been remarkably active in the early months of 1314, these activities had largely been in keeping with the general strategy of wearing down the English administration in Scotland through attrition while avoiding open battle. Moreover, King Robert does not appear to have played an active role in any of the actions that had occurred earlier in the year. The unusually aggressive reaction to the threatened English invasion might just as easily be ascribed to the king's lack of involvement in events, rather than that he was pursuing a new, more provocative strategy.

The most detailed surviving Scottish account of King Robert's reign, Barbour's *Bruce*, is explicit in presenting the deal as having been made on Carrick's initiative alone, adding that when his brother the king heard about it he judged it to have been 'unwisly doyn'.[6] For Barbour, the deal with Stirling represented a serious break with previous Scottish war policy: one undertaken on a personal basis by Edward Bruce, motivated by his own rashness. While the poet no doubt heightens the melodrama of the moment when King Robert learns of the deal – as much to reinforce the ongoing theme of the value of prudence and Edward Bruce's inferiority in comparison to his elder brother as anything else – the notion that the deal with Stirling Castle was a decision taken by Carrick and not the king would certainly fit with what we can tell about how the Scottish royal administration was being managed in the first half of 1314. Barbour's claim that King Robert did not approve this decision and was initially critical of it is also plausible. His subsequent decision to embrace the opportunity presented may have had less to do with his brother's hearty response to the challenge (which is what Barbour implies changed his mind) and rather more to do with cynical calculations about how to turn the deal to his advantage.[7]

King Edward's sudden need to relieve the garrison at Stirling meant that King Robert could now predict where the massive, slow-moving English army would be about or on 24 June. The English feudal host, with its enormous, cumbersome baggage train, could not move swiftly across country like the highly mobile guerrilla forces Bruce fielded. It would have to come via established roads, which meant that Bruce could now map their approach to Stirling more or less exactly. Armed with this intelligence, King Robert could begin to construct a battle plan to challenge them at a time and in a place that played to his strengths while simultaneously nullifying Edward's own. If he could do so successfully, he might well achieve the hitherto inconceivable goal of defeating the English king in battle. Moreover, if in defeating the English army King Robert could affect Edward's capture, he might well secure a means to end the entire war at a stroke, as the English king could then be traded for formal recognition of Bruce's rights as king. With his strength returning as his latest bout of ill-health came to an end – or perhaps he was simply stirred into action by the need to react to this latest development – the king was about to return and personally take charge, possibly for the first time since October. The end result would be the most remarkable military victory of his reign.

## 'Hys Ost Assemblit All Bedene': The Scottish Army and Their Preparations

By 1314, most of Scotland was back under Bruce's control, but we might reasonably doubt his ability to call out the full military capacity of the kingdom at this stage of his reign. We might, for example, expect the north-east and the south-west – traditional heartlands of Comyn and Balliol power – to be less than enthusiastic when responding to King Robert's call to arms. Bruce would have been primarily reliant on the armed followings of his leading subjects and long-standing allies, which at least meant these would be mostly experienced and battle-hardened veterans of the previous seven years of fierce guerrilla warfare. The downside was that there would be significantly fewer of them than the English could field. The short period of time in which Bruce had to raise his army – probably only the five weeks between the deal being struck and the English army's arrival at Stirling – would have exacerbated this problem. McDiarmid has suggested the Scots may have fielded as few as 3,500 in 1314.[8] The most influential estimate has been that of Prof. Barrow, who proposed a number anywhere between 7,000 and 10,000, though scholars such as McNamee and Phillips have preferred to argue this down to 5,000 to 6,000.[9] More recently, Dr David Caldwell has argued for as many as 15,000 to 25,000 Scots at Bannockburn, based on estimates for the army available to Wallace at Falkirk in 1298, and this interpretation has received support from Dr Penman as well.[10]

On balance, McDiarmid's assessment is probably too low, but the specific context of 1314 likely counts against Caldwell's higher estimates as well. Bruce had been unwilling to openly confront King Edward when the English army numbered less than 5,000 men in 1310 to 1311, suggesting he had fewer men than that then. For all King Robert's ability to call on the kingdom's manpower would have increased in line with his territorial control of his kingdom, this had probably not swelled his army to more than twice its previous size. Moreover, the likelihood that Bruce was seeking to avoid a direct confrontation until after the deal had been struck with the Stirling garrison suggests that whatever muster orders were issued would have gone out at short notice, meaning that numbers would be relatively low, at least compared to 1298. Bruce would therefore require a battle plan that would counteract this numerical disadvantage. Though we lack the kind of detailed records we have for Edward's army, we can draw at least some tentative conclusions about the composition of Bruce's army from several relevant sources.

In terms of identifying the personnel of the Scottish army, Barbour names a number of the leading Scots and offers clues about the presence of others. The list of individuals in attendance at the Cambuskenneth parliament of November 1314, though not complete, also provides some useful hints about the figures who may have responded to Bruce's summons in the summer.[11] The likely list of Bruce's key war leaders gives us another valuable insight into another of his advantages over his English counterpart. Prof. Michael Prestwich has argued that medieval battles should not be thought of as disorganized affairs, even though it can be difficult to reconstruct precisely how communications on the battlefield were carried out.[12] While ultimate responsibility for a battle plan would have rested with the two kings, moment-to-moment decisions would necessarily have to be made by 'junior' commanders as and when issues arose. There was plenty of experience among the leading men in King Edward's army, but their experiences of Edward's rule and their attitudes towards one another left them bitterly divided. Bruce's chief lieutenants were, for the most part, relatively young, at least by comparison with Edward's, though many of them had plenty of experience fighting in their king's vigorous guerrilla campaigns in the last seven years or so. Moreover, while they all shared the competitive tendencies that were a prerequisite for all medieval nobles, Bruce's subordinates must have been keenly aware that success for Bruce would empower him to reshape the community of the realm as he saw fit. If they could help to deliver that power, then they might reasonably expect to be the beneficiaries of the king's generosity when that time came. Thus, while the 'junior' war leaders in the Scottish army at Bannockburn might be expected to compete with one another as fiercely as their English counterparts, they were competing to prove their usefulness to their sovereign and thus, as it were, pulling in the same direction, whereas Edward's followers were generally at cross purposes.

First and foremost among Bruce's subordinates, the king's brother Edward Bruce, earl of Carrick, was apparently present at Stirling even before the king himself arrived to take charge of the situation. For all the poet emphasizes the disagreement between the Bruce brothers over the deal with the Stirling garrison, Barbour credits Carrick – 'Schyr Edward the worthy' – with the leadership of one of the main Scottish divisions at Bannockburn.[13] This would certainly fit with Carrick's status as the king's heir and would have served to reinforce the message sent by his appointment as earl of Carrick in October 1313. The other main Scottish division was led by the king's 'dearest nephew' Thomas Randolph, earl of Moray, according to Barbour.[14] Barbour initially describes Randolph's division as the vanguard ('vaward'), but on the second day of the battle has Carrick's division engage first, which may indicate that his – not Randolph's – was in fact the vanguard.[15] Randolph's presence is confirmed by Gray, who also describes his division as the vanguard (*auaunt garde*).[16]

It would certainly have been more appropriate in terms of the two men's status if Carrick had held the more prestigious position. Yet tensions between the king and his brother may have led the former to rebuke the latter with a less-respectable command. As well as stressing the king's dissatisfaction with Carrick's activities in 1314, Barbour claims that Carrick chose to lead an armed expedition to Ireland in the spring of 1315 because he 'Thocht that Scotland to litill wes/Till his brother and him alsua'.[17] Similarly, Barbour's contemporary, John of Fordun, claims that Carrick set out for Ireland because he 'would not dwell together with his brother in peace', giving an impression of considerable ill-feeling between the Bruce brothers in the wake of Bannockburn.[18] If King Robert did intend to insult his brother with this appointment, Randolph – as Bruce's most richly rewarded kinsman – would be an obvious choice to replace him as leader of the vanguard. Carrick's only known return to Scotland after April 1315 was to settle a dispute that had arisen between him and his brother over the generous patronage the king had extended to Randolph in granting him the lordship of Man (which otherwise would have been strategically valuable to Carrick in his efforts to extend Scottish influence in Ireland).[19] Yet the extent to which animosity between Robert and Edward Bruce influenced the Scottish expedition to Ireland has probably been exaggerated by later writers like Fordun and Barbour. On balance, it seems unlikely that King Robert would have done something so provocative as to deliberately alienate his brother and heir at such a crucial juncture. He would have enough problems to deal with facing the English invasion without creating domestic strife for himself.

Barbour invents another division that he places under the command of James Douglas and his cousin Walter Stewart.[20] Though Dr Sonja Cameron has persuasively argued that this 'phantom division' is entirely fabricated by the poet, the presence of Douglas and Stewart in the Scottish army at Bannockburn is believable.[21] As we have seen, like Carrick and Randolph, Douglas had already played a significant role in the Scottish military activities of 1314. Indeed, his impromptu assault on Roxburgh had arguably been the catalyst for the Bruce Scots' aggressive war policy in the early months of the year. Moreover, the author of the *Vita* notes Douglas's presence on the battlefield at Bannockburn, hinting that he may have served under Carrick.[22] Like Carrick and Randolph, Douglas would have brought with him a battle-hardened following 'usit in fechting', as

Barbour puts it.[23] Their extensive experience on the front lines of the war over the previous seven years or so would have been of enormous value to King Robert, even though Douglas had not yet achieved the social or political prominence he would attain by the end of the reign.

Stewart was young – 'bot a berdles hyne' (i.e., a beardless youth), to use Barbour's colourful expression – having been born circa 1296, but he boasted an extensive following drawn from ancestral lands in Ayrshire, Renfrewshire, and Kyle.[24] Moreover, the Stewarts had a long-standing association with the Bruces. Walter's late father, James, had been party to the so-called Turnberry Band with King Robert's father and grandfather in 1286 and served as an auditor for King Robert's grandfather during the Great Cause in 1291 to 1292.[25] James had joined the future king in his brief rebellion against the English in early 1297 and had almost certainly been present for Bruce's inauguration in 1306.[26] The Bruce-Stewart alliance was formalized in the immediate aftermath of Bannockburn when Walter married Marjory, Bruce's daughter from his first marriage, and thereafter became one of the king's closest councillors.[27] The marriage had not apparently taken place before King Robert held an assembly at Ayr in late April 1315, but the wedding may have taken place shortly afterwards at the nearby Stewart castle at Rothesay on Bute, perhaps in the wake of the expedition that King Robert led through his western dominions immediately following the assembly at Ayr.[28]

Both Stewart and Douglas were present at Cambuskenneth in November, as was another Scottish lord mentioned in *The Bruce* – Sir Robert Keith. Keith was a Lothian baron with a respectable history of service to the 'patriotic' cause during the recent Anglo-Scottish wars and was also the hereditary marischal of Scotland.[29] He had, however, remained cautiously aloof from Bruce initially. Partly this may have been influenced by the fact that from around 1303 he had been engaged in a legal dispute with Bruce's close ally Neil Campbell over wardship of Susannah and Alice Crawford, daughters of the late Andrew Crawford of Loudoun. Keith had bought the right to arrange marriages for the two young girls from John Balliol during his brief reign as king of Scots, but Neil and his kinsman Donald had apparently taken the girls into custody, forcing Keith to fruitlessly chase the Campbells through the English courts for several years.[30] By Christmas 1308, Keith had submitted to Bruce and quickly entered the king's inner circle.[31] The office of marischal had originally involved various responsibilities for the management of the king's household, but by the fourteenth century had become primarily a judicial role. Critically, it guaranteed Keith a role in the royal council, and he was thus regularly to be found in King Robert's entourage throughout the reign. Recent social network analysis has shown Keith to have appeared in more documents alongside the king than any other contemporary figure.[32] He seems to have remained physically close to King Robert on the battlefield too, at least if Barbour's testimony is to be believed. As a result, he played a small but tactically significant role at a critical moment in the fighting on the second day, as we will see in the following chapter.

Another long-standing ally of King Robert, Angus Óg ('the Younger') Macdonald of Islay, is also mentioned by Barbour, albeit somewhat obliquely as the lord of the Islemen in the king's division at the battle.[33] The odd phrasing has led Prof. A. A. M. Duncan to suggest that Macdonald was not present at Bannockburn, but his absence would be striking.[34] Following his defeats at the Battles of Methven and Tyndrum in 1306, it was to Macdonald that Bruce had chiefly looked to rebuild his shattered political networks, and it was with the assistance of Macdonald's Hebridean tenants that the king made his spirited comeback in the spring of 1307.[35] Macdonald's seal does not survive on the judgment passed at Cambuskenneth in November, though of course it may have been one of those damaged beyond recognition or lost altogether. There is some evidence of disputed leadership of the wider Macdonald kindred during this period, and it is also true that Bruce-Macdonald relations soured later in the reign as King Robert sought to restrain Macdonald's ambitions on the west coast.[36] Either of these issues may have interfered with Angus Macdonald's ability to appear in person at Bannockburn. Yet, it seems doubtful that his followers would serve in the army without his leadership.

Similarly, it is not entirely clear, but highly likely, that William, earl of Ross, joined Bruce in 1314. His eldest son, Hugh, was present at Cambuskenneth in November and his youngest son, Walter, is mentioned by Barbour as one of the three Scottish casualties that the poet elects to name over the two days of fighting.[37] Earl William's middle son, John, is not to be found either in *The Bruce* or at Cambuskenneth, but he was mentioned by name in the earl's submission to King Robert in 1308.[38] This suggests that, although he was married to a sister of John Comyn, earl of Buchan, John Ross was indeed in the Bruce camp by 1314 and was likely to have joined his brothers on the battlefield at Bannockburn.

Another kinsman, Thomas Ross, also attended the parliament at Cambuskenneth and thus may have been present in the Scottish army as well. Earl William had famously been responsible for the capture of the royal women at Tain in 1306.[39] However, the earl's northern powerbase had been easily isolated from his English allies during Bruce's earliest campaigns through northern Scotland and, under pressure from repeated assaults on his interests in the region, Ross submitted to King Robert in October 1308.[40] Despite his role in capturing the king's female relatives, Ross quickly emerged as one of the key magnates in the north of the kingdom – alongside Randolph and David Strathbogie, earl of Atholl, who was also present in the Scottish army at Bannockburn, according to Barbour.[41] Ross appears to have embraced this role, perhaps grateful of the king's magnanimity in the circumstances, whereas having his personal interests balanced with those of the other earls likely played a part in alienating Atholl, explaining his subsequent behaviour at Bannockburn.

The only other Scots mentioned by name by Barbour are those who were killed in the fighting. He mentions three in total, as well as an anonymous yeoman ('yuman') slain in the skirmishing on the first day. These are the aforementioned Sir Walter Ross, Sir William Vipont, and Sir William of Airth.[42] Vipont was likely the man of the same name who was granted the baronies of Bolton in East Lothian and Langton in Berwickshire by King Robert in 1309.[43] These should probably be considered speculative grants, intended to encourage Vipont to apply military pressure to his prospective tenants in these areas and bring them into the king's peace. Bruce's grants of the lordships of Galloway and Nithsdale to his brother Edward and nephew Thomas, respectively, and his acknowledgement of James Douglas as lord of Douglas around the same time were likely part of a similar policy of encouraging his more warlike subjects to press their newfound claims, and in doing so, extending Bruce's royal authority into the south.[44] At the time the grants to Vipont were made, the king was unable to guarantee physical possession of them; in 1312, Bolton was granted by Edward II to Alexander Mowbray, brother of the Philip Mowbray who in 1314 was leading the garrison at Stirling.[45] William of Airth is an otherwise obscure figure, but presumably he hailed from nearby Airth on the south shore of the Forth. A namesake appears in the Ragman Rolls of 1296, who may either be a relative or the man himself.[46] Possibly he was also a kinsman of the Hugh of Airth who witnessed a number of royal *acta* during Bruce's reign – including the king's grant to Inchaffray Abbey at Scotlandwell in February 1314.[47]

Arguably the most peculiar absence among those lords listed as present at Bannockburn in *The Bruce* (particularly peculiar because he is repeatedly acknowledged elsewhere in the text as a committed Bruce partisan) is Neil Campbell. Campbell was almost certainly in Bruce's army in 1314 and was probably present in the king's own division among – or indeed leading – the men of Argyll. He had been in Bruce's service even before the latter became king in 1306.[48] Barbour notes Campbell's presence among the survivors that fled the battlefield at Methven with King Robert and credits him with providing supplies and transport by boat to Kintyre while on the run after Tyndrum.[49] At an uncertain date, possibly even before 1314, he married King Robert's sister Mary, a powerful acknowledgement of the close political relationship between the two men.[50] Due to this long service, Campbell's 'mengye' ('followers') would, like those of Carrick, Randolph, Douglas, Macdonald, and others, have had extensive experience in warfare and thus been extremely valuable to Bruce as he faced the unprecedented prospect of a direct confrontation with the English royal host. Campbell was present at the Cambuskenneth parliament in November 1314, making his presence on the battlefield in June all the more likely.

Similarly, Gilbert Hay is another pre-1306 Bruce adherent who frequently appears in Barbour's *Bruce* but nonetheless goes unnamed in the poet's account of Bannockburn. Like Campbell, Hay did attend the Cambuskenneth parliament. Also like Campbell, Hay is identified by Barbour as one of the Scottish lords who narrowly escaped from Methven, and he later accompanies the fugitive king through his native Carrick.[51] Hay's lands had been forfeited after he came out in support of King Robert in 1306.[52] In 1308, he and Campbell – along with Alexander Seton – had sworn on the Eucharist at Cambuskenneth Abbey to protect the king's person.[53] He and Campbell may therefore have been physically close to King Robert on the battlefield at Bannockburn. The two men – along with Keith and Roger Kirkpatrick (another early Bruce partisan who may have been present at Bannockburn) – would form the first embassy dispatched by the Scots for peace talks with the English following Bannockburn.[54] Hay had been styled 'constable of Scotland' (*'constabularius Scotie'*) in 1309, a role that included responsibility for the king's personal safety, and he would be regranted the office on a hereditary basis before the end of 1314.[55] Penman has reasonably suggested that King Robert entrusted the practical responsibilities of the constable at Bannockburn to Hay, which may have played a role in alienating the holder of the office in June 1314 – David Strathbogie, earl of Atholl.[56]

Aside from the four earls mentioned above - Carrick, Moray, Atholl, and Ross - we can deduce the presence in the Scottish army in 1314 of several other magnates not mentioned by Barbour or associated with the Cambuskenneth parliament. Malcolm, earl of Lennox, had been one of the most frequent witnesses of royal acts in the first eight years of King Robert's reign.[57] Earl Malcolm's fidelity to Bruce is emphasized throughout *The Bruce*. Their tearful reunion after King Robert believed Lennox to have been captured or killed at Methven in 1306 is so emotionally charged that it leads Barbour to digress into a truly bizarre attempt to reassure his readers that men who appear to be weeping with joy are merely experiencing the water 'fra the hart' rising to wet their eyes.[58] Barbour acknowledges that in 1313, Malise, earl of Strathearn, had supported Bruce despite his father's refusal to do so and had been granted the earldom as a consequence of this, even though his father was still alive until around 1317.[59] If Barbour is correct, we might thus expect the earl to respond to Bruce's summons in 1314. Though not as high-ranking as Lennox or Strathearn, Sir John Menteith of Arran and Knapdale has been identified as a close councillor of the king in the years leading up to Bannockburn and the years that followed.[60] Barbour ignores Menteith's contribution to King Robert's affairs altogether, but this is perhaps reflective of the fact that Menteith had no descendants whom Barbour wished to appeal to with his writing. Alternatively, Menteith's absence may be linked to Sir John's awkward association with William Wallace's capture. Though he had done little more than been unfortunate enough to be the sheriff in whose jurisdiction Wallace happened to be arrested in 1305, a fiercely critical literary tradition had already emerged by the late fourteenth century that presented Menteith as having personally betrayed Wallace to his death.[61]

A portion of the troops drawn from the Western Isles may have been led by Ruairi MacRuairi, half-brother of King Robert's cousin Christina MacRuairi – though Barbour mentions neither Ruairi nor Christina in his account of Bannockburn and they are not found at Cambuskenneth either. Like Macdonald, Christina appears to have been one of the king's allies from the *Gàidhealtachd* who saved his skin – more or less literally – by providing shelter and support in the difficult winter of

1306 to 1307. Fordun is explicit in highlighting her early assistance to the king, and she may also be the unnamed kinswoman who Barbour claims provided Bruce with forty men and intelligence of the disposition of the local English forces on his return to the mainland in early 1307.[62] For her part, assisting her cousin in pursuit of his kingly ambitions offered the promise of royal patronage in her ongoing dispute with her half-brothers Lachlan and Ruairi over their father's lordship of Garmoran, which embraced a large parcel of lands in the north-west, including Moidart, Arisaig, Morar, and Knoydart on the mainland and the islands of Rum, Eigg, Barra, the Uists, and St Kilda. A precise chronology of the dispute is difficult to reconstruct, since most of the surviving documents concerning it are undated. However, a compromise was eventually reached, possibly before Bannockburn, by which Ruairi was acknowledged as lord of Gamoran but Christina's own son – also Ruairi – had been recognized as the heir to the lordship if the elder Ruairi died without offspring of his own.[63] For Bruce, this secured Ruairi's service – albeit at sea rather than on land necessarily – and maintained for Christina's son a strong claim on the disputed lordship. Ruairi's price for this may have been his recognition by the Scottish crown as *rí Innse Gall* ('king of the Hebrides'). This was a title that the descendants of Somerled – Clan Donald, Clan Ruairi, and Clan Dougall – had been competing over since the twelfth century. A MacRuairi *rí Innse Gall* was reputedly killed in battle at Faughart in Ireland alongside Edward Bruce in 1318, a fact that may have ignited a fresh round of uncertainty and royal interference over possession of the lordship of Garmoran.[64]

The list of barons and knights at the Cambuskenneth parliament in November suggests some other names that can tentatively be added to Bruce's likely supporters drawn from the lower ranks of the Scottish nobility in 1314. David Balfour was probably a kinsman of the John Balfour who served as a guarantor for Gilbert Hay in 1310, and if so may have fought for Hay in 1314.[65] Malcolm Balfour, also mentioned at Cambuskenneth, was likely his kinsman. Thomas Dishington belonged to a family whose interests were promoted in Forfarshire after 1314, surely a reflection of services provided to the Bruce cause.[66] Archibald Beaton was, no doubt, a member of the influential Beaton kindred of Fife and Perthshire, while Ranulph Lyle may have been an ancestor of the John Lyle who held lands in Stirlingshire and East Lothian from Bruce's successor David II.[67] Norman Leslie had enjoyed patronage from the English crown at the expense of Bruce's allies in 1305 but had witnessed a royal act at Perth in October 1308, so he had clearly submitted to Bruce well before Bannockburn.[68] Mornus de Muschamp is another difficult figure to identify, though a Lanarkshire Muschamp – to whom Mornus may have been related – appears in the Ragman Rolls of 1296.[69]

Not all of the attendees at the Cambuskenneth parliament were necessarily able or willing to join Bruce's army at Bannockburn, however. Andrew Murray was a posthumous child of the Andrew Murray who had fought with William Wallace at Stirling Bridge in 1297 and died soon afterward.[70] The younger Andrew was a prisoner in England at the time of the battle and thus could not have fought at the battle.[71] Duncan Wallace of Auchincruive in Ayrshire was, like Murray, probably quite young in 1314. A teenaged lord might find himself on a battlefield in the fourteenth century of course. As noted above, Walter Stewart would have been in his late teens in 1314 – about the same age as Andrew Murray – and was nonetheless present in Bruce's army. William, lord of Douglas, was also in his teens when he was killed fighting at Halidon Hill in 1333.[72] Yet Duncan was likely significantly younger even than this. He would, for example, later marry Eleanor, widow of Bruce's nephew Alexander Bruce, after 1332, and would still be active as late as 1370.[73] Interestingly, by that date he would be in possession of the lands of 'Ochtirbannock', that is, Bannockburn, but this may have been connected to his marriage to Eleanor rather than a reward for some service performed there in 1314.[74] John Sinclair of Herdmanston and Walter Haliburton both appeared at the Cambuskenneth parliament but may have been recent 'converts' to the Bruce cause, having reconsidered their allegiances because of Bruce's victory. Gray places John Haliburton, presumably Walter's kinsman, in the English army at Methven in 1306 and even has him almost capture Bruce in the fighting there.[75] Sinclair is a more difficult figure to associate with one side or the other. His kinsman Henry Sinclair of Rosslyn may have had a hand in the knightly education of Bruce's faithful lieutenant, James Douglas, and was certainly adhering to the Bruce cause by October 1313.[76] We must, however, be cautious about the likely loyalties of individuals whose landed interests were focussed close to the border and potentially on the route the English army might take into Scotland. The Berwickshire laird Alexander Seton also appeared at Cambuskenneth in November, and he was certainly not present in Bruce's army *before* the battle.

It is also worth considering the potential clerical contributions to Bruce's army in 1314. King Robert had enjoyed a good relationship with the Scottish clergy since the outset of his reign. An English observer at Forfar in May 1307 had for instance complained of the 'false preachers' who had promoted the Bruce cause to their congregations.[77] Maurice, abbot of Inchaffray, is mentioned as being present at Bannockburn by Bower, who had access to sources produced within Bruce's lifetime. One of these was apparently written by Bernard, abbot of Arbroath; as Bruce's chancellor, he would likely have remained close to the king throughout his preparations for battle to fulfil this office.[78] Both Abbot Bernard and Abbot Maurice were present at the Cambuskenneth parliament in November, as were the abbots of Scone, Kelso, Holyrood, Lindores, Newbattle, Coupar Angus, Paisley, Dunfermline, Inchaffray, Inchmaholme, Deer, and Sweetheart. So too were the bishops of St Andrews (Bruce's long-standing ally, William Lamberton), Dunkeld, the Isles, Brechin, Argyll, and Caithness, and the priors of Coldingham, Restenneth, St Andrews, Loch Leven, and perhaps also Pittenweem. It must be reiterated again that attendance at the Cambuskenneth parliament does not equate to participation in the battle, however, especially for clergymen. For instance, William de Gretham, prior of Coldingham, would surely have been more likely to associate himself with the English crown in June since the English army would be advancing perilously close to his border priory as they began their invasion of Scotland. Elias, abbot of Holyrood, may also have found it expedient to remain faithful to King Edward until after the battle. The English army would after all approach Stirling via Edinburgh and thus was well-placed to threaten Holyrood if not kept satisfied of the abbot's loyalty. Moreover, while they would no doubt have tenants who could be sent to join the army, we might reasonably doubt whether any of these churchmen would have personally contributed to the fighting. Barbour does credit one of these individuals – William Sinclair, bishop of Dunkeld – with leading the Scots into battle at Inverkeithing in 1317.[79] On another occasion, Barbour mentions 'a rycht sturdy frer [i.e., friar]' who assisted Douglas in luring an English force into an ambush near Melrose in 1322, and the poet clearly expected this individual to fight, as he describes him as wearing armour under his robe.[80] For the most part, however, any clergymen in the army would have largely provided moral support to the anxious troops.

In terms of the ordinary soldiers, no Scottish muster orders for 1314 survive. The only extant ordinance for raising soldiers from Robert I's reign was produced at a parliament at Scone on 3 December 1318, for an army to be ready for the following April.[81] There is little reason to suppose that Bruce's expectations had changed dramatically over those four years, however. In 1318, those with

£10 of goods were to serve with 'a sufficient aketon [a quilted jacket], a basinet [a conical helmet], and mailed gloves with a lance and sword'.[82] The aketon and bascinet could be substituted for a *hobirgellum* (a type of mail shirt) and an iron cap (*capellum de ferro*), but the emphasis was clearly on protection for the head, torso, and hands.[83] This equipment is particularly reminiscent of the description of the Scottish soldiers in the *Vita Edwardi Secundi*.[84] It is also reflective of how the Scots are armed in the illuminated initial of a charter of 1316 depicting the siege of Carlisle in the previous year.[85] The lower rank of the army in 1318 were described quaintly as 'anyone having the value of one cow in goods' ('*quicunque habens valorem unius vacce in bonis*'). These men were expected to bring with them 'a good lance or a good bow with a sheath of arrows, namely twenty-four arrows'.[86] There was apparently no expectation that the lower-class troops would have any armour whatsoever, although presumably they would protect themselves as best they could afford. Those who had been serving in Bruce's armies for a while may well have equipped themselves with better gear than they otherwise might by looting previous battlefields and captured castles. The penalty for failing to appear with the required equipment was the forfeiture of the person's goods, half of which would be retained by the crown while the remainder would be given to the delinquent individual's lord. The absence of any mention of horses is striking, but broadly fits with the tactics the Scots employed on the day of the battle. Many Scottish soldiers might ride to the battlefield, but they would fight on foot, as we will examine in more detail in the following chapter.[87]

Barbour claims that in 1314, Bruce mustered his army in the Torwood, a wide stretch of woodland and parkland located between the Bannock Burn to the north and the River Carron to the south.[88] Despite its name, this would not have been a single stretch of dense forest but would have encompassed large areas of parkland in which Bruce's army could train and prepare for the coming battle.[89] Bruce's preparations for the battle must have included surveying the landscape around Stirling on his arrival in the Torwood, which occurred at an uncertain date but probably within the last week of May, likely close to 27 May – the date when Edward learned of the deal with the garrison at Stirling. Many of those in the English army would have been familiar with the landscape around Stirling in a general sense. Stirling had after all been in English hands since 1304, and a number of those in the English army in 1314 had been present at the castle's fall – Edward II and Robert Bruce included.[90] Bruce, however, had the advantage

'To Reskew Strevillyne with Bataill' 113

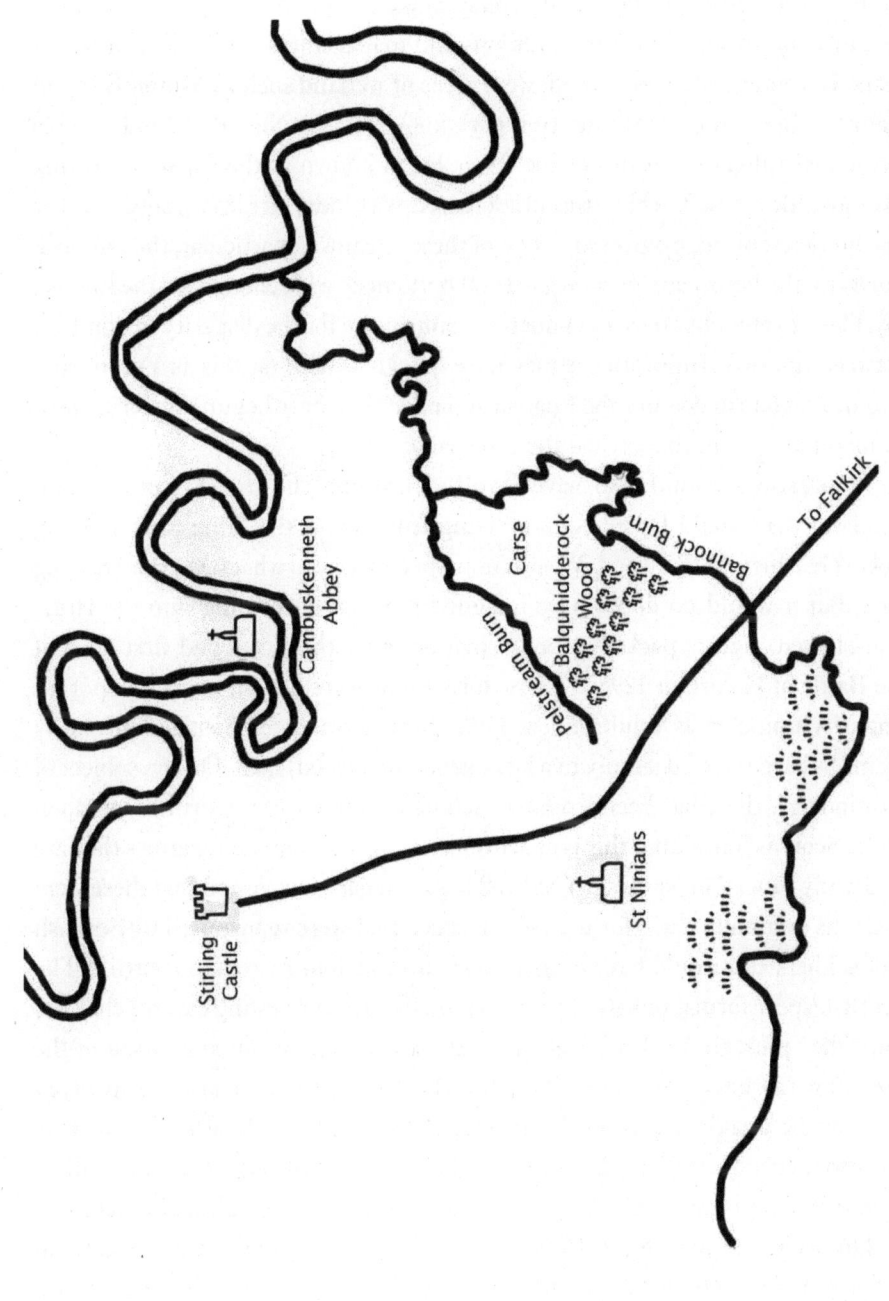

Map 2. The area immediately south and west of Stirling Castle, where Bruce chose to make his stand in 1314.

of being able to assess precisely what the landscape was like in the month or so ahead of the battle, noting – and capitalizing on – any minor changes brought about by the specific weather conditions and management of the land in recent years. Beyond the Torwood there were areas of wetland such as Milton Bog and Halbert's Bog, an enclosed hunting park known as the New Park, and a wide fertile plain along the banks of the River Forth known as the Carse of Stirling (also just 'the carse'), which was crisscrossed with tidal streams, many of these also bordered by boggy ground.[91] Two of these streams in particular, the Bannock Burn and the Pelstream, created a natural bottleneck wide enough for the English royal host to enter but narrow enough to compensate for the disparity in numbers between the two armies. Bruce may have quickly settled on this as a promising area in which to encounter the English and must then have begun pondering how he might lure them there when the time came.

Preparations would also have involved training the troops from around Scotland that would have begun arriving from about the same time as King Robert reached the Torwood. We can only speculate as to what form this training took, but it would no doubt have included practice in forming into the large, oval-shaped, tightly packed spear formations that the Scots had first used at the Battle of Falkirk in 1298.[92] These formations were known by contemporary English chroniclers as 'schiltrons', an Older Scots term that in Scotland primarily seems to have referred simply to a large group of (armed) men. On the subject of terminology, there has been a modern tendency to refer to the primary weapon of the Scots as 'pikes', but this is anachronistic. In contemporary sources they are invariably 'lances' or 'spears'.[93] Caldwell has reasonably suggested that these were weapons originally made for use on horseback that were repurposed by Scottish foot soldiers and would have been around three or four metres in length.[94] The Scottish spear formations were particularly effective at resisting cavalry charges, since they presented a dense wall of spears to their opponents regardless of the direction the enemy attacked. Possibly the training may also have involved some of the wealthier men in the army (i.e., those who could afford to fight on horseback) conducting mock charges at the spear formations to get the soldiers used to what was one of the most intimidating sights on a medieval battlefield.

However, the plan King Robert was concocting would not rely solely on defence. Being oval-shaped, early 'schiltrons' had been static formations, since moving in any given direction would require roughly half of the troops to march backwards! This inability to move had been their undoing at Falkirk, where the

English archers shot them to pieces.[95] As we have already seen, Edward II had summoned at least 4,000 archers (and probably more) to serve in his army in 1314. Bruce could thus not afford to rely on immobile units as Wallace had done sixteen years before. This would have made the area between the Bannock Burn and the Pelstream Burn an even more appealing site for the battle, since by forming up between the streams Bruce could cover his flanks and thus obviate the need to have spears pointing in any direction but forwards. To exploit this, though, he would need formations that could move so that they could trap the English in that narrow space and then squeeze them into an ever-tighter space as the battle progressed. The training the Scots undertook in the Torwood must therefore also have included practice at forming into units with all their spears pointing in the same direction and advancing slowly and methodically forward. Bannockburn would be an object lesson for early-fourteenth-century tacticians on the effectiveness of disciplined infantry in battle.[96]

As well as getting his troops used to the manoeuvres they would need to pull off on the battlefield, King Robert was almost certainly appraising their performance. A contemporary English chronicler named John of Trokelowe describes soldiers on the front line of the Scottish army at Bannockburn as *electi*, i.e., 'picked men'.[97] As well as limiting the number of Englishmen who could engage with the Scots at any one time, trapping the English among the streams of the carse had the added bonus that Bruce could now afford to be selective about who he put in the most important positions in his army. If anyone was suspected to not be up to the standard required to pull off his audacious plan, the king could make sure they were positioned further back in the army (or sent away entirely). Meanwhile, the toughest and most capable soldiers could be pushed forward so that they were the only Scots likely to have to engage in serious fighting. With the two armies on effectively even footing on the banks of the Bannock Burn, King Robert could rely on the experience and discipline of his veterans to triumph over the sheer numbers of the English.

## 'Marching with Great Pomp and Elaborate State': The English Response to the Deal

On 27 May, King Edward II was at Newminster in Northumberland. From here, he issued his first muster orders specifically mentioning the rescue (*rescussum*) of Stirling Castle, suggesting that it was on this day that he learned of the deal struck between the garrison and the besieging Scottish army a few days earlier.

Edward complained that 'the Scots, our enemies and rebels, are endeavouring, as far as they can, to assemble great numbers of foot in strong and marshy places, extremely hard for cavalry to penetrate, between us and our castle of Stirling'. Whether this meant that Edward had intelligence that the Scots were already mustering in the Torwood or if this was instead merely an expectation based on the English experience of 1310 to 1311 is unclear. Possibly, the information had been leaked by David Strathbogie, earl of Atholl, who had been treasonously in contact with the English since January.[98] Whatever the case, King Edward ordered royal officers from across England and Wales 'under the forfeiture of all the things which you will be able to forfeit to us...that you may provoke, hasten, and compel...infantry, by the measures and ways by which you will be able, to come to us...so that they are at Wark on Monday, the tenth day of June, near to come, well-armed, well prepared, and ready to advance, and ready to march thence against our enemies and our rebels'.[99] This was a reasonable precaution to take, since infantry would be better able to hunt for the Scots across rough terrain than heavy cavalry. It also challenges traditional assumptions about Edward II's supposed ignorance of military matters.[100]

A total of 21,540 troops from across England and Wales were summoned. No indication was given of how they were to be equipped, but Morris has argued that some deductions about how many were meant to be archers can at least be made based on the summonses of 9 March.[101] From Yorkshire, 4,000 troops were summoned, of whom perhaps 2,000 were expected to serve as archers. From Nottinghamshire and Derbyshire, 2,000 were summoned, and again fifty per cent of these were likely to be archers. From Northumberland, 2,500 were summoned, with maybe 1,000 being archers. From Shropshire and Staffordshire, 2,000 troops were called; 500 from Warwickshire and Leicestershire; and another 500 from Lancashire. From Lincolnshire, 3,000 were called on, of whom probably 500 would be archers, and the bishop of Durham was expected to provide a further 1,500 men. Edward also requested 2,000 men from northern Wales, 1,000 from southern Wales, 500 from Glamorgan, 200 from Brecknock, 200 from Abergavenny, 300 from the Welsh Marches, 500 from Powys, and forty men from Hope (in Flintshire). One James de Pirar was to furnish King Edward with 200 men; the Forest of Dean was to provide a further 100; while 500 were expected from Cheshire.

Instructions were issued to the sheriffs of York, Nottingham, Northumberland, Stafford, Warwick, Lancaster, and Lincoln, the bishop of Durham, the earls of

An apocalyptic battle in the 'Holkham Bible', an English picture book from c. 1320–30 (London, British Library, Add. MS 47682, f. 40r).

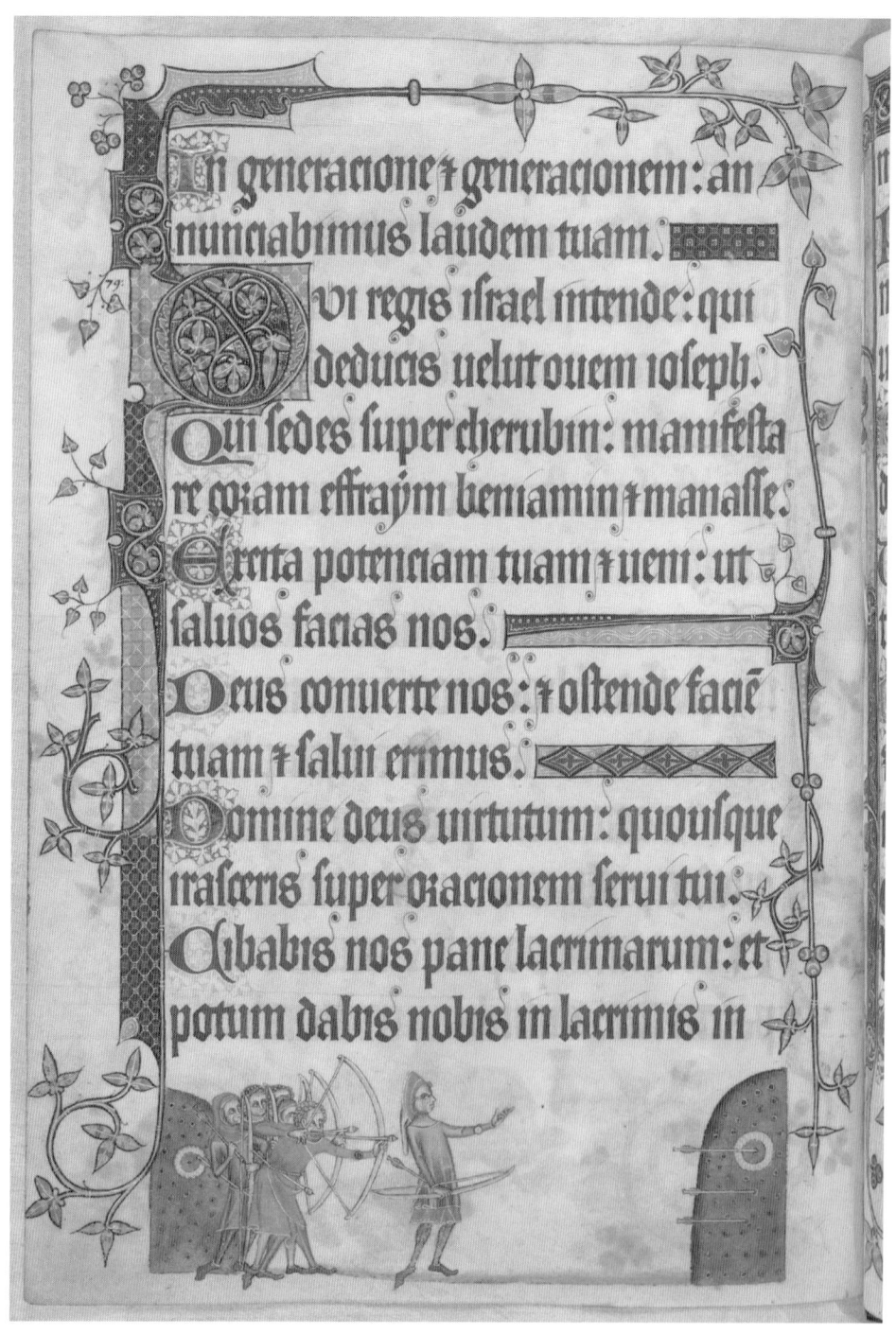

In generacione † generacionem: an
nunciabimus laudem tuam.
Qui regis israel intende: qui
deducis uelut ouem ioseph.
Qui sedes super cherubin: manifesta
re coram effraym beniamin † manasse.
Excita potenciam tuam † ueni: ut
saluos facias nos.
Deus conuerte nos: † ostende facie
tuam † salui erimus.
Domine deus uirtutum: quousque
irasceris super oracionem serui tui:
Cibabis nos pane lacrimarum: et
potum dabis nobis in lacrimis in

Archers practicing their craft in the 'Luttrell Psalter' from c. 1325-35 (London, British Library, Add. MS 42130, f. 147v).

Illuminated initial 'E'(dwardus) from a 1316 charter showing the successful defence of Carlisle from the Scots in 1315 (Cumbria Archive Centre, Carlisle)

The hill on which Roxburgh Castle once stood, with some of the fragmentary ruins visible to the left of the image. (Author's own)

Edinburgh Castle viewed from the north. (Author's own)

Stirling Castle. (© Crown Copyright: HES)

Roman *lilia* at Rough Castle. (© Crown Copyright: HES)

An aerial view across the area where the fighting on 24th June is most likely to have taken place, looking roughly south-west. (David Wilkinson, Scotdrone)

An aerial view across the area where the fighting on 24th June is most likely to have taken place, looking roughly north-west. (David Wilkinson, Scotdrone)

Bothwell Castle in Lanarkshire. (© Crown Copyright: HES)

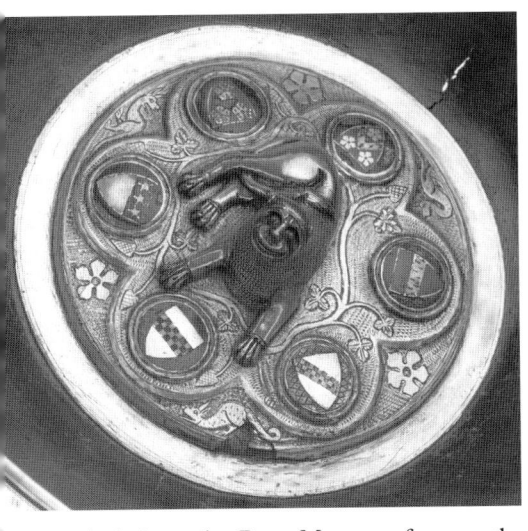

The 'print' from the Bute Mazer, a fourteenth-century communal drinking vessel, likely created during the reign of Robert I. (On loan from The Bute Collection at Mount Stuart. Image © National Museums Scotland)

Cambuskenneth Abbey on the north bank of the River Forth. (© Crown Copyright: HES)

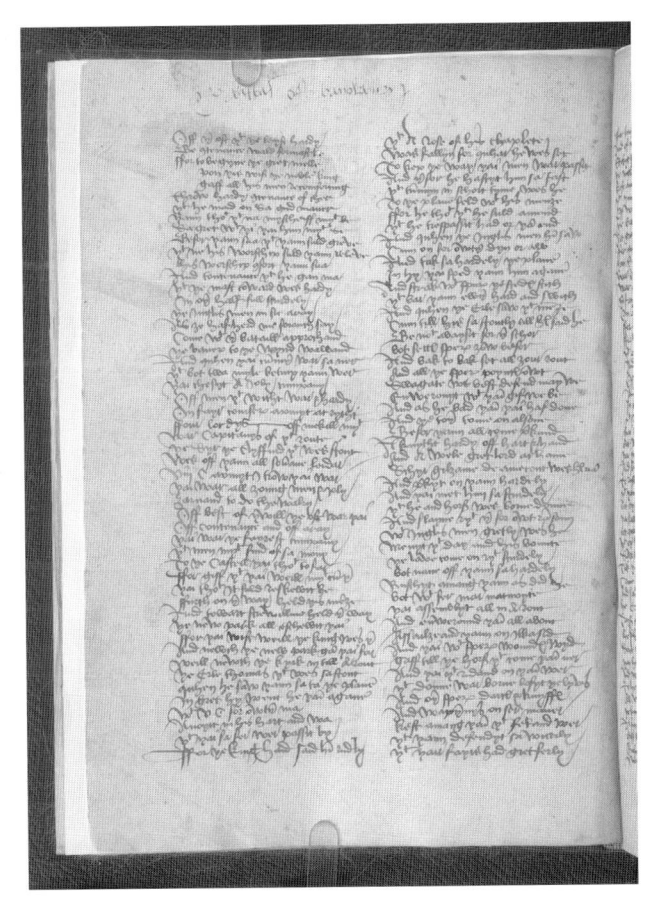

The oldest complete manuscript of Barbour's *Bruce* (Edinburgh, National Library of Scotland, Adv.MS. 19.2.2 f. 39v).

The earliest surviving illustration of the Battle of Bannockburn, from a copy of Walter Bower's *Scotichronicon* produced in the 1440s (Cambridge, Corpus Christi College, MS 171B, f. 265r).

The equestrian statue of King Robert outside the Battle of Bannockburn Visitor Centre near Stirling. (Author's own)

Gloucester and Hereford, and various other royal officers. This is certainly an impressive group, but it betrays a reduction in the scope of Edward's ambitions when it came to recruitment. Back in December, Edward had issued orders to seven earls and a further eighty-five barons, instructing them to gather 'with horses and arms and all service due to us' ready to make war in Scotland.[102] In May, Edward addressed his instructions to only two earls and a far smaller pool of lords as well. The king's half-brother – Thomas of Brotherton, earl of Norfolk – had been excused service due to his youth, being only in his early teens in 1314, but several others – most notably the king's cousin Thomas, earl of Lancaster – had refused to appear in person and sent only the minimum number of troops they were legally required to provide. Moreover, the king began by complaining that he 'had ordered the men to be ready by a date already passed'. This strongly suggests that these muster orders were not being made in addition to the early summonses, but rather in response to ongoing difficulties in recruitment.

It would appear then that in light of the deal with Stirling, which placed tighter restrictions on when he would need to set off, King Edward had decided not to press the issue with his political opponents and simply rely on those who would support him willingly. This was a gamble, but not an unreasonable one. If King Edward could bring Bruce to battle and defeat him – ideally killing or capturing him in the process – this would revolutionize the English position in Scotland and vindicate Edward's decision to launch his campaign in the first place. There is thus good reason to suppose that both kings saw the deal made in May as the fulcrum on which their fortunes turned in 1314, offering a tantalizing opportunity to turn the tide against their counterpart. The muster orders of 27 May give the impression of a determined and confident Edward II, a king who was facing difficulties in domestic politics but who was apparently hoping that a striking foreign policy success might help to solve his problems north and south of the border.

By 29 May, Edward had been joined at Newminster by Richard de Burgh, earl of Ulster and Robert Bruce's father-in-law. On that day Ulster testified that a clerk named Nicholas de Staveleye was trustworthy enough to carry out certain judicial duties for the English crown in Dublin, while on the following day the earl received letters of protection to facilitate his travels 'on the king's service to Scotland'.[103] His appearance alongside Edward in May 1314 serves as our best direct evidence for the presence of an Irish contingent at the Battle of

Bannockburn. As with the rest of the army, it is difficult to tell how large the Irish contingent was, but it was probably fewer than the long list of native Irish lords, prelates, civic leaders, and Anglo-Irish colonists Edward had summoned to serve back in March would suggest. As the 'captain' ('*capitaneum*') of the Irish portion of the army, Ulster would no doubt have brought with him whatever forces he had been able to muster, but it seems likely that some – possibly many – of the individuals summoned in March would have ignored the call or found excuses not to attend. It is unclear whether Ulster himself felt any tension between his status as King Robert's father-in-law and one of the English crown's leading allies in Ireland, though there is some evidence that Bruce himself held a grudge about it.[104]

Also on 29 May, King Edward granted Isolde ('Iseude'), widow of John de Rybille, wardship of his lands and the right to arrange a marriage for their son Richard. Rybille had been killed when James Douglas had attacked and captured Roxburgh in February.[105] Isolde had apparently approached Queen Isabella to intercede on her behalf, as the grant was made 'at the Queen's request'. This serves to demonstrate that Queen Isabella was still able to fulfil her traditional intercessory role as queen during this period. One of a medieval queen's main public roles was to hear the pleas of the king's subjects and then present worthy cases to the king, who in theory should always resolve the situation as she advised.[106] The breakdown of this arrangement, which only really began in the 1320s as Edward's favourites the Despensers muscled Isabella out of courtly activities, would directly lead to Isabella's estrangement from her husband and ultimately provoke her into overthrowing him altogether.[107]

Edward's magnates were also now beginning to step up their preparations for the campaign. On 1 June, Humphrey de Bohun, earl of Hereford, wrote to Adam Osgodby, keeper of the Great Seal, requesting a letter of protection for Sir Anthony Lucy, a Cumbrian knight due to serve in Hereford's following during the upcoming invasion of Scotland.[108] Hereford was an influential magnate and an experienced war leader, having accompanied Edward I on his Scottish campaigns since 1300. He had a vested interest in the successful conclusion of the Scottish war since Edward I had granted him the Bruce lordship of Annandale after Robert declared himself king of Scots in 1306.[109] The earl had also initially enjoyed a good relationship with Edward II. He attached one of the prince's spurs at his knighting ceremony in 1306, attended Edward II's marriage to Isabella of France at Boulogne, and carried the king's sceptre at the coronation in 1308.[110] However, like many English lords, he was alienated by the king's favouritism, particularly towards Piers Gaveston; as we have seen, Hereford refused to participate in Edward's campaign into Scotland in 1310 to 1311. This was particularly outrageous because Hereford was the hereditary lord constable of England, a title that effectively made him the senior military official in the kingdom after the king himself. This did nothing to smooth relations between Hereford and the royal party, and in 1312 Hereford was one of the cadre of magnates who approved the summary execution of Gaveston. However, wider distaste among the English political community at the dubious legality over their treatment of Gaveston forced Hereford and his allies to negotiate a settlement with Edward II, one which saw them effectively submit and renew their loyalty to the king.[111] Hereford's appearance in Edward's army in 1314 was reflective of his chastened status, even though his allies from 1312 did not participate.

Bitterness between King Edward and Hereford continued to cause problems during the 1314 campaign, although this probably was not apparent this early in June. At an uncertain date, possibly around the time the army finally set off into Scotland, the king appointed his own nephew, Gilbert de Clare, earl of Gloucester, as leader of the vanguard, the most prestigious command in the army and a position usually reserved for the lord constable (i.e., Hereford). As the contemporary author of the *Flores Historiarum* puts it:

> 'A furious discord (*effraenata discordia*) arose between Gilbert de Clare, earl of Gloucester, and Humphrey de Bohun, earl of Hereford, over the command of the vanguard and the office of constable [of the army], because the lord king, in contempt of the earl of Hereford, being fiercely moved (*felle commotus*), unjustly assigned both offices to the earl of Gloucester, notwithstanding that the said earl had the same duties from ancient times hereditarily through the line of succession by full right. This act, therefore, of plunder and spite (*spoliationis et livoris*) served as fuel for envy and hatred (*invidiae et odii*).'[112]

This obvious rebuke to the earl was exacerbated by the fact that Gloucester was relatively young (only 23 years old in June 1314) and thus less experienced than Hereford, and the two men were also regional rivals on the Welsh Marches.[113] In a weak attempt at compromise, King Edward appears to have given the two earls joint command of the vanguard.[114] This only served to confuse the command structure of the leading portion of the army. Someone like Sir Anthony Lucy could be expected to follow Hereford's orders, while Gloucester's followers would look to him for leadership. This would be bad enough, risking major divisions among the troops if the two earls did not coordinate their activities. But for anyone else in this force not already aligned with Hereford or Gloucester, if the two earls gave different or even contradictory orders, such men would have no way of knowing who to obey since both men were supposedly in command. This only added to the vanguard's problems when they encountered the well-drilled and disciplined Scots on 23 June. Lucy would also share in Hereford's unfortunate fate in the aftermath of the battle – discussed in a later chapter – which might lead us to conclude that Lucy would come to wish that Osgodby had denied him his letter of protection after all.

The following day, letters of protection were issued for William de Vaux and his three valets 'on his way to Scotland in the King's [i.e., Edward II's] service'.[115] William was probably the lord of Dirleton in East Lothian and was thus one of the Scots serving in the English army. There were several reasons a Scottish lord might find himself fighting for the English at Bannockburn. Many of them were relatives or allies of John Balliol, who had been king of Scots before Robert Bruce, and John Comyn, who Bruce had (in)famously killed in front of the high altar at Greyfriars Kirk in Dumfries in February 1306. Such was the case, for example, for John Macdougall, whose mother was apparently a Comyn.[116] We have seen already how Macdougall was deployed by Edward II in the west in the build-up to the 1314 campaign. Robert Umfraville, earl of Angus – whose mother was a Comyn – and his cousin, Sir Ingram Umfraville – whose mother or grandmother had been one of the Balliols of Redcastle – both fought on the English side at Bannockburn in defence of their kin's perceived rights.[117] Sir Ingram even fought wearing the arms of Balliols of Redcastle, physically displaying his motivation for opposing King Robert.[118]

The other reason a Scot might side with the English was expedience. If their lands were too close to the English border for the Bruce Scots to guarantee their safety, a Scottish lord might reasonably side with the English simply to protect their property. Vaux was most likely one of this latter group. He had no obvious connection to either the Bruces or to their rivals, but his lands, primarily based around Dirleton Castle in East Lothian, were within a day's ride of the border. This made them a relatively easy target for English recriminations if Vaux did not maintain good relations with the English crown. Dirleton was, for example, one of the castles targeted by the English army ahead of the Battle of Falkirk in 1298, at which point Vaux remained on the 'patriotic' side.[119] Moreover, his estates could be easily occupied and regranted to another, more trustworthy candidate if the English king came to doubt his fidelity. With no existing ties to Bruce, Vaux had no reason to risk his estates or livelihood by adhering to King Robert after he seized power in 1306, although there is some evidence to suggest that before 1314 Bruce power had extended sufficiently south-eastwards to mount a successful assault on Dirleton Castle itself.[120] Even so, the likely route of Edward's advance into Scotland in 1314 would bring him perilously close to Dirleton, so it was surely the sensible move for Vaux to make a public demonstration of support for the English war effort and reduce the threat to his estates. It is also likely that Vaux was one of the many Scottish lords who submitted to King Robert in the aftermath of Bannockburn, and his descendants certainly benefited from royal patronage in the reign of Bruce's son David II.[121]

A similar sense of pragmatism no doubt influenced the presence of Sir Alexander Seton in the English army in 1314. Seton's lands were also concentrated in the Lothians and Berwickshire, meaning he could not afford to alienate the English crown at this time. Yet he may still have personally favoured the Bruce cause. As noted above, in September 1308 Seton was one of three Scottish lairds who made a bond to protect King Robert bodily from all threats to his person.[122] We will see in the following chapter how fragile Seton's allegiance to the English was in 1314.

By 3 June, King Edward had finally arrived at Berwick, where his army had been assembling. Here, the king granted 100 marks to John Macdougall of Argyll as wages for himself and his men-at-arms.[123] The grant of 3 June described Macdougall and his men as 'going to the Irish ports on the king's affairs'. This does not necessarily mean the fleet and the plan to raid up the Scottish west coast – where Macdougall's landed interests had been before Bruce drove him out and where the locals might be expected to have residual loyalties to the exiled Scot – had been abandoned. Most of the men and supplies that King Edward had ordered for the fleet were apparently coming from Ireland, but it may be that these had not been forthcoming as quickly as had been hoped. When Richard de Burgh, earl of Ulster, had recently arrived in Northumberland to join the king for his campaign, he would surely have brought with him intelligence on the state of affairs in Ireland and perhaps on the reticence of the locals to serve in or supply Macdougall's fleet. This message would only have been reinforced if, as seems likely, Ulster was able to bring only a portion of the troops King Edward had initially summoned from Ireland in March. In these circumstances, the grant to Macdougall may represent additional payments for Macdougall and his men to appear in Ireland in person to hurry the preparations along. On the other hand, it may be that, now that he knew about the deal between the Scots and the English garrison at Stirling, King Edward was increasingly hopeful that he would find Bruce waiting for him at or near Stirling and thus the second front of his proposed two-pronged assault on the Scottish kingdom had lost some of its urgency.

Even though he was now at the muster point and was faced with a promising opportunity to secure the large-scale pitched battle he had been hoping for since 1310, King Edward could still not escape domestic issues surrounding the administration of justice within his kingdom. Thus, on 5 June, moved by 'the loud complaint of his people', he sought to address the maintenance of law and order during his absence on campaign. According to Edward, 'great outrages' had been committed by both nobles and common folk alike since he set out for Scotland. Wrongdoers had apparently 'confederated together, held conventicles and other unlawful assemblies, as well by day as night, committed assaults and murders, broke the parks both of the king and his subjects, and hunted the deer, which outrages have not been duly repressed by the sheriffs and other officers and ministers of the king'. Edward therefore appointed 'conservators of the peace' for each English county to investigate these incidents and bring the perpetrators to justice. The conservators were answerable to the royal council at Westminster, which had been given responsibility for governing the kingdom while Edward was away on campaign.[124]

While the sensationalist language may give an exaggerated view of the extent of lawlessness in England by mid-1314, this nevertheless offers a fascinating insight into how the king's absence from the kingdom could have a destabilizing effect on the administration of justice. This was particularly true in the case of a controversial king like Edward II. To some extent, the failure of 'the sheriffs and other officers and ministers of the king' might be accounted for by the fact that many sheriffs had responsibility for raising local levies and were thus probably by now on their way to Berwick or else already present in the army. Yet they would have appointed deputies to fill the functions of their offices in their absence. It seems likely that the complaints Edward had received reflected a general impression that either this had not happened or that those responsible for the administration of justice were perceived to be failing in this role. Moreover, as noted repeatedly, many of Edward's political opponents had refused to personally serve on the Scottish campaign of 1314. Even if they did not directly engage in or encourage the 'great outrages' that King Edward sought to curb, his domestic opponents might well exploit the perceived lawlessness as a means of undermining the king's position in an effort to force policy corrections in their favour. This placed even greater pressure on King Edward to secure not just a pitched battle but to score a resounding victory over the Bruce Scots. This, in turn, would undoubtedly influence Edward's decisions once the two armies came in sight of one another on 23 June.

9 June is the Feast of St Columba, which may have been a cause of pious celebration and devotion for the Scots in the Torwood. St Columba was remembered as having played a significant part in establishing monastic practices and embedding Christianity across the area encompassed by the kingdom of Scotland and his cult enjoyed considerable devotion among Scots in the early fourteenth century.[125] There is a long-standing tradition claiming that relics of St Columba were brought to the battlefield at Bannockburn.[126] The notion that the saint's relics were present at Bannockburn is believable enough, especially since a reliquary known as the *Breccbennach* was given to Arbroath Abbey by King Alexander II in the early thirteenth century.[127] It has been suggested that the *Breccbennach* was an object now known as the Monymusk reliquary – on display at the National Museum of Scotland in Edinburgh – although more recently Dr David Caldwell has cast considerable doubt on this.[128] Nevertheless, Bruce's chancellor was Bernard, abbot of Arbroath, and Bernard would have been well-placed to arrange for the *Breccbennach* to be brought to the Torwood to provide the army with potent intercession from one of Scotland's most celebrated saintly patrons. Either way, we would expect King Robert and his followers to view the fact that Columba's feast day occurred in the midst of their preparations for battle as portentous. They would surely have seized this opportunity to seek the saint's assistance in the coming enterprise.

Meanwhile, King Edward remained concerned with the affairs of those who were about to join him on his fast-approaching campaign into Scotland. On 12 June, he granted further patronage to one of his new favourites – Hugh Despenser 'the Younger'. Like his father and namesake, Despenser had been associated with Edward II since around 1306, before Edward became king. This association was strengthened by the younger Despenser's marriage to Eleanor de Clare, one of Edward's nieces and sister of another of the English lords preparing to join the campaign – Gilbert de Clare, earl of Gloucester.[129] The contemporary Lanercost chronicler claims that after the death of Edward's familiar Piers Gaveston in 1312, Despenser became to the king 'like his right eye', and the business conducted on 12 June goes some way towards supporting this conclusion.[130] Edward granted Despenser and Eleanor the lands forfeited by John Graham, described as 'the king's enemy and rebel'.[131] The lands in question were probably the lordships of Dalkeith and Abercorn. Edward's army would pass close by to the estates in question on its way to Bannockburn, and if Barbour's narrative is to be believed, Edward and Despenser would also flee past these lordships following the defeat, 'to their perpetual shame' in the opinion of the Lanercost chronicler.[132] Edward also granted Despenser lands forfeited by King Robert's nephew Thomas Randolph, earl of Moray, described as in identical terms to Graham.[133]

These grants were an early sign of Despenser's status as the king's latest favourite. Favouritism was the worst failing of a medieval king, since one of the king's primary roles was to act as the ultimate arbiter of patronage within the kingdom. In other words, it was his job to make sure that the leading lords in England got, more or less, their fair share when it came to landholding, rights, royal offices, income, etc. If a few individuals close to the king were receiving undue favour, and particularly if their rewards were given at the expense of others, this could create serious tensions between a monarch and his most powerful subjects. We have already seen how King Edward had frustrated the efforts of Sir Miles Stapleton and Sir Marmaduke Tweng to seek legal redress against Walter Fauconberg, one of the king's familiars. Edward's favouritism towards Gaveston had been the cause of much turmoil during the early years of the reign, and his preferential treatment towards the Despensers would cause similar – ultimately more serious – problems later in the reign as well.

Two days later, on 14 June, King Edward pardoned one John 'de Newebygging' 'for taking provisions and other goods to the Scottish enemy, and otherwise communing with them'.[134] Identifying precisely who this individual was is difficult. There were settlements called 'Newbigging' in Northumberland, Berwickshire, Roxburghshire, and Angus. Realistically, it was probably to one of the southern Newbiggings that John belonged. Interestingly, in 1316 there was a John, described as 'son of the late John son of Nigel', who King Robert confirmed in possession of lands associated with the Berwickshire Newbigging.[135] Possibly this John, or his father and namesake, was the John pardoned by Edward II in 1314, although this is necessarily speculative. Bruce's confirmation to John in 1316 described him as 'beloved and faithful', but this phrasing is conventional. It may well be that John had indeed provided material support for the Bruce Scots as they began to intrude their influence into the south-east, then sought to protect his local interests by reaching an accommodation with the English authorities in anticipation of Edward II's advance through the region in 1314, only to then submit to King Robert again once the outcome of Bannockburn became clear. We have already explored the reasons a Scot might find it expedient to switch sides, particularly in the build-up to an English campaign into Scotland. John's pardon in 1314 was apparently facilitated by the intercession of Sir Ralph Fitzwilliam, Edward's faithful keeper of Berwick, whose tenant John may have been. John's crime was straightforwardly treasonous, since supplying the enemy was one of the most common legal definitions of treason in the period.[136] In the circumstances however, King Edward may have felt that winning over another figure with potential influence in the south-east, perhaps one who might be able to arrange supplies for the increasingly beleaguered garrison at Berwick, may have been more valuable than sticking to the strict letter of the law.

The following day, Walter Stapledon, bishop of Exeter, was at his manor house, Farndon, in Hampshire. From here, he wrote to King Edward at Berwick, requesting letters of protection for his brother Richard and his nephew William Hereward 'who are starting for the Scottish war in haste, and await nothing but these'.[137] This indicates that there were still troops gathering this close to the start of the campaign. Edward had initially planned to set off on 10 June, suggesting that the bishop's relatives had been particularly slow in responding to the summons. Within two days, perhaps even before the bishop's letter had reached Berwick, King Edward would set off into Scotland. It is therefore doubtful that either Richard or William ultimately did serve in the English army that fought at Bannockburn. Edward's willingness to set off without waiting for the entirety of his army to assemble serves to demonstrate his decision to forge ahead with what support he could muster in the hopes that a victory over the Scots would give him leverage against his domestic opponents. It no doubt reflects his confidence that even with many of his subjects dragging their feet or ignoring their commitments altogether, he had still been able to muster a sufficiently large army to overwhelm whatever force King Robert had been able to gather. But most importantly of all, time was now beginning to tell against Edward's preparations. If he was to capitalize on the opportunity the deal between the besieging Scots and the Stirling garrison had given him, he would have to bring his army to Stirling soon. This newfound urgency would not prove conducive to achieving success in the subsequent campaign.

## 'The King…Hurried Day After Day to the Appointed Place': The Bannockburn Campaign

On or about 17 June, Edward II finally set off from Berwick, getting the campaign underway he had been planning since November 1313. The precise route that Edward took is unclear. Probably he and his cavalry worked their way upstream along the Tweed until they reached Wark Castle, where the infantry had been mustering, and then advanced more or less up the route of the modern A697 and A68. Alternatively, Edward's portion of the army may have travelled across country while the elements that had gathered at Wark passed along the suggested route, with both groups joining forces further north. On balance, the former seems more likely. Either way, it was no doubt an impressive army that King Edward had mustered, even if it was not perhaps as numerous as he had hoped. It would have been around 20,000-strong, with 2,500 to 3,000 heavy cavalry, around 4,000 archers (perhaps more), and the rest being mixed infantry. Dr Andrew Ayton has noted that these forces were raised separately, as we have seen in detail, and apparently expected to fight separately.[138] This lack of cohesion would play a significant role in their eventual defeat, as we will examine in the following chapter.

In terms of the English cavalry, no horse inventory or proffer roll for the Bannockburn campaign survives, both likely lost in the English camp after the battle was over. Simpkin has used those that survive from 1310 to develop at least a sense of the situation in 1314.[139] Morris has identified letters of protection for

830 men-at-arms, including 131 in Gloucester's service, eighty-six in Pembroke's, sixty-two between the two Despensers, forty-five in Hereford's following, twenty-six in Richard Gray's, twenty-four in John Mowbray's, twenty-nine in Beaumont's, and twelve in Clifford's.[140] Letters of protection were usually only obtained by wealthier, landed individuals who would be likely to serve as heavy cavalry, not foot soldiers.[141] Otherwise, however, we are forced to rely on narrative accounts to reconstruct the size of the English cavalry at Bannockburn. The author of the *Vita* offers only the rather vague figure of 'more than two thousand'.[142] Barbour, on the other hand, offers the utterly unbelievable claim that Edward brought 'fourty thousand' horsemen to Bannockburn. However, Barbour adds the detail that only 'thre thousand' of these were 'helyt [covered] hors in plate and mailye'.[143] If we suppose that Barbour's estimate for the number of those 'helyt' (that is, 'barded' with livery and perhaps even some light armour) represents the actual number of cavalry in the English army – and his claim for the overall number of cavalry is merely poetic exaggeration – this gives us, alongside the testimony in the *Vita*, at least a rough estimate of English cavalry numbers in 1314.

As far as the infantry was concerned, Edward had summoned a total of 4,000 archers from various English counties on 24 March, and while not all of these may have arrived on time, the numbers would likely have been augmented by subsequent muster orders as well.[144] The infantry muster orders that had gone out on 27 May had requested a little over 21,000 men.[145] Since these orders give the impression that they were a response to the failure of the previous muster orders to provide the expected number of troops, we might reasonably doubt that the later orders had been entirely successful either. Nevertheless, it seems likely that the various summonses produced between March and May 1314 would have at least swelled the numbers in the English army to around 20,000 men overall. The English infantry would likely have been divided into units of twenty and one hundred, led by *vintenars* or constables.[146]

Although a number of England's leading earls had refused to appear in person, the experienced earls of Pembroke and Hereford were both present, as was the king's young and energetic nephew Gilbert de Clare, earl of Gloucester. Pembroke was, alongside John Macdougall, one of only two individuals who could claim to have defeated Bruce in open confrontation.[147] Furthermore, several 'lesser' lords in the army were – like Pembroke and Hereford – veterans of Edward I's wars in Scotland and elsewhere. Robert Clifford, lord of Skipton, had fought in most of the major engagements of the war so far and had greatly expanded his landed interests in doing so.[148] So too had Sir Henry Beaumont, formerly a household knight of Edward I, who as noted previously was pressing the claim on the earldom of Buchan in north-east Scotland he had gained through his marriage to Alice Comyn circa 1310. In Beaumont's following was Sir Thomas Gray, a formidable knight from Northumberland. Gray was one of the few English survivors of William Wallace's attack on Lanark in 1297, had saved Beaumont's life at the siege of Stirling in 1304, and had since continued to distinguish himself in the Scottish wars.[149] Sir John Seagrave too had played a prominent role in the conflict, most (in)famously in bringing the remains of William Wallace north in 1305 for display at Newcastle, Berwick, Stirling, and Perth.[150]

The veteran Yorkshire knight Sir Marmaduke Tweng was the only English knight credited with fighting his way through the Scots and back across the bridge at the Battle of Stirling Bridge in 1297.[151] Though he would have been advancing in years by 1314 – and Edward's interference in Tweng's legal affairs cannot have endeared the king to him much – the presence of such a tough and experienced soldier was nonetheless a boon for the English army. King Edward's missives to Emperor Andronikos II in October 1313 had also been successful in securing the release from captivity in Salonika of Sir Giles d'Argentan, a famous crusader and by all accounts a formidable soldier, who would serve as the king's bodyguard on the coming campaign. The presence of Robert Baston, a Carmelite monk, in the English army reflects Edward's expectation of success. Baston was a celebrated poet in England. He had been invited north by the king to witness the victory that he expected to achieve and then compose a poem celebrating this event. His ultimate fate would provide a particularly bitter twist to the tale of the battle, as we shall see.[152]

There were also a number of Scottish lords in Edward's army. For example, Sir John Comyn, son and successor of the John Comyn, lord of Badenoch, who Bruce had killed before the high altar at Dumfries in February 1306, was in attendance. Though he had little military experience personally, he would no doubt have been eager to redress the wrongs done to his father. So too would his cousins Walter and Edmund Comyn of Kilbride, who also accompanied the English army into Scotland in 1314. Moreover, as the great-nephew of the still-living John Balliol, the young John Comyn boasted a respectable claim to the Scottish kingship in his own right, making him a potential alternate focus of authority that might serve to unnerve the Bruce regime.[153] As noted previously,

Robert Umfraville, earl of Angus, had refused to recognize Bruce due to the fact Angus's mother was a Comyn. He had served as royal lieutenant of Scotland in 1308 and had played a significant part both in the defence of the border and in diplomacy with the Bruce Scots. Angus's cousin Sir Ingram Umfraville had such a formidable martial reputation that even Barbour considered him to be 'Into the hycht off chevalry'.[154] Barbour attributes the tactics employed by the English army to defeat Bruce at Methven in 1306 to Sir Ingram, suggesting that he too ought to be included in that small group of war leaders who had ever bested the formidable King Robert on the battlefield.[155] There were, of course, southern Scottish lords – such as Alexander Seton and William de Vaux – who accompanied Edward out of convenience, while the English king may also have taken comfort from the knowledge that David Strathbogie, earl of Atholl, had – secretly for now – renewed his association with the English crown.

On 18 June, King Edward and his army were at Soutra, in what is now the Scottish Borders. He and his men likely stayed in and around the hospital at Soutra, where the religious community were dedicated to providing hospitality to travellers.[156] Here, King Edward issued instructions to the archbishop of Canterbury, who was managing the affairs of the royal council during Edward's absence on campaign, to examine a suit between the crown and Sir John Giffard concerning possession of King's Stanley in Gloucestershire.[157] Giffard had been in possession of the property in 1311, but by 1313 it was in crown hands. In 1315, Giffard received a pardon for having acquired King's Stanley without licence, after which he apparently regained the lands. But King's Stanley was forfeited again when Giffard joined King Edward's cousin and rival Thomas, earl of Lancaster, in rebellion against the king in 1322. In 1323, King's Stanley was regranted to Giffard's widow, Avelina, who held it until her death circa 1327. Giffard was present in the army with Edward at Soutra in 1314, and he would in fact be captured by the Scots at Bannockburn.[158] Possibly the two men used this opportunity to discuss the ongoing dispute over King's Stanley, and Edward's instructions to the archbishop and the 1315 pardon may reflect an accommodation they had reached during this time. The return of King's Stanley and the revenues it brought may also have helped to compensate Giffard for the ransom he would have had to pay to obtain his freedom from the Scots.

The following day, 19 June, was the Feast of the Translation of St Margaret – that is, the anniversary of the day when the remains of St Margaret were transferred into a new, even-more-impressive shrine at Dunfermline Abbey in 1250. St Margaret had been queen of Scots from her marriage to King Malcolm III in 1069 or 1070 until her death in 1093. She was buried at Dunfermline Priory, which was elevated to the status of an abbey by her youngest son, David I, in 1128, and her tomb quickly became the focus of a popular saint cult. It was not until the middle of the thirteenth century, however, following mounting pressure from the Scottish clergy, that Margaret was officially canonized by the pope. To celebrate her new status, the community at Dunfermline moved her into a richly decorated shrine at the east end of the abbey church, and the date that this was done became one of the dates that St Margaret's devotees routinely celebrated.[159] Robert Bruce was one of these devotees. On St Margaret's feast day (16 November) 1314, in the wake of Bannockburn and his triumphant parliament at Cambuskenneth, he would appear in person at Dunfermline to announce his intention to be buried at the abbey alongside his 'royal predecessors', chief among these St Margaret herself.[160] At least two – and probably all four – of his children with Queen Elizabeth would be born at Dunfermline Abbey, with the queen likely wearing St Margaret's 'birthing serk [shirt]' while in labour in the hope of securing the saint's intercession during this potentially dangerous time.[161] The abbey was in receipt of generous patronage throughout King Robert's reign, all of which was a reflection of Bruce's devotion to the cult of St Margaret.[162]

King Robert was still in the Torwood on the feast day, deep into the preparations for the battle. We do not know what he did to commemorate the Translation of St Margaret, but he almost certainly would have done so in some way. Dr Michael Penman has speculated that one of the relics associated with St Margaret, perhaps one of the pieces of the True Cross (known in Scots as the 'Black Rood') that she had owned during her lifetime and afterwards kept at Dunfermline Abbey, may have been brought to the battlefield at Bannockburn with the Scottish army.[163] St Margaret was almost certainly included among 'the saints of the Scottish nation' who Bruce apparently invoked ahead of the fighting on the second day of battle.[164] It seems highly unlikely that the king would miss an opportunity to appeal to the saint for intercession on one of her feast days.

While King Robert was making his spiritual and military preparations in the Torwood on 19 June, Edward II was arriving at Edinburgh. Possibly he set the 'masons, carpenters, and smiths' ('*cementariis, carpentariis, et fabris*') he had recruited on 27 March to work assessing the damage done by the Scots to the castle when they had captured and slighted it in March. He must also have dispatched scouts to locate Bruce's army and determine its intentions. Ironically, King Edward may also have shown his devotion to St Margaret in honour of the Translation. Margaret's cult was popular in England as well as in Scotland, and the English royal family traced their descent from her just as Bruce did. Edward's father had, for example, spent the winter of 1303 to 1304 at Dunfermline Abbey seeking St Margaret's intercession in his efforts to impose a final English settlement on Scotland.[165] Edinburgh Castle was where St Margaret had died in 1093, and a chapel there – founded by her son David I – was dedicated to her. A single saint was probably once again being invoked by both sides ahead of the battle.

The next day, 20 June, was the Feast of St Fillan (or Fáelán), another saint venerated by King Robert. St Fillan had been an eighth-century abbot of Iona and was reputedly buried at Strathfillan (meaning 'Valley of Fillan') in western Perthshire. While retreating westwards through Strathfillan in 1306, following his defeat at the Battle of Methven, Bruce and his army were ambushed by John Macdougall of Argyll near Tyndrum. The king seems to have credited his (narrow) escape from Tyndrum on St Fillan's intercession, and his devotion to the saint grew from there.[166] Two relics associated with St Fillan, both now held at the National Museum of Scotland, are traditionally believed to have been present with the Scottish army at Bannockburn. One is known as the *Quigrich* and is an ornate case containing the saint's crozier (i.e., his staff of office as abbot of Iona). The other is a hand bell known as the *Bernane*.[167] If these were indeed present at Bannockburn, the acts of devotion King Robert performed on the saint's feast day in 1314 may have revolved around them in some way.

The sixteenth-century Scottish chronicler Hector Boece identifies another striking (if somewhat dubious) connection between St Fillan and the Battle of Bannockburn. Boece states that Bruce owned a reliquary (the *Mayne*) containing an arm bone of St Fillan, which he apparently took everywhere with him. Unfortunately, Boece claims, the king's chaplain brought only the silver case in which the arm bone was kept to Bannockburn, leaving the arm bone behind in case the Scots lost the battle and the relic fell into English hands. But on the evening of the battle, when King Robert was unable to sleep and thus 'vacand [pacing] in his deuote contemplacioun', the chaplain heard the case suddenly open and then snap shut again. When he inspected the case, he discovered to his amazement that the arm bone had miraculously made its way back into the case![168] While we might be cautious about accepting Boece's remarkable tale uncritically, the notion that King Robert sought to secure St Fillan's protection in anticipation of the coming battle is certainly believable.

Finally, on 22 June, King Edward set off from Edinburgh towards Falkirk, on the penultimate leg of his fateful journey towards Bannockburn. When King Robert received word of this, he ordered his army to withdraw northwards out of the Torwood, across the Bannock Burn, and into the New Park, roughly two miles south of Stirling Castle.[169] Ross has speculated that the park had originally been created in part to enhance the approach to Stirling Castle, making it the most obvious route for the English army to take on their route north.[170] Once across the burn, Bruce had his men make some last-minute modifications to the landscape around the New Park to increase its defensive properties, and then settled in to await the arrival of the English. It is unclear whether Edward and his men received word of Bruce's withdrawal from the Torwood, but if they did it would have seemed to the English that this confirmed their suspicions that the Scots were planning to frustrate his ambitions for a decisive confrontation by refusing to give battle at all. This prospect would no doubt have continued to trouble the English army as they advanced towards Stirling from Falkirk on 23 June. In fact, King Robert had a far more daring plan in mind, but one that would be easier to pull off if the English believed he still wanted to avoid facing them in the field.

'To Reskew Strevillyne with Bataill' 133

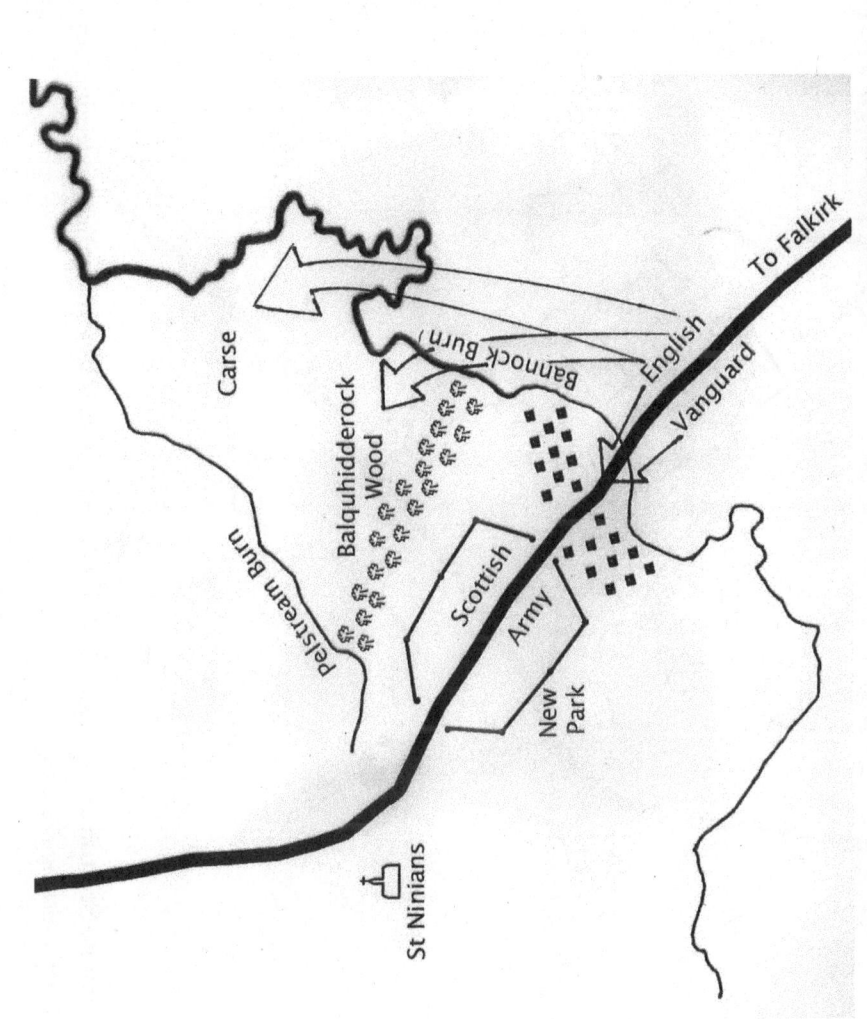

Map 3. 23 June – English attacks are repulsed at the mouth of the New Park and beneath Balquhidderock Wood, forcing the English army onto the Carse of Stirling.

134    1314: The Year of Bannockburn

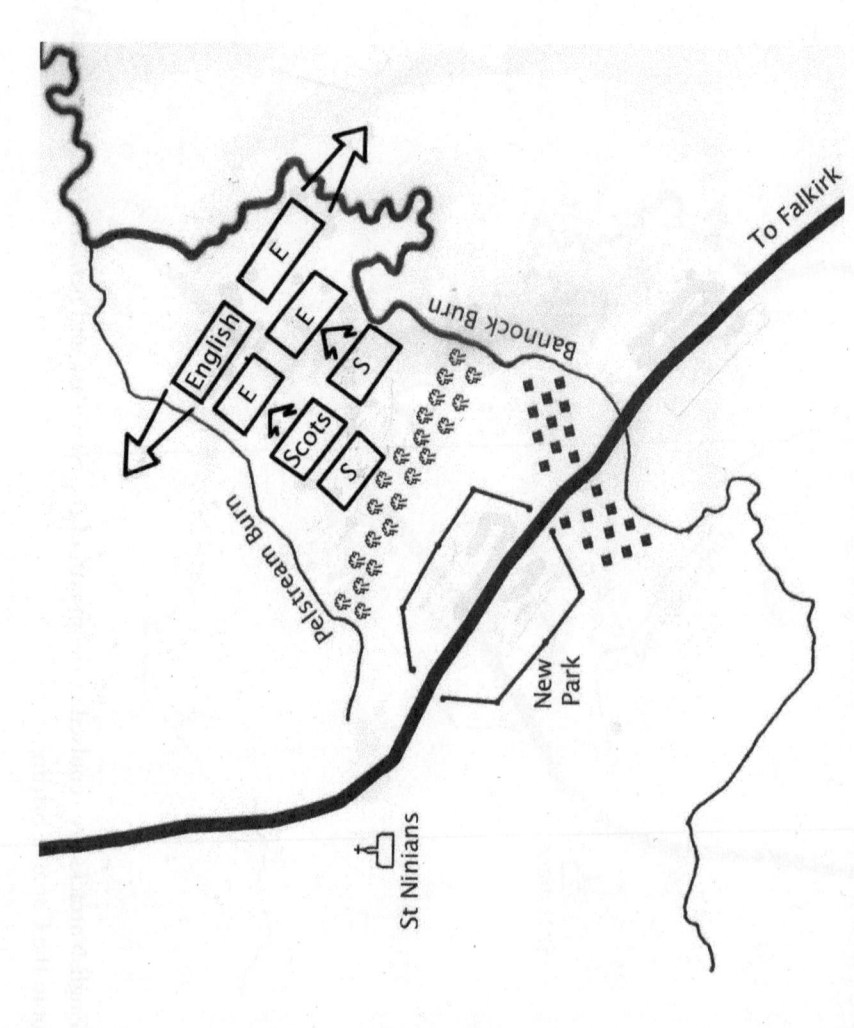

Map 4. 24 June – The entire Scottish army attacks the English army on the Carse of Stirling, squeezing them between the two streams and ultimately forcing them to flee.

*Chapter 6*

# 'Let the Retaliation of Scotland Depend on Her Foot-Soldiers':

## The Battle of Bannockburn, 23 to 24 June 1314

### 'Rebutyt Foulily Thai War': The Skirmish at the New Park

The English army appears to have arrived within sight of the Scottish army rather late on 23 June, 'after dinner' according to the Lanercost chronicler.[1] They would have had a good twelve miles or so to cover on their march from Falkirk, so this is perhaps unsurprising. According to Gray, once Edward II arrived within three leagues of the castle – which would have been long before the English king was within sight of the Scots – Mowbray was allowed through the Scottish lines to approach the king and warned him of at least some of the preparations made by the Scots. However, Gray insists that the 'young men' ('*ioenes gentz*') in the English army would not pause and instead pressed on to attack the Scots.[2] Here again we see the divisions among the English leadership, this time expressed in terms of the young lords contrasted with the wiser council of their more experienced elders, a common moralizing tool for medieval chroniclers.[3] As they emerged from the Torwood, the mounted English vanguard found the Scots awaiting them within the bounds of the New Park. The New Park was a royal hunting reserve, so called to distinguish it from the King's Park, an older hunting park just west of Stirling Castle.[4] Bounded to the north and south by steep-sided streams – the Pelstream and the Bannock Burn, respectively – the New Park had been enclosed for King Alexander III in 1264, with a new palisade (*palicii*) added as recently as between 1288 and 1290.[5] Given that this barrier was designed to keep deer in, it would have no trouble keeping the horses of the English out. Nonetheless, the author of the *Vita* claims that the Englishmen in the vanguard believed that the Scots intended to run, and assumed that they had caught their foes unaware, rather than finding the enemy ensconced in a strong defensive position.[6] They thus pressed on to engage them as quickly as possible.

The New Park did have a few entry points, one of which seems to have been in the southern side of the wall; it was probably close to Milton Ford, the main crossing point on the Bannock Burn south of Stirling. The English vanguard therefore surged forward and were soon splashing their way across the ford. On reaching the northern side of the burn, the English quickly discovered that they could not spread out to take full advantage of their numbers, as the Scots had dug a series of pits to further narrow the entrance to the New Park. Baston describes these as 'A contrivance full of evils...holes with stakes, so that they may not pass without disasters', while Barbour claims they were:

'Off a fute-breid round, and al tha
War dep up till a mannys kne,
Sa thyk that thai mycht liknyt be
Till a wax cayme that beis mais.'[7]

These pits – coupled with the palisade around the New Park – forced the English to hit the Scots on a narrow front. By dictating the space in which the fighting could take place, Bruce blunted the impact of the English cavalry charge and nullified any numerical superiority the English might otherwise have enjoyed. Moreover, if Barbour is correct in describing the leading division of the Scottish army as being composed of 'The men of Carrik halely/And off Arghile and of Kentyr/And off the Ilis', then the English vanguard found themselves facing some of the most experienced and battle-hardened troops in the Scottish army.[8] Far from finding the Scots unprepared, the English vanguard now discovered these veteran Scots were dug in and ready for a fight.

A number of striking setbacks befell the English army at the entrance to the New Park. Gloucester was unhorsed, apparently by an ordinary Scottish foot soldier.[9] This would have been embarrassing enough at the best of times but took on an additional level of humiliation given how controversial and fiercely contested his leadership of the vanguard had been. Yet Hereford too suffered what must have been a bitter personal blow in the fighting on 23 June. In one of the most famous moments of the entire battle, Hereford's relative Sir Henry de Bohun was killed, apparently by King Robert himself. Precise details of how the killing took place differ from source to source. The earliest account – from the *Vita* – has Sir Henry leading a body of Welsh infantrymen to scout the Scottish position at the mouth of the New Park. The author states that Sir Henry hoped to kill or capture the Scottish king. However, it quickly turned out that this was a trap, with Bruce and his followers suddenly attacking the approaching force. As the *Vita* puts it:

> 'the said Henry, seeing that he could not resist the multitude of Scots, turned his horse with the intention of returning to his companions; but Robert opposed him and struck him on the head with an axe that he carried in his hand.'

The author claims that the Scots even killed Sir Henry's squire as he tried to rescue his lord's body.[10] The purpose of this passage is, of course, to portray King Robert and his fellow Scots as brutish and uncouth villains, callously killing the bold Sir Henry as he attempted to flee and even slaying his (probably quite young) squire. Yet the fearsome resistance the English encountered at the entrance to the New Park may indeed have been sufficiently shocking to make them feel as if they had been ambushed (or at the very least misled).

Barbour – who identifies Sir Henry as Hereford's 'cusyne' – claims that it was Sir Henry who surprised King Robert.[11] The poet has Bruce making a last-minute inspection of the troops, riding along the front line 'apon a litill palfray'.[12] Barbour may also envisage the king as being only lightly armoured and not even displaying his heraldry at this point, since when Sir Henry spots Bruce he can only tell he is the king 'for that he saw/Him sua rang his men' and 'by the croune that wes set/Alsua apon his bassynet'.[13] The only weapon Barbour mentions the king as having is 'ane ax in hand', though elsewhere in the text Barbour insists that the king always carried a sword with him wherever he went.[14] By contrast, Sir Henry is described as approaching 'With helm on heid and sper in hand'.[15] The overall impression is clearly intended to emphasize Bruce's apparent vulnerability in an effort to heighten the tension for Barbour's audience. Barbour has Sir Henry, who he describes as 'a wycht knycht and a hardy', riding a bowshot ahead of the vanguard when he spots King Robert arranging his troops and hastens towards him.[16] Rather than fleeing, however, Barbour has Bruce mount a counter charge against his opponent and then split Sir Henry's helm and head open to the brains in one of the most dramatic passages in the poem:

> 'Sprent thai samyn intill a ling,
> Schyr Hanry myssit the noble king
> And he that in his sterapys stud
> With the ax that wes hard and gud
> With sua gret mayne raucht him a dynt
> That nother hat na helm mycht stynt
> The hevy dusche that he him gave
> That ner the heid till the harnys clave.
> The hand-ax schaft fruschit in twa,
> And he doune to the erd gan ga
> All flatlynys for him faillyt mycht.'[17]

Both the *Vita* and Barbour's account have their obvious problems. The *Vita* seeks to paint Bruce as an almost cartoonish villain while Barbour's version of events relies on the king being able to perform an essentially superhuman feat of strength by smashing through helmet and skull with a single blow. Yet the existence of both independent accounts suggests some truth to the tale. This is further corroborated by a third account – slightly confused but certainly more grounded –in Gray's *Scalacronica*. Gray states simply:

> Here [i.e., at the New Park], Piers Mountforth [sic], knight, was killed at the hands of Robert Bruce with an axe, it was said.[18]

This terse observation – while misidentifying Sir Henry – surely must be read as a confirmation of the more dramatic accounts preserved in the *Vita* and *The Bruce*. Word that the nearly 40-year-old king, who after all may have been only recently recovered from a serious bout of ill-health, had personally killed Sir Henry (and/or Sir Piers) would no doubt be a serious blow to English morale as it passed back through the English army, in much the same way as it would have boosted Scottish confidence. Impeded by the narrowness of the space, and many of them no doubt demoralized by what they had witnessed happening to

Sir Henry and Earl Gilbert, the English vanguard was driven back across the Bannock Burn.

## 'Whatever You Give Them Now, They Will Have All Too Soon': A Second Skirmish

While the English vanguard was making a spectacle of itself at the entrance to the New Park, another, smaller body of cavalry – 800 according to Barbour, but only 300 according to Gray, whose father and namesake was one of them – attempted to skirt around the Scottish position to the east.[19] Barbour describes these troops as 'all young men and joly/Yarnand to do chevalry', suggesting he shared Gray's association of youth with impetuousness and credited this in part with the disaster that was about to befall them.[20] The precise purpose of this manoeuvre is uncertain. The earliest account – found in the *Lanercost Chronicle* – states that the cavalry hoped 'to prevent the Scots escaping by flight'.[21] The notion that this force hoped to cut off a potential Scottish retreat is certainly in keeping with the general impression that the English were concerned that Bruce still intended to withdraw and deny them a pitched battle. Barbour on the other hand claims 'To the castell thai thocht to far[e]'.[22] We cannot rule out the possibility that they were hoping to invest (i.e., move troops into) the castle, but this seems less likely than the Lanercost chronicler's explanation. It is difficult to see what advantage getting a few extra men into the castle would give the English at this juncture. Such a manoeuvre makes even less sense if we accept the Lanercost chronicler's claim that Mowbray had already been allowed to leave the castle and deliver what intelligence he had to King Edward. Moreover, Gray's report of the terms of the deal indicates that the English army had fulfilled its side of the bargain when they were still some miles south of the Scottish army, obviating the need to get men into the castle itself.

Gray might be expected to offer some insight into this issue given his father's presence in this detachment, but frustratingly he does not offer an explanation for their movements. Instead, he blandly states that they 'went round the wood on the other side, towards the castle, keeping to open fields'.[23] The phrase 'towards the castle' ('*deuers le chastel*') might support Barbour's account, but this is hardly conclusive. Gray does at least furnish us with other details. He hints at similar divisions and disharmony among this cavalry unit as those that plagued the vanguard. For instance, he claims that it was under the joint leadership of Sir Robert Clifford and Sir Henry Beaumont. The difference in size between Beaumont and Clifford's contributions to the English army may explain this shared command. Morris has identified twenty-nine men in Beaumont's following, but only twelve in Clifford's.[24] If he had more men than Clifford, Beaumont may not have been willing to play second fiddle to him, but Clifford had more experience leading large companies onto the battlefield.[25] Placing them both in command of this cavalry division may thus have been another feeble compromise like that which had been attempted between Gloucester and Hereford. These two men had less to divide them than the two earls, but the lack of a single clear source of authority nevertheless still risked spreading confusion among the troops at critical moments.

In this case, Gray also notes disunity between the leaders and their men. On reaching the far side of the 'wood', by which it seems likely Gray means the New Park, Clifford and Beaumont's division was confronted by a contingent of spearmen led by King Robert's nephew Randolph.[26] No contemporary or near-contemporary source identifies precisely where the subsequent engagement took place, but Barbour's reference to them passing 'newth the kirk' has led most scholars to associate it with St Ninians or the modern village of Broomridge (now a suburb of Stirling), towards the northern end of Balquhidderock Ridge.[27] Gray claims that Randolph had heard about his uncle's engagement with the English vanguard on the south side of the park and was seeking a similar opportunity to win renown. Gray's father – who had saved Beaumont's life at the previous siege of Stirling in 1304 and thus might be expected to hold a privileged position within this force – advises against giving the Scots space to form up properly, leading Beaumont to accuse him of cowardice. This provokes the elder Gray and his comrade Sir William Deyncourt to charge headlong into the Scots, getting Deyncourt killed, Gray's horse pinioned by Scottish spears, and Gray himself taken prisoner. The experience of Gray and Deyncourt foreshadowed what was about to happen to the rest of the cavalry.

As usual, Barbour offers the most detailed account of this incident, though we must again be wary of accepting his narrative at face value. He reports that Randolph ordered his men 'bak to bak set all your rout/And all the speris poyntis out' and later describes the appearance of the resulting formation as looking 'as ane hyrchoune' ('like a hedgehog').[28] This would seem to fit with Walter of

Guisborough's description of the formations used by the Scots at the Battle of Falkirk in 1298, which Guisborough had described as 'made up wholly of spearmen, standing shoulder to shoulder in deep ranks and facing towards the circumference of the circle, with their spears slanting outwards at an oblique angle'.[29] Guisborough uses the Older Scots term 'schiltron' ('*scheltrouns*', as he puts it) to describe this formation. Gray also uses the term *schiltrome* to describe the Scottish formations at Bannockburn, while the Lanercost chronicler describes the decision of the Cumbrian knight Sir Andrew Harclay and his men to fight in a tightly packed formation on foot at the Battle of Boroughbridge in 1322 as fighting 'in schiltron, in the manner of the Scots' ('*in scheltrum, secundum modum Scottorum*').[30] The term has thus been adopted by modern historians to refer to the Scottish formations at Bannockburn.[31] Yet Barbour uses the term in a much more general sense, and (somewhat ironically) only ever applies it to groups of English soldiers.[32] It would appear then that this was a term that contemporary Scots likely applied to any large group (or group of soldiers), but that contemporary English writers had come to associate with a specifically Scottish way of fighting.

Regardless of the terminology used, the strength of fighting 'back-to-back' in a roughly circular formation of dismounted spearmen was that it presented to the enemy a bristling wall of spears in every direction. Barbour provides a typically vivid and visceral description of the subsequent fighting, offering a keen sense of how Clifford and Beaumont's men were left with no option but to circle the formation in a fruitless effort to identify or create a weak spot, with some exasperated Englishmen even hurling their weapons into the midst of the Scots in frustration:

> 'And thai with speris woundis wyd
> Gaff till the hors that come thaim ner,
> And thai that ridand on thaim wer
> That doune war borne losyt the lyvis,
> And other speris dartis and knyffis
> And wapynnys on ser maner
> Kast amang thaim that fechtand wer
> That thaim defendyt sa wittily
> That thar fayis had gret ferly,
> For sum wald schout out of thar rout
> And off thaim that assaylyt about

> Stekyt stedis and bar doun men.
> The Inglismen sa rudly then
> Kest amang thaim swerdis and mas
> That ymyd thaim a monteyle was
> Off wapynnys that war warpyt thar.'[33]

In these circumstances, it is unsurprising that ultimately the English cavalry was forced to withdraw, as by now the vanguard had done from the New Park. This did not prevent the author of the *Vita* critically describing Clifford and his men as having been 'disgracefully routed'.[34] Though it may not have seemed like it to the English at the time, this was a crucial engagement. Randolph and his men had denied the English access to the area west of Balquhiderock Ridge on 23 June, just as Bruce had done at the New Park. This limited their options for where to camp overnight and would encourage them to move into the position King Robert hoped to trap them in the following day.

Barbour includes another, rather dubious, detail concerning the engagement between Randolph's men and the English cavalry that deserves consideration here. The poet is keen to emphasize the desperate plight faced by Randolph and his men, being assaulted from all sides as well as suffering under the conditions of the warm June weather:

> 'Thar fayis demenyt thaim full starkly,
> On ather half thai war sa stad
> For the rycht gret heyt that thai had
> For fechtyn and for sonnys het
> That all thar flesche of swate wes wete,
> And sic a stew rais out off thaim then
> Off aneding bath of hors and men
> And off powdyr that sic myrknes
> Intill the ayr abovyne thaim wes
> That it wes wondre for to se.'[35]

As the fighting unfolds, Barbour reports how 'the noble renownyt king' coolly observes this development from the New Park, surrounded by his close companions – including Sir James Douglas.[36] We should be cautious about uncritically accepting

Barbour's presentation of Douglas's role at Bannockburn. As Dr Sonja Cameron has convincingly argued, Barbour wildly exaggerates Douglas's importance at the battle, giving him joint command of what Cameron has termed a 'phantom division' on the second day of the fighting, most likely to satisfy Douglas's various influential relatives among the poet's intended audience.[37] Prof. A. A. M. Duncan has plausibly suggested that Douglas may have been placed in charge of a small, lightly armed body of cavalry, which was intended to remain highly mobile and deploy at trouble spots around the battlefield as needed.[38] Duncan's interpretation certainly fits with Barbour's depiction of Douglas's activities on the first day of Bannockburn and in the immediate aftermath of the battle, and this is perhaps worth keeping in mind when discussing the episode in question, but even this may be overly generous to Barbour.

On seeing Randolph 'in perell', Douglas addresses Bruce with a request to assist the beleaguered earl.[39] However, according to Barbour, Randolph had been specifically instructed to guard against a manoeuvre like the one Clifford and Beaumont were attempting and had been so slow in reacting that 'the king haid said him [i.e., Randolph] rudly/That a rose of his chaplete [i.e., a wreath or garland awarded in recognition of a worthy achievement]/Was fallyn'.[40] Thus, Bruce dismisses Douglas's request out of hand:

> 'The king said, "Sa our Lord me se,
> A fute till him thou sall nocht ga,
> Giff he weile dois lat him weile ta.
> Quhatever him happyn, to wyn or los,
> I will nocht for him brek purpos."'[41]

The king's statement makes it clear that to assist Randolph would mean modifying Bruce's battle plan, which might of course have serious ramifications for the entire course of the battle. However, Douglas responds:

> '"Certis," said James, "I may na wis
> Se that his fayis him suppris
> Quhen that I may set help thartill,
> With your leve sekyrly I will
> Help him or dey into the payn."'[42]

The phrasing here is striking. Douglas does not appeal to the king based on the danger to Randolph and his men, nor does he address Bruce's reservations about deviating from the overall plan. Rather, Douglas reminds Bruce of the personal cost to Douglas's own reputation if he were to fail to help a fellow knight when he was able. More telling still is the fact that this plea works, as King Robert tells Douglas 'Do than and speid the sone agayn'.[43] In the event, this entire exchange proves irrelevant to the course of the battle, incidentally strengthening Cameron's case that Barbour largely invented Douglas's role at Bannockburn. On arriving at the scene of the fighting between Randolph and Clifford's men, Douglas sees that the earl has things well in hand and chooses not to engage for fear of diminishing the renown owed to the earl for having fought his way out of such desperate circumstances.[44]

While this incident may not have any impact on Barbour's narrative of the battle, it offers a fascinating insight into the political role that friendship played in noble life in late medieval Scotland. In Scotland, as in many contemporary kingdoms in western Europe, political decision-making was limited to a small group of people, with supreme executive authority resting – theoretically at least – with the king. Thus, a degree of intimacy and confidentiality with the king could translate into significant influence over policy and could give an individual considerable sway within the community of the realm.[45] Effective governance of a medieval kingdom was impossible without the advice and support of the magnates, the king's tenants-in-chief.[46] Barbour's presentation of the conversation between Bruce and Douglas illustrates this principle in practice. Douglas's close personal relationship with Bruce not only allows him to approach the king, but also enables him to convince King Robert to modify his plans in Douglas's favour.

Of course, Barbour shows this influence to be benign, a reflection of the great affection between the two men. This would also have had keen relevance to Barbour's contemporary audience among the Scottish aristocracy in the mid-1370s. Although Barbour's patron has traditionally been assumed to be King Robert II – based on the poet's undoubted years of service to the king in various roles – there is a reasonable case to be made that at least the elements concerning Douglas were inspired by Douglas's illegitimate son, Archibald 'the Grim'.[47] This was the same 'Schyr Archebald' who Barbour identifies as having commissioned a 'fair and fyne' alabaster tomb for his father at St Bride's Kirk.[48] By the time Barbour was writing, Archibald had risen to become lord of Galloway and was one of the most influential figures in south-western Scotland. He had already commissioned a significant refortification of Bothwell Castle (his favourite residence) and had begun construction of a fashionable new castle at Threave as well.[49] Archibald was thus more than capable of financing part or all of Barbour's work. He also had good cause to promote his family connections and his rights within the community.

Archibald was, after all, illegitimate, and therefore, at birth at least, he had no legal rights to any inheritance.[50] His father's property, and to some extent his father's legacy as the premier war leader in the Scottish Marches, belonged to Archibald's cousin William, first earl of Douglas.[51] By sponsoring a history of his father's exploits, Archibald may have hoped to cultivate an image for himself as the natural successor to 'the Good' Sir James. The emphasis on the friendship between Bruce and Douglas in *The Bruce* takes on added meaning if we suppose Archibald had a hand in patronizing the work. Archibald owed his predominance in the south-west to a close personal relationship with Bruce's son and heir, King David II, a 'frendschip' the two men developed from the early 1360s onward. The relationship between David and Archibald imitated – perhaps consciously – that between their fathers. Archibald's closeness to David cannot have endeared him to Robert II, however, since much of David's reign had been spent trying to thwart Robert's claim to succeed as king. Archibald had been associated with these efforts, and David's earliest promotion of Archibald as a major landed nobleman through marriage to the wealthy heiress Joanna Murray in 1362 came at the expense of Robert's son, Robert, earl of Fife.[52] Though, in practice, the fledgling Stewart regime would prove eager for compromise with the most powerful figures from David's reign, when Robert came to the throne in 1371, Archibald's position may have felt somewhat vulnerable.[53] The new king might be expected to use his newfound authority to reverse some of Archibald's gains, especially where Archibald's interests ran contrary to those of the Stewarts. Barbour dates the 'compiling' of his poem to 1375, four years after Robert became king.[54] It is therefore quite possible that Archibald contributed to Barbour's efforts to compose *The Bruce*, employing the services of a cleric with established connections to the new king in order to ingratiate himself with the incoming Stewart regime.

In this context, the close relationship of Bruce and Douglas – and the political implications of this – takes on new significance. Barbour was not merely seeking to explain the historical closeness of two of Scotland's 'patriotic' heroes. He was also advocating the idea of a natural association between their successors, in this case Robert II (Bruce's grandson) and Archibald the Grim (Douglas's illegitimate son). Randolph's most prominent descendants at the time Barbour was writing would have been his grandsons George Dunbar, earl of March, and John Dunbar, earl of Moray. Although they would regularly cooperate with him in border warfare against the English, domestically both men were natural rivals of Archibald in the south of the kingdom.[55] Therefore, Barbour's presentation of Randolph as having failed to live up to King Robert's expectations, and having Douglas step in to intercede for him to the king, reads as an effort to emphasize the chivalric reputation of Archibald's father at the expense of the Dunbars' grandfather. The incident in which Douglas persuades Bruce to adapt his plans can thus be read as an intrusion of contemporary socio-political concerns into the text of the poem. It can simultaneously be dismissed as offering any real insight into the actual events of 1314.

## Edward's Choice: Manoeuvring on the Evening of 23 June

Even before the minor defeats had been inflicted on the advance parties of his army, King Edward must have been forced to contemplate how to react to Bruce's decision to make his stand in the relative safety of the New Park. Unable to tackle the Scots head-on due to the natural narrowness of the entrance and the pits the Scots made between it and Bannock Burn, the English army would now have to find a way around the park in the hopes of establishing a clearer angle of attack. It may be that, far from trying to cut off a Scottish retreat or seeking to muscle their way into the castle, Clifford and Beaumont's division had actually been dispatched to scout out the possibilities for assaulting the Scottish position from an alternate direction. The reversal they had suffered had demonstrated the eastern extent of the area the Scots were effectively able to defend, which would require the English to take an even wider route in their efforts to circumvent the Scots. As explored in the previous chapter, the ground to the west of the New Park was low-lying and boggy, and further west still was the awkward bulk of Gillies Hill.[56] Navigating this area, particularly for the heavy, slow-moving English royal host, would be painstaking, laborious, and time-consuming. The delay this would inevitably cause would more-or-less guarantee the Scots time to withdraw further north again, diminishing Edward's chance of forcing the pitched battle he so desperately needed. With King Robert's banner probably in sight from the brow of the hill over which the English would have approached the New Park, King Edward could not afford to let this opportunity slip away. Two short skirmishes (both of which the English had lost) followed by a hasty Scottish retreat would not demonstrate the value of military intervention in Scotland to the English king's fractious magnates like Lancaster and Warwick, any more than his desultory meandering through southern Scotland had done in 1310 to 1311. Edward had to have a battle – now more than ever after the dismal showing his troops had made on the first day – and moving west would all but guarantee this would not happen.

East of the New Park, the Bannock Burn cut a deep ravine – some forty feet from the ridgeline down to the water below – through the landscape for roughly a mile and a half.[57] However, beyond this the burn debauched into a wide, flat area known as the Carse of Stirling. The carse – a mixture of meadowland and wetland – was crisscrossed with tidal streams, of which the Bannock Burn was one of the largest. These bodies of water were known in French as *polles* and in Scots as 'pows'. The Carse of Stirling extended as far as the banks of the River Forth itself, and the eastern portions (closest to the river) were probably as wet and marshy as the area around the foot of Gillies Hill.[58] However, the western parts of the carse, nearest the New Park, were meadowland, normally used for agricultural purposes.[59] It would certainly be firm enough for the English army to set up camp. Once the burn itself had been crossed – a slow but achievable aim – the carse would offer some further benefits to the English army. For a start, the streams themselves would provide fresh water for the men and horses who had travelled from Falkirk on 23 June in the midsummer heat. Beyond the Bannock Burn, the next major obstacle to the English army's progress northwards would be the Pelstream, which flowed together with the Bannock Burn on the Carse of Stirling before joining the River Forth. During the night, the Pelstream and the Bannock Burn would serve to protect the flanks of the English army, ensuring that if the Scots sought to raid into the English camp under cover of darkness, they could only realistically do so down a relatively narrow strip of land between the two streams. Though it was not where anyone in the English army would have originally envisioned spending the night, it was undoubtedly the best option the Scots had left open to the English. Edward thus marched his army eastwards towards the carse.

Crossing the Bannock Burn proved – predictably – to be a long and frustrating process for the English royal host. It was achieved in part, according to both the author of the *Vita* and Barbour, by pilfering doors and other materials from local farmhouses to use as makeshift bridges.[60] The passage of perhaps 20,000 pairs of English feet, plus the hooves of several thousand horses and an uncertain number of carts and wagons, churned the wetlands around the burn itself – described by Gray as 'an evil, deep, boggy stream' to begin with – into a morass.[61] This probably did not concern the English greatly once they had crossed it, however, since few if any of them would have expected to have to cross it again any time soon. They had, after all, only seen the Scots fighting defensively on the first day of battle and they likely still believed that Bruce favoured withdrawal over confrontation. If they awoke to find that the Scots intended to hold their ground for a second day, the English would be free to either attack the Scots from the east – in the hope that the Scots had not made similar preparations on this side of the New Park as they had done to the south – or more likely to move even further north across the Pelstream. In this latter case, the English would be able to form up on the firm ground between the Pelstream and Stirling, and would thus have cut Bruce off from his most likely escape route into the north-west.[62]

As strange as it may seem, given the frustrations of the first day and what was to come on the second, there was some cause for hope in the English camp on the evening of 23 June. Baston, who was present in the English camp, claims that the troops 'spent the night in braggartry and revelry with Bacchus', suggesting fairly high spirits.[63] Subsequent chroniclers – all of them aware of the disaster that was about to befall the English army and writing for audiences eager to excuse the defeat – paint a rather bleaker impression of the situation in the English camp between the two days of fighting. The author of the *Vita*, for instance, insists that the soldiers spent the night 'sleepless, expecting the Scots rather to attack by night than to await battle by day'.[64] Gray too states that many of the English chose to remain in their armour all night in fear of Scottish raiding and 'sadly lost confidence…being too much disaffected by the events of the day'.[65] Yet by the time the sun set on 23 June, the English army had overcome the most serious physical obstacle between them and the Scots (i.e., the Bannock Burn) and were now closer to the Scottish army than any English royal host had been since the beginning of either king's reign. Those leading the English army could be forgiven for hoping that the momentum of the encounter was gradually shifting in their favour. In fact, they had stepped neatly into the trap King Robert had been preparing for them for at least a month.

The atmosphere in the Scottish camp, which remained in the New Park, must have been more resolute by comparison. Thus far, the plan had proceeded precisely as King Robert had envisioned it. The Scots had held the direct route to the castle via the New Park, and this had forced the English down into the carse, where they would be vulnerable to a counterattack. Barbour sounds one sour note for the Scottish experience on the evening of 23 June, although he tactfully avoids mentioning it until near the end of his narration of the battle so that it does not disrupt the triumphant tone that he assumes in the bulk of his account. At an uncertain point 'apon Saynct Jhonys nycht', David Strathbogie, earl of Atholl, betrayed his uncle and attacked the Scottish supply camp at Cambuskenneth on the north side of the River Forth, killing Sir William Airth and 'with him men ma then ynew' before withdrawing.[66] Barbour attributes Atholl's treachery to a personal feud between the earl and King Robert's brother Edward, who had apparently jilted Atholl's sister Isabella in favour of a daughter of the earl of Ross.[67] As mentioned in previous chapters, Atholl had been in contact with the English since January, when none other than Sir Roger Mowbray, whose brother Philip was serving as captain of the garrison at Stirling, had been licenced to offer military aid to the earl 'against Edward de Brus, on account of the dissension between them'.[68] Yet any personal animosity between Atholl and Edward Bruce there may have been was most likely simply a pretext used by Atholl to justify his sudden shift in allegiance. Dr Penman has convincingly argued that Atholl's sudden defection was likely motivated by a number of more serious political concerns, most notably the squeezing of his landed interests in the Highlands by the likes of Thomas Randolph, earl of Moray, and his continuing difficulties in asserting his influence at the Scottish royal court.[69]

Another notable defection took place on the evening of 23 June, this time in the opposite direction. Again, at an uncertain point in the evening, possibly even while Atholl was making his assault on Cambuskenneth, Sir Alexander Seton crossed over from the English camp to the Scottish camp. Gray's *Scalacronica* is our only source for this tale.[70] But given that Gray's father had been captured in the skirmishing of the first day of the battle and was thus likely to have been present in the Scottish camp on the night of 23 June, we should not dismiss this testimony out of hand. As we have seen in the previous chapter, Seton was a Berwickshire laird who had dithered between English and Scottish allegiance throughout Bruce's reign.[71] His vacillation may simply have been a pragmatic response to the fact that his lands in the south-east were intensely vulnerable to destruction or confiscation by the English crown. What he had witnessed on 23 June had apparently now convinced him that the tide was turning and that his interests were therefore better served by a timely submission to King Robert. Gray reports that the Scots were 'on the point of decamping and moving into the Lennox, a more defensible country, when Seton arrived'.[72] Bruce had certainly reserved the option to withdraw after the engagements on the first day. The notion that he would make his retreat to Lennox if he chose to disengage is also eminently believable, since he had already spent some time there during Edward's previous invasion of Scotland in 1310.[73] We should be cautious about accepting Gray's implication that the intelligence delivered by Seton is what ultimately convinced Bruce to remain, however. The precise manoeuvrings of the Scots on 24 June suggest they were planned in advance rather than spontaneous. But tales of the misery and dissension in the English army told by Seton can only have emboldened the Scottish king to follow through on his preparations at this crucial juncture.

Barbour has King Robert consult with the other Scottish lords on whether they should stay or go following the skirmishing on 23 June, with the lords of course unanimously opting to fight.[74] Again, it is entirely plausible that a war council of some sort was held on the evening of the first day at which the decision to give battle the following morning was discussed. This council would serve to reassure any Scottish lords who remained uncertain of the wisdom of the king's proposed plan as well as securing at least the appearance of consensus for the decision to fight. However, the discussion would no doubt have been more carefully managed than Barbour's conventional literary presentation would suggest. Bruce would hardly have been willing to accept a decision that wasted the weeks of planning he had undertaken in the build-up to the battle or failed to capitalize on the successes of the first day of fighting. The king would no doubt have drawn on the same skills that Tanner has identified the king as using at his parliaments to ensure the war council reached the decision he wanted.[75] Bruce was now committed to the largest military enterprise of his reign.

## Caught in a Trap: The Second Day

As the sun rose on Monday, 24 June – St John the Baptist's feast day – the Scots would already have been deep into their preparations for the coming day of fighting.[76] There would have undoubtedly been a strong spiritual element to these preparations. Walter Bower, abbot of Inchcolm, suggests that mass was said by Maurice, abbot of Inchaffray, who 'put forward a short and effective statement on freedom and the defence of their right' and afterwards led the Scots to the battlefield barefoot and carrying a crucifix. Bower also preserves fragments from a chronicle that he attributes to Bruce's chancellor Bernard, abbot of Arbroath, which states that the Scots heard mass when they awoke.[77] He adds the detail that Bruce himself was shriven by Maurice, abbot of Inchaffray, and it seems likely that many other Scots – noble and common alike – would have made their confessions in anticipation of the dangers they were about to face.[78] Barbour too has the Scots hearing mass on the morning of 24 June, and adds that Walter Stewart, James Douglas, 'And other als of gret bounté' were knighted by the king.[79] The creation of knights before a battle was a common morale-boosting exercise. John de Warenne, earl of Surrey, had gone so far as to delay the initial English advance at the Battle of Stirling Bridge in 1297 in order to honour this tradition, while Douglas's nephew William, lord of Douglas, and illegitimate son Archibald would be knighted by King Jean II of France ahead of the Battle of Poitiers in 1356.[80]

Bernard's chronicle also recounts a speech reputedly given by Bruce at this juncture.[81] While the words themselves are likely Bernard's invention, it is worth noting that they were almost certainly written for recitation at King Robert's court. They thus represent at least what the king wished others to believe he said on the fateful day, and as such provide a useful insight into his outlook on the battle. The speech rehearses the justifications for the fight, laying emphasis on the hardships suffered by both the king and his subjects, the losses incurred, and the perceived arrogance of the English. Bernard has Bruce paraphrase Psalm 20:7 – 'Their glory is in their wagons and horses; for us the name of the Lord and victory in war is our hope' – and invoke St John the Baptist, whose feast day it was, St Andrew, and St Thomas Becket by name, as well as 'the saints of the Scottish nation' in offering protection to the Scots in the coming fight. Though to some extent the spread of Becket's posthumous popularity was due to the patronage of the English crown, the saint had been martyred as a result of his conflict with Edward's great-great-grandfather, King Henry II of England. Becket thus served Bruce – an ardent devotee of the cult of St Thomas – as a powerful symbol for resistance against a tyrannous English king seeking to expand his power beyond his legal rights.[82] The speech ends with the promise that service in this battle would earn remissions for anyone in the army currently accused of crimes against the crown. Remissions were a very specific – and often controversial – form of royal patronage whereby the king could forgive an individual of any wrongdoing, usually used as a means of raising funds.[83] Here we find Bruce drawing on the full extent of his royal powers to induce his troops to fight.

Barbour offers a much longer – and even more inventive – address by the king to his men ahead of the fighting on 24 June. As well as mirroring many of Bernard's points on the justification for the struggle, Barbour also includes a great deal of practical advice for the soldiers, much of it no doubt aimed at Barbour's contemporary audience and reflecting the poet's keen interest in the prudent prosecution of warfare. For instance, Bruce enjoins his followers:

> 'And I pray you als specially
> Bath mar and les commonaly
> That nane of you for gredynes
> Haff ey to tak of thar riches
> Ne presonaris for to ta
> Quhill ye se thaim contraryit sa
> That the feld anerly youris be,
> And than at your liking may ye
> Tak all the riches that thar is.'[84]

This concern over the taking of prisoners and seizing of booty before a battle is won is reflective of fourteenth-century military thinking, as demonstrated in, for example, Geoffrey de Charny's *Livre de chevalerie*.[85]

With these niceties observed, the Scots advanced out of the New Park and moved eastwards towards Balquhidderock Ridge, which overlooked that area of the carse where the English had spent the night. It was critical that they covered this distance before the English had time to manoeuvre themselves out of the space between the Bannock Burn and the Pelstream. Once the Scots had formed up along Balquhidderock Ridge, they had in effect trapped the English with the streams on three sides of them and the Scots on the other. The Scots formed up along the ridge in three divisions – one led by King Robert's brother Edward Bruce, earl of Carrick; one led by Bruce's nephew Thomas Randolph, earl of Moray; and a reserve led by the king. [86] The Scots were apparently all dismounted. The author of the *Vita*, no doubt drawing on information supplied by others of Edward's courtiers who were present at Bannockburn, offers a particularly vivid description of the Scottish army as:

> 'not one of them was on horseback, but each was furnished with light armour, not easily penetrable by a sword. They had axes at their sides and carried lances in their hands. They advanced like a thick-set hedge, and such a troop (*turma*) could not easily be broken.'[87]

Barbour confirms that the Scots chose 'To gang on fute to this fechting/Armyt bot in litill armyng'.[88] Gray too claims that the Scots fought on foot at Bannockburn and adds the detail that they were actively mimicking tactics employed by the Flemish militias that defeated a French royal host at Courtrai in July 1302.[89] The impression given is once again of tightly packed bodies of spearmen similar to that deployed by Randolph against Clifford and Beaumont's men. Now, however, they were probably formed up in rectangular blocks with their long spears pointed in the direction of the enemy, rather than in the circular or oval-shaped formation used on the first day. They would have no longer needed to worry about protecting their flanks or their rear from the English once they had them trapped in between the two streams. As soon as they were ready, the two divisions led by Carrick and Randolph advanced down into the Carse of Stirling. Pollen analyses have shown that Balquhidderock Wood, now known to locals as Bluebell Wood, was present in 1314, but would have been no larger than it is now.[90] There would have been nothing to prevent the Scots from cutting gaps through the trees ahead of the battle to avoid getting their spears entangled in the overgrowth as they passed through the wood. As they emerged onto the carse, the Scots would then have filled up the area between the Bannock Burn and the Pelstream, effectively sealing the English in the cramped space where the two streams flowed together.

It is unclear precisely when the English became aware of this sudden Scottish offensive. The Lanercost chronicler mentions some skirmishing between English and Scottish archers before the main fighting began, and it may be that this was used by both sides to give the main bodies of their armies time to get into position.[91] Barbour includes a passage – almost certainly designed as a mocking demonstration of the English king's arrogance – in which King Edward sees the Scots kneeling in prayer ahead of the fighting and assumes that the Scots are asking for mercy, only to be corrected by Sir Ingram Umfraville – a Balliol relative serving in the English army – that 'Thai ask mercy bot nane at you,/ For thar trespas to God thai cry'.[92] This would imply that the two armies were formed up in front of one another before the action began. Certainly, while the Scots seem to have caught the English off-guard, the English were apparently able to get their mounted vanguard ready to fight before the Scots had advanced far onto the carse. As on 23 June, the vanguard was led jointly by the earls of Gloucester and Hereford, with the former no doubt still nursing his frustrations about being unhorsed at the New Park the previous afternoon.

The English cavalry charged directly into the division led by Carrick, their aim apparently to create a gap in the formation through which the rest of the army could try to muscle their way out of the trap in which they found themselves. Instead, they smashed ineffectively against the disciplined Scottish infantry. This is a somewhat predictable outcome given that the tightly packed Scottish spear formations had been developed precisely to counter heavy cavalry charges. A number of the English lords at Bannockburn had received first-hand experience of this at the Battle of Falkirk some sixteen years earlier. Yet the tactical lessons of Falkirk were probably not as obvious to those who had fought in it as they are to us with hindsight. After all, while the Scottish spearmen at Falkirk had been picked apart by archery and missile troops after an initial cavalry charge had foundered against their spears, it was a second cavalry charge that finally swept the Scots from the field.[93] To veterans of Falkirk like Sir Robert Clifford – who may have been one of those English lords killed in the opening charge at Bannockburn – it may well have seemed as though their contribution, rather than that of the common archers, had brought victory in 1298. Thus, they expected to do so again in 1314. They were to be grievously – and in many cases fatally – disappointed.[94]

Unable to break through the Scottish formation, and having no doubt spent some time riding back and forth along the line looking in vain for a weak point to exploit, the English cavalry was ultimately left with no choice but to pull back. One of their leaders – Gloucester – may well have been killed during or shortly after the initial charge, which would no doubt have undermined their morale (though it may also have simplified the English chain of command somewhat). Much attention was paid to Gloucester's death in subsequent English chronicles, and none more so than in the *Vita*. Somewhat unconvincingly, the author claims that Gloucester's division managed to penetrate the Scottish line, a notion likely intended to present the English as at least having had some small degree of success in the fighting. However, having claimed that Gloucester's horse was killed under him, the author states that he was:

'borne down by the weight of his body armour [and] he could not easily arise, and of the five hundred cavalry whom he had led to battle at his own expense...they stood astonished and brought him no aid.'[95]

Not content with heaping blame on Gloucester's feckless followers, the writer also includes an alternate explanation for Gloucester's death – his own rashness. Geoffrey le Baker, whose account of the battle is, for the most part, deeply confused, also hints at Gloucester's rashness by claiming that he was killed because he had failed to put on his surcoat and thus the Scots did not know to save him for ransom.[96] The motivation for the inclusion of these apparently contradictory explanations of Gloucester's death in the *Vita* may simply be a reflection of the author's eagerness to launder Edward II's reputation by comparison with his inept subordinates. Crucially, in doing so the *Vita* highlights the dispute between Gloucester and Hereford over command of the vanguard as a source of tension within the English army, offering a valuable insight into the continuing disunity among the English leadership into the second day of the fighting and the part this played in cementing their defeat.

By disengaging from the Scots, the English cavalry might have hoped to regroup for a renewed assault on the Scottish spearmen, or perhaps more likely to allow the infantry to advance and engage with the Scots on a more equal footing. The 'schiltrons' they had encountered at Falkirk sixteen years earlier had, after all, been entirely stationary formations and had fallen victim to precisely this tactic.[97] Even Randolph's spear formation, which had turned Clifford's cavalry back on themselves on the first day of Bannockburn, had not moved since taking up position to block the cavalry's advance. However, on 24 June, the Scottish spearmen revealed yet another unexpected benefit of the weeks of training they had enjoyed in Torwood ahead of the battle – they began to advance inexorably towards the retreating English.[98] This was an unmitigated disaster for the English and the most devastating aspect of the trap Bruce had prepared for them. With their own cavalry still ahead of them, the English infantry could not reach the Scots to have an impact on the fighting. Neither could their archers shoot at the advancing Scots for fear of hitting their own men. Sandwiched between the advancing Scots and their own infantry, the cavalry found themselves with less and less space in which to manoeuvre or to attack the spearmen, against whom they had already proven useless even when at full strength and with a long run-up. Every effort by the cavalry and the infantry to let one another past diluted their strength further and moreover led to the breakdown of the cohesion of the English army as a whole, spreading confusion and panic through the English ranks. Soon the English were no longer able to act a functional army at all and had degenerated into a confused and disorientated mass of men and horses struggling to have any impact on events as they unfolded around them.

Someone in the English army may have still been making intelligent tactical decisions as the situation worsened. Whether or not this was King Edward or not is unclear. But according to Barbour, at a certain point in the fighting some archers seem to have formed up, perhaps on the flank of the English army, and began to shoot into the tightly packed Scottish spear formations.[99] Given time – and assuming the archers could form up in sufficient numbers – this might disrupt the Scottish formations enough for the English to break through them, creating more space in which the English could bring their superior numbers to bear against the Scots at last. However, before they could achieve this, the archers were scattered by Sir Robert Keith, the Scottish marischal, and about 500 men on 'lycht hors'. It may be that Keith and his 'lycht' (here meaning 'fast') cavalry had been assigned to screen one flank of the Scottish army specifically to counter this eventuality.[100] However, Barbour states that Bruce 'Ordanyt forouth the assemble/Hys marschell with a gret menye.../For to pryk amang the archeris', which suggests that Keith had remained with the king among the reserve at the rear of the Scottish army with the intention of fighting on foot until he was ordered to mount up and disperse the archers.[101] Either way, the removal of these archers from the field seems to have ended any hope for the English to extricate themselves from Bruce's trap by force.

The Lanercost chronicler, whose account of the battle was most likely drawn from conversations with ordinary English soldiers who had escaped the battlefield and fled to the Cumbrian priory, sums up the dilemma facing the English succinctly:

> 'when both armies engaged each other, and the great horses of the English charged the spears of the Scots, as it were into a dense forest, there arose a great and terrible crash of spears broken and of destriers wounded to the death; and so they remained without movement for a while. Now the English in the rear could not reach the Scots because the leading division was in the way, nor could they do anything to help themselves, wherefore there was nothing for it but to take to flight.'[102]

Eventually, King Robert judged that the English were close to a breaking point and decided to commit his reserve to the fighting.[103] Assuming that Barbour's observations on the make-up of the king's division on the first day of battle held true for the second, the reserve would have been composed of battle-hardened troops from Carrick, the western Highlands, and the Hebrides. Barbour also claims that around this point in the battle the 'Yomen and swanys and pitaill [i.e., rabble]' who had been left in the New Park to guard the Scots camp, seized by patriotic fervour, took up what makeshift arms they could improvise and charged onto the battlefield. The poet even goes so far as to claim that these were mistaken for additional reinforcements and contributed to the panic already spreading through the English army.[104] The spontaneous and seemingly democratic nature of this incident has excited a great deal of interest both in popular and academic histories of the battle.[105] Yet given that no English source mentions the intervention of the so-called 'small folk' – and early English chroniclers were naturally eager to include any excuse they could for the collapse of their countrymen's morale at the battle – we should be highly cautious about accepting Barbour's claim at face value. Yet the late Prof. A. A. M. Duncan has rather brilliantly suggested that a kernel of truth may be gleaned from Barbour's observation that the 'small folk' selected a 'Capitane' from among their number before leaving the park.[106] Scottish soldiers were not paid a wage in the fourteenth century but did have the right to a share of the booty that was taken following a successful engagement. Specifically, they appear to have been allowed to take two-thirds of whatever they could recover from the battlefield, while owing the remaining third to their immediate commander (or captain).[107] Thus, the appointment of a captain among the 'small folk' and their sudden rush to the battlefield may have been an attempt by the army's ancillary staff to stake a claim to the loot that they knew was about to be taken, which Barbour sought to retroactively give a less cynical sheen.

Committing the reserve at this crucial moment was designed to do more than simply shatter what remained of English morale. Bruce must now surely also have hoped to capture King Edward. Doing so would almost certainly end the war altogether, since the Scots could deny Edward his freedom until he agreed to recognize Bruce's rights as king. That the Scots ultimately hoped to capture Edward is suggested by the amount of physical danger the English king appears to have been in during the second day of fighting. In spite of his subsequent reputation for lacking military skills, Edward II probably did more fighting than his Scottish counterpart at Bannockburn. He had a horse killed under him, and many members of the royal household were either killed or captured defending the king.[108] Edmund Mauley, the steward of the royal household, was killed, while Mauley's brother Robert was captured, as was the keeper of the privy seal, Roger Northburgh.[109] All three men were likely fighting in King Edward's own division at Bannockburn. One of the men closest to the king on the battlefield was Sir Giles d'Argentan, who, as we saw earlier, had only been recently released from captivity, probably specifically so that he could serve as Edward's bodyguard. Sir Giles's physical closeness to the king is confirmed by the *Vita*, Gray, and Barbour, but the latter two reserve particular reverence for Sir Giles's actions at this critical juncture.[110]

According to the author of the *Vita*, Sir Giles left Edward's side when he saw Gloucester had been unhorsed by the Scottish spearmen. Although Sir Giles ultimately could not rescue Gloucester, the *Vita* states that he was killed alongside the earl, 'thinking it more honourable to perish with so great a man than to escape death by flight'.[111] It should be noted that the author of the *Vita* reserves no obvious criticism for Sir Giles, but his actions are elevated to even more heroic heights by Gray and Barbour. According to these accounts, Sir Giles dragged the king from the battlefield, but once Edward was a safe distance from the fighting, Sir Giles turned around and returned to the fighting, having never fled from battle before and refusing to do so now. Gray puts the following speech into Sir Giles's mouth:

> 'Sire, your rein was committed to me; you are now in safety, there is your castle where your person may be safe. I am not accustomed to fly, nor am I going to begin now. I commend you to God.'[112]

Barbour offers the most detailed description of Sir Giles's demise:

> 'He prikyt, cryand, 'the Argenté!'
> And thai with speris sua him met
> And sua fele speris on him set
> That he and hors war chargyt sua
> That bathe till the erd gan ga
> And in that place thar slane wes he.'[113]

Barbour, who might otherwise be considered a hostile witness, states that his death was a source of 'gret pité' even among the Scots due to his prowess and renown as a crusader.[114]

Once the king himself was on the run, the entire English army – seeing the royal banner vanishing northwards – quickly began to fall apart as well.[115] Those on the northern side of the battlefield fled north in the same direction as Edward. Barbour describes some of the retreating Englishmen even scaling the steep sides of Castle Hill in their desperation to reach the safety of the castle.[116] Most of the army, however, seems to have taken the route south, retracing the steps they had taken to arrive on the battlefield on the evening of 23 June.[117] For many of the English troops, particularly those who had never served in Scotland before, this may have seemed like the most obvious route home given that it was the way they had taken the previous day. But it would prove to be a fatal error for a significant number of them. The burn's banks were steep, and in crossing the Bannock Burn on the first day, the English army had churned the already wet ground on either side of the burn into a quagmire. Anyone who slipped and fell trying to traverse this treacherous area in a panic on the second day would struggle to regain their footing with 20,000 of their fellows pressing on behind and around them in their eagerness to escape. By the end of the day, so many had been trampled and drowned in the mud and the water – so Barbour claims – that:

> 'And Bannokburne betwix the brays
> Off men and hors sua stekyt wais
> That apon drownyt hors and men
> Men mycht pas dry out-our it then.'[118]

Among those who did escape – possibly over the backs of their hapless comrades – were the Gloucestershire knight Sir Maurice Berkeley and his Welsh infantry, who Barbour describes as being 'wele ner all nakyt' after shedding any clothing that might weigh them down or identify them as soldiers from the defeated English army.[119] While this detail may simply be a cruel joke on Barbour's part, the *Vita* confirms the English fear of recrimination from the Scottish commons as they made their way to the border.[120] Also among the English escapees were: Humphrey de Bohun, earl of Hereford; Aymer de Valence, earl of Pembroke; Hugh Despenser; and Henry Beaumont. Hereford does not appear to have overcommitted himself in the initial cavalry charge as Gloucester had done, and even managed to rally a substantial following of fellow noblemen with whom he retreated to the apparent safety of Bothwell Castle.[121] The circumstances of Pembroke's escape are disputed in the surviving sources. The Lanercost chronicler has him escaping 'on foot...with the fugitive Welsh', but according to Barbour he fled with the king, having been appointed – like Sir Giles – to bodily protect Edward on the battlefield.[122] Despenser and Beaumont likely escaped alongside the king as well, although the Lanercost chronicler is in no doubt that they did so 'to their perpetual shame'.[123]

Not all of the English sought to flee the field when the cohesion of the army began to collapse. Sir Marmaduke Tweng – who, despite his exotic-sounding name and even more exotic-looking heraldry featuring three green popinjays (parrots), was from Yorkshire – was a veteran of several earlier campaigns and engagements, including the battles of Stirling Bridge in 1297 and Falkirk in 1298.[124] Tweng apparently recognized the danger in trying to escape southwards across the Bannock Burn. He must also have been too far south on the battlefield to reliably make for the castle. Instead, he resolved to hide himself out of the way of the potentially vengeful Scots until he saw King Robert himself pass by. Tweng then presented himself to the king and surrendered himself into Bruce custody. As it happened, Tweng's mother had been Lucy Bruce, a descendant of Bruce's own ancestor and namesake, Robert Bruce, first lord of Annandale (d. 1142). He may well have gambled that his status as Bruce's kinsman would afford him special treatment from the king, and if so, he was to be proven absolutely correct. Bruce invited Tweng to reside for a time with the royal household, gave him gifts, and eventually sent him home to England 'Arayit weile but ransoun fre'.[125] Tweng was certainly at liberty again by 4 January 1315, when the old warrior was once again dispatched to the border – alongside several other barons – in anticipation of further Scottish raiding.[126]

Similarly courteous treatment was given to Sir Ralph Monthermer, a knight from County Durham.[127] Bruce's generosity towards Monthermer is less obviously explicable – they do not seem to have been kinsmen – but their friendship may have dated to Bruce's time in English allegiance from 1302 to 1306. John of Fordun credits 'the earl of Gloucester' with having warned Bruce of an English plan to arrest him in 1306.[128] Monthermer used this style in right of his wife Joan of Acre, Edward II's aunt, from 1297 until Joan's death in 1307, which has generally been taken to mean that he was the man about whom Fordun was writing. If Monthermer had assisted Bruce in evading capture, his release in 1314 may be seen as a form of compensation for this valuable service. As the victorious Scots tore through the abandoned English camp, plundering – as Barbour tells us – 'silver gold clathis and armyng/With veschall [i.e., tableware]' – they also found a Carmelite monk named Robert Baston.[129] Baston had been brought north by King Edward himself with the intention of witnessing Edward's anticipated victory, but now found himself swept up in the ruin of the English king's army. When eventually brought before King Robert, the hapless Baston was apparently informed that he could buy his freedom by composing his promised poem, now celebrating Bruce's victory over Edward instead.[130]

While his subjects were scattering, drowning, or bargaining for their lives, Edward II was engaged in a frantic flight of his own. The English king appears to have initially withdrawn northwards in the direction of Stirling Castle, but either recognized the inherent risk in this or was warned off by the garrison (perhaps the last service Mowbray provided to Edward before his submission to Bruce).[131] If Edward had taken shelter in the castle, it would surely have enabled the Scots to take him into custody, which was, after all, their primary goal in the first place. Even if the garrison initially refused to surrender the castle to Scots (perhaps arguing that the terms of the deal had technically been met by Edward's arrival on 23 June), there would be nothing to stop the Scots encircling the castle once again and starving out those inside. This would been made easier by the fact that the garrison's supplies were probably fairly tight even when Carrick had laid siege to the castle in late April or early May and would not be able to sustain the vast number of Englishmen who had come to the castle in the wake of the English defeat. Having crossed the Pelstream, Edward and his followers seem to have looped round behind the Scots, escaping down the western side of the battlefield across land that the Scots had abandoned in order to press their attack against the English in the carse. Edward was shadowed by Sir James Douglas and about sixty Scottish horsemen, too few to surround and overwhelm the king and his company, but certainly enough to harass any stragglers who fell behind. Barbour, who provides the numbers for Douglas's horsemen, plausibly suggests that Bruce was understandably cautious about allowing too many of his men to give chase to the English beyond the Bannock Burn or the Pelstream since the number of Englishmen who had escaped the field probably still outnumbered the Scottish army by some way.[132] Edward covered the nearly seventy miles from the battlefield to Dunbar within the day.[133] While Patrick Dunbar, earl of March – one of the complainants who had induced Edward to mount his campaign into Scotland in the first place – allowed the English king to take ship to safety in England, he afterwards submitted to King Robert, bringing most of the southeast under Bruce's control and further eroding what remained of English power in Scotland.[134]

This was undoubtedly the most remarkable victory of King Robert's career to date and would prove to be the most significant military success of his entire reign. He had accomplished something that no other Scottish monarch had before or since: defeating the king of England in open battle (albeit by stretching the definition of 'open battle'). This would add tremendous moral and diplomatic weight for the Bruce cause going forward, both domestically and internationally. Robert and Edward had contested the right to govern in Scotland on the battlefield, and God had selected Bruce as the victor. Bruce's 'native' opponents among the Scots, his English enemies, and potential Continental allies would have to take account of this in their future dealings with the king. There was also tremendous material reward for victory. Baston notes that, as a result of the booty taken and ransoms exchanged after Bannockburn, many Scots were 'enriched and exalted who at first had been lowly'.[135] The author of the *Vita* estimates the value of the English baggage train plundered by the Scots at a staggering £200,000.[136] The English chronicler Thomas Walsingham – writing later in the century – reports that King Robert 'generously distributed' ('*distribuit larga*') the booty taken among the ordinary soldiers. Barbour too claims that:

'So gret a riches thair thai fand
That mony man mychty wes maid
Off the riches that thai thar haid.'[137]

Yet there were also material limitations to Bruce's success. For all of the death and destruction wrought on the English army at Bannockburn, most of Edward's troops had escaped the battlefield. While they might be hesitant to return to military service in the near future, they remained a resource that Bruce could neither match nor eliminate. Moreover, the prisoners taken on the day of the battle seem to have been relatively few and low status compared to those who had been killed – such as Gloucester – and those who had escaped – like Hereford. Worst of all, King Edward himself had avoided capture, all but guaranteeing that the war would continue indefinitely. If this was truly to be Bruce's greatest military achievement, he would have to use it as leverage to further his wider political and diplomatic aims. This process would begin almost immediately after King Robert's victory became apparent.

*Chapter 7*

# 'Eftre the Gret Journé'

# The Aftermath of Bannockburn, June to October 1314

## Picking Up the Pieces: The Immediate Aftermath

By the afternoon of 24 June, with the fighting over and the English clearly routed, King Robert would likely have already begun to assess the extent of his success and started to plan how he could capitalize on it to consolidate his power. The first order of business was the slighting of Stirling Castle itself, which had duly surrendered to the Scots once the fighting was over. King Robert could afford neither the men nor the resources to hold a castle for long periods. Neither could he afford to allow the English to reoccupy them, since the castle would serve as a base from which the English could extend their influence across a given area. By slighting the castles that he took, King Robert was essentially denying the English an easy method of maintaining control in a region without diminishing his own power. According to Barbour, at Stirling the Scots undermined the walls and towers so that they collapsed 'Rycht till the ground'.[1] They may also have burned any of the wooden components of the castle's structure, as Douglas had reportedly done following the infamous 'Douglas Larder'.[2] The primary aim when slighting a castle was to neutralize the castle's military capacity, rather than demolishing it altogether, and the process may have been assisted by locals who might reuse materials taken from the castle.[3] King Robert's decision to slight Stirling demonstrates that Bannockburn did not radically change Scottish policy overnight.

How the bodies would have been disposed of is not entirely clear. In all likelihood, the Scots would have seen to their own dead, perhaps even ensuring they were returned to their families for burial. Both armies would have been organized largely along local lines, and so any casualties no doubt would have had friends from their home regions with an interest in seeing that their remains were respectfully treated.[4] Scottish losses were probably negligible anyway. Barbour notes the deaths of only three knights and a yeoman, though this can hardly be considered an exhaustive list.[5] The dead English lords might expect to enjoy a certain amount of respectful treatment from the victorious Scots. Although he notes that 200 pairs of red spurs were looted from the dead knights, Barbour also insists that King Robert was 'sumdele anoyit' ('somewhat saddened') when he learned of Gloucester's death.[6] Walsingham states that Bruce had the bodies of Gloucester and Clifford 'conveyed [to Berwick] free of charge, to be buried at the royal will', and Barbour claims that King Robert saw to it that other English lords were given a decent burial in a nearby 'haly place'.[7] Whether the Scottish army felt it was their responsibility to deal with the common English dead – or whether this was left to the locals to deal with once the army had looted the corpses and moved on – is uncertain. Barbour mentions the digging of 'gret pyttis' into which these bodies were buried.[8] The poet offers no indication where precisely these pits were dug, and no evidence of them has so far been found. It seems likely, however, that they would not be far from where the fighting had taken place, since whoever was responsible for these burials would be unlikely to drag the bodies a long distance simply to throw them into a mass grave. Pains would, no doubt, have been taken to ensure they were at least far enough from the streams so as to avoid tainting the water that the locals and their animals would have relied on in their daily lives.

There was also the matter of the prisoners taken. The garrison were likely protected by the terms of the deal and may thus have been allowed to return safely to England. The only member of the garrison we can name – the captain Sir Philip Mowbray – submitted to King Robert, however, and there may have been other Scots among the garrison who chose to expeditiously switch sides in the hopes of preserving their private interests within Scotland. We know from the *Vita* that there were some among the English political community who questioned whether Mowbray had not been colluding with the Scots all along, although if he had been, he would surely not have saved Edward from capture by turning him away – a point even the author of the *Vita* concedes.[9] Any Englishmen who had fled to the castle would not have been covered by the deal and would thus have become Bruce's prisoners. Other men would have surrendered themselves on the battlefield rather than fighting to the death or face having to flee desperately through the choking mud on the banks of the Bannock Burn. Some assessment of the value of the prisoners would thus have begun on the afternoon of 24 June as well. Becoming a prisoner was not the worst outcome for a soldier on a medieval battlefield, although it could be expensive since you would then have to buy back your freedom. Yet Walsingham notes that Bruce ensured that the prisoners taken at Bannockburn were 'so civilly treated, and so honourably guarded, that he inexpressibly converted the hearts of many into his love'.[10]

The extreme courtesy the Scots showed in dealing with their prisoners after Bannockburn should be understood as a deliberate policy decision by the Bruce regime designed to counteract the continued refusal of the English crown to recognize Robert's rights as king. Even as late as 1314, the 'official' English perspective on the struggle with Scotland was that it was a rebellion led by an unruly vassal of the English crown. As we have seen, Scotland was routinely described as the 'land' of Scotland rather than the 'kingdom' of Scotland, and Bruce was at best grudgingly acknowledged as formerly the earl of Carrick but never given the title 'king of Scots'.[11] While this might naturally engender similar ill-will on the part of the Bruce Scots, King Robert and his ministers wisely recognized that the most effective way to counter this was to behave in as civil a manner as possible. This served to undermine the English insistence that the Scots were merely rebellious subjects of the English crown while simultaneously reinforcing the moral rectitude of the Scottish cause to international onlookers – most importantly, the king of France and the pope. The Scots' general good treatment of their prisoners and the repatriation of Gloucester and Clifford's bodies all served to further this policy, in stark contrast to the brutality with which, for instance, King Robert's brothers Neil, Alexander, and Thomas had been met when captured by the English in 1306 and 1307.[12]

Aside from the prisoners taken on the battlefield, a significant number of Englishmen had been rallied by Humphrey de Bohun, earl of Hereford, whose kinsman, Henry, had been killed by King Robert on the first day of the battle. Among Hereford's following as he left Bannockburn, according to the Lanercost chronicler, were: Robert Umfraville, earl of Angus, and his kinsman Sir Ingram Umfraville, Sir John Seagrave, and Sir Anthony Lucy.[13] Humphrey led these men to Bothwell Castle in Lanarkshire, a little under thirty miles south-west of the battlefield. Bothwell was, at that point, held for the English by a Scot named Sir Walter Fitz Gilbert.[14] Walter's motivations for serving the English crown in 1314 are somewhat difficult to reconstruct. He appears to have previously been an adherent of the Stewarts, who were closely allied to Bruce throughout this period, and he would be associated with them after 1314 as well.[15] Whatever his reasons for remaining in English allegiance until 1314, Walter swiftly changed his mind when he heard about the outcome of the battle. Walter allowed the Englishmen into the castle, immediately took them prisoner, and sent word to Bruce informing him that the castle and the prisoners within were now his if he wanted them.[16]

The exact chronology is difficult to reconstruct – Barbour merely says 'syne' after Bannockburn – but surely within a matter of days, King Robert's brother Edward Bruce, earl of Carrick, arrived at Bothwell to receive Walter's submission, take possession of his prisoners, and begin the process of slighting Bothwell just as was done at Stirling. Walter was rewarded for his timely defection with the barony of Cadzow (now Hamilton) in Lanarkshire in March 1315.[17] The family, whose influence among the Scottish political community would increase considerably in the fifteenth century, later adopted the surname Hamilton, and the modern Dukes of Hamilton – who built Brodick Castle on the Isle of Arran – are descended from him. Once again, most of the prisoners taken at Bothwell would be exchanged for cash, but Hereford was important enough for Bruce to attempt something a little more audacious. Hereford was, after all, the lord constable of England. In light of his disastrous defeat at Bannockburn, King Edward could not afford to further alienate Hereford's large and highly militarized following by leaving the earl to languish in Scottish captivity for long.

While King Robert was at Stirling looking for ways to capitalize on his success, King Edward was at Berwick-upon-Tweed trying to mitigate the damage done by his defeat. Barbour claims that Edward had sailed from Dunbar to Bamburgh before making his way north to Berwick again, whereas the relevant English chroniclers are unanimous in stating that he sailed directly to Berwick.[18] Although he had suffered a shocking defeat at Bannockburn, the king remained in northern England to manage the situation there – and perhaps to postpone facing the inevitable backlash from his domestic opponents in response to his latest failure. Active royal leadership in the immediate aftermath of the battle may have been particularly vital, as Madicott has argued that civil administration in the north effectively collapsed for two years following Bannockburn.[19] On 27 June, King Edward wrote from Berwick to various royal officers around the kingdom and its dominions, informing them that 'Because our privy seal is far from us' ('*Quia privatum sigillum nostrum a nobis est elongatum*') they should have it proclaimed that no one should act on any mandate produced under the privy seal unless they had additional confirmation of its authority from the king.[20]

The privy seal was used for king's personal correspondence and usually held by the controller of the wardrobe.[21] The king's privy seal was thus a tremendously important object because, in an era before individuals signed documents in their own hand, it was used to authenticate all his private correspondence. Its loss therefore raised the very serious possibility that it might be used to promulgate inauthentic documents and have them accepted and acted upon by the king's agents and subjects. It was this eventuality that King Edward was so eager to prevent with his letter to the royal officers. Since he now lacked a privy seal of his own, King Edward was forced to borrow Queen Isabella's privy seal to authenticate the document. By July, acts were once again being produced under the king's own privy seal, which likely indicates that a new one had been made for him.[22] The reason the king's privy seal was far from him was because he had been forced to leave it behind in the camp when he abandoned the battlefield on 24 June. It was recovered by the Scots and eventually returned to King Edward in the custody of Sir Ralph Monthermer, according to Nicholas Trivet's continuer.[23] Ostensibly, this was a gesture of good will from Bruce, a reflection of their shared status as fellow sovereigns. It was another expression of the Bruce regime's policy of seizing any opportunity it could to emphasize the parity of the two kingdoms, and of the two kings in particular. However, there was also surely a veiled rebuke behind Bruce's generosity in returning King Edward's seal. As well as demonstrating his benevolence towards a fellow monarch, it also served as a stinging reminder of the humiliating position into which Bruce's victory at Bannockburn had placed Edward II.

## Making the Best of a Bad Situation: Defending the North and Dealing with Prisoners

7 July was the Feast of the Translation of St Thomas Becket. Bruce probably commemorated the feast annually anyway. But in 1314, he no doubt utilized this event to connect the intercession of St Thomas to his recent victory at Bannockburn. He had, after all, invoked St Thomas by name on the morning of 24 June according to Abbot Bernard's chronicle.[24] Edward had visited St Thomas's shrine at Canterbury Cathedral ahead of the battle, presumably to seek

St Thomas's intercession as well, but it is unclear how – or if – he commemorated the feast in the wake of Bannockburn. Perhaps a show of contrition may have been in order, but this is necessarily speculative.

The English king may have had less-spiritual priorities in July 1314. As early as 30 June, Edward had summoned no fewer than 362 lords to muster at Newcastle by the middle of August in a desperate, and ultimately futile, attempt to bolster the morale of Edward's northern subjects in the wake of this latest military blunder.[25] The cumulative impact of repeated humiliations in war during the 1310s and 1320s were probably more significant than any one defeat.[26] Yet the lasting psychological impact of Bannockburn in particular is shown in the almost euphemistic way Le Bel refers to the battle in his work, despite the fact he was probably writing in the 1350s.[27] The size of the English army at Bannockburn increased the impact of the defeat on the whole English community as veterans returned to their home regions, bringing with them first-hand accounts of the disaster.[28] King Edward would experience difficulty in recruiting troops for the remainder of his reign. The army he led into Scotland in 1319 has been estimated at around 10,000 infantry and 400 to 500 cavalry, about half the size of the English force at Bannockburn.[29] The army he raised for his final invasion of Scotland in 1322 has been estimated at 12,000 from county levies, 6,800 from towns, and a further 2,000 raised separately in Cumberland and Westmoreland, pushing numbers back towards Bannockburn levels. This reflected the dramatic removal of Lancaster as a focus of political dissent, though it would have no more success on campaign than Edward's earlier forces.[30]

On 12 July, Dougal Macdowell was dispatched by the sheriff of Cumberland – almost certainly Andrew Harclay, though no name is given in the surviving document – from Carlisle to York to appraise King Edward of the situation along England's western border.[31] Macdowell was a Scot, but as a representative of one of the leading kindreds of Galloway (a lordship formerly controlled by Bruce's rivals, the Balliols), he was a staunch opponent of King Robert. In fact, he is even credited by the Lanercost chronicler with having captured King Robert's brothers Alexander and Thomas in 1307.[32] Macdowell was to report that the Scots were expected to enter England via the West March on Tuesday 14 July and assault Carlisle with 'ladders and other engines, as he [the sheriff] knows by certain spies'. This serves as a potent reminder of the importance that intelligence played in the border conflicts of the fourteenth century, a fact that is reflected in Barbour's account of the war as well.[33] Macdowell was also told to warn King Edward that if the Scots did not besiege Carlisle 'they intend to approach the king, wherever he may be'. This would suggest that the Scots still harboured hopes of capturing King Edward even though he had escaped them at Bannockburn. This was an understandable ambition given that the capture of King Edward would almost certainly guarantee a swift end to the war and formal recognition of Bruce's rights as king by the English royal administration. At an uncertain point in July, Harclay (this time named in the document and identified as sheriff) informed the king through John de Halton, bishop of Carlisle, that the Scots were attacking Cumberland 'by day and night' and warned the king that the funds being raised by the local baillies were 'insufficient to pay his forces'.[34]

There is no evidence that the anticipated 14 July assault on Carlisle took place. Possibly the intelligence Harclay had received was incorrect, or possibly the Scots altered their plans on realizing their intentions had become known to the English. However, as we shall explore in more detail, in early August the Scots launched a destructive *chevauchée* through Northumberland, County Durham, North Yorkshire, and Cumbria. Harclay and his men would play a part in resisting the Scots' progress through northern England in August, although they do not appear to have enjoyed much success in doing so. Carlisle would then suffer a sustained Scottish assault in July 1315.[35] The successful defence of the town is commemorated in the illuminated initial at the top of a charter produced in 1316, and this does indeed show the Scots utilizing 'ladders and other engines' just as the sheriff's spies had predicted in 1314. The situation along the border was already rough before Bannockburn, but Bruce's victory only seems to have made matters worse.

By 18 July, King Edward had moved south to York but was still dealing with the fallout from Bannockburn. To that end, he paid £288 to Sir William d'Argentan, nephew and heir of the Sir Giles d'Argentan who had recently been killed at Bannockburn, in payment of the crown's outstanding debts to Sir Giles. This substantial sum was granted to help Sir William 'defray his uncle's debts and discharge his soul', indicating that the payment was a direct consequence of the battle. It is also notable that the grant was ratified 'under the Queen's privy seal, his own not being at hand', indicating that King Edward had not yet received his privy seal back from King Robert, nor had he had a new one made.[36] As we saw in the first chapter, Sir Giles had been a prisoner at Salonika in October 1313, having been captured while on crusade in the eastern Mediterranean. However, Edward had personally written to the emperor, Andronikos II, at Constantinople to arrange Sir Giles's ransom. According to three separate sources – the *Vita*, the *Scalacronica*, and Barbour's *Bruce* – Sir Giles had 'the king's rein' at Bannockburn.[37] This meant that it was his job to ride alongside the king, ready to seize the reins of the king's horse and lead him to safety if things began to go wrong. It seems likely then that King Edward had arranged Sir Giles's release from captivity specially so Sir Giles could serve as the king's bodyguard at Bannockburn. Indeed, according to Gray and Barbour, Sir Giles had sacrificed his life while protecting the king's retreat.[38] In these circumstances, it is perhaps no wonder that Edward was so generous in his recompense of Sir Giles's relatives after the battle.

As well as dispensing patronage to Sir Giles's bereaved kinsman King Edward was by now anticipating the exchange of prisoners held by the English crown since 1306 for those captured by the Scottish crown as a result of the battle. Thus, Edward ordered the following to be brought to him at York: Robert Wishart, bishop of Glasgow; Elizabeth de Burgh, styled 'wife of Robert Bruce'; Donald, earl of Mar; 'and other Scots in England'. Similarly, he instructed the prior of Sixhills in Lincolnshire 'to deliver Cristiana sister of Robert de Brus, widow of Cristophor [sic] de Seton, to the sheriff of Lincoln to be brought to him [i.e., Edward] at York.'[39] Elizabeth, Cristiana (referred to as Christian elsewhere in this book), and Bishop Wishart, along with King Robert's daughter from his first marriage, Marjory, would eventually be exchanged for Humphrey de Bohun, earl of Hereford, who as noted above had been taken prisoner by the Scots in the immediate aftermath of Bannockburn.

Donald 'of Mar' was Bruce's nephew, probably through an older sister whose exact identity is otherwise lost to us but also through the king's first wife, Isabella of Mar (sister of Donald's father, Gartnait). Like his aunts Christian and Elizabeth and his cousin Marjory, he had been taken prisoner by the English soon after King Robert's inauguration in 1306, when Donald was still a minor.[40] He effectively grew up in the household of Edward II and seems to have enjoyed the English king's friendship and patronage. He received a respectable allowance of 15d. per day for his service in the English king's household from 8 July 1312 until 31 January 1313, totalling a sum of £13.[41] Thus, Donald made it only as far north as Newcastle-upon-Tyne before deciding to remain in England, where he continued to receive the favour of King Edward.[42] His decision may already have been known to King Edward by the end of the month, since on 26 July the king instructed the steward of his household to accompany *Douenaldus de Mar* to Westminster the following Monday (29 July) for discussions with the royal council.[43] In November 1319, Edward granted the manor of Long Bennington in Lincolnshire to Donald 'that he may remain more becomingly in the king's service'.[44]

In fact, Donald would not ultimately return to Scotland until 1327, and he did so specifically to seek his uncle's help in restoring Edward II to the English throne following his deposition by his queen Isabella of France. King Robert appears to have warmly welcomed Donald back into the fold, probably not least because as a nephew of the king, Donald had a claim to the Scottish kingship and thus served to bolster the still-fragile Bruce line of succession.[45] Donald even served as guardian of Scotland for a brief period in 1332, although continuing suspicions of the earl's loyalties are emphasized by Scottish sources as a reason for the earl's defeat and death at the Battle of Dupplin Moor in that year.[46] Even if Mar would not return to Scotland in 1314, the promise of the release of the royal women after eight years in English captivity was a major success for King Robert, since it made settling the dynastic uncertainty that had plagued the Bruce regime that much more likely.

Further prisoner-related business was conducted on 22 July, when King Edward learned that Sir Ingram Umfraville was *en pleine vie* (i.e., still alive) but a prisoner of the Scots, having been captured at the battle. Two days later, Edward issued protections and safe conducts for Ingram's brother William and John and Simon de Gourlay for a proposed visit to France 'in quest of money for the ransom of Sir Ingram Umfraville, a prisoner with the Scots'.[47] It may well have been the trio of William, John, and Simon who brought news of Umfraville's survival to the king, and the issuing of the safe conducts was likely the result of discussions about how the English crown could assist in Umfraville's release. As previously noted, Umfraville was a cousin of the Umfraville earls of Angus, and through his mother or grandmother had a strong claim to part of the baronies of Redcastle in Angus and Urr near Kirkcudbright. However, these female relatives were Balliols, and this naturally made Umfraville an enemy of the Bruces. Indeed, the arms Umfraville adopted and would likely have worn at Bannockburn were those of the Balliols of Redcastle, differentiated with a blue label.[48] He had already had quite an active career before Bruce became king in 1306. He may have been already considered an adult by 1279, making him Bruce's senior by a good ten or fifteen years.[49] He had served as an auditor for the Balliols during the Great Cause, supporting their claim against the Bruces, and had briefly replaced Bruce as joint-guardian (alongside another of Umfraville's kinsmen John Comyn).[50] Following Bruce's inauguration as king in 1306, Umfraville emerged as an active opponent of King Robert in south-west Scotland.

Barbour places Umfraville in close proximity to King Edward in his account of the Battle of Bannockburn. On the second day, Barbour has Umfraville sagely suggest that the English use a feigned retreat to lure the Scots into breaking formation, only for this advice to be rejected by the impetuous king. Shortly afterwards, when the Scots kneel in prayer ahead of the fighting, King Edward mistakenly assumes they are asking for mercy. Barbour has Umfraville correct the king that the Scots are merely seeking mercy from God, apparently for the English blood they are about to spill.[51] As we have seen in the previous chapter, Edward's personal household came under a lot of pressure on the battlefield at Bannockburn, with several of them being slain or captured and Edward himself having a horse killed under him. Thus, if Umfraville was physically close to King Edward on the battlefield, it would certainly explain the initial confusion over Umfraville's fate and the king's assumption that Umfraville had probably been killed protecting Edward's retreat.

Despite William and the Gourlays' planned trip to France to raise money for Umfraville's release, Umfraville ultimately submitted to King Robert, either before or shortly after he was ransomed.[52] This appears to have been in return for the half of the barony of Redcastle that Umfraville had a claim to through his mother or grandmother.[53] Bruce's recognition of Umfraville's rights did not necessarily reflect a warming of relations between the two men, and Umfraville – like many former Balliol and Comyn adherents – seems to have struggled to secure further royal patronage after his submission. Umfraville does appear – as 'Ingelramus de Umfreuile' – among the barons named in the so-called Declaration of Arbroath in 1320.[54] However, as with many of those named in that document, his presence may be as much a signal of the Bruce regime's continued suspicion of his motives as a sign of his closeness with the royal administration. Indeed, by January 1321, Umfraville was back in England, his time in Scotland conveniently excused as a period of imprisonment.[55] Barbour presents Umfraville's return to England as being a principled response to his objections to the treatment of Sir David Brechin, who had been executed for knowing about a conspiracy to overthrow King Robert but not reporting it, even though he had apparently not been actively involved in the plot.[56] However, this is likely another curious instance of Barbour presenting Umfraville's actions in the most favourable light. More likely, Umfraville had fled Scotland because he had been implicated in the conspiracy himself.[57] Barbour also credits Umfraville with advising Edward to make the thirteen-year truce that was agreed to between Scotland and England in 1323, but in this Barbour is surely mistaken, since Umfraville disappears from the written record in February 1321 and almost certainly died in that year.[58]

On 28 July, still at York, King Edward granted the manor of Aylsham ('Eylesham') in Norfolk to Sir Richard Lovel as surety for the whopping sum of £96, 16s. 8d. owed by the crown to Lovel for wages for him and his men and for 'his eleven chargers lost in the Scottish war'.[59] The eleven horses in question might have either been killed or taken as booty by the Scots at Bannockburn, although this may represent losses incurred across several years of service in Scotland.[60] Lovel himself was apparently captured in the fighting (or in the immediate aftermath), since on 21 November 1314 Sir John Soules, a cousin of Lovel's Scottish wife, Muriella, received a safe conduct from the English crown to travel to Scotland to arrange Lovel's release.[61] Probably then the payment of July 1314 was intended by Edward to alleviate the financial burden that Lovel's ransom would inevitably place on his kin. As the daughter of a former guardian of Scotland John Soules, Muriella had strong claims to several Scottish estates, which likely influenced Lovel's willingness to participate in the war of 1314. He had traded Muriella's claim on the manor of Old Roxburgh to the English crown in return for Bradninch in Devon, as part of Edward II's preparations for the summer campaign.[62] But had King Edward succeeded in overwhelming the Bruce administration in 1314, Lovel might have been able to assert his control over Muriella's other Scottish estates.

Aylsham had come into royal hands only recently due to the death of King Edward's nephew, Gilbert de Clare, earl of Gloucester, at Bannockburn. The grant of July 1314 therefore demonstrates that Edward was already using lands belonging to those killed at Bannockburn to relieve the financial burdens that the defeat had placed upon the English crown. On its own, this serves as an illustration of Edward's adaptability and shrewdness, traits that he is often said to be lacking in popular histories of his reign. However, in December 1314, Lovel would receive a further 295 marks from the king, this time to be taken from fines enforced on unnamed criminals from Bristol. Once again, this was said to be 'for the wages of his knights and squires and for restitution of his horses lost in the Scottish war'. But the later grant adds the detail that, in the intervening months, Aylsham had been regranted to David Strathbogie, earl of Atholl, forcing Edward to find another means of compensating for his losses.[63] Atholl had of course betrayed Bruce on the night of 23 June, attacking the Scottish supply camp at Cambuskenneth Abbey while the two armies were encamped ahead of the second day of fighting at Bannockburn. The earl had been in talks with the English crown from at least January, but his decision to openly switch sides in June cost him dearly in material terms. Bruce's victory at Bannockburn cut Atholl off from his Scottish possessions, including his earldom. To ensure the earl's continued support – and to repay him for this considerable sacrifice – it is perhaps unsurprising that Edward was willing to transfer lands from a minor lord such as Lovel. However, it also illustrates the considerable pressure Edward was under to balance the various interests of those who had suffered as a result of the defeat at Bannockburn, highlighting the intense strain the defeat had placed upon King Edward's relationship with his subjects.

The following day, Edward pardoned Sir James de Perriers a fine of 100 marks he owed to the crown for having married Ela Audley, widow of Sir Griffith de la Pole, without royal permission. The reason Edward gave for this apparently random act of generosity was that Perriers 'has been since made prisoner in Scotland and ransomed'.[64] The document does not explicitly link Perriers capture to Bannockburn, but the timing is suggestive. Given that he appears to have been a relatively low-value prisoner, his ransom seems to have been arranged quite quickly. According to the contemporary Lanercost chronicler, 'From day-to-day sundry prisoners were released from the hands of the Scots, but only through very heavy pecuniary ransoms'.[65] It would appear Perriers's pardon represents an effort by the crown to alleviate some of the financial burden the ransom placed on Perriers and his family. This, coupled with the other examples examined above, illustrates the point that the crown acknowledged a degree of responsibility for the predicament its hapless subjects found themselves in as a result of the disaster at Bannockburn.

The most serious business of 29 July was the summoning of parliament, which was to meet at York on 9 September specifically to discuss matters relating to Scotland.[66] This was no doubt a reluctant decision, since this would inevitably be a forum in which the king would have to face the music from his domestic enemies over his defeat at Bannockburn. On 29 September, at the York parliament, Aymer de Valence, earl of Pembroke, quitclaimed to Lancaster all his rights in Thorpe Waterville in Northamptonshire and New Temple in London. Then on 6 October, Pembroke and Lancaster drew up an indenture by which Pembroke accepted compensation from Lancaster for these disputed estates. This was an early indication that the king's enemies intended to exploit the recent defeat at Bannockburn to settle personal scores with the king's allies.[67] One small ray of hope of King Edward came on 30 July, two days after he had summoned the parliament, when one Nicholas Bradley, thanks to the intercession of John Mauleverer, was permitted to return to the king's peace after a stint in service to the Scots in return for participating in the future defence of the Marches.[68] Apparently not everyone who could do so treated King Robert's victory as a signal to ingratiate themselves with the Bruce regime.

This was, however, a minor blip in a period otherwise dominated by less encouraging royal business. On 2 August, still at York, Edward took a break from dealing with the ongoing need to alleviate the financial pressures on those captured at Bannockburn and instead sought to resolve issues arising from the death of another of his subjects in the battle. Thus, the English king granted Nicholas de la Beche and Hugh Audley 'the Younger' the lands of Edmund Comyn of Kilbride. Edmund Comyn was a distant cousin of John Comyn, lord of Badenoch, who Bruce had killed at Greyfriars Kirk in Dumfries in February 1306 shortly before becoming king. Nicholas was also to have the right to marry off the 8-year-old Euphemia, the elder of Edmund's two daughters (who were also his co-heirs), while Hugh was to have that of Edmund's younger daughter, the 2-year-old Mary.[69] It was normal practice in a case where an individual had only female heirs for their property to be shared among the heiresses rather than simply passing to the eldest daughter (as would have been the case if there had been a son to inherit). Typically, the property would not be shared evenly, with the eldest daughter receiving the most and then the younger daughters receiving progressively less.

There is evidence of considerable controversy over the settlement of the late Edmund Comyn's inheritance, however. On 24 October ('Thursday before All Saints' Day'), Edmund's widow Mary was tried by a jury of twelve at Newcastle-upon-Tyne, having been accused of having 'maliciously removed' her eldest daughter, Euphemia, against the king's wishes.[70] Although Mary was absolved of any wrongdoing, the fact that such a legal hearing was necessary may indicate that Mary had sought to use physical possession of her eldest daughter to secure some form of concession to ensure her own welfare in the wake of her husband's death. A further inquest on 5 October found that one of the late Edmund's tenants had apparently tried to cheat the Comyn sisters over on the rent of lands in Suffolk that he had previously held from their father in dubious legality. On the same day as the verdict was passed concerning Mary's supposed abduction of her daughter, Edward issued instructions to his royal officers to ensure the widow received her 'terce' (i.e., the third of the revenues she was owed as a widow) from lands in Suffolk, Hertfordshire, and Northumberland.

This did not settle Mary's problems, however. In 1316, Mary would request safe conduct to travel to Scotland, but in April 1318 King Edward had come to believe that she had entered King Robert's peace, resulting in the English king regranting Mary's English lands to William de la Beche.[71] This William was apparently the son and heir of the Nicholas who had been given wardship of Mary's daughter Euphemia in 1314, since by 1318 William was married to Euphemia.[72] In the same year, Mary wrote to the king explaining that she had remained in Scotland because Gilbert Middleton, one of Edward's rapacious household knights, had exploited her absence to devastate her property. She pleaded with King Edward to let her return, apparently 'in fear for her life' if she remained in Scotland. Mary clearly got no joy from Edward II, because as late as October 1331 she dispatched an almost identical missive to his son Edward III, who finally gave her permission to return to England in 1333 – the year in which her son-in-law William died – and even provided her with a living from her terce lands again.[73] This vividly demonstrates the potential difficulties facing the female relatives of those who had been killed in the fighting at Bannockburn.

## 'He Dared Not Leave His Post for the Scottish Attacks by Day and Night': Scottish Retaliation and Mounting Pressure on the English Administration

Even as Edward was trying to settle the issue of Edmund Comyn's inheritance, the Scots were militarily pressing the advantage their recent victory at Bannockburn had given them. The second Scottish *chevauchée* of 1314 began around 1 August, causing two English tax collectors named Richard and Robert to flee from Morpeth in Northumberland shortly before a Scottish force descended on the town. According to the two officials, the leaders of the Scottish army were King Robert's younger brother, Edward, and King Robert's nephew Thomas Randolph, earl of Moray.[74] As we have seen, these were certainly two of King Robert's most prominent lieutenants. Both had played a leading role in Scottish raids into northern England before (and indeed after) Bannockburn, and they had of course led the two main divisions of the Scottish army at the recent battle. The contemporary Lanercost chronicler reports the Scottish leaders as being Edward Bruce, Sir James Douglas, and John Soules.[75] Douglas was – like Edward Bruce and Randolph – an experienced and capable war leader. He had been knighted by King Robert on the morning of 24 June, and in the years after Bannockburn would become an influential member of King Robert's court. His presence as a leader of the Scottish army is therefore not hard to reconcile with what we know about the makeup of the Bruce party at this time.

John Soules stands out as somewhat unusual. He and his elder brother, William, were the sons of Margaret Comyn, a kinswoman of Bruce's great rivals, and thus were initially opposed to Bruce. The brothers do appear to have reconciled themselves to Bruce as a result of Bannockburn and must have done so remarkably quickly if one of them played a leading role in the first-known Scottish raid across the border following the battle. Dr McNamee and Prof. Duncan have both reasonably proposed that it was in fact William, not John, who played a senior role in the 1314 raid.[76] William was the lord of Liddesdale, a significant border lordship in the Middle March, which gave it an important strategic role in the defence of the realm. This fact may have been what enabled the Soules brothers to ensure their rapid rehabilitation with the Bruce regime. Liddesdale could even have played a role in the *chevauchée* of 1314, with McNamee suggesting that this was the route by which the Scots ultimately recrossed the border once the raid was over.[77]

According to the Lanercost chronicler, the Scots entered England 'by way of Berwick' and 'devastated almost all Northumberland with fire'. They then progressed south into County Durham, where the locals bought to a truce to save themselves from a similar fate. The Scots advanced as far south as Richmond without meeting any resistance, which the Lanercost chronicler attributes to the fact that 'nearly all men fled to the south or hid themselves in the woods, except those who took refuge in the castles'. From Richmond, which they did not attack, the Scots swept north-westward again via Swaledale and over the Pennines.[78] There, on 4 August, they were finally confronted by Andrew Harclay, sheriff of Cumberland, and his men from the Carlisle garrison. Harclay was a minor knight from north-west England who, like many men in a similar position, had seized upon the Scottish wars as an opportunity for social and financial aggrandizement.[79] Having presumably had word of the Scottish movements in the east, Harclay and his men issued forth from Carlisle in order to offer battle to the Scots. This would become the standard policy for English border defence in the fourteenth century: deploy one or more of the local garrisons to force the Scots into battle, with the aim of defeating and scattering the raiders.[80] More often than not, the Scots would simply avoid battle and slip back across the border, but if they were forced to do so before they had caused too much mayhem, then this could still be considered a success for the policy as a whole.

This does not, however, appear to have been the case in 1314, when the Scots not only met the English in the field but also seem to have had the better of the ensuing engagement. We have no direct evidence of the outcome of this encounter, but the king's receiver of victuals at Carlisle was later forced to request the replacement of twenty-two horses lost on 4 August, losses that hardly speak to a resounding victory.[81] Moreover, the Scots subsequently burned Brough, Appleby, and Kirkoswald, threatened Penrith, and destroyed a watermill at Salkeld, all targets that suggest they were able to continue their progress westwards after the confrontation at Stainmore. Shortly after the Scots returned home, the community of Copeland in southern Cumbria paid 600 marks to prevent their return before the following midsummer.[82]

This first major raid into England following the Scottish victory at Bannockburn serves as an early illustration of the ways in which victory both changed and did not change subsequent Scottish raiding practices. The overall strategy did not alter significantly after 1314. The Bruce Scots had already been terrorizing the communities of northern England from as early as 1307, and the extraction of blackmail from these communities had always been a major aim of these attacks. Similarly, the Bruce Scots had long specialized in highly mobile, inventive, and unpredictable raiding patterns to make it as difficult as possible to plan a defence against them. What had noticeably changed was the extent and ambition of the raids the Scots were carrying out. Richmond is in

North Yorkshire, further south than the Bruce Scots had penetrated before, and raids this far south (and further) would become increasingly common in the years that followed. This, in turn, is reflective of the major morale boost that Bannockburn had given to the Bruce Scots. The more confident and ambitious Scottish raiding became after Bannockburn, the less faith the English northern communities would have in the ability of their king to defend them. In theory, this would increase the pressure on Edward II to accept a peace deal. However, Dr Alistair Macdonald has argued convincingly that the physical separation of these northern communities and the English administration, based as it was primarily in the south, limited the effectiveness of raiding as a tool for forcing the English crown to the negotiating table.[83] Nevertheless, on 10 August, King Edward issued a safe conduct for the servants of the abbot of Newminster to move the abbey's livestock south 'on account of the inroads of the Scots' into Northumberland, powerfully illustrating the pressure the Bruce Scots were once again putting on the communities of northern England.[84]

## 'To See How and in What Way Agreement and Friendship Could Be Between Us': Edward's Return South and Diplomatic Discussions

On the same day as Edward allowed the abbot of Newminster to send his animals out of harm's way, he also appointed Aymer de Valence, earl of Pembroke, 'captain and guardian' ('*capitaneum et custodem*') of the region between the Trent and the Tweed. Pembroke's primary responsibility was 'to restrain the Scots, our enemies and rebels' ('*ad refraenandam Scotorum, inimicorum et rebellium nostrorum*').[85] The choice of Pembroke should hardly be surprising. He had, after all, served as lieutenant of the king while his army had been mustering earlier in the year and had served Edward faithfully – if unspectacularly – on the battlefield at Bannockburn.[86] The timing of this appointment is perhaps indicative of the fact that Edward was planning to focus on the parliament he had summoned to meet at York in September, and that he therefore wished to delegate the management of military matters to Pembroke. King Edward would surely expect that the main business of this assembly would revolve around the summer's military failure. He had delayed facing his leading subjects in 1311 due to concerns about the Ordinances. He can hardly have cherished the prospect of answering to his

'Eftre the Gret Journé'   181

domestic opponents following outright military defeat at Bannockburn. He could not put it off forever, however, and the scope of the disaster that he had suffered in 1314 may have made it vital for him to begin to repair the damage done to his domestic reputation sooner rather than later.

On 13 August, the mayor, bailiffs, and community of Berwick-upon-Tweed wrote to King Edward.[87] Although much of the later part of the letter is damaged and illegible, what survives offers a fascinating insight into the situation along the border in the months immediately after Bannockburn. The letter opens on a strikingly positive note. The community thanks Edward for 'taking every precaution for the safety of the town'. This is broadly confirmed by the Lanercost chronicler and the safe conduct issued to the abbot of Newminster's servants, both of which suggest Northumberland, and not Berwick, took the brunt of the Scottish *chevauchée* in 1314. However, they quickly go on to report that 'Since his late departure they have not suffered so much from the Scottish enemy as from some people of Northumberland'. The letter then rehearses a shockingly long list of apparently local people who had recently been tried and executed for plotting 'to betray and sell the town to the enemy [i.e., the Scots]'. The document also names a substantial group of men who were now harassing the king's officers and had reportedly 'sworn to kill any Berwick man found in Northumberland' in revenge for the executions. This provides a valuable insight into how divided the community at Berwick was becoming, and these divisions were in turn surely a symptom of how the town had become increasingly vulnerable as a result of the Scottish successes of 1314. As the last Scottish town left in English hands, the denizens must have recognized that the recovery of Berwick, which had already come under attack from the Bruce Scots in late 1312 and been saved only by the inopportune barking of a dog, would now be high among King Robert's priorities.[88] Many of them may have preferred to assist King Robert in speedily and bloodlessly retaking the town rather than risking a prolonged siege or assault. The tensions within the community at Berwick would only become more acute as time wore on and ultimately Berwick would fall to the Bruce Scots in 1318 precisely because of the assistance offered to them by a local burgess named Peter Spalding.[89]

On 16, King Edward granted the manors of Manfield ('Mannfeld') in North Yorkshire, Geddington ('Geytinton') in Northamptonshire, and Harwell ('Harewell') in Berkshire to Margaret, widow of John Comyn, 'for the support of herself and their son Adomar...as possessed by her late husband, slain in the king's service in Scotland'.[90] John Comyn was the son and heir of the John Comyn, lord of Badenoch, who Robert Bruce had killed in front of the high altar at Dumfries in February 1306. The younger John Comyn appears to have been a minor at the time of his father's death and was sent south by his mother, Joan de Valence, into the care of Sir John Weston, guardian of the royal children for the English crown and later chamberlain of Scotland on behalf of Edward II.[91] During John's absence from Scotland, his father's political networks were gradually unravelled by the Bruce Scots, denying the younger Comyn his father's former influence. Nevertheless, the younger John Comyn represented a potential focus of authority for the Balliol/Comyn Scots in opposition to the Bruce Scots. His great-uncle had been King John (Balliol) of Scotland, and through him he had a not-insignificant claim on the Scottish throne, especially while Balliol's own son, Edward, appears to have been more interested in consolidating his position within the English political community rather than pursuing any ambitions in Scotland.[92]

Even ignoring any potential claim on the kingship, the younger John Comyn could potentially command a considerable amount of loyalty from the Balliol/Comyn Scots simply by association with his famous father, who had effectively led the Balliol/Comyn cause following Balliol's forced abdication in 1296.[93] The younger Comyn's presence at Bannockburn suggests that he had at least some interest in reviving his family's fortunes in Scotland, even if a personal bid for the kingship still seemed remote. However, the younger John Comyn's death in the fighting dramatically curtailed any hopes for a Comyn revival. The young Adomar, likely named after his great-uncle Aymer (i.e., Adomar) de Valence, earl of Pembroke, again appears to have been a minor at the time. While the grant of August 1314 shows some effort to provide for the pair on the part of the English crown, Adomar would have no further impact on politics either north or south of the border because he died before November 1316, when his property was divided between his aunts.[94] The removal of effective Comyn-led resistance to Bruce power represented a marked boost to King Robert's prospects, and this should be understood as one of the secondary benefits of Bruce's victory at Bannockburn in 1314, at least in the short term.

By the beginning of September, the Scots were ready to start pushing for a diplomatic solution, capitalizing on whatever advantage they could get from their recent battlefield victory in any negotiations that took place. On 5 September, King Robert was at 'Faryngleghe' (possibly Fairnilee near Selkirk), where he issued a letter of credence to a friar named Ralph Chilton, who was due to travel south into England deliver an offer of peace talks to Edward II.[95] Bruce was, as was usually the case in his diplomatic correspondence, effusive in his tone. He insisted that 'the thing we desire most is that we may have complete agreement and friendship from you'. Brother Ralph was enjoined 'to see how and in what way agreement and friendship could be between us' and then report back to King Robert. We can infer some other details of the representations Chilton had been instructed to make based on Edward's response, made at an English parliament at York in September. Here, on 18 September, Edward issued safe conducts for a Scottish embassy composed of Sir Neil Campbell, Sir Roger Kirkpatrick, Sir Robert Keith, and Sir Gilbert Hay so that they could visit Durham on 20 October to discuss a prisoner exchange and, less hopefully, peace terms.[96]

The personnel of the Scottish embassy comprised a group of men close to King Robert himself, who could therefore no doubt be relied upon to faithfully represent the king's personal wishes in any negotiations. All four of them were likely present at Bannockburn and had probably remained close to the king throughout the battle. Campbell and Kirkpatrick had been Bruce adherents since before Robert had become king, while Hay had immediately supported Bruce's bid for power in 1306. Kirkpatrick has traditionally been directly associated with Bruce's killing of John Comyn, lord of Badenoch, in February 1306, the later Kirkpatrick motto 'I mak siccar' reputedly being in reference to Kirkpatrick having dealt the killing blow to Comyn.[97] The impression given by the Scottish embassy of 1314 is certainly of a group selected for their closeness with King Robert and thus their familiarity with his diplomatic priorities in the immediate aftermath of his victory at Bannockburn. The presence of Keith (and perhaps Hay too) was likely also intended to provide the additional endorsement of one (or two) of Scotland's highest-ranking officers of state, adding weight to the Scottish case. Dr Michael Penman has speculated that Campbell's presence may also indicate that negotiating the release of Bruce's sister Mary – who would marry Campbell at an uncertain date – from English captivity was high on the embassy's list of priorities.[98] However, the fact that Mary is not mentioned by name in any of the documents concerning the release of prisoners after Bannockburn, coupled with the fact that negotiations for her release appear to have been attempted in 1310 and 1312, may indicate that she had been released before Bannockburn.[99] Even if Mary was already at liberty by 1314, Penman is surely correct that the embassy had been instructed to focus on arranging a prisoner exchange, and in particular securing the release of the royal women as a means of alleviating the dynastic pressure on the Bruce regime.

Various matters relating to Scottish affairs were undertaken at the York parliament in September 1314, although the author of the *Vita* claims that actual discussion of how to proceed with the conflict was postponed due to concerns over the number of prisoners still in Scottish custody. The author adds that the most vocal expression of these anxieties came from the king's own sister Elizabeth, who was married to Humphrey de Bohun, earl of Hereford.[100] It was perhaps to allay his sister's fears somewhat that on 19 September – the day after he had approved the proposed Anglo-Scottish peace talks at Durham – that he instructed the keeper of the stores at Carlisle to dispatch 'a *toneu* of flour, and 5 *toneux* of wine' to Hereford while he remained in captivity. The writ described the earl as 'the king's brother and liege Sir Humphrey de Bohun earl of Hereford, a prisoner with the Scots enemies'.[101] Interestingly, the man who was to receive the goods from the keeper of the stores and deliver them to Earl Humphrey was John Walwayn, a long-standing crown servant and one of the individuals who has been proposed as the author of the *Vita*.[102] This might explain the *Vita*'s emphasis on Elizabeth's concerns at the York parliament. On 24 September, King Edward also gifted another tun of wine from the stores at Carlisle to the executors of Sir Robert Clifford, 'who is with God', as Edward put it.[103] Clifford had, of course, met his maker in the fighting at Bannockburn, and this gift no doubt served as an acknowledgment of the debt the English crown owed him for his sacrifice.

The only (surviving) indication that Edward still harboured military ambitions towards Scotland was his confirmation of John Macdougall as 'captain and admiral' ('*capitaneo et admirallo*') of the king's navy.[104] The fact that the fleet, which Edward had commanded to assemble at the same time as his earliest specific orders had gone out for the Bannockburn campaign in March 1314, had not apparently set off as expected meant that these naval resources remained intact for Edward to call upon when needed. It was no doubt with these that Macdougall was able to recover the Isle of Man in early 1315.[105] Nevertheless, defeat at Bannockburn had clearly placed Edward on the back foot, and in the months that remained of 1314, a series of events would unfold that serve to demonstrate the major benefits of victory at Bannockburn for the Bruce Scots.

*Chapter 8*

# 'King Robert Now Wes Wele at Hycht'

# The Benefits of Bannockburn, October to November 1314

## The Return of the Queen: The Prisoner Exchange

On 2 October 1314, King Edward was still at York. From here, he issued instructions that 'Robert [Wishart], Bishop of Glasgow, [Elizabeth de Burgh] the Countess of Carrick, wife of Robert Bruce, Donald [earl] of Mar, [Christian?] sister of Robert Bruce, and [Marjory] a certain daughter of Robert himself' were to be brought to Carlisle Castle, from which they would then be released as part of a prisoner exchange in return for Humphrey de Bohun, earl of Hereford.[1] Bishop Wishart had been one of the fiercest proponents of Scottish independence during the build-up to and in the early years of the conflict. As a member of the Scottish clergy, he was eager to ensure that the Scottish church maintained its ability to make direct representations to the pope, which would be compromised if Scotland ceased to be independent. He had served as a guardian following Alexander III's death in 1286, had publicly rebuked Edward I over his demand for recognition of English overlordship in 1291, and was still sufficiently a figure of suspicion for the English to be required to remove himself from Scotland for a time following the general Scottish surrender of 1304.[2]

Wishart also had a long association with the Bruces. His diocese encompassed both the Bruce earldom of Carrick (which Robert claimed through his mother, Marjory) and the Bruce lordship of Annandale, making him the main ecclesiastical figure within the Bruce family's sphere of influence. The bishop had supported the Bruce claim to the throne during the Great Cause from 1291 to 1292, and Dr Michael Penman credits Wishart with encouraging the future King Robert to join the initial Scottish rebellion against the English occupation in 1297.[3]

Certainly, he was instrumental in Bruce's early successes when he made his bid for power in 1306. Wishart absolved Bruce for killing his rival John Comyn (despite the killing happening in a church) in return for assurances that the new king would guarantee the Scottish clergy a say in the governance of the realm, leading to him being described by one contemporary English observer as 'the wicked bishop...his [i.e., Bruce's] chief adviser' at that time.[4] He even provided Bruce with enthronement robes supposedly kept hidden from the English when they invaded in 1296.[5] However, in early June Wishart was captured by the English and had remined in custody ever since. According to Barbour, he had gone blind during his captivity, and he would be dead within eighteen months of his return to Scotland.[6] Nevertheless, the release of his old ally (and probably friend) must have felt like a significant personal boost to King Robert.

Donald, earl of Mar, was, as noted in the previous chapter, the son of one of Bruce's sisters (whose name sadly has not survived to us) and Garnait, earl of Mar, the brother of Bruce's first wife, Isabella. Still a minor at the time of Bruce's inauguration as king in 1306, he was captured soon afterwards and was taken into the English royal household, even serving as a page to Edward II. Through this, Donald appears to have developed a preference for English aristocratic life, ultimately refusing to return to Scotland. He would choose not to return to Scotland until after Edward II had been deposed. Donald's decision in 1314 must have been a personal disappointment to King Robert, who might otherwise have included the young earl in his efforts to clarify the line of succession. Nevertheless, it did not apparently diminish his uncle's opinion of him, and Mar even served briefly as guardian of the realm for King David II before being killed at the Battle of Dupplin Moor in 1332.

The release of the royal women was arguably the most important short/medium-term benefit that victory at Bannockburn brought King Robert. Elizabeth was the most important of the prisoners released in the wake of Bannockburn, since as well as being countess of Carrick she was also queen of Scots – despite the unwillingness of the English scribe to style her as such. She was accompanied north by Sir Stephen Blount, who afterwards received £8 in compensation for two casks of wine, described as 'expenses of the Lady de Bruys coming as far as Carlisle towards Scotland in October this year'.[7] The marriage between Elizabeth and Robert had originally been arranged to consolidate long-standing Bruce political connections across the Irish Sea and to help reconcile Bruce with the English crown after several years of resisting English ambitions in Scotland. The significance of her return to Scotland in the aftermath of Bannockburn was that she gave an enormous boost to Bruce's ambition to establish a lasting dynasty. The couple had no children before she was captured in 1306, and so long as she remained a prisoner, Bruce had no hope of producing a legitimate heir to succeed him as king on his death. In the thirteen years between Elizabeth's release and her death, they would have at least two daughters – Margaret and Maud – and twin sons, John and David.[8] David would ultimately succeed his father as David II in 1329.

It is unclear whether Christian was older or younger than King Robert, though given that he likely had two other older sisters – Donald of Mar's mother and Isabella, later queen of Norway – it seems unlikely that his parents could have had three children before Robert was born in 1274.[9] She had certainly married before her brother became king in 1306. Her husband, Sir Christopher Seton, is credited by Barbour with saving King Robert from capture at the Battle of Methven in June 1306.[10] Seton was captured when Loch Doon Castle fell to the English later that year and was executed at Dumfries.[11] Christian had spent her captivity in the nunnery at Sixhills in Lincolnshire, where she received 3d. per day for her expenses.[12] Following her return to Scotland, Christian did not immediately remarry, unusual given the value a strategic marriage would have brought for the Bruce regime. There is no evidence of any breakdown in the relationship between King Robert and his sister, however, and at some point after her return he granted Christian the lordship of Garioch in the north-east to provide her with an independent income.[13]

Possibly Christian remained in mourning for her late husband, and as late as December 1324 she founded a chapel dedicated to the Holy Cross on the spot where he had been executed.[14] She did eventually remarry in 1326 to Sir Andrew Murray, who would serve as a particularly successful guardian during the Second War of Scottish Independence. Christian herself played an important role in that conflict, successfully defending Kildrummy Castle in Mar (ironically the castle from which Christian had fled before her capture at Tain in 1306) from a force led by David Strathbogie, earl of Atholl, in 1335. This was the son and namesake of the earl who had abandoned King Robert on the evening of 23 June, attacked the Scottish supply camp at Cambuskenneth, and withdrawn. Christian's stout defence of Kildrummy bought her husband valuable time to march an army north and defeat and kill Atholl at the Battle of Culblean.[15] She retained possession of Kildrummy even after Murray's death in 1338, and died in 1356, aged around 80.

Marjory was the only surviving child from King Robert's marriage to Isabella of Mar, and in 1314 she remained the king's only legitimate child. Marjory thus was technically Bruce's only direct heir. Probably born around 1296, she would have still been a child when captured in 1306, and due to her youth she was kept in custody at a nunnery in Watton in Norfolk.[16] She would still have only been a teenager on her release, but her return to Scotland enabled Bruce to clarify both the line of succession and also to secure another strategic marriage for one of his closest female relatives. In April 1315, at an assembly in Ayr, King Robert entailed the kingdom in the male line.[17] Strictly speaking, this moved Marjory further down the line of succession by privileging the king's male relatives. The reasoning behind this move was to increase the chances of an adult, experienced war leader becoming king in the event of Robert's death. This was the same fundamental principle that we identified at work in the Dundee parliament of October 1313, examined in the opening chapter. In both cases, the chief beneficiary had been the king's brother Edward Bruce. This arrangement would have seemed vital to a Scottish political community in the midst of a war that had dragged on now for almost twenty years and showed no sign of ending any time soon. If Bruce could not end the war with victory at Bannockburn, then he would at least use it to reassure his leading subjects that the Bruce regime offered their best hope for continued, effective resistance to English ambitions in Scotland.

Marjory's consent was, of course, required to ratify this arrangement, and her seal was the third to be attached to the document produced in 1315 (after her father's and her uncle's). Her absence from Scotland prior to 1314 had prevented the formal recognition of King Robert's preferred succession settlement, hence the awkward compromise he had pursued in October 1313. Following her release, he was now able to gain legal acknowledgement of the new succession plan. In both cases, ensuring that the arrangements were made in an assembly of the community of the realm secured their approval – at least notionally – of the new status quo. This is a typical example of Bruce's talent for wringing the maximum value out of political developments as they occurred. Moreover, shortly after the assembly at Ayr, Marjory married Walter, sixth high steward of Scotland.[18] Walter had been knighted by her father at Bannockburn, and their marriage cemented long-standing political connections between the Bruces and the Stewarts. The couple's only child – named Robert after his grandfather – would inherit the kingdom as Robert II in 1371, beginning 343 years of Stewart rule in Scotland and later Great Britain. Marjory, however, would be described as 'the lady Marjory of honourable memory' in December 1318, meaning her death had occurred at some point during the intervening period.[19]

Prisoner-related business would continue well into the following year, though none of it would be quite as significant as the release of the royal women. On 3 November, King Edward was at Ashbeach ('Assebethe') near Ramsey in Cambridgeshire. Here, he instructed royal officials at the exchequer to assist one of the king's sergeants-at-arms, Alan of Wallingford, in ransoming his son Robert, 'a prisoner with the Scots'.[20] The document does not state explicitly that Robert had been captured at Bannockburn, but the timing and the fact that his father at least was in direct service to the king is certainly suggestive. Simpkin has demonstrated that sergeants-at-arms were particularly active in this stage of the conflict, as the loss of castles in Scotland reduced their opportunities for serving in English garrisons.[21] Robert's ransom had apparently been set at £100, which seems extortionate for someone of relatively low social standing. Possibly the Scots felt that his connection to the English crown, however tenuous, meant they could demand such a high price for his return. If so, it appears they would be disappointed. The exchequer gave Wallingford £10 on 9 December, and a further £21 2s. 6d. on 4 November 1315. These were still substantial sums of money, but they fell far short of the overall total of Robert's ransom. Moreover, the date of the second payment implies that poor Robert was still imprisoned a year after Edward's original instruction to his officers of the exchequer had been issued.

On 20 November, various royal officers across the kingdom were enjoined to turn over their Scottish prisoners to Stephen Seagrave so that he could trade them for his father John, who had been one of those English lords taken at Bothwell Castle in the immediate aftermath of the battle. Among the Scots included in this exchange were Thomas Morham ('Morram'), Andrew Murray, and brothers David, Reginald, and Alexander Lindsay.[22] Morham was an East Lothian laird who had been a prisoner at the Tower of London since at least 1311.[23] Murray's father and namesake had played a crucial role in reviving Scottish resistance to the English in 1297 shortly before his death. The elder Murray had shown no obvious association with the Bruce faction, and it is unclear precisely when the younger Murray had been taken into English custody.[24] However, the young man could surely be expected to be grateful to his benefactor King Robert for securing his release, and Murray would be present at Bruce's first post-Bannockburn parliament at Cambuskenneth in November 1314.[25] The Lindsay brothers were the sons of Alexander Lindsay of Barnweill, of Crawford, and of the Byres, who had been a Bruce supporter even before the reign began.[26] They had apparently been captured when Kildrummy Castle fell to the English in late 1306.[27] The father had been released by the time of King Robert's first parliament in March 1309, when he was named in the barons' letter to King Philippe IV of France.[28] He does not seem to have lived to see his sons return to Scotland, but the family would prosper under the Bruce regime, with David – the eldest son – becoming a regular witness to royal *acta* after 1314.[29]

The post-Bannockburn prisoner exchange serves as a useful illustration of both the benefits *and* the limits of Bruce's victory in 1314. On the one hand, the release of the royal women enabled King Robert to further consolidate his political networks and cement his legacy. This latter point would have far-reaching consequences for the history of the fourteenth century and beyond. The extortion of ransoms from the families of those captured also seems to have ensured a steady flow of cash well into the following year, much of this likely going directly into the royal coffers. Yet, on the other hand, none of this brought the war closer to a conclusion. Bannockburn was thus primarily significant for the leverage it gave King Robert in reshaping the situation within Scotland to best suit his ambitions. A key element of Bruce's success was his ability to exploit every opportunity to its fullest potential, and this did not end at getting the maximum value from his captives.

## Diplomacy Is Never Just About One Thing: Peace Talks and Compensating the Soon-to-Be 'Disinherited'

While Bruce looked to secure the future of his dynasty, Edward was still not free from the business of dealing with prisoners taken at Bannockburn. On 4 October, the English king issued a safe conduct for Roger Comyn to enter Scotland to negotiate for the release of Gilbert 'of Glenkerne' (possibly the Gilbert Glencairnie who Bruce had besieged at Elgin in late 1307), and the same for Margaret 'of Brighbyn' to negotiate for the release of her husband, David.[30]

Then on 6 October, King Edward ratified a general truce between England and Scotland to last until the following spring.[31]

Edward was keen to present this truce as having been achieved through the intercession of King Philippe IV of France, 'our very dear father and friend' as Edward calls him in the documents confirming the truce. It is certainly plausible that Philippe had interceded on behalf of the Scots. Good relations with France would be – alongside cultivating papal support – one of the main priorities of the Scottish kingdom throughout the late medieval period. Indeed, the immediate precursor to hostilities in 1296 had been the conclusion of a Franco-Scottish defensive pact in 1295.[32] As early as July 1309, King Philippe had shown a willingness to style Bruce 'king of Scots' ('*regem Scotorum*') in his private correspondence with Edward II.[33] Philippe was the father of Edward's queen Isabella and thus Edward's father-in-law, a relationship that – in theory at least – gave Philippe a certain amount of influence in such matters. Yet Edward's emphasis of Philippe's role surely also served to obscure the fact that the English crown badly needed at least a temporary cessation of hostilities in the wake of Bruce's victory at Bannockburn. The *chevauchée* through the northern English counties that the Scots had mounted in August had proven that the Scots had been emboldened by their earlier success and intended to capitalize on it by increasing military activity along the border, damaging property, rustling cattle, and extorting cash from the already war-weary communities there. Even as Edward was arranging this truce, doubts lingered among his northern subjects over their king's ability to guarantee their safety, as would be powerfully demonstrated at Durham a few days later.

Meanwhile, on the same day as the truce was ratified, Edward commissioned an embassy headed by Sir John Botetourt to represent him in the upcoming peace talks with the Scots he had agreed to on 18 September.[34] Botetourt had been a faithful servant of the crown during the reign of King Edward I and had seen extensive service in the Scottish wars during that period. However, Botetourt's relationship with the crown declined after Edward II's accession in 1307. He became increasingly associated with the king's cousin Thomas, earl of Lancaster, from 1307 onwards, and was one of the barons implicated in the summary execution of Edward's favourite Piers Gaveston in 1312.[35] Botetourt's leadership of the embassy therefore may be a sign of the 'Lancastrian' party's resurgence after the disastrous defeat at Bannockburn destabilized Edward's position once more.

That being said, Botetourt had proven himself able to use his earlier ties to the crown to reconcile himself with Edward in times of relative peace between the king and his leading domestic opponents. The aftermath of Gaveston's execution was one such period, when the backlash against this brutal act forced the rebels to temper their opposition.[36] Moreover, the deaths of pro-Lancaster sympathizers like Robert Clifford, Miles Stapleton, and John Grey at Bannockburn had weakened Earl Thomas's faction as well.[37] This, coupled with the very real threat of renewed Scottish assaults on northern England (where Lancaster's landed interests were focused), may have inclined Lancaster and his allies to willingly cooperate in the defence of the realm, at least in the immediate aftermath of the battle. Thus, Botetourt's position within the English embassy in 1314 could reflect the last lingering vestiges of the post-Gaveston détente between Edward and his chief baronial rebels. With negotiations due to take place at Durham on 20 October, there was surely value in selecting a candidate that both the king and his cousin could find acceptable. On paper, at least, the talks proposed in late 1314 sounded ambitious and far-reaching, with Edward describing their goal as 'perpetual peace' ('*pace perpetua*'). In practice, however, the outcome would be far less impressive.

While making these preparations for, if not peace, then at least a temporary cessation of the fighting, King Edward was also working to maintain the support of the Balliol faction in anticipation of further conflict in the future. Thus, on 8 October, he granted the manors of Aylsham ('Aylesham'), Cawston ('Causton'), and Fakenham ('Fakenhamdam') in Norfolk to David Strathbogie, earl of Atholl, 'until he recovers his Scottish possessions'.[38] As previously noted, Strathbogie occupied an interesting position astride the warring factions in the struggle for the kingship of Scotland in the early fourteenth century, with ties of kinship to both the Bruce and Balliol parties. He had exploited his divided allegiance to abandon the Bruce Scots at what he surely calculated was a critical moment during the course of the battle. Strathbogie's assault on Cambuskenneth on the evening of 23 June, while no doubt shocking to the Scots at the time, does not appear to have had any impact on the course of the battle, and it certainly did not deter King Robert from following through in his attack on the English the next morning. Defection did, however, have serious repercussions for Strathbogie's interests in Scotland. The earldom of Atholl was granted to John, the son of Sir Neil Campbell, a close ally of King Robert who had served him since before the war, while the constableship was granted to another long-standing Bruce ally, Sir Gilbert Hay.[39] The grant of these three manors in 1314 were explicitly intended as compensation for the losses Strathbogie had incurred for switching sides at Bannockburn. The earl would receive a modest but steady stream of patronage in the years that followed.[40] His son and namesake would, until his death in 1335, play a significant role in the early stages of the Second War of Scottish Independence, demonstrating his father's (and, for that matter, his great-uncle Robert's) capacity for and willingness to play both sides in the conflict.[41] Ultimately though, Strathbogie's decision to defect in 1314 should be seen as a miscalculation in the long run.

The ongoing business of preparing for the upcoming peace talks with the Scots continued in the meantime. On 9 October, the day after the grants to Strathbogie, Edward commissioned a notary named Andrew of Tong to be present at the peace talks and to record the negotiations. For this, Andrew was to receive £10 from the keeper of the king's wardrobe.[42] Apparently born in the village of Tong in West Yorkshire, Andrew was a cleric associated with the diocese of York and had an established history of service to the English crown. He had accompanied the English royal court as they paraded the defeated John Balliol around north-west Scotland and produced copies of the *Ragman Rolls*, a record of submissions by numerous Scottish lords collected by Edward I in the 1290s.[43] Andrew also made copies of records relating to the Great Cause – Edward I's mediation in the Scottish succession crisis from 1291 to 1292 – in the years after Bannockburn.[44] He last appears in the written record in 1319, by which point he had been captured by the Scots and his son Richard received payment from the English crown to pay for his ransom.[45] His experience as a notary made Andrew an understandable choice to record the negotiations in 1314.

Yet, at the same time, King Edward was also making provisions for further conflict, suggesting that at least some in England did not place much faith in the negotiations. On the same day, Edward commissioned Sir Robert Holland to raise troops from Lancashire in anticipation of future hostilities. The document described the Scots as 'our enemies and rebels' (*'inimicorum et rebellium nostrorum'*), the conventional terminology used throughout the reign, including when Edward was mustering his army ahead of the Bannockburn campaign. Edward also complained of the 'depredations, fires, sacrileges, and other innumerable evils' (*'depraedationes, incendia, sacrilegia, et alia mala innumera'*) caused by Scottish raiding. Holland was to raise 'both cavalry and infantry' (*'tam equites, quam pedites*') for the defence of the county, implying a substantial force.[46] However, the fact that it was Robert Holland who was assigned to muster this force may indicate that the instructions were being issued against Edward's will. Unlike Botetourt, who had served both Edward and Edward's cousin, Holland was unequivocally a servant of Thomas, earl of Lancaster, having even served as Lancaster's valet on the campaign that led to the Battle of Falkirk in 1298. Holland's commission in 1314 may reflect an effort by Lancaster to create an effective fighting force to defend his own interests in northern England in the event of further Scottish raiding. In the period from 1314 to 1318, Lancaster would grow increasingly bold in asserting his own influence over the governance of England on the basis that the disaster at Bannockburn demonstrated Edward's inability to govern on his own.

The military build-up on the border continued for the rest of the year. On or about 3 November, the exchequer clerks inspected a list of twenty-three knights, fifty-nine squires, fifteen sergeants-at-arms, twenty-seven squires of the household, and 'other attendants' who had been serving at Berwick between 17 August and 3 November under the command of the warden Sir William Montague.[47] The list was apparently being inspected so that payment could be arranged for their services, although no breakdown of costs survives. Among those named in the list was a spy ('*exploratrix*') named Juliana 'de Goldyngham' and her maid. Juliana's presence on the list serves as a valuable reminder of the value of intelligence gathering for both sides in the conflict.[48] On 19 November, the mayor and bailiffs of York were instructed to raise forty crossbowmen equipped with aketons and bascinets ready to serve at Berwick for forty days from 'the morrow of St Andrew's day next' (1 December) at a rate of 4d. per day. In any event, only twenty crossbowmen seem to have been provided, although their wages, equipment, and transport from York to Berwick cost the English exchequer £33, 4d. nonetheless.[49]

There was further evidence on 9 October that not everyone in England looked to the upcoming peace talks with great optimism. At the same time that Edward was issuing his instructions from York, King Robert's nephew Thomas Randolph, earl of Moray, was at Durham. Here, the prior of the cathedral and convent there, acting on behalf of 'the community of the bishopric of Durham', agreed to pay Randolph 800 marks in return for protection from further Scottish raiding until 'the octave of St Hilary' (i.e., 20 January). This sum was to be paid at Jedworth in two instalments, the first due on 18 November and the second on 8 January.[50] This is particularly remarkable given the general truce that King Edward had ratified a mere three days earlier. It seems unlikely that news like this had not reached Durham from York by this time. Yet the community of Durham apparently still preferred to buy their own private truce rather than rely on one made by the crown.

This is reflective of the way in which mounting Scottish successes undermined the confidence of the northern communities of England in their king's ability to guarantee their safety. It further demonstrates the point that the community of Durham cannot have invested much faith in the upcoming peace talks either, even though they would be hosting them! Strikingly, the prior styled Bruce 'king of Scotland' ('*regis Scociae*'). This was a title that King Edward was unwilling to extend to Bruce when ratifying the truce at York three days earlier. However, the Scots likely insisted on this style, and it probably seemed like a small concession to the community at Durham, whose priority was clearly guaranteeing their own safety from Scottish depredations during the coming winter. The Durham truce might also suggest that the Scots themselves did not hold out great hopes for the upcoming negotiations for a lasting peace. Alternatively, whatever their expectations for the peace talks, the Scots would be unlikely to turn their noses up at such a hefty sum of money. Cash was, after all, one of the main commodities that Scottish raiding activities in this period were designed to generate.

The increasingly desperate outlook of Edward's northern subjects was also vividly on display at Berwick-upon-Tweed. While not directly related to the aftermath of Bannockburn as such, an incident took place there on 12 October that serves as a useful, and rather depressing, illustration of the level of paranoia gripping the community in the last major Scottish town in English hands following King Edward's defeat in 1314.[51] William Montague, warden of Berwick, John Weston, chamberlain of Scotland, and a jury of thirteen burgesses gathered on that date – 'Saturday next before the Translation of St Edward king and martyr, in the 8th year' – to hear the charges against a rather surprising pair of defendants. Richard, aged eleven, and his brother Roland, aged eight, were the sons of a burgess named William of Roxburgh. One Sir Nicholas Kingston had accused them of 'trafficking with the Scots rebels'. Apparently, Henry Bentley, the local coroner, had recently left Berwick 'to harass the Scots' and stayed for a while at nearby Lamberton. During Bentley's unusually long absence, rumours began to circulate that he had been killed and some of the townsfolk gathered on the walls to look out for him, Richard and Roland included. They and a third boy – Bentley's son – left the town to play in 'the field of St Mary Magdalene', but on returning, Richard realized he had lost his songbook, which apparently was for use in his lessons. The two boys went back out to search for the songbook, fruitlessly as it turned out. On returning to the town a second time, they were met and questioned by Kingston, who took them into custody and was still holding them at the time of the trial.

Naturally, the jury acquitted the boys, but the incident strikingly illustrates the paranoid atmosphere that prevailed at Berwick in the wake of Bruce's victory at Bannockburn. The locals had good reason to feel nervous, although this hardly justifies the treatment received by poor Richard and Roland. At the beginning of the year, the English held the royal castles of Stirling, Edinburgh, and Roxburgh, and the formidable Lanarkshire fortress of Bothwell Castle, while the earldom of March (centred around Dunbar) provided an effective buffer zone between the town and the Bruce Scots. Since then, however, each of these strongholds had fallen to King Robert's forces. Moreover, Bruce's victory at Bannockburn had convinced Patrick Dunbar, earl of March, to submit to King Robert. Berwick had thus become the only Scottish town left in English hands, and its denizens must have known that Bruce would be eager to secure its recovery sooner rather than later. It would ultimately take until 1318 for the Bruce Scots to seize the town, but the inhabitants were nevertheless clearly already on edge, a state of affairs that would get worse before it got better.[52]

On 20 October, the negotiations for a lasting peace between the two kingdoms were due to get underway at Durham. It is unclear whether the talks took place at all, but if they did, it is obvious that they failed. Negotiations of some sort did take place at Dumfries in December, with the English ambassadors returning on 26 December not only having failed to achieve a settlement, but also bringing with them rumours of an imminent renewed assault on northern England.[53] The failure to find a diplomatic resolution in late 1314 is perhaps unsurprising given the low expectations that both sides appear to have had for the peace talks. Probably the major sticking point was Bruce's insistence that he be formally recognized as king of Scots as part of any enduring peace deal. Bruce had apparently insisted on the style when making truces with the community at Durham in August 1312 and as recently as 9 October.[54] In 1317, Bruce would even mildly rebuke envoys representing Cardinals Luca Fieschi and Gaucelin d'Eauze over the pope's decision to address him as 'governor' (*'gubernatoris'*) of Scotland rather than king.[55] When the final peace was agreed in 1328, Robert would assume no less an exalted style that 'the magnificent prince the lord Robert by the grace of God illustrious king of Scots', and to gain formal English recognition of this, Bruce was willing to commit to the marriage of his only legitimate son and heir and sacrifice a cool £20,000 in war reparations.[56] Controversy over the issue would provide the pretext for the English to start the next war in the 1330s, with Edward Balliol's coronation in 1332 enabling Edward III to present his invasion in 1333 as being in support of a more legitimate claim than David II's.

Securing such a major concession was all but impossible in 1314. The English royal administration had, after all, maintained throughout the conflict that Scotland had never been an independent kingdom, and that the king of Scots had merely been a subject of the English crown who had been allowed to use that style. Thus, to acknowledge Bruce as king in his own right was to admit that the entire premise of the English war effort since 1296 had been false. No English monarch was likely to admit that willingly, while Bruce could accept nothing less to maintain the prestige of the Scotland crown. Bruce had proven himself capable of vigorously defending his own kingdom, and apparently had the northern communities of England terrified. But a single defeat – even on the unprecedented scale of Bannockburn – was insufficient to apply enough material pressure to the English royal administration that they would roll back nearly twenty years of policy. That he was able to do so before the end of his reign – however briefly it may have lasted – is a remarkable testament to King Robert's energy and ambition.

## 'They Should Be Considered as the King and Kingdom's Enemies Henceforth': The Cambuskenneth Parliament and the Bruce Resettlement of Scotland

If there is a single event that best illustrates the long-term significance of Bruce's victory at Bannockburn, then it is the parliament that King Robert held in November at Cambuskenneth Abbey, within sight of the field where he had defeated his English counterpart in June. On 6 November, the opening day of the assembly, Bruce issued a piece of legislation that paved the way for him to begin reshaping and rebuilding the community of the realm to suit his own purposes, which would have an enormous impact on Scottish society, politics, and warfare well into the next century. Styling himself 'Lord Robert by the grace of God illustrious king of Scots', he secured parliamentary approval for a sentence of forfeiture against anyone 'who died outside the faith and peace of the said lord king in the war or otherwise, or who had not come to his peace and faith on the said day'.[57] In other words, if anyone wanted to hold lands or titles in Scotland, they would have to formally acknowledge Bruce as king of Scots first. If they had a claim to estates in Scotland but still refused to recognize Bruce's rights as king, those estates would revert to the crown. Bruce was then free to retain the lands and enjoy their revenues or regrant them to another lord as he saw fit. The document codifying this judgment was witnessed by at least seven bishops, thirteen abbots, five priors, and twenty secular noblemen, most of whom had probably fought at Bannockburn less than five months earlier and some of whom most certainly had.

As explored in the first chapter, historians have traditionally seen the forfeiture of 1314 as the culmination of an ultimatum that Bruce had issued a year earlier, perhaps at the assembly he had held at Dundee in 1313. This is largely based on the fact that Barbour, writing in the 1370s, claims that Bruce gave Scottish landowners 'twelf moneth' in which to come and submit to him following Bannockburn.[58] Historians have sought to associate Barbour's ultimatum with an earlier assembly because the document produced at Cambuskenneth in November 1314 makes it clear that the judgment of forfeiture was to take effect immediately. Barbour, on the other hand, strongly implies that the twelve-month period in which Scottish landowners had to submit began around the time of (indeed perhaps at) the Cambuskenneth parliament.[59] The Cambuskenneth forfeiture does, however, state that those to whom it applied 'had been often summoned and lawfully expected', which may explain Barbour's confusion. It seems likely that Bruce had issued warnings about forfeitures at every assembly he had held before 1314, which would, of course, have included the one at Dundee in October 1313. What had changed in 1314 was that, following his victory at Bannockburn, Bruce was now in a position to make good on these threats.

In principle at least, this revolutionized Bruce's position. It placed enormous pressure on any Scottish landowner who had not yet submitted to Bruce to make their peace with the king. Their only alternatives would be to either live off any

English estates they might have or else rely on the charity of the English crown and hope that Bruce was ousted – either by the English or Bruce's Balliol rivals or a combination of the two – at some point in the near future. The possibility of that must have seemed particularly remote in the wake of Bannockburn. In the case of any landowner who remained intransigent, whether out of principle or because they had an alternate source of income, Bruce could now simply reclaim their estates to deal with as he liked. In the course of eight years of warfare, Bruce had built up considerable debts with those lords who had fought in service of his ambitions. Long-standing Bruce allies like Gilbert Hay, Neil Campbell, James Douglas, Robert Keith – all of whom witnessed the sentence of forfeiture – and others could now look forward to reaping the material rewards for their efforts. In redistributing these lands, Bruce was also able to drive forward a programme of military reform. Many forfeited lands were regranted for archer or galley service in an effort to modernize Bruce's army and swell his naval forces as well.[60]

Yet there was not, in 1314 at least, an immediate rush among Bruce partisans to carve up Scotland. King Robert seems to have favoured reconciliation over retribution at this stage. There certainly were some forfeitures, and the process of redistribution got underway, albeit slowly. For example, the constableship, forfeited from Strathbogie, was regranted to Gilbert Hay a mere six days after the sentence of forfeiture was passed.[61] This time the constableship would be granted hereditarily, meaning it would be held by Hay's successors as well, essentially guaranteeing Hay and his heirs a position on the royal council in perpetuity. As noted above, it is entirely possible that Hay was already acting as *de facto* constable by September 1314, if not sooner. Bruce, however, likely wished to wait until the Cambuskenneth parliament to formalize the grant, since by doing so he could secure the wider recognition of the community of the realm – and thus additional legitimacy – for Hay's status. Similarly, in February 1315, Sir Andrew Gray was granted lands in Perthshire and Angus that had previously belonged to Sir Edmund Hastings.[62] Hastings, whose wife, Isabella, was a daughter of the late Walter Comyn, earl of Menteith, had been granted lands within the earldom of Menteith in May 1306; served Edward II as 'wardens beyond the Scottish sea [i.e., the River Forth] between the Forth and Orkney' in 1308; commanded the garrison at Perth in 1309 and Berwick in 1312; and had then been killed at Bannockburn.[63] Walter Fitz Gilbert, whose timely defection had ultimately delivered the royal women from English custody, was given the former Comyn tenement of Machan in Lanarkshire in March 1315.[64] However, many others were welcomed back into the king's peace. Sir Ingram Umfraville, who had been captured while fighting for the English at Bannockburn, submitted to Bruce and received the half of the barony of Redcastle in Angus that he laid claim to through his Balliol mother or grandmother. As late as August 1315, Duncan, earl of Fife, who had remained in England throughout Bruce's reign so far, was back in Scotland to cut a deal with King Robert in order to retain his earldom.

It was only after the discovery of the so-called 'Soules conspiracy' in 1320, which resulted in the execution or exile of most of the rump Balliol faction, that King Robert seems to have committed himself to a more thoroughgoing redistribution of lands to his most faithful followers.[65] This somewhat mysterious plot – mysterious because the Bruce regime seems to have gone to some lengths to obscure the nature and extent of the conspiracy – was exposed and brutally suppressed before it was fully formed.[66] Yet it consisted apparently exclusively of former Comyn and Balliol adherents and likely aimed to assassinate Bruce and replace him with Edward Balliol, a rival claimant to the kingship.[67] The execution and forfeiture of the conspirators furnished the king with yet more lands that could be parcelled out to his more trustworthy supporters. Moreover, the fact that so many members of the Comyn/Balliol faction had been implicated seems to have convinced him of the long-term value in creating a network of dedicated followers whose livelihoods relied on the survival of the Bruce dynasty beyond his own lifetime. Though Douglas had become a close councillor of the king shortly after Bannockburn, most of the landed rewards he received for service to the Bruce cause seem to have come after 1320.[68] By 1324, these gifts of lands, titles, and rights had effectively elevated him to magnatial status, though without the rank of earl.[69] Like Douglas, Keith was a regular member of the royal council, but it is not until the 1320s that we have clear evidence of significant territorial aggrandizement in return for his service to King Robert.[70] It is unclear when the Strathbogie earldom of Atholl was regranted to John, the son of Bruce's sister Mary and Neil Campbell. However, the confirmation of John's possession of certain Atholl estates in July 1323 may indicate that King Robert did not commit to transferring the earldom until after the 'Soules conspiracy' had been blown.[71] The earldom of Angus was also not apparently regranted until the late 1320s.[72] In this case, the decision not to identify a new earl may have been in deference to Sir Ingram Umfraville, whose kinsmen would have lost out in such an event.

The Bruce resettlement of the kingdom was not without its problems. While the likes of Umfraville and Earl Duncan proved willing to make their peace with Bruce rather than face forfeiture in the months following the battle, there were plenty of other Scottish lords who refused to do so. Umfraville's cousin Robert, earl of Angus, was of course one of them. The redistribution of lands forfeited after Bannockburn in 1314 and after the failure of the 'Soules conspiracy' in 1320 only exacerbated the problem. The process created a body of men – known collectively as 'the Disinherited' – who were fervently committed to the destruction of the Bruce administration, since this was their only hope of regaining their Scottish possessions. The demands of the Disinherited to be restored to their former holdings within Scotland went unsatisfied in the peace deal that was ratified in 1328.[73] They played a key role in the outbreak of the Second War of Scottish Independence, even launching what amounted to a private invasion of Scotland in 1332 in order to crown Edward Balliol – son of the deposed John Balliol – as king of Scots.[74]

In this later conflict, the Bruce regime came perilously close to total collapse. Yet it was no mistake that the personnel who led the resistance to the Balliol faction and their English allies in the 1330s and 1340s were individuals who had either directly or indirectly benefited from the Bruce resettlement of the kingdom. As well as creating the Disinherited, Bruce had also developed a loose coalition of kindreds – including the Randolphs, the Stewarts, the Douglases, the Murrays, the Keiths, the Hays, the Campbells, and others – who could not reconcile themselves with either the English or the Balliols, since the lands and titles they had accrued in service to Bruce would be returned to their previous owners in the event that the Bruces were supplanted.[75] Figures like Duncan, earl of Fife, and Patrick Dunbar, earl of March, might – and did – abandon the Bruce cause when the Balliols were in the ascendency.[76] Even Bruce's own grandson Robert the Steward would temporarily make his peace with the Edward Balliol in 1335.[77] Yet, there were many who could not. There was little the Balliols or the English crown could offer the likes of John Randolph, earl of Moray, Andrew Murray of Bothwell, or William Douglas of Lothian, since most or all of the landed interests they were fighting to retain would be returned to their original owners in the event that the Bruce dynasty was decisively ended. Even the Steward's brief defection seems to have been primarily a method of buying himself time to regroup after a series of recent reversals for the Bruce Scots and may even have been modelled after his grandfather's vacillations before 1306. The Steward could not exploit this strategy to the same degree that Bruce himself had done from 1296 to 1306, and nor indeed could any other Scottish lord. The Bruce resettlement made it impossible to have two masters in Scotland.

Moreover, Bruce had furnished his party with an effective and efficient model of waging war that equipped them to successfully resist England's superior military resources. Later chroniclers emphasize the guerrilla tactics the Bruce Scots employed in forcing the submissions and undermining the authority of their opponents.[78] This clearly built on King Robert's own ruthless approach to warfare. Though occasional large-scale confrontations would occur in later conflicts, successful Scottish war leaders tended to avoid pitched battles and focused instead on the guerrilla warfare preferred by Robert I.[79] In the 1370s, when Barbour sought to instruct his contemporary audience in how to establish military ascendency over England, it was to Bruce's reign that he looked for inspiration and came to the conclusion that, if they truly wished 'to cum to purpos', then they should proceed 'Umquhile with strenth and quhile with slycht'.[80] The kindreds King Robert had favoured fought fiercely to maintain the Bruce dynasty, even when the Bruces were unable to provide active personal leadership. As a consequence, there was never a point after 1314 – indeed, after 1306 and 1307 – when there was not an independent Bruce administration active in Scotland, despite the fact that David II was a minor (and absent altogether from 1334 to 1341) and in spite of the occupation of large areas of the kingdom after 1333 by either the Balliol faction or the English crown. This ensured the survival of the Bruce dynasty during the so-called Second War of Scottish Independence and shaped the attitudes of the Scottish political community well into the fifteenth century, as seen in the vigorous promotion of Bruce propaganda by later historians such as Barbour, Wyntoun, and Bower. The gradual process of rebuilding the political community to ensure the preservation of the Bruce regime began at Cambuskenneth Abbey in November 1314. However, King Robert could not have begun this process at Cambuskenneth in November had he not defeated Edward at Bannockburn in June.

# Appendix: Image Decriptions

An apocalyptic battle in the 'Holkham Bible', an English picture book from c. 1320-30 (London, British Library, Add. MS 47682, f. 40r). Though an essentially fanciful scene, the arms and armour depicted offer a valuable insight into the types of equipment potentially available to both the noble and non-noble soldiers from both kingdoms who fought at Bannockburn in 1314. (From the British Library archive)

Archers practicing their craft in the 'Luttrell Psalter' from c. 1325-35 (London, British Library, Add. MS 42130, f. 147v). King Edward summoned at least 4,000 archers for the Bannockburn campaign, although they would ultimately be neutralised when King Robert's forces trapped them behind the English cavalry. (From the British Library archive)

Illuminated initial 'E'(dwardus) from a 1316 charter showing the successful defence of Carlisle from the Scots in 1315. This represents the only surviving depiction of Scottish soldiers produced during the reign of Robert I. The lightweight armour the Scots are shown wearing here strongly resonates with the author of the *Vita*'s description of the appearance of Bruce's army at Bannockburn. (Cumbria Archive Centre, Carlisle)

The hill on which Roxburgh Castle once stood, with some of the fragmentary ruins visible to the left of the image. Complaints about the indiscipline of the Roxburgh garrison played a major role in Edward II's decision to invade Scotland in 1314. The fall of the castle to the Bruce Scots in February signalled the beginning of a more aggressive Scottish response to this threat than had been the case during Edward's 1310 campaign into Scotland. (Author's own)

Edinburgh Castle viewed from the north. It is from this direction that the Lanercost chronicler claims the Bruce Scots ascended the cliffs in secret to overwhelm the garrison in March. The fall of Edinburgh left Stirling woefully isolated and made it a tempting target for attack in the near future. (Author's own)

Stirling Castle. The deal struck between the besieging Scottish army and the beleaguered garrison here in late May put the two armies on a collision course. Yet once the two kings were on the battlefield, the castle became something of a red herring, with the real prize being the capture (or death) of their opposite number. (© Crown Copyright: HES)

Roman *lilia* at Rough Castle. The *concava* described by Baston and the 'pottis' described by Barbour likely had a similar appearance. At Bannockburn, they served to create an artificial bottleneck at the entrance to the New Park, ultimately forcing the English army into the natural bottleneck between the Bannock Burn and Pelstream Burn. (© Crown Copyright: HES)

An aerial view across the area where the fighting on 24th June is most likely to have taken place, looking roughly south-west. Balquidderock Ridge, where the Scottish army likely formed up at dawn, is the wooded ridge in the right of this image. The Scots would have advanced eastwards through the now built-up area beneath the ridge. The Bannock Burn itself can be seen in the centre of the image, in the crook between the railway tracks to the right and the A91 to the left. The Scots would have kept their right flank anchored against the burn as they advanced. (David Wilkinson, Scotdrone)

An aerial view across the area where the fighting on 24th June is most likely to have taken place, looking roughly north-west. Balquidderock Ridge is once again visible as a wooded ridge to the left of the image. The thin line of trees to the right of the image traces the modern line of the Pelstream Burn, against which the Scots would have anchored their left flank. On a hill in the distance, Stirling Castle is visible, reinforcing its dominance of the local landscape. Edward II's flight from the battlefield may have initially been made towards the castle before diverting southwards behind the Scots. (David Wilkinson, Scotdrone)

Bothwell Castle in Lanarkshire. A substantial number of English escapees from Bannockburn sought refuge here in the aftermath of the battle, only to be turned over to Bruce as prisoners when the Scottish garrison commander promptly switched allegiance. (© Crown Copyright: HES)

The 'print' from the Bute Mazer, a fourteenth-century communal drinking vessel, likely created during the reign of Robert I. The stylised lion in the centre of the print may represent the king himself, while at least two of the individuals represented by the enamelled arms surrounding it are known to have been present at Bannockburn in 1314. Walter Stewart – whose arms are positioned between the lion's paws – was knighted by King Robert ahead of the fighting on 24$^{th}$ June, as was his cousin James Douglas (clockwise from Stewart). Sir John Menteith (anti-clockwise from Stewart) was also likely present, while Susannah Crawford (anti-clockwise from Menteith) may have contributed troops to King Robert's army from her estates in Ayrshire. Furthermore, the timely defection of Sir Walter Fitz Gilbert (clockwise from Douglas) in the immediate aftermath of the battle delivered several valuable prisoners into Bruce's custody, giving the king valuable diplomatic leverage in the closing months of 1314. (On loan from The Bute Collection at Mount Stuart. Image © National Museums Scotland)

Cambuskenneth Abbey on the north bank of the River Forth. It was at the parliament King Robert held here in November 1314 that the long-term significance of the recent victory at Bannockburn began to become clear. (© Crown Copyright: HES)

The oldest complete manuscript of Barbour's *Bruce* (Edinburgh, National Library of Scotland, Adv.MS. 19.2.2 f. 39v). Though it was written in the 1370s – and this manuscript transcribed in 1489 – *The Bruce* offers a valuable and detailed early Scottish perspective on the event, one that continued to resonate with Scots through the fourteenth- and fifteenth-centuries and beyond. (Reproduced with the permission of the National Library of Scotland)

The earliest surviving illustration of the Battle of Bannockburn, from a copy of Walter Bower's *Scotichronicon* produced in the 1440s (Cambridge, Corpus Christi College, MS 171B, f. 265r). The steep-sided Bannock Burn in the foreground offers a sense of what a substantial barrier to movement it was in the medieval period. Perhaps the most striking element of the image is the face-off between King Robert and Sir Henry de Bohun (the mounted figures in the centre of the picture). This is particularly noteworthy because Bower does not reference this confrontation in the text of his chronicle, highlighting the popularity of the tale among Scottish audiences, largely derived from Barbour's colourful account (which Bower had certainly read). (The Parker Library, Corpus Christi College, Cambridge.)

The equestrian statue of King Robert outside the Battle of Bannockburn Visitor Centre near Stirling. Perhaps the most enduring modern image of the king, it was commissioned in 1964 to celebrate the battle's 650$^{th}$ anniversary. (Author's own)

# Bibliography

**Primary Sources:**

Allmand, C., *The De Re Militari of Vegetius: The Reception, Transmission and Legacy of a Roman Text in the Middle Ages* (Cambridge: Cambridge University Press, 2011).

Bain, J. (ed), *Calendar of Documents Relating to Scotland*, 5 vols. (Edinburgh, 1881–1888).

Barbour, J., *The Bruce*, ed. and trans. A. A. M. Duncan (Edinburgh: Canongate, 1997).

Barbour, J., *The Bruce: A Fredome Is a Noble Thing!*, eds. M. P. McDiarmid and J. A. C. Stevenson, 3 vols. (Edinburgh: Scottish Text Society, 1985).

Bede, *Ecclesiastical History of the English People*, ed. D. H. Farmer (London: Penguin, 1990).

Boece, H., *The Chronicles of Scotland*, ed. R. Chambers and E. Batho (Edinburgh: Scottish Text Society, 1938–1941).

Bonet, H., *The Tree of Battles of Honoré Bonet*, ed. and trans. G. W. Coopland (Liverpool, 1949).

Bower, W., *Scotichronicon*, ed. D. E. R. Watt, et al., 9 vols. (Aberdeen, 1987–1999).

Broun, Taylor, et al. (eds), The Dynamic Edition of the Declaration of Arbroath, online at *The Community of the Realm in Scotland, 1249–1424: History, Law and Charters in a Recreated Kingdom*, https://cotr.ac.uk/texts.

Brown, K. M., et al. (eds), *The Records of the Parliaments of Scotland to 1707* (St Andrews, 2008), www.rps.ac.uk.

*Calendar of Chancery Warrants. Vol. I, Hen. III - Edw. II.* (London: HMSO, 1920).

*Calendar of Inquisitions Post-Mortem and Other Analogous Documents Preserved in the Public Records Office. Vol. 4. Edward I.* (London: HMSO, 1912).

*Calendar of Patent Rolls, Edward II*, 5 vols. (London: HMSO, 1894–1904).

Charny, G., *The Book of Chivalry*, ed. and trans. R. Kaeuper and E. Kennedy (Philadelphia, 1996).

Cuttino, G. P. and J. P. Trabut-Cussac (eds) *Gascon Register A*, 3 vols. (British Academy, 1975).

Fraser, W., *The Douglas Book*, 4 vols. (Edinburgh, 1885).

Fraser, W., *The Red Book of Menteith*, 2 vols. (Edinburgh, 1880).

Given-Wilson, C, P. Brand, S. Phillips, M. Ormrod, G. Martin, A. Curry, and R. Horrox (eds) *Parliament Rolls of Medieval England* (Woodbridge, 2005), *British History Online*, http://www.british-history.ac.uk/no-series/parliament-rolls-medieval.

Hardy, T. D. (ed), *Registrum Palatinum Dunelmense: The Register of Richard de Kellawe, Lord Palatine and Bishop of Durham, 1311–16, Volume 1* (London, 1873).

Luard, H. (ed), *Flores Historiarum*, 3 vols. (Rolls Series, 1890).

Innes, C. (ed), *Registrum Monasterii de Passalet* (Glasgow: Maitland Club, 1832).

King, A. (ed), *Sir Thomas Gray: Scalacronica (1272–1363)* (Surtees Society, 209, 2005).

Mac Airt, S. (ed) *The Annals of Inisfallen* (Dublin, 1951).

Macpherson, D. (ed), *Rotuli Scotiae in Turri Londinensi et in Domo Capitulari Westmonasteriensi Asservati*, 2 vols. (London, 1814–1819).

Maxwell, H. (ed), *The Chronicle of Lanercost, 1272–1346* (Glasgow, 1913).

Palgrave, F. (ed), *Parliamentary Writs and Writs of Military Summons*, 2 vols. (London, 1827–1834).

Preest, D. (ed and trans) *The Chronicle of Geoffrey Le Baker of Swinbrook* (Woodbridge: Boydell, 2012).

Raine, J. (ed), *Historiae Dunelmensis Scriptores Tres*, (London, 1839).

Raine, J. (ed), *Historical Papers and Letters from the Northern Register* (London, 1873).

Riley, H. T. (ed), *Johannes de Trokelowe and Henrici de Blandeford, Chronica et Annales* (Rolls Series, 1866).

Riley, H. T. (ed), *Thomae Walsingham, quondam monachi S. Albani, Historia Anglicana, Vol. 1* (London, 1863).

Riley, H. T. (ed), *William of Rishanger, Chronica et Annales* (Rolls Series, London, 1865).

Rymer, T. (ed), *Foedera, Conventiones, Litterae et Cuiuscunque Generis Acta Publica*, 20 vols. (London, 1704–1735).

Skene, F. (ed), *Liber Pluscardensis*, 2 vols. (Edinburgh, 1877–1880).

Skene, W. F. (ed), *Johannis de Fordun, Chronica Gentis Scotorum*, 2 vols. (Edinburgh, 1871–1872).

Stones, E. L. G. (ed) *Anglo-Scottish Relations, 1174–1328: Some Selected Documents* (London, 1965).

Thomson, J. M. and J. B. Paul (eds), *Registrum Magni Sigilii Regum Scotorum*, 11 vols. (Edinburgh, 1882–1914).

Thomson, T. (ed), *Instrumenta publica, sive processus super fidelitatibus et homagiis Scotorum domino regi Angliae factis, A.D. MCCXCI–MCCXCVI* (Edinburgh: Bannatyne Club, 1768–1852).

Trivet, N., *Nicolai Triveti Annalium Continuatio* (Oxonii: E Theatro Sheldoniano, 1722).

Wright, T., *Political Songs of England* (London: Camden Society, 1839).

Wyntoun, A., *The Original Chronicle of Andrew of Wyntoun*, ed. F. Amours, 6 vols. (Edinburgh: Scottish Text Society, 1903–1914).

**Secondary Sources:**

Althoff, G., 'Friendship and Political Order', in J. Haseldine (ed), *Friendship in Medieval Europe* (Sutton, 1999), pp. 91–105.

Altschul, M., *A Baronial Family in England: The Clares* (Baltimore, 1965).

Ayton, A., 'English Armies in the Fourteenth Century', in *Arms, Armies and Fortifications in the Hundred Years War*, ed. A. Curry and M. Hughes (Woodbridge: Boydell, 1994), pp. 21–38.

Ayton, A., 'In the Wake of Defeat: Bannockburn and the Dynamics of Recruitment in England', in *Bannockburn 1314–2014: Battle and Legacy*, ed. Michael Penman (Donington: Shaun Tyas, 2016), pp. 36–56.

Barnes, P. and G. W. S. Barrow, 'The Movements of Robert Bruce between September 1307 and May 1308', *The Scottish Historical Review*, vol. 49, no. 147 (1970), pp. 46–59.

Barrow, G. W. S., *Robert Bruce and the Community of the Realm of Scotland* (Edinburgh: Edinburgh University Press, 1976).

Beam, A., '"At the Apex of Chivalry": Sir Ingram de Umfraville and the Anglo–Scottish Wars', in A. King and D. Simpkin (eds), *England and Scotland at War, c.1296–c.1513* (Leiden: Brill, 2012), pp. 53–76.

Beam, A., *The Balliol Dynasty, 1210–1364* (Edinburgh: John Donald, 2008).

Beam, A., J. Bradley, D. Broun, J. R. Davies, Ma. Hammond, N. Jakeman, M. Pasin, A. Taylor, et al. (eds), *People of Medieval Scotland: 1093–1371* (Glasgow and London, 2019) www.poms.ac.uk.

Bellamy, J. G., *The Law of Treason in England in the Later Middle Ages* (Cambridge: Cambridge University Press, 1970).

Bennett, M., 'Development of Battlefield Tactics in the Hundred Years' War', in *Arms, Armies and Fortifications in the Hundred Years War*, eds. A. Curry and M. Hughes (Woodbridge: Boydell, 1999).

Benz St. John, L., *Three Medieval Queens: Queenship and the Crown in Fourteenth-Century England* (New York: Palgrave Macmillan, 2012).

Blakely, R., *The Brus Family in England and Scotland, 1100–1295* (Woodbridge: Boydell Press, 2005).

Boardman, S. 'Chronicle Propaganda in Fourteenth-Century Scotland: Robert the Steward, John of Fordun and the "Anonymous Chronicle"', *The Scottish Historical Review* 76, no. 201 (1997), pp. 23–43.

Boardman, S., '"Thar Nobill Eldrys Gret Bounte": The Bruce and Early Stewart Scotland', in S. Boardman and S. Foran (eds), *Barbour's Bruce and its Cultural Contexts* (Cambridge: D. S. Brewer, 2015), pp. 191–212.

Boardman, S., *The Campbells: 1250–1513* (Edinburgh: John Donald, 2006).

Boardman, S., *The Early Stewart Kings: Robert II and Robert III 1371–1406* (East Linton: Tuckwell Press, 1996).

Borthwick, A. and H. MacQueen, *Law, Lordship and Tenure: The Fall of the Black Douglases* (Strathmartine Press, 2022).

Bradbury, J., *The Medieval Archer* (Woodbridge: Boydell, 1985).

Broun, D., 'A New Letter of Robert I to Edward II', http://www.breakingofbritain.ac.uk/blogs/feature-of-the-month/june-2013/; Accessed: 23/1/23.

Broun, D., 'New Information on the Guardians' Appointment in 1286 and on Wallace's Rising in 1297', on *The Breaking of Britain: Cross-Border Society and Scottish Independence 1216–1314*; Accessed: 19/03/23, http://www.breakingofbritain.ac.uk/blogs/feature-of-the-month/september-2011-the-guardians-in-1286-and-wallaces-uprising-in-1297.

Brown, C., *Bannockburn 1314: The Battle 700 Years On* (Stroud: Spellmount, 2013).

Brown, M., *Bannockburn: The Scottish War and the British Isles 1307–1323* (Edinburgh: Edinburgh University Press, 2008).

Brown, M., *The Black Douglases: War and Lordship in Late Medieval Scotland, 1300–1455* (East Linton: Tuckwell Press, 1998).

Brown, M., *The Wars of Scotland, 1214–1371* (Edinburgh: Edinburgh University Press, 2004).

Bryant, N. (trans), *The True Chronicles of Jean Le Bel, 1290–1360* (Woodbridge: Boydell & Brewer, 2015).

Bumke, J., *Courtly Culture: Literature and Society in the High Middle Ages* (Berkeley: University of California Press, 1991).

Caldwell, D., 'Bannockburn: The Road to Victory', in *Bannockburn 1314–2014: Battle and Legacy*, ed. Michael Penman (Donington: Shaun Tyas, 2016), pp. 15–35.

Caldwell, D., 'Scottish Spearmen, 1298–1314: An Answer to Cavalry,' *War in History* 19, no. 3 (2012), pp. 267–289.

Caldwell, D., 'The Monymusk Reliquary: The Breccbennach of St. Columba', *Proceedings of the Society of Antiquaries of Scotland*, 131 (2000), pp. 262–282.

Cameron (Vathjunker), S., 'A Study of the Career of Sir James Douglas: The Historical Record versus Barbour's Bruce', unpublished PhD thesis, University of Aberdeen, 1992.

Cameron, S., 'Keeping the Customer Satisfied: Barbour's *Bruce* and the phantom division at Bannockburn', in E.J. Cowan and D. Gifford (eds), *The Polar Twins* (Edinburgh: John Donald Pub., 1999), pp. 61–74.

Carradice, P, *Robert the Bruce: Scotland's True Braveheart* (Barnsley: Pen & Sword Books, 2022).

Childs, W. R., 'Resistance and Treason in the *Vita Edwardi Secundi*', in M. Prestwich, R.H. Britnell and Robin Frame (eds), *Thirteenth Century England, VI: Proceedings of the Durham Conference* (Woodbridge, Suffolk: Boydell & Brewer, 1995), pp. 177–191.

Childs, W. R. (ed), *Vita Edwardi Secundi* (Oxford, 2005).

Christison, P., 'Bannockburn – 23rd and 24th June, 1314: A Study in Military History', *Proceedings of the Society of Antiquaries of Scotland*, 90 (1959), pp. 170–179.

Cook, M., *Bannockburn and Stirling Bridge: Exploring Scotland's Two Greatest Battles* (Stirling: Extremis Publishing, 2021).

Cornell, D., *Bannockburn: The Triumph of Robert the Bruce* (London: Yale University Press, 2009).

Cowan, I. B. and D. E. Easson, *Medieval Religious Houses: Scotland* (2nd edn, London, 1976).
Crouch, D., *Tournament* (London and New York: Hambledon and London, 2005).
Dean, L., 'Projecting Dynastic Majesty: State Ceremony in the Reign of Robert the Bruce', in *International Review of Scottish Studies*, vol. 40 (2015), pp. 34–60.
Denholm-Young, N., 'The Authorship of *Vita Edwardi Secundi*', *The English Historical Review* 71, no. 279 (1956), pp. 189–211.
DeVries, K., *Infantry Warfare in the Early Fourteenth-Century: Discipline, Tactics, and Technology* (Woodbridge: Boydell, 1996).
Doherty, P., *Isabella and the Strange Death of Edward II* (London: Robinson, 2004).
Duffy, S., 'The Bruce Brothers and the Irish Sea World, 1306–29', in Seán Duffy (ed), *Robert the Bruce's Irish Wars: The Invasions of Ireland 1306–1329* (Stroud, 2002), pp. 45–70.
Duffy, S., 'The "Continuation" of Nicholas Trevet: A New Source for the Bruce Invasion', ed. S. Duffy, *Proceedings of the Irish Academy*, xci, 12 (Dublin, 1991), pp. 303–315.
Duggan, A., 'Becket Is Dead! Long Live St Thomas', in M.-P. Gelin (ed.), *The Cult of St Thomas Becket in the Plantagenet World, c.1170–c.1220*, pp. 25–52.
Dunbar, A. H., *Scottish Kings: A Revised Chronology of Scottish History 1005–1625* (2nd edn., Edinburgh, 1906).
Duncan, A. A. M., 'A Question about the Succession, 1364', *Scottish History Society Miscellany*, xii (Edinburgh, 1994), pp. 12–57.
Duncan, A. A. M. (ed), *Regesta Regum Scottorum, v: The Acts of Robert I, 1306–29*, (Edinburgh, 1986).
Duncan, A. A. M., 'The War of the Scots, 1306–23: The Prothero Lecture', *Transactions of the Royal Historical Society* 2 (1992), pp. 125–151.
Eeles, F., 'The Monymusk Reliquary of Brecbennoch of St Columba', in *Proceedings of the Society of Antiquaries of Scotland*, 68 (1934), pp. 433–438.
Fairbank, F., 'The Last Earl of Warenne and Surrey', *Yorks. Arch. Journal*, xix (1906–7), pp. 193–264.
Fawcett, R., *Scottish Medieval Churches: Architecture & Furnishings* (Stroud: Tempus, 2002).
Fenton, A. (ed), *Angels, Nobles and Unicorns: Art and Patronage in Medieval Scotland* (Edinburgh: National Museum of Antiquities of Scotland, 1982).
Fisher, A., *William Wallace* (Edinburgh: John Donald, 2002).
Foran, S. and Boardman, S., 'Introduction: King Robert the Bruce's Book', in S. Boardman and S. Foran (eds), *Barbour's Bruce and its Cultural Contexts* (Cambridge: D. S. Brewer, 2015), pp. 1–32.
Fraser, C. M., 'The Pattern of Trade in the North-East of England, 1265–1350', in *Northern History*, iv (1969), pp. 44–66.

Freeman, A. M. (ed), *The Annals of Connacht* (Dublin, 1944).
French, M., 'Christina Bruce and Her Defence of Kildrummy Castle', *Royal Studies Journal*, 7(1) (2020), pp. 22–38.
Fryde, N., 'Antonio Pessagno of Genoa, King's Merchant of Edward II', *Studi in memoria di Federigo Melis*, 2 (Naples, 1978), pp. 159–79.
Gilbert, J., *Hunting and Hunting Reserves in Medieval Scotland* (Edinburgh, 1979).
Grant, A., 'Bravehearts and Coronets: Images of William Wallace and the Scottish Nobility', in E. J. Cowan (ed), *The Wallace Book* (Edinburgh: John Donald, 2007), pp. 86–106.
Grant, A., *Independence and Nationhood: Scotland, 1306–1469* (Edinburgh, 2001).
Grant, A., 'Royal and Magnate Bastards in the Later Middle Ages: The View from Scotland', working paper, Lancaster University, Lancaster.
Grant, A., 'The Death of John Comyn: What Was Going On?', in *Scottish Historical Review*, Vol. 86, No. 2 (2007), pp. 176–224.
Guy, J. A., *Thomas Becket: Warrior, Priest, Rebel, Victim: A 900-Year-Old Story Retold* (London: Penguin, 2012).
Hallam, E., *The Itinerary of Edward II and His Household, 1307–1328* (London, 1984).
Hammond, M., 'Breaking Down Robert's Reign', *The Community of the Realm in Scotland, 1249–1424: History, Law and Charters in a Recreated Kingdom*, 21 Nov. 2019, https://cotr.ac.uk/social-network-analysis-political-communities-and-social-networks/networks-robert-i-king-scots-1306-29/breaking-down-roberts-reign.
Hammond, M., 'Robert I's Charter Witnesses', *The Community of the Realm in Scotland, 1249–1424: History, Law and Charters in a Recreated Kingdom*, 21 Nov. 2019, https://cotr.ac.uk/social-network-analysis-political-communities-and-social-networks/networks-robert-i-king-scots-1306-29/robert-is-charter-witnesses.
Hardy, R., *Longbow: A Social and Military History* (5th edn. Sparkford: Haynes, 2012).
Hay, D., 'Booty in Border Warfare', *Transactions of the Dumfriesshire and Galloway Antiquarian Society*, third series, 31 (1952–3), pp. 145–66.
Jones, M. K., 'The Battle of Verneuil (17 August 1424): Towards a History of Courage', *War in History 9* (2002), pp. 375–411.
Jordan, A., 'The St Thomas Becket Windows at Angers and Coutances: Devotion, Subversion and the Scottish Connection', in M. P. Gelin (ed), *The Cult of St Thomas Becket in the Plantagenet World, c.1170–c.1220*, pp. 171–207.
Kaeuper, R., *Chivalry and Violence in Medieval Europe* (Oxford: Oxford University Press, 1999).
Kaeuper, R. W., 'The Frescobaldi of Florence and the English Crown', *Studies in Medieval and Renaissance History*, 10 (1973), pp. 41–95.
Keen, M., *Chivalry* (London: Yale University Press, 1984).
Loades, M., *War Bows* (London: Osprey Publishing, 2019).
Lydon, J., 'The Impact of the Bruce Invasion', in Seán Duffy (ed), *Robert the Bruce's Irish Wars: The Invasions of Ireland 1306–1329* (Stroud, 2002), pp. 119–152.

Macdonald, A. J., *Border Bloodshed: Scotland and England at War, 1369–1403* (East Linton: Tuckwell Press, 2000).

Macdougall, N., *James IV* (East Linton: Tuckwell, 1997).

Macdougall, N.A.T, *James III: A Political Study* (2nd edn., Edinburgh: John Donald, 2009).

MacInnes, I. A., 'Shock and Awe: The Use of Terror as a Psychological Weapon during the Bruce–Balliol Civil War, 1332–8', in A. King and M. A. Penman (eds), *England and Scotland in the Fourteenth Century: New Perspectives* (Woodbridge: Boydell Press, 2007), pp. 40–59.

MacInnes, I., *Scotland's Second War of Independence, 1332–1357* (Woodbridge: The Boydell Press, 2016).

Mackay, J., *William Wallace: Brave Heart* (Edinburgh: Mainstream, 1995).

Mackenzie, G., *The Lives and Characters of the Most Eminent Writers of the Scots Nation* (Edinburgh, 1708–1722).

Maddicott, J. R., *Thomas of Lancaster, 1307–1322: A Study in the Reign of Edward II* (London: Oxford University Press, 1970).

Marner, D., *St Cuthbert: His Life and Cult in Medieval Durham* (London: British Library, 2000).

Marshall, S., *Illegitimacy in Medieval Scotland, 1100–1500* (Boydell, 2021).

Maxwell-Irving, A., *The Border Towers of Scotland. Volume II: Their Evolution and Architecture* (Stirling, 2014).

Maxwell-Lyte, H. C. (ed), *Calendar of Close Rolls, Edward II: Volume 2, 1313–1318* (London: HMSO, 1893).

McGladdery, C., 'The Black Douglases 1369–1455', in R. Oram & G. Stell (eds), *Lordship and Architecture in Medieval and Renaissance Scotland* (Edinburgh: John Donald, 2021), pp. 161–187.

McGuigan, N., 'Cuthbert's relics and the origins of the diocese of Durham', in *Anglo-Saxon England* 48, December 2019, pp. 121–162.

McNamee, C., *Robert Bruce: Our Most Valiant Prince, King and Lord* (Edinburgh: Birlinn, 2012).

McNamee, C., *The Wars of the Bruces: Scotland, England and Ireland 1306–28* (East Linton, 1997).

McNamee, C., 'William Wallace's Invasion of Northern England, 1297', *Northern History*, xxvi (1990), pp. 40–58.

McNutt, R. 'Finding Forgotten Fields: A Theoretical and Methodological Framework for Historic Landscape Reconstruction and Predictive Modelling of Battlefield Locations in Scotland, 1296–1650', unpublished PhD thesis, University of Glasgow, 2014.

Moffat, A., *Bannockburn: The Battle of a Nation* (Edinburgh: Birlinn, 2016).

Moffat, R. (ed), *Medieval Arms and Armour: A Sourcebook – Volume I, The Fourteenth Century* (Woodbridge: Boydell Press, 2022).

Moor, C. (ed), *Knights of Edward I*, vol. 4, Harleian Society, 83 (1931).
Morris, J., *Bannockburn* (Cambridge: Cambridge University Press, 1914).
Neville, C. J., *Land, Law and People in Medieval Scotland* (Edinburgh: Edinburgh University Press, 2010).
Neville, C. J., 'Widows of War: Edward I and the Women of Scotland during the War of Independence', in *Wife and Widow in Medieval England*, ed. S. Walker (Michigan, 1993), pp. 109–139.
Nubacher, A., *1314: Bannockburn* (Stroud: Tempus, 2005).
Oram, R., 'Bruce, Balliol and the Lordship of Galloway: South-Western Scotland and the Wars of Independence', in *Transactions of the Dumfriesshire and Galloway Natural History and Antiquarian Society*, vol. 67 (1992), pp. 29–47.
Owen, D. D. R., *William the Lion, 1143–1214: Kingship and Culture* (East Linton: Tuckwell, 1997).
Palgrave, F. (ed), *Documents and Records Illustrating the History of Scotland* (London, 1837).
Pascual, L., 'The de Bohun Dynasty: Power, Identity and Piety, 1066–1399', unpublished PhD thesis, Royal Holloway, 2017.
Penman, M., '"A Fell Coniurecioun Agayn Robert the Douchty King": the Soules Conspiracy of 1318–1320', in *The Innes Review*, Vol. 50, no. 1 (Spring 1991), pp. 25–57.
Penman, M., *David II, 1329–1371* (Edinburgh: John Donald, 2004).
Penman, M., *Robert the Bruce: King of the Scots* (New Haven: Yale University Press, 2014).
Phillips, J. R. S., *Aymer de Valence, Earl of Pembroke, 1307–1324: Baronial Politics in the Reign of Edward II* (Oxford: Clarendon Press, 1972).
Phillips, J. R. S., *Edward II* (London: Yale University Press, 2010).
Pollard, T., 'A Battle Lost, A Battle Found: The Search for the Bannockburn Battlefield', in *Bannockburn 1314–2014: Battle and Legacy*, ed. Michael Penman (Donington: Shaun Tyas, 2016), pp. 74–95.
Powicke, M., *Military Obligation in Medieval England. A Study in Liberty and Duty* (Oxford, 1962).
Prestwich, M., *Armies and Warfare in the Middle Ages: The English Experience* (London: Yale University Press, 1996).
Prestwich, M., 'Cavalry Service in Early Fourteenth Century England', in *War and Government in the Middle Ages*, eds. J. Gillingham and J.C. Holt (Woodbridge: Boydell Press, 1984), pp. 147–158.
Prestwich, M., *The Three Edwards: War and State in England, 1272–1377* (London: Weidenfeld and Nicolson, 1980).
Prestwich, M., *War, Politics and Finance under Edward I* (Aldershot, 1991).
Rose, A., *Kings in the North: The House of Percy in British History* (London: Weidenfeld & Nicolson, 2002).

Ross, A., 'Men for All Seasons? The Strathbogie Earls of Atholl and the War of Independence, Part 1 – Earl John (1266x1270–1306) and Earl David III (c.1290–1326)', *Northern Scotland*, 20 (2000), pp. 1–30.

Ross, A., 'Recreating the Bannockburn Environment and Climate', in *Bannockburn 1314–2014: Battle and Legacy*, ed. Michael Penman (Donington: Shaun Tyas, 2016), pp. 96–110.

Rothwell, H. (ed), *Chronicle of Walter of Guisborough* (Camden Society, Third Series, lxxxix, London, 1989).

Rothwell, H. T. (ed) *English Historical Documents*, 12 vols. (London, 1953–1977).

Salter, M., *The Castles and Tower Houses of Northumberland* (Malvern: Folly Publications, 1997).

Sayles, G. (ed), *Documents on the Affairs of Ireland before the King's Council* (Irish Manuscripts Commission, 1979).

Sayles, G., 'The Guardians of Scotland and a Parliament at Rutherglen in 1300', *Scottish Historical Review* 24, no. 96 (1927), pp. 245–250.

Sharpe, R., 'The Late Antique Passion of St Alban', in *Alban and St Albans: Roman and Medieval Architecture, Art and Archaeology*, eds. M. Henig and P. Lindley (Leeds: British Archaeological Association, 2001), pp. 30–37.

Simpkin, D., 'The English Army and the Scottish Campaign of 1310–11', in A. King and M. Penman (eds) *England and Scotland in the Fourteenth Century: New Perspectives* (Boydell Press, 2007) pp. 14–39.

Simpkin, D., 'The King's Sergeants-at-Arms in Scotland, 1296–1322', in A. King and D. Simpkin (eds), *England and Scotland at War, c. 1296–c.1513*, pp. 77–117.

Smout, T. C. and M. Stewart, *The Forth: An Environmental History* (Edinburgh, 2012).

Stevenson, J. (ed), *Documents Illustrative of the History of Scotland*, 2 vols. (Edinburgh, 1870).

Strickland, M., 'Treason, Feud and the Growth of State Violence: Edward I and the "War of the Earl of Carrick"', 1306–7, in C. Given-Wilson, A. J., Kettle, and L. Scales (eds), *War, Government and Aristocracy in the British Isles, c.1150–1500: Essays in Honour of Michael Prestwich* (Woodbridge: Boydell Press, 2008), pp. 84–113.

Stones, E. L. G., and G. Simpson, *Edward I and the Throne of Scotland, 1290–1296: An Edition of the Record Sources for the Great Cause* (Oxford, 1977–1978).

Stuart, J. et al. (eds), *The Exchequer Rolls of Scotland*, 23 vols. (Edinburgh, 1878–1908).

Stubbs, W. (ed) *Chronicles of the Reigns of Edward I and Edward II*, Rolls Series, vol. 76:1 (London, 1882).

Spinks, S., *Edward II the Man: A Doomed Inheritance* (Stroud: Amberley, 2017).

Stevenson, J. H., 'The Bannatyne or Bute Mazer and its Carved Bone Cover', in *Proceedings of the Society of Antiquaries of Scotland*, vol. 65 (1931), pp. 217–255.

Stevenson, K., *Chivalry and Knighthood in Scotland, 1424–1513* (Woodbridge: Boydell Press, 2006).

Stones, E. L. G., 'The Records of the "Great Cause" of 1291–92', *The Scottish Historical Review* 35, no. 120 (1956), pp. 89–109.

Tanner, R. J., 'Cowing the Community? Coercion and Falsification in Robert Bruce's Parliaments, 1309–1318', in K. M. Brown and R. J. Tanner (eds), *The History of the Scottish Parliament , vol. 1: Parliament and Politics in Scotland, 1235–1560* (Edinburgh University Press: Edinburgh, 2004), pp. 50–73.

Taylor, C., *Chivalry and the Ideals of Knighthood in France during the Hundred Years War* (Cambridge: Cambridge University Press, 2013).

Taylor, S., P. McNiven, and E. Williamson, *Place Names of Kinross-shire* (Donington, 2017).

Tipping. R., et al., 'Landscape Dynamics and Climate Change as Agents at the Battle of Bannockburn', in *Bannockburn 1314–2014: Battle and Legacy*, ed. Michael Penman (Donington: Shaun Tyas, 2016), pp. 111–128.

Tout, T. F., *Chapters in the Administrative History of Mediaeval England: The Wardrobe, the Chamber and the Small seals* (6 vols., London, 1920–33).

Turpie, T., *Kind Neighbours: Scottish Saints and Society in the Later Middle Ages* (Leiden: Brill, 2015).

Vernier, R., *The Flower of Chivalry: Bertrand du Guesclin and the Hundred Years' War* (Woodbridge: Boydell Press, 2003).

Wærdahl, R. B., 'A Well-Adjusted Immigrant: Isabella Bruce, Queen Dowager of Norway, 1299–1358', in *Gender and Mobility in Scotland and Abroad*, eds. S. Dye, E. Ewan, and A. Glaze (Guelph: Centre for Scottish Studies, 2018), pp. 31–48.

Warner, K., *Edward II: The Unconventional King* (Stroud: Amberley, 2015).

Watson, F., 'Sir William Wallace: What We Do – and Don't – Know', in E. J. Cowan (ed), *The Wallace Book* (Edinburgh: John Donald, 2007), pp. 26–41.

Watson, F., *Under the Hammer: Edward I and Scotland* (2nd edn., Edinburgh: Birlinn, 2022).

Webster, P., 'Crown versus Church after Becket: King John, St Thomas and the Interdict', in M.-P. Gelin (ed), *The Cult of St Thomas Becket in the Plantagenet World, c.1170–c.1220*, pp 147–170.

Woolgar, C. M., *The Great Household in Late Medieval England* (London: Yale University Press, 1999).

Yeoman, P., 'War and (in) Pieces: Stirling Castle, June 1314', in *Bannockburn 1314–2014: Battle and Legacy*, ed. Michael Penman (Donington: Shaun Tyas, 2016), pp. 129–138.

Young, A., *Robert the Bruce's rivals: The Comyns, 1212–1314* (East Linton: Tuckwell Press, 1997).

# Notes

## Introduction

1. Morris, *Bannockburn*; Christison, 'Bannockburn – 23rd and 24th June 1314: A Study in Military History'; DeVries, *Infantry Warfare*; Nusbacher, *The Battle of Bannockburn*; Brown, *Bannockburn: The Scottish War and the British Isles 1307–1323*; Cornell, *Bannockburn: The Triumph of Robert the Bruce*; C. Brown, *Bannockburn 1314*; Penman, *Bannockburn 1314–2014*; Moffat, *Bannockburn: The Battle of a Nation*; Murray Cook, *Bannockburn and Stirling Bridge*.
2. Barrow, *Robert Bruce and the Community of the Realm*; McNamee, *Robert Bruce: Our Most Valiant Prince, King and Lord*; Penman, *Robert the Bruce*; Carradice, *Robert the Bruce*; Prestwich, *Three Edwards*; Phillips, *Edward II*; Warner, *Edward II: The Unconventional King*; Spinks, *Edward II The Man*.
3. For the suggestion that there were initially seven guardians, cf. Broun, 'New information on the Guardians' appointment'.
4. *RPS*, 1290/7/1.
5. Stevenson, *Docs.*, i, no. 12; Penman, *Robert the Bruce*, pp. 26–27.
6. Barrow, *Robert Bruce and the Community of the Realm*, p. 110.
7. Penman, *Robert the Bruce*, pp. 48–51.
8. *CDS*, ii, no. 1978.
9. Phillips, *Edward II*, p. 33, 40; Fordun gives the date of Bruce's birth as 'In twelve seven four since Christ our manhood wore,/And at the feast when Benedict deceased', i.e., 11 July 1274, *Chron. Fordun*, p. 300.
10. *CDS*, ii, no. 1191.
11. Tipping et al., 'Landscape Dynamics', p. 112.
12. Watson, *Under the Hammer*, p. 225.
13. Brown, *The Wars of Scotland*, pp. 196–197.
14. Palgrave, *Docs.*, no. 146 (2).
15. The seminal work on this episode in Bruce's life remains A. Grant, 'The Death of John Comyn: What Was Going On?', *The Scottish Historical Review* 86, no. 222 (2007), pp. 176–224.
16. *Chron. Fordun*, pp. 330–331; *The Bruce*, Bk. 1, ll. 477–514; Barbour even offers potential insight into the nature of Bruce's offer to Comyn, suggesting that he would exchange his existing lands and titles for Comyn's support for his kingship,

a similar offer to that which Bruce's grandfather had briefly mooted with Floris, count of Holland, during the 'Great Cause', Stevenson, *Docs.*, i, no. 255.
17. *The Bruce*, Bk. 2, ll. 43–48.
18. Dean, 'Projecting Dynastic Majesty', p. 34; Bishop Lamberton played his part by celebrating Palm Sunday Mass for the king at Scone two days after the inauguration ceremony.
19. Penman, *Robert the Bruce*, p. 92.
20. *Anglo-Scottish Relations*, no. 34.
21. For instance, it would appear that James Douglas, who would afterwards become renowned as one of Bruce's most fearsome partisans, was still trying to negotiate his submission to the English – 'dickering to desert', as Prof. A. A. M. Duncan once put it – until Bruce's victory at Loudoun Hill convinced him otherwise; *CDS*, ii, no. 1979; Duncan, *The Bruce*, p. 305.
22. *The Bruce*, Bk. 9, ll. 295–301.
23. *Chron. Bower*, vi, pp. 319–321.
24. *English Historical Documents*, iii, pp. 529–539.
25. That is, those who had composed the Ordinances.
26. *Vita Edward Secundi*, pp. 39–41.
27. Maddicott, *Thomas of Lancaster*, pp. 130–131.
28. *Chron. Bower*, vi, p. 349; *The Bruce*, Bk. 9, ll. 387–394.

## Chapter 1

1. Phillips, *Edward II*, pp. 212–213.
2. *RRS*, v, nos. 35–37.
3. *RRS*, v, nos. 29–33.
4. Penman, *Robert the Bruce*, p. 135; Boardman, *Early Stewart Kings*, p. 22; David may also have used the title to identify his cousin Alexander Bruce as heir presumptive for a brief period in the 1330s, Penman, *David II*, pp. 40–41.
5. *RMS*, i, no. 45.
6. Tanner, 'Cowing the community?', pp. 50–73.
7. *RPS*, 1315/1.
8. *RPS*, 1318/30.
9. Borthwick and MacQueen, *Law, Lordship and Tenure, passim* but esp. chaps. 1-3.
10. *The Bruce*, Bk. 20, ll. 75–78.
11. Barrow and Barnes, 'The Movements of Robert Bruce', p. 58; *The Bruce*, Bk. 9, ll. 33–62.
12. *Chron. Lanercost*, p. 238; *Vita Edwardi Secundi*, pp. 163–167; *The Bruce*, Bk. 17, ll. 491–530.
13. '...*si febles et si defait qil ne durra mie tauntque a cel oure ove leide de Dieu, car il ne poait guerps mover forsque la lange*', Sayles, *Affairs in Ireland*, no. 155.

14. The Lanercost chronicler, for instance, describes him as *'leprosus'*, *Chron. Lanercost*, p. 257; Le Bel states that he suffered from *'la grosse maladie'* ('the unclean sickness'), *Chron. Le Bel*, p. 34; Gray claims that he died *'de lepre'* ('of leprosy'), *Scalacronica*, p. 107; Dr Michael Penman has presented a particularly valuable discussion of the issues surrounding the king's final illness, Penman, *Robert the Bruce*, pp. 302–304.
15. His last known act was the inspection of a charter concerning lands in Peebleshire a mere week before his death, *RRS*, v, no. 383.
16. Duncan, *The Bruce*, p. 406n.
17. That who-so claimed to have [the] right/To hold land or property in Scotland,/That they should within twelve months/Come and claim it and therefore do/Homage to the king/And if they did not come within that year/Then should without doubt/[their representations] should be heard thereafter; *The Bruce*, Bk. 13, ll. 734–741.
18. *RPS*, 1314/1; this assembly will be examined in detail in the concluding chapter.
19. Duncan, 'War of the Scots', p. 149.
20. Penman, *Robert the Bruce*, p. 136.
21. *RPS*, 1314/1.
22. *RPS*, 1308/1.
23. *RPS*, 1309/1–3.
24. Penman, *Robert the Bruce*, pp. 332–333.
25. *CDS*, iii, no. 332.
26. Maxwell-Irving, *Border Towers of Scotland*, ii, p. 4.
27. *CDS*, iii, p. 406.
28. Ibid., no. 333; T. F. Tout and J. S. Hamilton. 'Fitzwilliam, Sir Ralph (c. 1256–1316/17), baron.' *ODNB*, 23 Sep. 2004.
29. *Cal. Close Rolls*, 1313–18, p. 76.
30. The third best knight that men knew living in his day; *The Bruce*, Bk. 13, ll. 321–322; writing in the 1440s, Walter Bower, Abbot of Inchcolm, would claim that this reputation was traceable to Edward II's own court, although Bower does not cite a source for this claim, cf. *Chron. Bower*, vii, pp. 51–57.
31. *Scalacronica*, p. 77; Barbour too emphasises the physical closeness of Sir Giles and King Edward on the battlefield, cf. *The Bruce*, Bk. 13, ll. 299–302.
32. *CDS*, iii, no. 336.
33. *Rot. Scot.*, i, 114.
34. *CDS*, iii, no. 337.
35. It is difficult not to suspect a certain amount of excuse-making on the bishop's part here, since Bishop William Lamberton of St Andrews had since 1312 at the latest abandoned any pretence of supporting the English and begun to openly serve the Scottish royal administration.
36. McNamee, *Wars of the Bruces*, ch. 3.
37. T. Tout & J. Hamilton, Fitzwilliam, Sir Ralph (c. 1256–1316/17), baron, *ODNB*.

38. *Foedera*, ii, I, p. 237.
39. '*festum Nativitatis Sancti Johannis Baptistae proximo futurum.*'
40. *Parl. Writs*, II, ii, pp. 120–125.
41. '*contra inimicos et rebelles nostros illarum partium progressuri.*'
42. Simpkin, 'The English Army and the Scottish Campaign, 1310–11', pp. 23–24.
43. Phillips, *Edward II*, pp. 218–219.

## Chapter 2

1. *RRS*, v, no. 38.
2. He would for instance spent his final Christmas at Glenkill on the Isle of Arran, a short boat trip from Ayr; *ER*, i, p. 213.
3. The most detailed scholarly summaries of Edward's campaign of 1310 to 1311 and the Scottish response to it can be found in McNamee, *Wars of the Bruces*, pp. 47–55 and Simpkin, 'The English Army and the Scottish Campaign, 1310–11', pp. 14–39.
4. *CDS*, iii, no. 95.
5. For Lamberton's release from English captivity, cf. *CDS*, iii, no. 61; for Lamberton's attendance at the March parliament, cf. *RPS*, 1309/2. Date accessed: 24 January 2023; Edward II still expected the bishop's attendance at an English parliament at Stanford in Norfolk in June 1309, *CDS*, iii, no. 94.
6. Phillips, *Edward II*, p. 168.
7. Ibid., p. 166.
8. *Chron. Lanercost*, p. 190; Phillips, *Edward II*, p. 169.
9. *Vita Edwardi Secundi*, p. 23, 27.
10. Simpkin, 'The English Army and the Scottish Campaign, 1310–11', pp. 17–23; Phillips, *Edward II*, p. 169.
11. *Rot. Scot.*, i, pp. 83, 90, 92, 93.
12. *Itinerary*, pp. 64–76.
13. McNamee, *Wars of the Bruces*, p. 49.
14. *CDS*, iii, no. 168.
15. *CDS*, iii, no. 176; both Fitz Gilbert and Mowbray would later play significant roles in the events of 1314, as examined in later chapters.
16. *Vita Edwardi Secundi*, p. 23.
17. BL Cotton Titus A XIX, f. 87r, transcribed and translated in Broun, 'A New Letter of Robert I to Edward II'; Dr Michael Penman has argued that the letter was actually the product of the diplomatic offensive undertaken by the Scots during the two-year truce of 1319 to 1321, Penman, *Robert the Bruce*, pp. 120–121, 228–229.
18. *CDS*, iii, no. 166.
19. *The Bruce*, Bk. 18, ll. 243–258.
20. *Chron. Lanercost*, p. 191.

21. *The Bruce*, Bk. 17, ll. 500–530; McNamee, *Wars of the Bruces*, pp. 90–91; Penman, *Robert the Bruce*, pp. 207–208.
22. *Rot. Scot.*, i, 96.
23. *CDS*, iii, no. 197.
24. McNamee, *Wars of the Bruces*, pp. 51–52; Phillips, *Edward II*, p. 170; both Phillips and McNamee have both argued that the mysterious arrest of the royal clerk John Walwayn – a possible author of the *Vita* – for apparently conducting secret talks with Bruce, mentioned in *CDS*, v, no. 554 may have been related to the negotiations concerning Gaveston, hinted at in the *Vita* and by the Lanercost chronicler; Penman, however, has cast doubt on this: Penman, *Robert the Bruce*, pp. 122–123.
25. Simpkin, 'The English Army and the Scottish Campaign, 1310–11', p. 26; Phillips, *Edward II*, p. 171.
26. *CDS*, iii, no. 202.
27. *Vita Edwardi Secundi*, p. 27.
28. *Chron. Lanercost*, pp. 194–195; the Lanercost chronicler claims the second raid occurred around 'the feast of the Nativity of the Blessed Virgin' (i.e., 8 September), but Bishop Richard Kellaw of Durham reported at the time that it took place on 16 September, *RPD*, i, pp. 92–93.
29. Simpkin, 'The English Army and the Scottish Campaign, 1310–11', pp. 27–28.
30. *Chron. Le Bel*, p. 62; *Scalacronica*, p. 57.
31. Duncan, 'A Question about the Succession, 1364', p. 25 (my italics).
32. '*Bernardus abbas de Abirbroth...quondam monachum Abirbothoc*'; *Chron. Bower*, viii, pp. 13–15; the late Prof. D. E. R. Watt has done valuable work in distinguishing these three separate sources based on the formulae they use for expressing dates, Ibid., vi, pp. xvii–xviii.
33. Ibid., vi, p. 321.
34. *The Bruce*, Bk. 13, ll. 708, Bk. 20, ll. 597–600; Barbour also mentions having based his narrative of an encounter in Galloway on the testimony of one Sir Alan Cathcart, but it is unclear whether Cathcart was still alive at the time Barbour was writing; for discussions of Barbour's potential association with Archibald 'the Grim', cf. McDiarmid, *The Bruce*, Vol. 1, pp. 7, 10–11; Duncan, *The Bruce*, pp. 2–3; for detailed discussion of the likely sources of patronage for *The Bruce*, cf. Boardman, and Foran, 'Introduction: King Robert the Bruce's Book', pp. 4–5, 13–16.
35. A. A. M. Duncan, 'Barbour, John (c. 1330–1395), ecclesiastic and verse historian', *ODNB*, 23 Sep. 2004; Accessed 29 Jan. 2023.
36. Won great esteem for chivalry; Renowned in several lands; *The Bruce*, Bk. 1, ll. 21–36.
37. For an in-depth discussion of this process, cf. Macdonald, *Border Bloodshed*, ch. 1.
38. S. Boardman, 'Thar nobill eldrys gret bounte', pp. 191–212.
39. *The Bruce*, Bk. 6, ll. 323–374.

40. And no man can be worthy/Unless he has intelligence to guide his actions/And to see what can and cannot be accomplished.
41. Ibid., Bk. 16, ll. 339–341.
42. The term 'slycht' appears twenty-one times in *The Bruce*, while the related terms 'sley' or 'slely' appear a further eleven times.
43. So it was here, but he was intelligent/And saw he might in no way/Fight his foes with even numbers/Therefore he decided to *proceed with cunning*; *The Bruce*, Bk. 5, ll. 266–270 (my italics).
44. Ibid., Bk. 9, ll. 677–681.
45. But the good king who was always intelligent/In all his deeds/Saw the stone walls were so strong/And saw the defence [those inside] were ready to make/And how hard the town would be to take/With open assault, strength, or might./Therefore he decided to *proceed with cunning*,/And in all the time he lay there/He spied and cleverly assessed/Where the ditch was shallowest/Until at last he found a place/That men might wade across [with the water] up to their shoulders; Ibid., Bk. 9, ll. 346–357 (my italics).
46. Therefore, men who make war/Should set their purpose evermore/To stand against their foes' might/Sometimes with strength and sometimes with cunning/And always seek to succeed; Ibid., Bk. 3, ll. 259–263.
47. But after he heard how Roxburgh had been/Taken by ruse, all his effort/And intelligence and industry I promise/He set [out] to find some stratagem/That might help him, through physicality/Mixed with high chivalry,/To win the wall of the castle/By some sort of ruse, for he knew well/That no power might openly take it/While those within had men and supplies; Ibid., Bk. 10, ll. 517–527 (my italics); for the importance of competition in chivalric society in late medieval Europe, cf. Keen, *Chivalry*, pp. 97–101; Kaeuper, *Chivalry and Violence in Late Medieval Europe*, pp. 149–155; Stevenson, *Chivalry and Knighthood in Scotland*, ch. 4; both the capture of Roxburgh and Edinburgh Castles will be explored in greater detail.
48. For in his time, as men tell me,/Thirteen times he was defeated/And he had fifty-seven victories./He thought it unseemly to lie idle for long,/He had no concerns apart from his labour,/*[and] it is reasonable for men to love him [for it]*; *The Bruce*, Bk. 8, ll. 431–436 (my italics).
49. Ibid., Bk. 19, ll. 361–369; Geoffrey de Charny devoted a considerable portion of his treatise on chivalry to the value of renown in a chivalric context, which in turn serves to highlight the relevance of Douglas's reputation for cunning to his knightly virtue, cf. Charny, *The Book of Chivalry*, pp. 85–99.
50. *The Bruce*, Bk. 20, ll. 373–396.
51. Taylor, *Chivalry and the Ideals of Knighthood in France during the Hundred Years War*, pp. 139–148.
52. '*Il n'y regardant profit, ne avantage pour leurs amis, ne a la grant grievance de leurs ennemis*'; Charny, *The Book of Chivalry*, p. 150.

53. H. Bonet, *Tree of Battles*, p. 122.
54. Vernier, *The Flower of Chivalry*, pp. 67–68; Taylor, *Chivalry and the Ideals of Knighthood in France*, pp. 46–51.
55. '*die Lunae proximo ante festum Sancti Barnabae Apostoli… cum equis et armis, et toto servito nobia debito*'; *Foedera*, II, i, pp. 238–239.
56. '*tam nostra quam fidelium nostrorum castra, fortalicia, villas, & terras, in terra nostra Scoc*', *ac aliis terris nostris adjacentibus, invaserunt & occuparunt; homicidia, depraedationes, incendia, sacrilegia, et alia innumera facinora inhumaniter perpetrando.*'
57. *Foedera*, II, i, p. 239.
58. Prestwich, *War, Politics and Finance*, pp. 69–70 for the pay situation during the 1300 campaign into Galloway; Simpkin, 'The English Army and the Scottish Campaign, 1310–11', p. 29 for the 1310 campaign.
59. Powicke, *Military Obligation in Medieval England*, p. 141.
60. Maddicott, *Thomas of Lancaster, passim*.
61. *Vita Edwardi Secundi*, pp. 45–47; Valence had also been party to the capture of Gaveston, but his outrage at Gaveston's treatment in spite of the assurances given to him on his surrender pushed Valence firmly into the royal camp thereafter, Phillips, *Aymer de Valence*, pp. 36–37.
62. Fairbank, 'The last earl of Warenne and Surrey', pp. 198–199.
63. S. L. Waugh, 'Warenne, John de, seventh earl of Surrey [earl of Surrey and Sussex, Earl Warenne] (1286–1347), magnate', *ODNB*, 23 Sep. 2004; Accessed 29 Jan. 2023.
64. Phillips, *Edward II*, p. 227; Ayton has, however, suggested that some of those who might otherwise have served in the retinues of these magnates may still have fought at Bannockburn, albeit in the service of other lords, Ayton, 'In the Wake of Defeat', p. 40.
65. *Foedera*, II, i, p. 239.
66. Crouch, *Tournament*, pp. 31, 53.
67. Ibid., p. 130; Phillips, *Edward II*, pp. 40, 73.
68. *Cal. Close Rolls*, ii, p. 35; coincidentally Roger and Alexander were brothers of the Philip Mowbray, who, at this time, was serving as constable of Stirling Castle for Edward II.
69. Ross, 'Men for All Seasons?', pp. 10–20; F. Watson, 'Strathbogie, David, styled tenth earl of Atholl (d. 1326), magnate and soldier', *ODNB*, 23 Sep. 2004; Accessed 30 Jan. 2023.
70. *Chron. Guisborough*, p. 369; *Flores Historiarum*, iii, pp. 134–135; *Scalacronica*, p. 55; the Lanercost chronicler states that his remains were displayed higher than those of other Scottish 'rebels', *Chron. Lanercost*, p. 179.
71. Joan is described as being 24 years old in November 1316, which would make her 21 or 22 in January 1314, *CDS*, iii, no. 512.

72. *CDS*, ii, no. 1979; *CDS*, iii, no. 200.
73. *CDS*, iii, no. 108 and p. 404; *Rot. Scot.*, i, p. 107; Barnes and Barrow, 'The Movements of Robert Bruce', pp. 57–59; Barrow, *Robert Bruce and the Community of the Realm*, pp. 171–172.
74. *CDS*, iii, no. 200.
75. *RRS*, v, no. 24.
76. The king's confirmation in October 1312 of an agreement between Hay and Sir Michael Scot of Balweary concerning lands in Perthshire and an undated grant of land at Slains in Aberdeenshire may have been intended as compensation for Hay's loss of the constableship in favour of Strathbogie, *RRS*, vi, nos. 23, 474; Ross, 'Men for All Seasons?', p. 15.
77. *Scalacronica*, p. 73.
78. For discussion of the likelihood of an actual marriage between Isabella Strathbogie and Edward Bruce, cf. Penman, *Robert the Bruce*, pp. 135–136.
79. *The Bruce*, Bk. 13, ll. 488–494.
80. Ross, 'Men for All Seasons?', p. 17.
81. Penman, *Robert the Bruce*, p. 136.
82. For the terms of the grant of the earldom of Moray, cf. *RRS*, v, no. 389; for King Robert's efforts to promote Randolph as a counter-balance to Strathbogie power in the Highlands, cf. Penman, Robert the Bruce, pp. 128–129.
83. A sense of the sheer scale of Douglas's landed holdings in the south can be seen in the so-called 'Emerald Charter' of 1324, which granted him regality rights within the bounds of these estates, most of which he had accumulated through service to King Robert, *RMS*, i, App. 1, no. 38; yet at the same time, Randolph's possession of the lordships of Annandale and Nithsdale in the south-west and Stichill in the south-east served to temper Douglas's regional dominance, as did Edward Bruce's claim on the lordship of Galloway (at least until his death in 1318); for the expansion of Stewart and Campbell interests in the west under Robert I, cf. Boardman, *The Campbells*, pp. 42–48, Penman, *Robert the Bruce*, pp. 165, 299.
84. *CDS*, iii, no. 351.
85. For a detailed reconstruction of Douglas's life and career, cf. Cameron, 'A Study of the Career of Sir James Douglas'.
86. '*pro salute anime nostre et pro salute animarum predecessorum et successorum nostrorum regum Scocie*'; *RRS*, v, no. 39.
87. Barrow, *Robert Bruce and the Community of the Realm*, p. 151; Penman, *Robert the Bruce*, pp. 98, 101.
88. *Chron. Bower*, vi, p. 363.
89. *RRS*, v, no. 134; *RRS*, v, no. 135; *RRS*, v, no. 138.
90. Taylor, McNiven, and Williamson, *Place Names of Kinross-shire*, p. 540.
91. *MRH: Scotland*, p. 93.

92. For Bruce's devotion to the cult of St Thomas, see below; for his veneration of St Serf, cf. Penman, *Robert the Bruce*, p. 131.
93. *Cal. Close Rolls*, ii, p. 51.
94. F. Barlow, 'Becket, Thomas [St Thomas of Canterbury, Thomas of London] (1120?–1170), archbishop of Canterbury', *ODNB*, 23 Sep. 2004; Accessed 31 Jan. 2023.
95. Guy, *Thomas Becket*, pp. 337–338.
96. Duggan, 'Becket is Dead', p. 42.
97. Owen, *William the Lion*, pp. 59–60; Turpie, *Kind Neighbours*, p. 72.
98. Penman, *Robert the Bruce*, pp. 17–18.
99. *CDS*, v, no. 492u.
100. *Chron. Guisborough*, p. 295.
101. *Chron. Rishanger*, p. 191.
102. *Chron. Bower*, vi, pp. 363–365.
103. A. A. M. Duncan, 'Douglas family (per. c. 1170–c. 1300), barons', *ODNB*, 23 Sep. 2004; Accessed 31 Jan. 2023.
104. *CDS*, ii, nos. 1054, 1055; *CDS*, iii, no. 682.
105. *The Bruce*, Bk. 1, ll. 345–359; Duncan has suggested that Douglas may actually have entered the bishop's service around the time of his father's death, and thus his three-year stint in France can be identified as being due to Bishop Lamberton's extended diplomatic missions to the Continent between 1301 and 1304, Duncan, *The Bruce*, p. 62. The entire matter is complicated by the fact that a James Douglas appears as a valet of either Sir Henry Sinclair or Sir Robert Keith at Linlithgow sometime between February 1307 and July 1307, *CDS*, v, no. 492p; this individual has generally been assumed to be James Douglas of Lothian, but on little other basis than an unwillingness to contradict Barbour, as argued in Cameron, 'A Study of the Career of Sir James Douglas' (PhD thesis, University of Aberdeen, 1992). It may be that Barbour based the youthful adventures of his hero on that of Douglas's son – and Barbour's potential patron – Archibald 'the Grim', Brown, *The Black Douglases*, p. 53.
106. *The Bruce*, Bk. 1, ll. 407–444; Cameron, 'A Study of the Career of Sir James Douglas', pp. 33–37.
107. Brown, *The Black Douglases*, pp. 17–19.
108. *The Bruce*, Bk. 10, ll. 358.
109. He had Simon Ledhouse/A crafty and skilful man/Make ladders out of hempen ropes/With wooden steps so [tightly] bound/That they would not break for any reason./A strong and sturdy iron/hook they made at the end [of the ropes]/That when placed in an embrasure [in a castle wall]/The ladder [would] therefore hang straight down/And remain securely upright [against the wall]; Ibid., Bk. 10, ll. 363–372.
110. *Chron. Lanercost*, p. 201.

111. *The Bruce*, Bk. 10, ll. 373–379.
112. *Chron. Lanercost*, p. 204; *Vita Edwardi Secundi*, p. 85; *Scalacronica*, p. 71.
113. *The Bruce*, Bk. 10, ll. 380–381, 384–385.
114. Without a doubt/He [i.e., the farmer] shall make merry tonight though they [i.e., his cattle]/ Will be led away by Douglas; [Douglas] has paid good attention/To their speech; Ibid., Bk. 10, ll. 388–402.
115. Ibid., Bk. 10, ll. 408–422.
116. *Scalacronica*, pp. 71–73; *The Bruce*, Bk. 10, ll. 377; the Lanercost chronicler broadly confirms this by stating that it occurred 'at the beginning of Lent', *Chron. Lanercost*, p. 204.
117. *The Bruce*, Bk. 10, ll. 442–467.
118. Ibid., Bk. 10, ll. 473–494; Gray implies that Fiennes was killed immediately by the arrow, but this is hardly a troubling contradiction, *Scalacronica*, p. 73.
119. *The Bruce*, Bk. 10, ll. 497–498.
120. Ibid., Bk. 10, ll. 499–506.
121. Prestwich, *Armies and Warfare in the Middle Ages*, p. 209.

# Chapter 3

1. *Cal. Close Rolls*, ii, p. 40.
2. *Chron, Guisborough*, pp. 271–272.
3. *Cal. Inq. P.M.*, iv, no. 427.
4. *CDS*, iii, no. 199.
5. *CDS*, iii, no. 282.
6. See above, n4.
7. *Cal. Close Rolls*, ii, p. 38.
8. Phillips. *Edward II*, p. 219.
9. *CDS*, iii, nos. 353, 367; the fact that the document of 5 July excused Joanna of debts she owed concerning her estates at Faxfleet may also indicate that Edward's judicial officers had failed to bring the aforementioned 'evil-doers' to justice and she was thus being compensated for her losses.
10. J. R. Maddicott, 'Beaumont, Sir Henry de (c. 1280–1340), baron', *ODNB*, 23 Sep. 2004; Accessed 1 Feb. 2023.
11. Young, *Robert the Bruce's Rivals: The Comyns*, pp. 206–207.
12. *CDS*, iii, no. 233; already by this point Joanna had been granted her lands at Faxfleet because 'her lands in Scotland were lost through the war'.
13. Penman, *David II*, pp. 29–30, 46–48; MacInnes, *Scotland's Second War of Independence*, pp. 151, 211.
14. *Cal. Chancery Warrants*, i, pp. 395–396.
15. *Cal. Chancery Warrants*, i, p. 270; *CDS*, ii, no. 17, iii, no. 1636.

16. *Foedera*, II, i, p. 244; Edward's earlier effort to prohibit an unlicenced tournament at Blyth can be found in Ibid., p. 239, and is discussed earlier.
17. Morris, *Bannockburn*, p. 40.
18. Bradbury, *The Medieval Archer*, pp. 71–138; Hardy, *Longbow: A Social and Military History*; Loades, *War Bows*, pp. 78–87; Prof. Kelly DeVries has questioned the extent of the supremacy of the longbow in the fourteenth century, DeVries, *Infantry Warfare*, pp. 5–6.
19. *Chron. Rishanger*, p. 188; Barrow, *Robert Bruce and the Community of the Realm*, pp. 102–103.
20. DeVries has drawn a direct connection between the tactics employed at Bannockburn and Edward III's deployment of archers at the Battle of Halidon Hill in 1333, DeVries, *Infantry Warfare*, pp. 127–128.
21. *Cal. Close Rolls*, ii, p. 42; *Rot. Scot.*, i, p. 115.
22. Fraser, 'The Pattern of Trade in the North-East of England, 1265–1350', in *Northern History*, iv (1969), p. 47.
23. *Chron. Lanercost*, p. 199.
24. McNamee, *Wars of the Bruces*, p. 79.
25. Salter, *The Castles and Tower Houses of Northumberland*, p. 38.
26. *Rot. Scot.*, i, pp. 114–115; for Convers as the 'king's clerk', cf. *Cal. Close Rolls*, iv, p. 102.
27. CDS, iii, nos. 403, 438.
28. *RMS*, i, App. I, no. 80; for Stephen's probable relationship to William, cf. Penman, *Robert the Bruce*, p. 262.
29. *Rot. Scot.*, i, p. 115.
30. McNamee, *Wars of the Bruces*, p. 62 (2,000 cavalry); Phillips, *Edward II*, p. 226 ('over' 2,000 cavalry); Morris, *Bannockburn*, p. 35 (2,000 to 2,500 cavalry); Barrow, *Robert Bruce and the Community of the Realm*, p. 206 (2,000 to 3,000 cavalry); Penman, *Robert the Bruce*, p. 141 (2,000 to 3,000 cavalry).
31. *Cal. Patent Rolls*, ii, mem. 20.
32. Phillips, *Edward II*, pp. 166, 185.
33. *Foedera*, II, I, p. 129.
34. For Gloucester's war record in Scotland, cf. McNamee, *Wars of the Bruces*, pp. 51–52; Phillips, *Edward II*, pp. 113, 153–154, 170–171.
35. M. Altschul, 'Clare, Gilbert de, eighth earl of Gloucester and seventh earl of Hertford (1291–1314), magnate', *ODNB*, 23 Sep. 2004; Accessed 5 Feb. 2023.
36. Maddicott, *Thomas of Lancaster*, pp. 133–134; Phillips, *Edward II*, pp. 197–201.
37. M. Altschul, *A Baronial Family in Medieval England: The Clares*, p. 39.
38. *Rot. Scot.*, i, pp. 115–116.
39. G. W. S. Barrow, 'Elizabeth [née Elizabeth de Burgh] (d. 1327), queen of Scots', *ODNB*, 23 Sep. 2004; Accessed 7 Feb. 2023.

40. Barrow, *Robert Bruce and the Community of the Realm*, p. 123-4; McNamee, *Wars of the Bruces*, p. 27; Penman, *Robert the Bruce*, p. 66, 72.
41. *Aestimo quod rec aestivalis sis; forsitan hyemalis non eris*; *Flores Historiarum*, p. 130.
42. *Chron. Fordun*, pp. 334–335; *The Bruce*, Bk. 4, ll. 39–56; for Isabella's status in Norway, cf. Wærdahl, 'A Well-Adjusted Immigrant'.
43. '*bien d'age et nyent gayes*'; Palgrave, *Docs*, no. 155.
44. G. W. S. Barrow, 'Elizabeth [née Elizabeth de Burgh] (d. 1327), queen of Scots', *ODNB*, 23 Sep. 2004; Accessed 7 Feb. 2023.
45. *CDS*, iii, no. 169; *Foedera*, ii, I, p. 155.
46. *Foedera*, ii, I, p. 201; *CDS*, iii, no. 323, 324; for the members of Queen Elizabeth's household, cf. *Foedera*, ii, I, p. 247.
47. Ibid., p. 244.
48. Another of King Robert's sisters, Mary Bruce, had been captured in 1306. Mary is not mentioned in any of the documents concerning the prisoner exchanges after Bannockburn, but she was at liberty to marry Sir Neil Campbell and later Sir Alexander Fraser in the years before her death sometime before September 1323. A document drawn up on 8 February 1312 indicates that the English crown proposed to exchange her for the captive Richard Mowbray, brother of Sir Philip Mowbray, suggesting that she may have been released before Bannockburn, *CDS*, iii, no. 244.
49. *CDS*, iii, nos. 159, 254, 330.
50. *Vita Edwardi Secundi*, p. 85.
51. *The Bruce*, Bk. 10, ll. 327–340.
52. *Scalacronica*, p. 73.
53. *RRS*, v, no. 84; Gray states that Lebaud had been 'hanged and drawn' ('*pendre et treyner*') because King Robert 'believed that [Lebaud] had always been English at heart, and was waiting for his best chance to harm [Bruce]', *Scalacronica*, p. 73.
54. *The Bruce*, Bk. 10, ll. 311–326.
55. *Scalacronica*, p. 73; *Chron. Fordun*, p. 339; Fordun was likely working from an earlier, pro-Bruce source as discussed in Boardman, 'Chronicle Propaganda in Fourteenth-Century Scotland'.
56. *RRS*, nos. 101, 389; although repeatedly identified by Bruce as his nephew, the fact Randolph was not included as a potential successor to the kingship in either of the entails concerning the kingship of Scotland in 1315 or 1318 indicates that Randolph's mother cannot have been a blood relative of King Robert's father, from whom the Bruce claim proceeded, *RPS*, 1315/1., 1318/30. Date accessed: 7 February 2023.
57. *CDS*, ii, no. 1807; *Scalacronica*, pp. 53–55; *The Bruce*, Bk. 2, ll. 408–409, 466–467, Bk. 6, ll. 509–513, Bk. 7, ll. 87–90.
58. Ibid., Bk. 9, ll. 722–762.
59. Boardman and Foran, 'Introduction', pp. 7–8; this trend will be discussed in greater detail in chapter 6.

60. *RRS*, v, no. 389; *RPS*, 1309/1. Date accessed: 7 February 2023; *RMS*, i, App. 1, no. 34.
61. *The Bruce*, Bk. 10, ll. 517–534.
62. Barbour does at least claim that Randolph acted 'with the consent off the king' in laying siege to Edinburgh Castle, *The Bruce*, Bk. 10, ll. 311.
63. *Instrumenta Publica*, pp. 139–141.
64. *The Bruce*, Bk. 10, ll. 556–557; Duncan has suggested that Barbour's Francis was the knight named William Francis who served as constable of Kirkintilloch before 1306 and received lands at Sprouston circa 1322, but Barbour never identifies Francis as a knight, Duncan, *The Bruce*, p. 388.
65. *The Bruce*, Bk. 10, ll. 535–592.
66. Ibid., Bk. 10, ll. 591.
67. *Chron. Lanercost*, p. 204; the eastern side of the castle would have been the least steep angle from which the Scots might approach, but possibly it was felt by the Scottish war leaders that an assault on the opposite side to Randolph's ascent – while potentially more hazardous to the attackers – gave Randolph (or Francis's) ploy greater chance of success.
68. *Scalacronica*, p. 73.
69. *The Bruce*, Bk. 10, ll. 625-42.
70. Ibid., Bk. 10, ll. 741–760; St Margaret's Chapel had in fact been founded by her son, David I (r. 1124–1153), Fawcett, *Scottish Medieval Churches*, p. 27.
71. An 'ayre' was the practice of making a royal progress through a particular region so that the monarch could personally hear local legal cases and directly dispense royal justice, thereby consolidating their personal authority in the localities, *The Bruce*, Bk. 10, ll. 772–779.
72. *CDS*, iii, no. 355.
73. *Cal. Close Rolls*, p. 51.
74. Blakely, *The Brus Family in England and Scotland*, p. 65.
75. A. A. M. Duncan, 'Brus [Bruce], Robert de, lord of Annandale (d. 1194?), baron', *ODNB*, 23 Sep. 2004; Accessed 7 Feb. 2023.
76. Moor, *Knights of Edward I*, iv, pp. 278–280.
77. Maddicott, *Thomas of Lancaster*, p. 269.
78. Phillips, *Edward II*, p. 216.
79. Prestwich, *The Three Edwards*, pp. 90–93; Phillips, *Edward II*, pp. 275–276, 294–297, 608.
80. *Rot. Scot.*, i, p. 117.
81. Fryde, 'Antonio Pessagno of Genoa, king's merchant of Edward II', p. 161.
82. Kaeuper, 'The Frescobaldi of Florence and the English crown', pp. 82–83.
83. Phillips, *Edward II*, p. 219.
84. '*ad festum Nativitatis de Sancti Johannis Baptiste proximo futuruam.*'

85. *Foedera*, ii, I, p. 245.
86. Prestwich, *Edward I*, p. 131; *Foedera*, ii, I, pp. 238–239.
87. *Chron. Bower*, vii, pp. 151–153; Rose, *Kings in the North*, p. 328.
88. *Foedera*, ii, I, p. 187.
89. Beam, *The Balliol Dynasty*, pp. 203–204.
90. Phillips, *Edward II*, pp. 432–450.
91. *CDS*, iii, no. 740.
92. *Flores Historiarum*, p. 233.
93. S. L. Waugh, 'Thomas [Thomas of Brotherton], first earl of Norfolk (1300–1338), magnate', *ODNB*, 23 Sep. 2004, Accessed 7 Feb. 2023; Stone (ed. and trans.), *Medieval English Verse*, pp. 113–114.
94. *Rot. Scot.*, i, p. 117.
95. Ibid., p. 96; *CDS*, iii, no. 203; as in 1314, the fleet does not appear to have made any traceable impact if indeed it did attempt to land in the west, cf. McNamee, *Wars of the Bruces*, p. 52.
96. *Cal. Patent Rolls*, ii, mem. 18.
97. S. L. Waugh, 'Vescy, William de, Lord Vescy (1245–1297), baron', *ODNB*, 23 Sep. 2004; Accessed 8 Feb. 2023; she was not the Isabella de Vescy who was a close companion of Edward's queen Isabella and sister of Henry Beaumont, another Bannockburn participant; Doherty, *Isabella and the Strange Death of Edward II*, pp. 49, 61.
98. *Foedera*, II, i, p. 245.
99. *Cal. Patent Rolls*, ii, pp. 120–121.
100. This would be confirmed in a separate document a mere four days later on 26 March, in which Edward expressed his trust 'in the full fidelity of the aforesaid earl' ('*de fidelitate praedicti comitis ad plenum confidentes*') and described him as 'our beloved and faithful Richard de Burgh, earl of Ulster' ('*dilectum et fidelem nostrum, Richardum de Burgo comitem Ultoniae*'); *Foedera*, II, i, p. 246.
101. '*Risderd a Brucc Iarla Ulad ar fut Erenn cin tren cin tresi ri hed na bliadna-sin*'; *Ann. Connacht*, p. 241.
102. Duffy, 'Bruce Brothers', p. 61; Lydon, 'The Bruce Invasion of Ireland', pp. 74, 80; McNamee, *Wars of the Bruces*, p. 170; Penman, *Robert the Bruce*, pp. 164, 173.
103. *Chron. Bower*, vi, pp. 385–403.
104. *Ann. Inisfallen*, pp. 419–420.
105. McNamee, *Wars of the Bruces*, pp. 182–184.
106. Ibid., p. 174; Duffy, 'Bruce Invasion of Ireland', pp. 16–17; Lydon, 'The Impact of the Bruce Invasion', p. 133.
107. Duffy, 'Bruce Invasion of Ireland', p. 31.
108. *The Bruce*, Bk. 14, ll. 329–382.
109. *Cal. Close Rolls*, ii, p. 95.

110. *Parl. Writs*, II, I, pp. 424–425; *Rot. Scot.*, i, pp. 119–120.
111. Prestwich, *Armies and Warfare in the Middle Ages*, pp. 128–129.
112. Macdonald, *Border Bloodshed*, pp. 170–171.
113. '*custodi terrae Scotiae*'; *Foedera*, II, i, pp. 245–246.
114. *CDS*, ii, no. 1754.
115. *Chron. Lanercost*, p. 177; *Scalacronica*, pp. 53, 57; *Chron. Fordun*, p. 334; *The Bruce*, Bk. 2, ll. 195–470, Bk. 8, ll. 126–370; Phillips, *Aymer de Valence*, p. 25.
116. *Rot. Scot.*, i, p. 121.
117. *CDS*, ii, no. 1755.
118. *Rot. Scot.*, i, p. 121.
119. *CDS*, iii, nos. 203, 420–1.
120. W. D. H. Sellar, 'MacDougall, John, lord of Argyll (d. 1316), magnate', *ODNB*, 23 Sep. 2004; Accessed 10 Feb. 2023; Barbour identifies Comyn as Macdougall's 'emys' ('uncle') but is perhaps conflating the Comyn killed by Bruce in 1306 with his father and namesake who had died circa 1302, *The Bruce*, Bk. 3, ll. 3–4.
121. *Chron. Fordun*, pp. 334–335, 338; *The Bruce*, Bk. 3, ll. 1–54, Bk. 10, ll. 1–130.
122. *Rot. Scot*, i, p. 121.
123. McNamee, *Wars of the Bruces*, p. 202 n74.
124. Penman, *Robert the Bruce*, p. 223.
125. Broun, Taylor, et al. (eds), *The Dynamic Edition of the Declaration of Arbroath*, online at The Community of the Realm in Scotland, 1249–1424: History, Law and Charters in a Recreated Kingdom (https://cotr.ac.uk/texts).
126. *Chron. Fordun*, p. 341; *Chron. Bower*, vii, p. 3.
127. *Rot. Scot.*, i, p. 121.
128. Young, *Robert the Bruce's Rivals*, p. 193.
129. *Rot. Scot.*, i, p. 122.
130. *Cal, Close Rolls*, p. 44.
131. Ibid., p. 46.
132. *Rot. Scot.*, i, p. 122.

# Chapter 4

1. Phillips, *Edward II*, p. 49.
2. *Historia Anglicana*, i, p. 138; the gift was made on *Vigilia Palmarum*, that is, 'the Vigil of Palm Sunday', with Palm Sunday falling on 31 March in 1314.
3. R. Sharpe, 'The late antique passion of St Alban', pp. 30–37.
4. *Chron. Lanercost*, p. 206.
5. *Rot. Scot.*, i, p. 122.
6. Woolgar, *The Great Household in Late Medieval England*, pp. 20, 190.
7. *Rot. Scot.*, i, p. 122.
8. Phillips, *Edward II*, pp. 177, 217–219.

9. *Cal. Close Rolls*, ii, p. 46.
10. '*Skymburnesse... in festo Nativitatis Sancti Johannis Baptistae proximo sequenti*'; *Foedera*, II, i, p. 246.
11. *Chron. Trokelowe*, p. 83.
12. '"*Scis*" – inquit – "*quod fratres mei apud Sanctum Albanum corpus ejusdem Martyris putant veraciter se habere, et in hoc loco dicunt monachi se dicti Santi corpus tenere; per animam*" – inquit, – "*Dei, volo videre in quo loco reliquias sancti corporis debeo potissimum vererari*"'; *Historia Anglicana*, pp. 138–139.
13. *Chron. Lanercost*, p. 206.
14. *Rot. Scot.*, i, p. 123.
15. *Cal. Close Rolls*, pp. 46, 47.
16. *Rot. Scot.*, i, p. 123.
17. *Parl. Writs*, II, i, pp. 425–426.
18. *Cal. Close Rolls*, pp. 46–47.
19. *Cal. Patent Rolls*, ii, mem. 14.
20. Grant, *Independence and Nationhood*, pp. 148, 161–162; Neville, *Land, Law and People*, pp. 13–14; for the difficulties that could arise when a king was perceived to be failing in his responsibility to carry royal authority into the localities, cf. Macdougall, *James III*, p. 145.
21. On the same day, Edward II was at Crowland in Lincolnshire, where he issued instructions for the sheriffs of Hereford and Worcester to recover armour and other goods taken from one Richard Talbot, who was due to accompany the king on campaign, *Cal. Chancery Warrants*, i, p. 397.
22. *Chron. Lanercost*, pp. 205–206; the chronicler nonetheless insists that hostages had been taken as surety for the eventual payment of the disputed sum. Given the highly disciplined and systematic nature of the Bruce Scots' raiding activities from 1307 to 1328, it seems unlikely that they would breach a truce without cause, since this would jeopardize similar arrangements with the beleaguered northern English communities in the future.
23. *Cal. Patent Rolls*, i, p. 2.
24. *Cal. Close Rolls*, i, p. 42.
25. *Rot. Scot.*, i, pp. 77–78.
26. *Chron. Lanercost*, pp. 194–195.
27. Ibid., pp. 199–200.
28. '*le noble prince monsire Robert, par le grace de Dieu, roi d'Escoce*'; *RPD*, i, pp. 204–205.
29. McNamee, 'William Wallace's Invasion of Northern England, 1297'; Guisborough also recounts a noteworthy incident in which William Wallace was unable to adequately protect the canons of Hexham Priory from harassment from his men despite extending a letter of protection to the priory; *Chron. Guisborough*, pp. 305–306.
30. *Chron. Lanercost*, p. 194.

31. Ibid., p. 213; *Chron. Guisborough*, p. 396.
32. He had been with the king at St Albans on 1 April but must have moved swiftly north soon afterwards, Phillips, *Aymer de Valence*, p. 326.
33. McNamee, *Wars of the Bruces*, p. 75.
34. Ross, 'Recreating the Bannockburn Environment', pp. 108–110.
35. McNamee, *Wars of the Bruces*, p. 109.
36. *Chron. Lanercost*, pp. 216–217.
37. McNamee, *Wars of the Bruces*, p. 75.
38. The relevant passage can be found in *Chron. Le Bel*, chap. 10, pp. 39–40.
39. Modern accounts of the campaign in which Le Bel served can be found in Barrow, *Robert Bruce and the Community of the Realm*, pp. 252–253; McNamee, *Wars of the Bruces*, pp. 241–242; Penman, *Robert the Bruce*, pp. 280–282.
40. *Chron. Lanercost*, p. 205.
41. Barrow, *Robert Bruce and the Community of the Realm*, pp. 243–244; McNamee, *Wars of the Bruces*, pp. 98–101; Penman, *Robert the Bruce*, pp. 237–238.
42. For examples of Barbour's critical attitude towards Edward Bruce, cf. *The Bruce*, Bk. 9, ll. 665–676, Bk. 11, ll. 37–53, Bk. 16, ll. 246–258, 325–334, Bk. 18, ll. 175–184.
43. *Cal. Close Rolls*, ii, p. 49; he did make a concession to Sempringham Priory at the request of Sir Henry Beaumont, but there is no obvious link between this and Beaumont's service on the approaching campaign, *Cal. Chancery Warrants*, i, p. 398.
44. '*die Domenica proxima ante festum Pentecostes proximo futurum*'; *Rot. Scot.*, i, p. 124.
45. *Foedera*, II, i, p. 247.
46. Penman, *David II*, p. 202.
47. *Cal. Patent Rolls*, ii, mem. 15.
48. J. S. Hamilton, 'Despenser, Hugh, the elder, earl of Winchester (1261–1326), administrator and courtier', *ODNB*, 23 Sep. 2004; Accessed 12 Feb. 2023.
49. *Chron. Lanercost*, p. 208.
50. Phillips, *Edward II*, pp. 482–486, 512–513.
51. Penman, *Robert the Bruce*, p. 139 dismisses this possibly, based on the lack of direct evidence of the banner's collection in 1314.
52. Bede, *Hist. Eccl.*, 4.23; 5.2–6, 24.
53. D. M. Palliser, 'John of Beverley [St John of Beverley] (d. 721), bishop of York', *ODNB*, 23 Sep. 2004; Accessed 12 Feb. 2023.
54. *Cal. Close Rolls*, ii, p. 53.
55. *Chron. Lanercost*, p. 206.
56. *Cal. Close Rolls*, ii, p. 56.
57. *Cal. Patent Rolls*, ii, mem. 11.
58. Ibid., mem. 11.
59. Prestwich, 'Cavalry Service in Early-Fourteenth-Century England', p. 152.

60. *The Bruce*, Bk. 20, ll. 601–611.
61. Marner, *St Cuthbert*, pp. 12–16.
62. McGuigan, 'Cuthbert's relics and the origins of the diocese of Durham', pp. 151–158.
63. *Chron. Lanercost*, p. 206.
64. Penman, *David II*, p. 129; Macdougall, *James IV*, p. 273.
65. Blakely, *Brus Family*, App. 3, nos. 118, 119, 137 identify charters from the Bruces to Durham Cathedral.
66. *CDS*, iii, no. 357.
67. *Chron. Fordun*, p. 323.
68. *The Bruce*, Bk. 9, ll. 722–730.
69. *CDS*, iii, no. 356.
70. *PROME*, Parliament Roll of 1315, item 23.
71. *Cal. Close Rolls*, ii, p. 56.
72. Macdonald, *Border Bloodshed*, p. 192.

# Chapter 5

1. *Scalacronica*, p. 73.
2. *The Bruce*, Bk. 10, ll. 486–491.
3. *Scalacronica*, pp. 115–117; *Chron. Fordun*, p. 348; *Chron. Wyntoun*, Bk. 8, ll. 3831–3836; *Chron. Bower*, vii, p. 91; MacInnes, *Scotland's Second War of Independence*, pp. 16–17.
4. Jones, 'The Battle of Verneuil', p. 378.
5. Penman, *Robert the Bruce*, pp. 137–138.
6. *The Bruce*, Bk. 10, ll. 818-30, Bk. 11, ll. 37–52; Barbour also claims that the deal was made on 24 June 1313, giving the English an entire year to prepare for the relief of the castle, but this is surely a mistake on Barbour's part, perhaps – as Duncan and King have suggested – due to the poet's confusion over the unusually short period of time before the deal's negotiation and the deadline it set, Ibid., p. 402n; *Scalacronica*, p. 228 n11.
7. For Carrick's response to his brother's criticism and the king's acceptance of the challenge the deal posed, cf. *The Bruce*, Bk. 11, ll. 53–68.
8. McDiarmid, *Barbour's Bruce*, p. 88.
9. Barrow, *Robert Bruce and the Community of the Realm*, pp. 208–209; McNamee, *Wars of the Bruces*, p. 62; Brown, *Bannockburn*, p. 109; Phillips, *Edward II*, p. 229.
10. Caldwell, 'Bannockburn: The Road to Victory', pp. 29–30; Penman, *Robert the Bruce*, p. 140.
11. *RPS*, 1314/1.
12. Prestwich, *Armies and Warfare in the Middle Ages*, p. 306.
13. Ibid., Bk. 11, ll. 321–327.

14. Ibid., Bk. 11, ll. 312–320.
15. Ibid., Bk. 11, ll. 313, Bk. 12, ll. 497–507.
16. *Scalacronica*, pp. 73–75.
17. Thought that Scotland was too little/For his brother and him also; *The Bruce*, Bk. 14, ll. 1–7.
18. *Chron. Fordun*, p. 340.
19. *RRS*, v, no. 101; Penman, *Robert the Bruce*, p. 171.
20. *The Bruce*, Bk. 11, ll. 328–236.
21. Cameron, 'Keeping the Customer Satisfied', pp. 65–66.
22. *Vita Edwardi Secundi*, p. 91.
23. *The Bruce*, Bk. 11, ll. 227–229.
24. Ibid., Bk. 11, ll. 223–226.
25. Fraser, *Menteith*, ii, no. 12; *Edward I and the Throne of Scotland*, ii, pp. 80–85.
26. Palgrave, *Docs.*, no. 109; James Stewart was forced to resubmit to Edward I in October 1306, having come out in support of Bruce's sudden bid for power, *Foedera*, II, i, p. 1001.
27. *The Bruce*, Bk. 13, ll. 699–701.
28. For the assembly at Ayr and Marjory's marital status in April 1315, cf. *RPS*, 1315/1; for Bruce's western progress in spring 1315, cf. *The Bruce*, Bk. 15, ll. 266–318; Penman, *Robert the Bruce*, p. 166.
29. C. A. McGladdery, 'Keith family (per. c. 1300–c. 1530), nobility', *ODNB*, 23 Sep. 2004; Accessed 26 Feb. 2023.
30. *CDS*, ii, no. 1406, v, no. 523.
31. Penman, *Robert the Bruce*, p. 108; the fact that in January 1318 King Robert granted to Susannah – now married to Donald's son Duncan Campbell – her father's lordships of Loudoun and Stevenston suggests that Bruce had nevertheless settled the long-standing legal dispute in favour of his more established allies, *RRS*, v, no. 128.
32. M. Hammond, 'Robert I's charter witnesses', *The Community of the Realm in Scotland, 1249–1424: History, Law and Charters in a Recreated Kingdom*; Accessed 26 Feb. 2023.
33. *The Bruce*, Bk. 11, ll. 341–343.
34. Duncan, *The Bruce*, p. 420.
35. *The Bruce*, Bk. 3, ll. 659–669; McNamee, *Wars of the Bruces*, pp. 36–37.
36. Penman, *Robert the Bruce*, pp. 102–103, 245–246.
37. *The Bruce*, Bk. 13, ll. 475–477.
38. *RPS*, 1308/1.
39. *Chron. Fordun*, pp. 334–335.
40. McNamee, *Wars of the Bruces*, pp. 43–44.
41. Penman, *Robert the Bruce*, pp. 129–130.

42. *The Bruce*, Bk. 13, ll. 474–477, 495–500.
43. *RRS*, v, no. 10.
44. *RPS*, 1309/1.
45. *CDS*, iii, no. 263.
46. *Instrumenta Publica*, p. 152.
47. *RRS*, v, nos. 20, 39, 48, 77, 90.
48. Boardman, *The Campbells*, pp. 22–27.
49. *The Bruce*, Bk. 2, ll. 490–498, Bk. 3, ll. 391–404, 567–574.
50. *RMS*, i, App. 1, no. 72; Neil and Mary's son, John, was probably born after Bannockburn, his name likely being a reference to the fact the battle took place on St John the Baptist's Day. However, Mary may have been free to marry Neil from around 1312, when she was probably released from English captivity.
51. *The Bruce*, Bk. 2, ll. 490–498; Bk. 6, ll. 69–70.
52. Palgrave, *Docs.*, pp. 301, 313.
53. Mackenzie, *Lives and Characters*, iii, pp. 210–211.
54. *Rot. Scot.*, i, p. 131.
55. *RPS*, 1309/1; *RRS*, v, no. 42.
56. Penman, *Robert the Bruce*, p. 140.
57. M. Hammond, 'Breaking down Robert's reign', *The Community of the Realm in Scotland, 1249–1424: History, Law and Charters in a Recreated Kingdom*; Accessed 27 Feb. 2023.
58. *The Bruce*, Bk. 3, ll. 481-534.
59. Ibid., Bk. 9, ll. 341-3, 437-42; C. J. Neville, 'Strathearn, Malise, sixth earl of Strathearn (b. c. 1261, d. in or before 1317), magnate', *ODNB*, 23 Sep. 2004; Accessed 27 Feb. 2023.
60. M. Hammond, 'Breaking down Robert's reign', *The Community of the Realm in Scotland, 1249 -1424: History, Law and Charters in a Recreated Kingdom*; Accessed 27 Feb. 2023.
61. Watson, 'Sir William Wallace: What we do – and don't – know', p. 41; *Chron. Fordun*, p. 332; *Chron. Wyntoun*, Bk. 8, ll. 2965–2972; *Chron. Bower*, vi, pp. 313–315; *The Wallace*, Bk. 12, ll. 824–830.
62. *Chron. Fordun*, p. 335; *The Bruce*, Bk. 5, ll. 133–146.
63. *RMS*, i, App. 1, no. 9; Lachlan had died circa 1307.
64. For the presence of the MacRuairi *rí Innse Gall* at Faughart, cf. Duffy, 'The "Continuation" of Nicholas Trevet: A New Source for the Bruce Invasion', ed. S. Duffy, *Proceedings of the Irish Academy*, xci, 12 (Dublin, 1991), p. 312; for the subsequent politicking concerning Garmoran, cf. Boardman, *The Campbells*, pp. 46–48.
65. *RRS*, v, no. 23.
66. Penman, *Robert the Bruce*, p. 154.

67. *RMS*, i, nos. 230, 238.
68. *RRS*, v, no. 4.
69. *Instrumenta Publica*, pp. 148–150.
70. Murray was described as two years old in November 1300, *CDS*, ii, no. 1178.
71. *CDS*, iii, no. 402.
72. *Scalacronica*, p. 117; William was the son and heir of the James Douglas who had captured Roxburgh Castle in 1314 and would afterwards fight at Bannockburn.
73. Grant, 'Bravehearts and Coronets', p. 92; *RMS*, i, nos. 314, 356, 358.
74. *RRS*, vi, no. 474.
75. *Scalacronica*, p. 53; Gray may, in fact, have intended this passage to appeal to Sir Walter Haliburton, who, by the time he was writing, was a significant figure at the court of David II, where Gray had been inspired to begin his chronicle, Penman, David II, p. 93; Barbour includes a similar passage in which it is Sir Philip Mowbray, the future captain of the Stirling garrison, who almost captures Bruce; as Duncan has previously noted, both incidents may have happened, *The Bruce*, Bk. 2, ll. 414–428, p. 100.
76. *CDS*, v, no. 492p; *RRS*, v, no. 389.
77. *CDS*, ii, no. 1926.
78. *Chron. Bower*, vi, pp. 363–365.
79. *The Bruce*, Bk. 16, ll. 580–682; as it happens, Bishop Sinclair may only have submitted to Bruce *after* Bannockburn, and had certainly been in King Edward's peace as late as February 1313, *CDS*, iii, no. 301.
80. *The Bruce*, Bk. 18, ll. 300–319.
81. *RPS*, 1318/29.
82. '*unam sufficientem aketonam, unum bacinetum et cyrotecas de guerra cum lancea et gladio*'.
83. For the possible construction of the *chapelle de fer*, cf. Moffat, *Medieval Arms and Armour: A Sourcebook*, p. 236.
84. *Vita Edwardi Secundi*, p. 91.
85. CA/6/1 Charter Roll 9 Edw.2.
86. '*unam bonam lanceam vel unum bonum arcum cum uno schapho sagittarum videlicet viginti quatuor sagittis cum pertinentiis*'.
87. Bower also offers some potential insight into the command structures of the Scottish army, claiming that during William Wallace's guardianship at least the 'less robust' ('*inferioribus*') troops had been split into groups of five, with one of the five in command as a *quaternion*, while the 'more robust and effective' ('*robustiores et valenciores*') troops would also be subdivided into tens, twenties, and so on, *Chron. Bower*, vi, p. 85; however, in this case Bower may simply have been imposing a classical model drawn from writers such as Vegetius in an effort to inflate the reputation of one of his heroes, Vegetius, *De Re Militari*, Bk. 2, chs. 13–14.

88. *The Bruce*, Bk. 11, ll. 211–218.
89. In 1327, for instance, King Robert confirmed the right of the burgesses of Stirling to common pasture for horses and wood in the Torwood, a right that they had enjoyed 'in the time of his predecessors' as well; *RMS*, i, app. 1, 41.
90. *CDS*, ii, no. 1509; Palgrave, *Docs.*, no. 146 (2).
91. Pollard has argued that the granting to locals of rights to gather peat from Skeoch in 1327 indicates the extent to which the peat had receded by the early fourteenth century, Pollard, 'A Battle Lost, A Battle Found', p. 85.
92. *Chron. Guisborough*, p. 328.
93. *lanceis* in Guisborough's description of the formations at Falkirk, Ibid., p. 328; *hasta* in the verses Bower attributes to Bernard and *lancea/haste* in Baston's poem, *Chron. Bower*, vi, p. 320, 368, 370; *lancea(m)* in the only surviving ordinance of Bruce's reign, *RPS*, 1318/29; *lanceas* in the *Vita Edwardi Secundi*, p. 90; *launces* in Gray's Anglo-Norman French, *Scalacronica*, p. 74; 'speris' in e.g., *The Bruce*, Bk. 12, ll. 506.
94. Caldwell, 'Scottish Spearmen', p. 274.
95. Barrow, *Robert Bruce and the Community of the Realm*, pp. 102–103; Fisher, *William Wallace*, pp. 154–156; Watson, *Under the Hammer*, pp. 83–84.
96. Prestwich, *Armies and Warfare in the Middle Ages*, p. 115.
97. *Chron. Trokelowe*, p. 84.
98. *Cal. Close Rolls*, ii, p. 35.
99. *Rot. Scot.*, i, p. 126-7; *Foedera*, II, i, p. 248; *Parl. Writs*, II, i, p. 427.
100. For criticism of Edward's military talents, cf. Morris, *Bannockburn*, p. 19, 39; Prestwich, *Three Edwards*, p. 262.
101. Morris, *Bannockburn*, p. 40.
102. *Foedera*, II, i, pp. 238–239.
103. *Cal. Patent Rolls*, ii, mem. 7; *Cal. Chancery Warrants*, i, p. 402.
104. *Ann. Connacht*, p. 241; McNamee, *Wars of the Bruces*, p. 242.
105. *CDS*, iii, no. 358.
106. Benz St. John, *Three Medieval Queens*, pp. 12–13.
107. Phillips, *Edward II*, pp. 481–483.
108. *CDS*, iii, no. 359.
109. *CDS*, ii, no. 1842.
110. Phillips, *Edward II*, pp. 110, 135; *Foedera*, II, i, p. 36.
111. For a detailed summary of the earl's career pre- and post-Bannockburn, cf. J. S. Hamilton, 'Bohun, Humphrey de, fourth earl of Hereford and ninth earl of Essex (c. 1276–1322), magnate and administrator', *ODNB*, 23 Sep. 2004; Accessed 18 Feb. 2023.
112. *Flores Historiarum*, iii, p. 158; the chronicler in question is most likely Robert of Reading, a monk at Westminster, J. Catto, 'Reading, Robert (d. 1317), Benedictine

monk and historian of Westminster Abbey', *ODNB*, 23 Sep. 2004; Accessed 18 Feb. 2023.
113. Altschul, *A Baronial Family in Medieval England: The Clares*, pp. 163–164.
114. *Vita Edwardi Secundi*, p. 89; *The Bruce*, Bk. 11, ll. 169–173.
115. *CDS*, iii, no. 360.
116. W. D. H. Sellar, 'MacDougall, John, lord of Argyll (d. 1316), magnate', *ODNB*, 23 Sep. 2004; Accessed 20 Feb. 2023.
117. F. Watson, 'Umfraville, Gilbert de, seventh earl of Angus (1244?–1307), baron', *ODNB*, 23 Sep. 2004; Accessed 20 Feb. 2023; Beam, 'At the apex of chivalry', pp. 54–56.
118. These were certainly the arms he displayed on his seal, cf. PoMS matrix record, no. 9568 & 9731 (www.poms.ac.uk/record/matrix/9563/ & www.poms.ac.uk/record/matrix/9731/; accessed 20/02/23)
119. *Chron. Guisborough*, pp. 324–325.
120. McNamee, *Wars of the Bruces*, p. 59, 70 n124.
121. *RMS*, i, nos. 103, 121.
122. Mackenzie, *Lives and Characters*, iii, pp. 210–211.
123. *CDS*, iii, no. 355.
124. *Cal. Patent Rolls*, ii, mem. 6.
125. Turpie, *Kind Neighbours*, pp. 21, 133.
126. Barrow, *Robert Bruce and the Community of the Realm*, p. 225; Penman, *Robert the Bruce*, p. 139.
127. *RRS*, ii, no. 499.
128. Eeles, 'The Monymusk Reliquary or Brecbennoch of St Columba', pp. 433–438; Fenton (ed.), *Angels, Nobles and Unicorns*, pp. 9–10; Caldwell, 'The Monymusk Reliquary: The Breccbennach of St. Columba', pp. 262–282.
129. *Ann. Londoniensis*, p. 146.
130. *Chron. Lanercost*, p. 208.
131. *CDS*, iii, no. 361.
132. For the likely route of Edward's retreat from Bannockburn, cf. *The Bruce*, Bk. 13, ll. 565–620; *Chron. Lanercost*, pp. 208–209.
133. *CDS*, iii, no. 362.
134. Ibid., no. 363.
135. *RMS*, i, no. 18; *RRS*, v, no. 95.
136. Bellamy, *The Law of Treason in England*, pp. 116–123; Childs, 'Resistance and Treason in the *Vita Edwardi Secundi*', p. 188; Strickland, 'Treason, Feud and the Growth of State Violence', p. 94.
137. *CDS*, iii, no. 364.
138. Ayton, 'English Armies in the Fourteenth-Century', p. 31.

139. Simpkin, 'The English Army and the Scottish Campaign, 1310–11', p. 28.
140. Morris, *Bannockburn*, pp. 34–35; Ayton has found references to 884 named individuals present in the English army in 1314, Ayton, 'In the Wake of Defeat', p. 37.
141. Simpkin, 'The English Army and the Scottish Campaign, 1310–11', p. 38.
142. *Vita Edwardi Secundi*, p. 89; the *Vita* also claims that the English army set off 'On the sixth or seventh day before the feast of St John the Baptist', the seventh day before 24 June being 17 June.
143. *The Bruce*, Bk. 11, ll. 106–116.
144. *Rot. Scot.*, i, p. 120.
145. Ibid., i, pp. 126–127; *Foedera*, II, i, p. 248.
146. Simpkin, 'The English Army and the Scottish Campaign, 1310–11', p. 30.
147. Pembroke at Methven and Macdougall at Tyndrum, both in 1306; *Scalacronica*, p. 53; *The Bruce*, Bk. 2, ll. 305–448, Bk. 3, ll. 1–60.
148. H. Summerson, 'Clifford, Robert, first Lord Clifford (1274–1314), soldier and magnate', *ODNB*, 23 Sep. 2004; Accessed 21 Feb. 2023.
149. *Scalacronica*, pp. 41, 47, 69–71.
150. *Cal. Patent Rolls*, 29 September 1305; quoted in Mackay, *William Wallace*, p. 267, & Fisher, *William Wallace*, p. 248.
151. *Chron. Guisborough*, pp. 301–302.
152. *Chron. Bower*, vi, p. 367.
153. Young, *Robert the Bruce's Rivals: The Comyns*, p. 208; of course, the extent to which the English crown was willing to embrace or promote the Comyn claim at this point in time is debatable.
154. At the apex of chivalry; *The Bruce*, Bk. 9, ll. 513.
155. Ibid., Bk. 2, ll. 255–304.
156. *MRH: Scotland*, pp. 192–193.
157. *CDS*, iii, no. 365.
158. *Vita Edwardi Secundi*, p. 97.
159. Penman, *Robert the Bruce*, p. 139.
160. *RRS*, v, no. 44.
161. *Chron. Bower*, vii, pp. 13–15; Penman, *Robert the Bruce*, p. 233; Turpie, *Kind Neighbours*, p. 103.
162. *RRS*, v, nos. 43, 125, 188, 199, 234, 305, 331, 406, 407, 411, 413.
163. Penman, *Robert the Bruce*, p. 139.
164. *Chron. Bower*, vi, p. 365.
165. *Itinerary of Edward I*, part II, pp. 217–23.
166. Penman, *Robert the Bruce*, p. 101-2; Turpie, *Kind Neighbours*, p. 128.
167. Fenton (ed.), *Angels, Nobles and Unicorns*, pp. 10–11.
168. *Chron. Boece*, ii, pp. 273–274.
169. *The Bruce*, Bk. 11, ll. 359–366.
170. Ross, 'Recreating the Bannockburn Environment', p. 103.

## Chapter 6

1. *Chron. Lanercost*, p. 207.
2. *Scalacronica*, p. 73.
3. Taylor, *Chivalry and the Ideals of Knighthood in France during the Hundred Years War*, p. 233.
4. Gilbert, *Hunting and Hunting Reserves in Medieval Scotland*, pp. 82–83.
5. *ER*, i, pp. 24, 38.
6. *Vita Edwardi Secundi*, p. 51.
7. One foot broad, and all [of] them were/As deep as a man's knee/[and were] So thickly spread that they might be likened/To a wax comb that bees make; *Chron. Bower*, vi, p. 373; *The Bruce*, Bk. 11, ll. 372–375.
8. All of the men of Carrick/And of Argyll and of Kintyre/And of the [Western] Isles; *The Bruce*, Bk. 11, ll. 340–342; it was, after all, from these regions that Bruce had drawn support for his 'comeback' in the spring of 1307.
9. *Vita Edwardi Secundi*, p. 91.
10. Ibid., p. 91; Prestwich has argued that, in the early fourteenth century, a knight would initially be accompanied to the battlefield by a pair of squires, one carrying his lance and the other leading his spare horses. Once the engagement was about to begin, the second squire would withdraw with the unneeded horses while the lance-bearer would hand over the knight's weapon and then follow him into battle, ready to give up his horse to him if the knight's horse was injured or killed. In this case, Sir Henry's luckless squire had presumably been fulfilling the role of the lance-bearer, Prestwich, *Armies and Warfare in the Middle Ages*, p. 49.
11. *The Bruce*, Bk. 12, ll. 31; a discussion of Sir Henry's parentage can be found in Pascual, 'The de Bohuns', unpublished PhD thesis, pp. 93–94.
12. *The Bruce*, Bk. 12, ll. 18; a palfrey was a long-legged and short-bodied horse bred to give an even gait and therefore be more comfortable to ride over long distances, and was thus more suited for travelling than warfare.
13. Ibid., Bk. 12, ll. 35–38; a 'bassynet' ('bascinet') was a conical helmet, usually with an open face or visor.
14. Ibid., Bk. 12, ll. 20, Bk. 5, ll. 576–577.
15. Ibid., Bk. 12, ll. 28.
16. Ibid., Bk. 12, ll. 29–34.
17. They rushed together in a [straight] line,/[but] Sir Henry missed the noble king/ And he [i.e., Bruce] stood in his stirrups/With an axe that was hard and good/ With such great might struck him such a blow/That neither hat nor helm might stop/The heavy blow that he delivered/That nearly cleaved [Sir Henry's] head to the brains./The axe shaft splintered in two,/And he [i.e., Sir Henry] fell down to the ground/Completely prostrate because his strength had gone; Ibid., Bk. 12, ll. 49–59.

18. *Scalacronica*, p. 73; it is not impossible that Gray is describing a separate incident in which an entirely different English knight was killed by Bruce during the fighting on the first day of the battle. However, given that no Sir Piers Mountforth has ever been identified in contemporary records, and taken alongside the accounts in the *Vita* and *The Bruce*, it seems likely that this is a third variation on the story of Sir Henry.
19. *Scalacronica*, p. 73; *The Bruce*, Bk. 11, ll. 530.
20. All young and light-hearted men/Yearning to perform [acts of] chivalry; *The Bruce*, Bk. 11, ll. 531–532.
21. *Chron. Lanercost*, p. 207.
22. Thought to reach the castle; *The Bruce*, Bk. 11, ll. 537.
23. *Scalacronica*, p. 73.
24. Morris, *Bannockburn*, p. 35.
25. Clifford had, for example, led the armed force that confronted Bruce, the Steward, and Robert Wishart, bishop of Glasgow, at Irvine in July 1297; Stevenson, *Docs.*, ii, no. 447, 452; Palgrave, *Docs*, no. 109–110.
26. Barbour too places Randolph in command of the Scottish 'vaward' early in his account of the battle, but later contradicts this by having Edward Bruce's division be the first of the Scottish divisions to encounter the English on the second day of the battle; *The Bruce*, Bk. 11, ll. 313, Bk. 13, ll. 499–500.
27. Ibid., Bk. 11, ll. 545; Barrow, *Robert Bruce and the Community of the Realm*, p. 219; Penman, *Robert the Bruce*, p. 141; Murray Cook, *Bannockburn and Stirling Bridge*, pp. 66–68; Duncan has offered an alternative interpretation, suggesting that this encounter happened before the rest of the fighting near Plean, south of the Bannock Burn, Duncan, *The Bruce*, pp. 443–444.
28. *The Bruce*, Bk. 11, ll. 571–572, Bk. 12, ll. 353.
29. *Chron. Guisborough*, p. 328.
30. *Scalacronica*, p. 75; *Chron. Lanercost*, p. 232.
31. For detailed analysis of the Scottish spear formations utilized in the early fourteenth century, cf. D. H. Caldwell, 'Scottish Spearmen, 1298–1314: An Answer to Cavalry', *War in History*, 19(3) (2012), pp. 267–289.
32. The English army is described as being only able to form up in a single dense 'sc(h)ilthrum' on the second day of Bannockburn, *The Bruce*, Bk. 12, ll. 431, 435, 446; Barbour also describes a column of retreating English raiders as 'a childrome' while recounting an incident that occurred in 1316, *The Bruce*, Bk. 15, ll. 360; to complicate matters further, in both cases Barbour uses the term to describe groups of soldiers including cavalry, whereas English chroniclers associate the term exclusively with dismounted formations.
33. And they with their spear points wide wounds/They dealt to the horses that came near,/And they that rode on them/That were borne to the ground lost their lives,/And other spears, darts, and knives/And weapons of other sorts/Were cast

among them that were fighting [in the Scottish formation]/[and] They defended themselves so smartly/That their foes were greatly astonished,/For some would dash out from the formation/And stabbed the horses of the attackers and bore men down./The Englishmen thus violently/Threw among them [i.e., the Scots] swords and maces/[so] That amid them [i.e., the Scots] a pile of abandoned weapons began to form; *The Bruce*, Bk. 11, ll. 594–609.

34. *Vita Edwardi Secundi*, p. 51.
35. Their foes fiercely assaulted them/On each side they were so pressed/For the very great passion that they had/For fighting and for [the] sun's heat/That their flesh was wet with sweat/And such a stench rose of them then/Due to the breathing of horses and men/And [their movements] kicked up so much dust/Into the air above them/That it was marvellous to behold; *The Bruce*, Bk. 11, ll. 616–625.
36. Ibid., Bk. 11, ll. 634–638.
37. Cameron, 'Keeping the Customer Satisfied', pp. 65–66.
38. Duncan, *The Bruce*, p. 445.
39. Ibid., Bk. 11, ll. 639–647.
40. Ibid., Bk. 11, ll. 552–554; Beam has noted an incident recorded by the late-fourteenth-century chronicler Jean Froissart in which Sir Eustace de Ribemont was awarded with a *chappellet* by Edward III for acquitting himself bravely (*vaillemment*) at the Siege of Calais, reinforcing the association between this type of headgear and chivalric accomplishment, Beam, 'At the apex of chivalry', p. 64.
41. The king said, 'As our Lord sees me,/You shall not go a foot towards him,/If he does well, let him take well. /Whatever happens to him, win or lose,/I will not change my plans for him'; *The Bruce*, Bk. 11, ll. 648–652.
42. 'Certainly', said James, 'I may [in] no way/See his foes ambush him/When I might provide assistance,/With your leave I will without delay/Help him or die in the attempt'; Ibid., Bk. 11, ll. 653–657.
43. Do [so] then and return swiftly; Ibid., Bk. 11, ll. 658.
44. Ibid., Bk. 12, ll. 119–126.
45. Althoff, 'Friendship and Political Order', p. 95.
46. Bumke, *Courtly Culture*, p. 203.
47. *The Bruce*, p. 8; Boardman, 'Thar nobill eldrys gret bounte', pp. 191–212.
48. *The Bruce*, Bk. 20, ll. 595–600.
49. C. McGladdery, 'The Black Douglases 1369–1455', pp. 161–167.
50. Marshall, *Illegitimacy in Medieval Scotland*, p. 29; in Archibald's case, he was nevertheless ultimately to lay claim to his father's patrimony through a combination of royal service, legal wrangling, and military prowess, Ibid. pp. 180–182; Grant, 'Royal and Magnate Bastards', pp. 15–18.
51. For William's emergence as the chief figure within the wider Douglas kindred, cf. Brown, *Black Douglases*, pp. 43–49.

52. Penman, *David II*, pp. 270–271.
53. Boardman, *Early Stewart Kings*, p. 49.
54. *The Bruce*, Bk. 13, ll. 709–714.
55. Macdonald, *Border Bloodshed*, pp. 76–77.
56. Tipping et al., 'Landscape Dynamics', p. 115.
57. Pollard, 'A Battle Lost, A Battle Found', p. 88.
58. For discussion of likely extent of the area known as 'the carse' in 1314, drawing on place-name evidence such as Polmont, Polmaise, even the Pelstream itself, see Barrow, *Robert Bruce and the Community of the Realm*, p. 212.
59. Smout and Stewart, *The Forth*, ch. 7; Tipping et al., 'Landscape Dynamics', p. 114; the 'Big Dig' conducted ahead of the 700th anniversary of Bannockburn in 2014 identified fragmentary evidence of farmsteads on the carse near the likely site of the battle, Pollard, 'A Battle Lost, A Battle Found', p. 89; Ross has argued that agricultural use of the carse – including salt panning, peat extraction, and grazing – would have created 'artificial and uneven land surfaces' that may have hindered English progress further, Ross, 'Recreating the Bannockburn Environment', p. 97-9.
60. *Vita Edwardi Secundi*, p. 51; *The Bruce*, Bk. 12, ll. 395–397.
61. *Scalacronica*, p. 75.
62. McNutt, 'Finding Forgotten Fields', p. 161.
63. *Chron. Bower*, vi, p. 369.
64. *Vita Edwardi Secundi*, p. 91.
65. *Scalacronica*, p. 75.
66. *The Bruce*, Bk. 13, ll. 495–500.
67. Ibid., Bk. 13, ll. 488–494.
68. *Cal. Close Rolls*, ii, p. 35.
69. For Penman's thoughts on the range of Atholl's anxieties in 1314, see Penman, *Robert the Bruce*, pp. 135–136.
70. *Scalacronica*, p. 75.
71. For a full account of his career pre- and post-Bannockburn, see C. McGladdery, 'Seton family (per. c. 1300–c. 1510), nobility', *ODNB*, 23 Sep. 2004.
72. *Scalacronica*, p. 75.
73. A letter from Bruce to Edward II dated 5 October 1310 is preserved in London, British Library, MS Cotton Titus A XIX, f. 87r.
74. *The Bruce*, Bk. 12, ll. 165–206.
75. Tanner, 'Cowing the Community', p. 65.
76. Gray states that the Scots began their attack 'at sunrise' ('*au solail leuaunt*') on 24 June, *Scalacronica*, p. 75.
77. *Chron. Bower*, vi, p. 363; the chronicle was likely composed sometime between May 1323 and February 1327, since it mentions the thirteen-year truce that was ratified

on 30 May 1323 and broken on 1 February 1327 as still being in effect at *Chron. Bower*, vii, p. 37.
78. Ibid., p. 365; Bower does not cite a source for this but, given that it follows an extended excerpt from Bernard's chronicle, it may be that this is where Bower had gleaned this information.
79. *The Bruce*, Bk. 12, ll. 409–420.
80. *Chron. Guisborough*, p. 301; *Liber Pluscardensis*, i, p. 300.
81. *Chron. Bower*, vi, pp. 363–365.
82. Webster, 'Crown versus Church after Becket', pp. 154–155; Jordan, 'The Becket Windows at Angers', p. 195.
83. Remissions would become a particular point of contention in the late fifteenth century and a source of repeated parliamentary complaints, Macdougall, *James III*, pp. 141–142; *RPS*, 1473/7/10, 1484/2/34.
84. And I encourage you all especially/Both common and noble/That none of you because of greed/Have an eye to take their riches/Nor to take prisoners/While you [can] see them still resisting/Until the field is entirely yours/And then at your discretion you may/Take all the plunder that there is; *The Bruce*, Bk. 12, ll. 303–311.
85. Charny, *The Book of Chivalry*, p. 99; Honoré Bonet strenuously condemns the breaking of ranks before a battle is settled, although in his case he connects this to the settling of personal scores rather than the taking of prisoners and booty, H. Bonet, *Tree of Battles*, p. 132.
86. *Chron. Lanercost*, p. 207, *The Bruce*, Bk. 12, ll. 498–501, 533–547; the Lanercost chronicler notes that the Scots advanced in three 'columns', with two approaching the English abreast while the third remained in the rear as a reserve. The writer attributes command of the reserve to King Robert but declines to name the commanders of the two leading divisions. Perhaps this is because the sight of the Scottish royal banner situated on the ridge above the action would have been particularly striking to an English soldier located further back in the English army, whereas the banners of the Scots in the front line may have been obscured by the mass of men in front of him.
87. *Vita Edwardi Secundi*, p. 91.
88. *The Bruce*, Bk. 11, ll. 297–298.
89. *Scalacronica*, p. 75; drawing inspiration from earlier tactics would certainly resonate with the later claim that the well-read Bruce's interest in (quite recent) history influenced his actions 'both in wartime and in peacetime', A. A. M. Duncan, 'A Question about the Succession, 1364', *Scottish History Society Miscellany*, xii (Edinburgh, 1994), p. 25.
90. Tipping et al., 'Landscape Dynamics', p. 116.
91. *Chron. Lanercost*, p. 207; the chronicler also notes that the Scottish archers came off the worst in this skirmish, but as long as they had given the spearmen time to

block the space between the two streams they would have achieved their primary aim.

92. They ask for mercy but not from you,/They cry to God [to forgive] their trespasses; *The Bruce*, Bk. 12, ll. 482–490; the Lanercost chronicler and Bower also suggest the Scots knelt in prayer immediately before the fighting began; *Chron. Lanercost*, p. 207, *Chron. Bower*, vi, p. 365.
93. *Chron, Rishanger*, p. 188.
94. It was defeats like the one inflicted on them at Bannockburn in 1314 and the repeated reversals they suffered at the hands of Robert Bruce and his key lieutenants that would encourage the English military community to rely more heavily on their infantry – and in particular their archers – by the 1330s, driving the so-called 'infantry revolution' of the fourteenth century, as convincingly argued in Ayton, 'English Armies in the Fourteenth-Century', pp. 21–38.
95. *Vita Edwardi Secundi*, p. 52; an anonymous English lament concerning the battle, written during the reign of Edward II's son Edward III, also lays the blame on the inaction of the earl's followers and even goes so far as to accuse Sir Bartholomew Badlesmere of intentionally betraying Gloucester to his death, Wright (ed.), *Political Songs*, pp. 262–267.
96. *Chon. Baker*, p. 8.
97. Barrow, *Robert Bruce and the Community of the Realm*, pp. 102–103.
98. *Vita Edwardi Secundi*, p. 52; *Scalacronica*, p. 75.
99. *The Bruce*, Bk. 13, ll. 41–49; Barrow has suggested that the archers may have crossed the Pelstream in order to circumvent the embattled English cavalry, an interpretation echoed by Bennett and Caldwell; Barrow, *Robert Bruce and the Community of the Realm*, p. 227; Bennett, 'Development of Battlefield Tactics', p. 4; Caldwell, 'Bannockburn: The Road to Victory', p. 34.
100. Robert Baston, for instance, refers to 'cavalry and infantry' present in the Scottish army at Bannockburn, *Chron. Bower*, vi, p. 370.
101. Sent instruction through the army/[that] The marshal with a great following.../To ride among the archers; *The Bruce*, Bk. 13, ll. 50–59.
102. *Chron. Lanercost*, p. 208.
103. *The Bruce*, Bk. 13, ll. 112–134.
104. Ibid., Bk. 13, ll. 225–264.
105. Barrow, *Robert Bruce and the Community of the Realm*, p. 228; Armstrong, *Bannockburn* (Osprey), p. 69; Moffat, *Bannockburn*, pp. 124–125; Murray Cook, *Bannockburn and Stirling Bridge*, p. 96.
106. Duncan, *The Bruce*, p. 490n.
107. Hay, 'Booty and Border Warfare', p. 157-63; the strong incentive for the Scots to loot the battlefield has, along with the moisture and acidity of the soil on the carse,

been used to explain the lack of archaeological evidence for the location of the battlefield, Pollard, 'A Battle Lost, A Battle Found', p. 86.
108. *Scalacronica*, p. 77.
109. The most extensive list of those killed and captured at Bannockburn can be found in *Chron. Trivet (Cont.)*, p. 14-5.
110. *Vita Edwardi Secundi*, p. 53, *Scalacronica*, p. 77, *The Bruce*, Bk. 13, ll. 299-319; in the *Vita*, Sir Giles abandons King Edward in a futile effort to rescue the stricken earl of Gloucester.
111. *Vita Edwardi Secundi*, p. 93.
112. *Scalacronica*, p. 77.
113. He spurred [his horse] crying, 'd'Argentan!'/And they [i.e., the Scots] met him with spears/And set so many spears on him/That he and [his] horse were so pressed/That both were brought to the ground/And in that place he was slain.
114. *The Bruce*, Bk. 13, ll. 299-327.
115. The significance of the king's banner being seen to leave the battlefield is emphasized particularly in the *Vita*; *Vita Edwardi Secundi*, p. 95.
116. The Bruce, Bk. 13, ll. 428-434.
117. *Chron. Lanercost*, p. 208; *Vita Edwardi Secundi*, p. 95; *Scalacronica*, p. 75.
118. And the Bannock Burn between the banks/Was so stuffed with men and horses/That men might pass over it dry-shod/Upon drowned horses and men; *The Bruce*, Bk. 13, ll. 337-340.
119. Ibid., Bk. 13, ll. 417-422.
120. *Vita Edwardi Secundi*, p. 95.
121. *Chron. Lanercost*, p. 209, *The Bruce*, Bk. 13, ll. 401-412; the Lanercost chronicler numbers Robert Umfraville, earl of Angus, and his kinsman Ingram, Sir John Seagrave, Sir Anthony Lucy, 'a great crowd of knights', 600 mounted men-at-arms, and 1,000 infantrymen among Hereford's companions on his flight to Bothwell, but these numbers may be an exaggeration.
122. *Chron. Lanercost*, p. 208, *The Bruce*, Bk. 13, ll. 294-298; the Lanercost chronicler's connection of 'the fugitive Welsh' to Pembroke evokes a similar image as that associated with Berkeley in *The Bruce*, possibly suggesting that one of the two writers was confusing the two men.
123. *Chron. Lanercost*, p. 208.
124. For a summary of Tweng's career, cf. N. Vincent, Thwing [Thweng], Sir Robert of [alias William Wither] (d. 1245x57), knight, *ODNB*.
125. Well-equipped but ransom-free; *The Bruce*, Bk. 13, ll. 518-539.
126. *Parl. Writs*, II, i, p. 139.
127. *Historia Anglicana*, p. 141.
128. *Chron. Fordun*, p. 331.

129. *The Bruce*, Bk. 13, ll. 447–448.
130. The tale of Baston's capture and the poem he composed are preserved in *Chron. Bower*, Vol. 6, pp. 367–375.
131. *The Bruce*, Bk. 13, ll. 359–381.
132. Ibid., Bk. 13, ll. 382–392, ll. 437–439.
133. *Chron. Lanercost*, pp. 208–209; *Vita Edwardi Secundi*, p. 55; *Scalacronica*, p. 77, *The Bruce*, Bk. 13, ll. 611–620.
134. *Scalacronica*, p. 77, *The Bruce*, Bk. 13, ll. 616.
135. *Chron. Bower*, vi, p. 375.
136. *Vita Edwardi Secundi*, p. 55.
137. Such great riches they found there/That many a man was made wealthy/From the plunder that they took; *The Bruce*, Bk. 13, ll. 450–452.

## Chapter 7

1. *The Bruce*, Bk. 13, ll. 667–668.
2. Ibid., Bk. 5, ll. 411–415.
3. Yeoman, 'War and (in) Pieces', pp. 133, 137.
4. Caldwell, 'Bannockburn: The Road to Victory', p. 26.
5. *The Bruce*, Bk. 12, ll. 151, Bk. 13, ll. 474–477, 495–500.
6. Ibid., Bk. 13, ll. 467–468, 512–517.
7. *Historia Anglicana*, p. 142; *The Bruce*, Bk. 13, ll. 672–674.
8. Ibid., Bk. 13, ll. 675–676.
9. *Vita Edwardi Secundi*, p. 95.
10. *Historia Anglicana*, p. 142.
11. *CDS*, iii, nos. 48, 165.
12. *Chron. Lanercost*, pp. 179–180; *Scalacronica*, p. 55.
13. *Chron. Lanercost*, p. 209.
14. *CDS*, iii, nos. 229, 243.
15. He appears, for instance, as a witness to a charter by James, fifth high steward of Scotland, in January 1295, *Paisley Registrum*, pp. 92–96.
16. *Chron. Lanercost*, p. 209; *The Bruce*, Bk. 13, ll. 401–412, 679–688.
17. Penman, *Robert the Bruce*, p. 158.
18. *The Bruce*, Bk. 13, ll. 611–631; *Chron. Lanercost*, pp. 208–209; *Vita Edwardi Secundi*, p. 95; *Scalacronica*, p. 77.
19. Maddicott, *Thomas of Lancaster*, p. 161.
20. *Foedera*, II, i, p. 249.
21. *Itinerary*, p. 7.
22. Tout, *Chapters in the Administrative History of Medieval England*, ii, p. 295.
23. *Chron. Trivet (Cont.)*, p. 16.
24. *Chron. Bower*, vi, pp. 363–365.

25. *Parl. Writs*, II, i, pp. 427–430.
26. Maddicott, *Thomas of Lancaster*, p. 323.
27. *Chron. Le Bel*, pp. 22, 35.
28. Ayton, 'In the Wake of Defeat', p. 40.
29. Maddicott, *Thomas of Lancaster*, p. 244.
30. Prestwich, *Armies and Warfare in the Middle Ages*, p. 117; Phillips, *Edward II*, pp. 425–426.
31. *CDS*, iii, no. 369.
32. *Chron. Lanercost*, p. 179.
33. *The Bruce*, Bk. 5, ll. 133–146, Bk. 10, ll. 535–545, Bk. 17, ll. 22–38.
34. *CDS*, iii, no. 379; we get a sense of the resources available to Harclay from the accounts of Gilbert of Bromley, the king's receiver at Carlisle, for the period of 8 July to 30 November 1314. Harclay was assisted by four other knights – including Sir Thomas Torthorald and, perhaps, Sir John Lancaster – fifty men-at-arms, fifteen squires, thirty hobelars, and 150 archers (forty of whom were from Ireland). Furthermore, an additional 176 archers were assigned to guard the town's three gates – sixty at the Caldew Gate in the west, fifty-six at 'Bokard's Gate' in the south (suggesting four recent desertions or injuries), and sixty at 'Ricard's Gate' in the east; Ibid., iii, no. 403.
35. *Chron. Lanercost*, pp. 213–216.
36. *CDS*, iii, no. 370.
37. *Vita Edwardi Secundi*, p. 93; *Scalacronica*, p. 77; *The Bruce*, Bk. 13, ll. 299–302.
38. *Scalacronica*, p. 77; *The Bruce*, Bk. 13, ll. 299–327.
39. *Foedera*, II, i, p. 251.
40. Palgrave, *Docs.*, no. 154.
41. *CDS*, iii, no. 302.
42. *Chron. Lanercost*, p. 211.
43. *Parl. Writs*, II, ii, p. 80.
44. *CDS*, iii, no. 671.
45. Penman, *Robert the Bruce*, pp. 268–269, 275.
46. MacInnes, *Scotland's Second War of Scottish Independence*, pp. 112–113.
47. *CDS*, iii, no. 373–374.
48. PoMS matrix record, no. 9568 & 9731 (www.poms.ac.uk/record/matrix/9563 & www.poms.ac.uk/record/matrix/9731; accessed 05/03/23.)
49. *CDS*, ii, no. 156.
50. *Edward I and the Throne of Scotland*, ii, 80–5; Sayles, 'The Guardians of Scotland', p. 246.
51. *The Bruce*, Bk. 12, ll. 452–490.
52. Penman, *Robert the Bruce*, p. 158.
53. *RMS*, i, App. 1, no. 76.

54. *RPS*, 1320/4/1.
55. *CDS*, iii, no. 721.
56. *The Bruce*, Bk. 19, ll. 73–118.
57. Penman, *Robert the Bruce*, p. 225.
58. *The Bruce*, Bk. 19, ll. 158–186.
59. *CDS*, iii, no. 378.
60. Lovel had, for instance, served with three squires in the garrison at Roxburgh in January 1310, Ibid., no. 121.
61. *Rot. Scot.*, i, p. 134.
62. *CDS*, iii, no. 352.
63. *Cal. Close Rolls*, ii, p. 130.
64. *CDS*, iii, no. 381.
65. *Chron. Lanercost*, p. 211.
66. *Parl. Writs*, II, ii, pp. 126–135.
67. Phillips, *Aymer de Valence*, pp. 81–82.
68. *Cal. Patent Rolls*, ii, mem. 28.
69. *CDS*, iii, no. 383.
70. Ibid., no. 387; All Saints' Day (1 November) was a Friday, making 31 October technically the 'Thursday before', but given the surviving instructions for the provision of her rights dated Thursday, 24 October, this is probably the date the verdict was passed (see following footnote).
71. Ibid., no. 395, 398, 506, 595.
72. On 12 February 1317, King Edward had given explicit approval for the marriage of Euphemia to one of Nicholas's heirs; *Cal. Patent Rolls*, ii, mem. 29.
73. *CDS*, iii, no. 627, 1041, 1084, 1092.
74. McNamee, *Wars of the Bruces*, p. 72.
75. *Chron. Lanercost*, p. 210.
76. McNamee, *Wars of the Bruces*, p. 72; Duncan, *The Bruce*, p. 606; as noted above, John Soules was involved in arranging the release of his cousin's husband Richard Lovel in November, possibly indicating he remained in English service as late as that.
77. McNamee, *Wars of the Bruces*, p. 74.
78. *Chron. Lanercost*, pp. 210–211.
79. H. Summerson, 'Harclay [Harcla], Andrew, earl of Carlisle (c. 1270–1323), soldier', *ODNB*, 23 Sep. 2004; Accessed 6 Mar. 2023.
80. Macdonald, *Border Bloodshed*, p. 47.
81. *CDS*, iii, no. 403.
82. *Chron. Lanercost*, p. 211.
83. Macdonald, *Border Bloodshed*, p. 202.
84. *Cal. Patent Rolls*, mem. 28.
85. *Foedera*, II, i, p. 252.

86. Ibid., pp. 245–246; *Chron. Lanercost*, p. 209; *The Bruce*, Bk. 13, ll. 294–298.
87. *CDS*, iii, no. 384.
88. *Chron. Lanercost*, pp. 200–201.
89. *Scalacronica*, p. 79; *The Bruce*, Bk. 17, ll. 22–38; Barbour misnames Spalding as 'Syme' ('Simon'), but the individual in question was probably the same Peter Spalding who was granted various lands in Berwickshire and Angus in May 1319, possibly as a reward for his part in assisting in the capture of the town the previous year, *RRS*, v, no. 150.
90. *CDS*, iii, no. 385.
91. *CDS*, ii, no. 1798.
92. Beam, *Balliol Dynasty*, p.
93. Watson, *Under the Hammer*, pp. 141, 278.
94. *CDS*, iii, no. 512.
95. *RRS*, v, no. 40.
96. *Rot. Scot.*, i, p. 131.
97. I make sure; Barrow, *Robert Bruce and the Community of the Realm*, p. 148.
98. Penman, *Robert the Bruce*, p. 150.
99. *Foedera*, ii, I, p. 105; *CDS*, iii, no. 244.
100. *Vita Edwardi Secundi*, pp. 100–101.
101. *CDS*, iii, no. 388.
102. Denholm-Young, 'The Authorship of Vita Edwardi Secundi', p. 196.
103. *CDS*, iii, no. 389.
104. *Rot. Scot.*, i, p. 132.
105. *CDS*, iii, no. 420–421.

## Chapter 8

1. *Foedera*, II, i, p. 255.
2. A. A. M. Duncan, 'Wishart, Robert (c. 1240–1316), bishop of Glasgow', *ODNB*, 23 Sep. 2004; Accessed 8 Mar. 2023.
3. *Edward I and the Throne of Scotland*, ii, 80–85; Penman, *Robert the Bruce*, pp. 48–50.
4. *Anglo-Scottish Relations*, no. 34, p. 131.
5. Dean, 'Projecting Dynastic Majesty', p. 36.
6. *The Bruce*, Bk. 13, ll. 693.
7. *CDS*, iii, no. 403.
8. Dunbar, *Scottish Kings*, pp. 141–142.
9. Fordun strongly suggests that Robert's parents were married in or around 1271 and gives the year of his birth as 'twelve seven four'; *Chron. Fordun*, pp. 299–300.
10. *The Bruce*, Bk. 2, ll. 414–428.
11. *Chron. Lanercost*, p. 178; *Scalacronica*, p. 55; *The Bruce*, Bk. 4, ll. 16–31.

12. *CDS*, iii, no. 27; *Cal. Close Rolls, 1301–7*, p. 503.
13. *RMS*, i, App. 1, no. 70.
14. *RRS*, v, no. 262.
15. French, 'Christina Bruce and Her Defence of Kildrummy Castle', pp. 22–38.
16. Neville, 'Widows of War', p. 125.
17. *RPS*, 1315/1.
18. The assembly at Ayr was followed by a royal progress, perhaps in a military capacity, through the Hebrides and western Highlands, but may have culminated with Marjory and Walter's wedding at the Stewart castle at Bute on Rothesay; the 'Bute Mazer', currently on display at the National Museum of Scotland, may even have been made for use at this event; Stevenson, 'The Bannatyne or Bute Mazer and its Carved Bone Cover,' p. 249; Fenton (ed.), *Angels, Nobles and Unicorns*, pp. 37–38.
19. *RPS*, 1318/30.
20. *CDS*, iii, no. 399.
21. Simpkin, 'The King's Sergeants-at-Arms in Scotland, 1296–1322', p. 102.
22. *CDS*, iii, no. 402.
23. Ibid., no. 322.
24. An inquest by the English royal administration into the inheritance of Murray's great-uncle William in November 1300 indicates that, at that point, he was at liberty and living 'among the king's enemies' in Moray, *CDS*, ii, no. 1178.
25. *RPS*, 1314/1.
26. He had, for instance, been one of the mainpernors for Bruce following the 'capitulation' at Irvine in 1297, Palgrave, *Docs.*, no. 110.
27. *CDS*, ii, no. 1829, v, no. 472.
28. *RPS*, 1309/1.
29. *PoMS*, no. 14048 (https://www.poms.ac.uk/record/person/14048; accessed 11 March 2023).
30. *Rot. Scot.*, i, p. 132; Bruce had, in fact, besieged two Gilbert Glencairnies - a father and son - in 1307: the father at Inverness and the son at Elgin, Barrow, and Barnes, 'The Movements of Robert Bruce', p. 58.
31. *Foedera*, II, i, p. 255.
32. *CDS*, ii, nos. 719–720; *Chron. Lanercost*, pp. 114–115.
33. *Gascon Register A*, ii, no. 71.
34. *Rot. Scot.*, i, p. 133.
35. Maddicott, *Thomas of Lancaster*, pp. 127–128.
36. Phillips, *Edward II*, p. 216.
37. Maddicott, *Thomas of Lancaster*, p. 158.
38. *CDS*, iii, no. 396.
39. Though he was not styled 'earl of Atholl' at this point, a grant of lands in Atholl to John and his mother Mary at a parliament at Scone in 1323 may indicate that

he had received the earldom by that point, *RPS*, A1323/7/2; Hay was granted the constableship on 12 November 1314 at the first parliament King Robert held after his victory at Bannockburn, *RRS*, v, no. 42.
40. Ross, 'Man for all seasons?', pp. 18–20.
41. Penman, *David II*, pp. 57–58, 60–62; MacInnes, *Scotland's Second War of Independence*, pp. 21–24.
42. *CDS*, v, no. 593.
43. Stevenson, *Docs*, ii, no. 372; *Instrumenta Publica*, 60–113.
44. Stones, 'The Records of the 'Great Cause' of 1291-92', pp. 94–95.
45. *CDS*, iii, no. 680.
46. *Foedera*, II, i, p. 256.
47. *CDS*, iii, no. 400.
48. Barbour, in particular, emphasises the value of intelligence to the Scottish war effort, *The Bruce*, Bk. 4, ll. 550–559, Bk. 5, ll. 133–146, Bk. 10, ll. 535–541, Bk. 17, ll. 22–38.
49. *CDS*, iii, no. 401.
50. *Historiae Dunelmensis*, p. cxiii.
51. *CDS*, iii, no. 397.
52. The garrison were threatening to desert altogether one year later in October 1315, while in February 1316 a substantial portion of the garrison were killed on an unsanctioned foray up the Tweed valley for supplies; *CDS*, ii, no. 452, 470; *Scalacronica*, p. 77; *The Bruce*, Bk. 15, ll. 319–417.
53. *Northern Registers*, no. 153.
54. *RPD*, i, pp. 204–205; *Historiae Dunelmensis*, p. cxiii.
55. *Foedera*, II, i, p. 340.
56. *RPS*, A1328/3; *RRS*, v, no. 345.
57. *RPS*, 1314/1.
58. *The Bruce*, Bk. 13, ll. 731–741.
59. Barbour claims that after issuing his ultimatum King Robert 'our-raid [overrode] all Northummyrland', probably referring to the *chevauchée* the king led into northeast England in June 1315; *The Bruce*, Bk. 13, ll. 742–748; McNamee, *Wars of the Bruces*, pp. 79–80.
60. Barrow, *Robert Bruce and the Community of the Realm*, pp. 287–289.
61. *RRS*, v, no. 42.
62. Ibid., no. 47.
63. *CDS*, ii, no. 1771, iii, nos. 47, 116, 192, 273; *Chron. Trivet (Cont.)*, p. 14.
64. *RRS*, v, no. 51.
65. Penman, *Robert the Bruce*, p. 312.
66. *Chron. Fordun*, p. 341; *The Bruce*, Bk. 19, ll. 1–72.
67. Penman, 'A fell coniurecioun agayn Robert the douchty king', pp. 25–57.

68. Hammond, 'Breaking down Robert's reign'; Accessed 13/03/2023.
69. *RMS*, i, App. 1, no. 38.
70. *RRS*, v, no. 261; *RMS*, i, App. 1, no. 47.
71. *RPS*, A1323/7/2.
72. Gray claims that 'John the Steward [John Stewart of Bonkyl]…called himself Earl of Angus' from August 1327, and he used that style in a charter dating from around 1329; *Scalacronica*, p. 99; *Douglas Book*, iii, no. 314.
73. *RRS*, v, nos. 342–345.
74. Penman, *David II*, pp. 47–50; MacInnes, *Scotland's Second War of Independence*, pp. 11–14.
75. A more exhaustive list of these kindreds has been compiled in Penman, *Robert the Bruce*, pp. 313–314.
76. *Chron. Fordun*, p. 347; *Chron. Lanercost*, p. 281.
77. Penman, *David II*, pp. 60–61.
78. *Chron. Lanercost*, pp. 298–301; *Chron. Fordun*, pp. 353-355; *Chron. Wyntoun*, Bk. 8, ll. 5001–5036, 6301–6308; *Chron. Bower*, vii, pp. 125–127, 137, 271; Oram, 'Bruce, Balliol and Galloway', p. 43; MacInnes, 'Shock and Awe', *passim*.
79. The most notable confrontations after Bruce's reign were Hallidon Hill in 1333 and Neville's Cross in 1346, both catastrophic defeats for the Scots; the Battle of Otterburn in 1388, though on a smaller scale than the other two, was at least comparable and, like Bannockburn, was a rare success for the Scots.
80. *The Bruce*, Bk. 3, ll. 259–263.

# Index

Aberdeen, 14, 77, 78
Abernethy, Sir Alexander, 29, 76
Abingdon, Richard, abbot of, 95–96
Airth, Sir William of, 106–107, 149
Alexander III, King of Scots (r.1249–86), 3, 16, 135, 185
Alfonso XI, King of Castile (r.1312–1350), 39
Andrew, bishop of Argyll, 66
Andronikos II, 'emperor of Constantinople', (d.1332), 20, 128, 171
Antwerp, 77, 78
Appleby (Cumbria), 179
Arbroath Abbey (Forfarshire), 34, 48
Archers, 56–57, 115, 156, 246 n94
Argentan, Sir Giles d' (d.1314), 20–21, 128, 158–159, 170–171
Argentan, Sir William d' (Sir Giles' nephew), 170–171
Arran, Isle of, 9, 167, 220 n2
Arundel, Edmund Fitzalan, earl of (d.1326), 41, 42
Audley, Ela, 175
Aylsham (Norfolk), 174, 192
Ayr, 15, 28

Baker, Geoffrey le, English chronicler, 155
Balfour, Sir David, 109
Balliol, Edward, pretender King of Scots (r.1332–1356), 69, 197, 200, 201
Balliol, John, King of Scots (r.1292–1296), 4, 6, 104, 120, 128, 182, 201

Balquhidderock Ridge, 140, 142, 152–153
Bamburgh (Northumberland), 167
Bannock Burn, 114, 115, 132, 135, 136, 146, 147, 148, 152, 153, 159, 160, 162
Barbour, John (d.1395), archdeacon of Aberdeen, poet, author of *The Bruce*, 17, 18, 35–39, 44, 50, 51, 62–65, 73, 99–100, 102, 103, 105, 106, 107, 108, 111, 112, 127, 129, 136, 137–138, 139, 140–146, 150, 152, 153, 156, 157, 158–159, 160, 162–163, 164, 165, 167, 171, 173, 174, 186, 198, 202, 217–218 n16, 219 n31, 225 n105, 234 n6, 242 n32
Baston, Robert, English poet, 128, 136, 148, 161, 162
Beaton, Sir Archibald, 109
Beauchamp, Guy, earl of Warwick (d.1315), 12, 29, 41, 42, 147
Beaumont, Sir Henry, titular earl of Buchan (d.1340), 54–55, 127, 128, 140–142, 143, 146, 153, 160
Bel, Jean le, Hainault chronicler (c.1290–1370), 34, 88–89, 169, 219 n14
Bellard, Peter of Sleperdam, merchant, 77
Bentley, Henry, coroner, 195
Berkeley, Sir Maurice, 160, 243 n122
Bernard (d.1331), abbot of Arbroath, chancellor, 34–35, 111, 123, 151–152, 168

Berwick-upon-Tweed, 11, 13, 17, 20, 22, 23, 24, 30, 32, 40, 62, 66, 69, 70, 83, 85, 87, 93, 98, 99, 121, 125, 128, 165, 167, 178, 181, 194, 195–196, 199
Bevercotes, William de, English chancellor of Scotland, 54
Beverley (Yorkshire), 91–93
Biggar, 30, 31
Blount, Sir Stephen, 58, 186
Blyth (Northumberland), 42
Boece, Hector, Scottish chronicler (c.1465–1536), 131–132
Bohun, de, Henry de (d.1314), 136–139, 166
Bonet, Honoré (d.c.1410), French monk and writer, 40
Booty, 32, 87, 152, 157–158, 162–163
Boroughbridge, Battle of (1322), 141
Bosco, Walter de, 21
Botetourt, Sir John, 191–192, 194
Bothwell Castle, 30, 145, 160, 166–167, 196
Bower, Walter, abbot of Inchcolm (d.1449), Scottish chronicler, author of *Scotichronicon*, 34, 111, 151, 219 n30, 237 n87
Bradley, Nicholas, 176
Bristol, 92, 175
Brodick Castle, 167
Brough (Cumbria), 179
*Bruce, The*, poem, see Barbour, John
Bruce, Alexander (King Robert's brother, d.1307), 9, 166, 169
Bruce, Alexander (Edward Bruce's illegitimate son, d.1333), 44, 110, 218 n4
Bruce, Christian (King Robert's sister, d.1356), 9, 61, 171, 185, 187–188
Bruce, Edward (King Robert's brother, d.1318), lord of Galloway, earl of Carrick:

granted lordship of Galloway (1309), 11, 106
created earl of Carrick, 14–16
'dissension' with David Strathbogie, 42–45, 149
slights Roxburgh Castle (February 1314), 52
possible role in the capture of Edinburgh Castle (March 1314), 62, 64
raids into Cumbria (April 1314), 85, 89–90, 91, 96
makes deal with the Stirling garrison? (May 1314), 97–100
leading role at Bannockburn (June 1314), 102–103, 153, 154, 178
raids northern England (August 1314), 177–180, 181, 191
position in line of succession clarified (April 1315), 188
killed at Dundalk (1318), 109
criticism in *The Bruce*, 99
Bruce, Isabella (King Robert's sister, d.1358), queen dowager of Norway, 9, 60, 187
Bruce, John (King Robert's son, d.1326), 187
Bruce, Lucy (Marmaduke Tweng's mother), 66, 160
Bruce, Margaret (King Robert's daughter), 187
Bruce, Marjory (King Robert's daughter, d.c.1317), 9, 16, 61, 104, 171, 185, 188–189, 252 n18
Bruce, Mary (King Robert's sister, d.1323), 9, 183, 200, 228 n48
Bruce, Maud (King Robert's daughter), 187
Bruce, Neil (King Robert's brother, d.1306), 9, 166

# Index  257

Bruce, Robert (VI) (King Robert's father, d.1304), earl of Carrick, 3, 4
Bruce of Skelton, family, 66–67
Bruce, Thomas (King Robert's brother, d.1307), 9, 48, 166, 169
Burgh, Elizabeth de, Queen of Scots (r.1306–27):
  sister Mathilda, 59
  marries Robert Bruce (1302), 6, 49
  captured (1306), 9
  experience of imprisonment, 60–61
  moved to Rochester Castle (March 1314), 61
  household at Rochester, 91
  release, 58, 171, 185, 186–187

Cambuskenneth Abbey (Stirlingshire), 8, 107, 149, 175, 197, 202
Campbell, John (d.1333), earl of Atholl, 192, 200
Campbell, Sir Neil, of Lochawe (d.1316), 104, 107, 183, 192, 199, 200
Canterbury (Kent), 48, 53, 54, 168
Carlisle (Cumbria), 89, 112, 169–170, 179, 184, 185, 186
Carlisle, Henry of, 21
Carrick, earldom, 15, 44, 185
Carrick, earls of, *see* Bruce, Edward, Bruce, Robert (VI), Robert I
Carrick, Marjory, Countess of (King Robert's mother), 3, 185
Carse of Stirling, 114, 147, 153
Charny, Sir Geoffrey de (d.1356), 40, 152, 218 n49
Chasteleyn, Richard le, clerk, 79
Cheyne, Henry, bishop of Aberdeen, 14
Chilton, Ralph, 183
Chivalry, 36–40
Clement V, Pope (1305–14), *see* Papacy

Clifford, Sir Robert (d.1314), 5, 12, 31, 127–128, 140–142, 143, 144, 146, 153, 154, 155, 165, 166, 184, 192
Colville, Sir Robert, 22
Comyn, Adomar (Aymer, d.c.1316), 181–182
Comyn, Alexander, earl of Buchan (d.1289), 22
Comyn, Alice (wife of Henry Beaumont), 55, 128
Comyn, Sir Edmund of Kilbride, 128, 176–177
Comyn, Joanna (*née* Latimer), 54–55, 222 n9
Comyn, Isabella, 199
Comyn, Sir John, lord of Badenoch (d.1306), 5, 7, 8, 43, 53, 74, 75, 120, 128, 173, 176, 182, 183, 186
Comyn, Sir John, of Badenoch (d.1314), 53–54, 128, 181–182
Comyn, John, earl of Buchan (d.1308), 9, 55, 105
Comyn, Margaret, 178
Comyn, Marjory, 22
Comyn, Mary (widow of Edmund Comyn of Kilbride), 176–177
Comyn, Roger, 190
Comyn, Walter, earl of Menteith (d.1258), 199
Comyn, Sir Walter, 128
Convers, Alexander le, clerk, 58, 79
Corbridge (Northumberland), 57, 86, 87
Couper, Adam, valet, 81
Courtrai, Battle of (1302), 7, 153
Craftsmen, 77, 130–131
Crawford, Susannah, 104
Crowland (Lincolnshire), 232 n21
Culblean, Battle of (1338), 188
Culross (Fife), 31

David II (Bruce), King of Scots
(r.1329–71), 15, 34, 69, 91, 95, 109,
121, 145, 186, 187, 197, 202
'Declaration of Arbroath' (1320), 76, 173
Despenser, Hugh the Elder (d.1326),
91–92, 118, 127
Despenser, Hugh the Younger (d.1326),
92, 124, 127, 160
d'Eauze, Gaucelin, cardinal, 197
Deyncourt, Sir William, 140
Dirleton (East Lothian), 120, 121
Dishington, Thomas, 109, 118
Donewithy, Alan de, 21
Douglas, Sir Archibald 'the Grim'
d.1400), lord of Galloway, 35,
144–146, 151
Douglas, Sir James, 'the Good' (d.1330)
youth and early career, 49, 110,
225 n105
'Douglas Larder' (1307/8), 37, 164
possible reaction to King Robert's
ill-health, 47
captures Roxburgh Castle
(February 1314), 38, 49–52, 118
possible influence on the fall of
Edinburgh Castle (March 1314),
63–64
present at Bannockburn (June 1314),
103–104, 143
knighted (24th June), 151
pursues Edward II from the battlefield,
162
raids northern England (August 1314),
177–180, 181, 191
rewarded for his service by King
Robert, 199, 200, 220 n83
raids northern England (1319), 17
skirmishes with English near
Melrose (1322), 111
raids through Weardale (1327), 39

chivalric reputation in *The Bruce*,
37, 38–39, 63, 142–146
Douglas, Sir William 'the Hardy'
(d.1297), 49
Douglas, William (Sir James's son,
d.1333), 110
Douglas, William of Lothian (d.1353), 201
Douglas, William, earl of (d.1384), 145, 151
Dover (Kent), 82
Draper, Warin le, merchant, 78
Dumfries, 13, 187, 196
Dunbar (East Lothian), 66, 162, 167, 196
Dunbar, George, earl of March
(d.1455x7), 146
Dunbar, John, earl of Moray (d.1391/2),
146
Dunbar, Patrick, earl of March (d.1369):
petitions Edward II for direct
support in Scotland (October 1313),
22–24
aids Edward II's escape from
Bannockburn (June 1314), 162
submits to King Robert after
Bannockburn, 162, 196
shifting allegiance during Second
War of Scottish Independence, 201
Dunbar, Battle of (1296), 26
Dundee, 14
Dunfermline Abbey, 130, 131
Dunstaffnage Castle, 76
Dupplin Moor, Battle of (1332), 172, 186
Durham, 57, 86, 93–95, 183, 184, 191,
192, 194–195, 196

Easingwold (North Yorkshire), 93
Edgefield, Thomas de, 58
Edinburgh, 30, 111, 130, 196
castle, 38, 62–66, 74, 95, 96, 131, 132
Edward I, King of England (r.1272–1307),
3, 6, 7, 10, 53, 55, 57, 118, 185, 191, 193

# Index

Edward II, King of England (r.1307-1327):
  betrothed to Margaret, Maid of Norway (1290), 3
  early campaigning experience in Scotland, 6
  present for the fall of Stirling Castle (1304), 7
  knighted (1306), 118
  becomes King of England (1307), 10, 119
  favouritism, 10, 66–68, 91–92, 124, 128
  first invasion of Scotland (1310), 11–12, 28–32, 40, 84, 93, 119, 147, 150
  initial response to March and Gordon's petition (November 1313), 25–26
  financial preparations, 26–27
  reacts to the deal between the Scots and the Stirling garrison (May 1314), 115–116, 122, 126
  concerned about lawlessness in English during his absence (June 1314), 122–123
  under personal threat at Bannockburn, 158, 173
  flight from the battlefield, 158, 161–162, 163
  loses privy seal, 167–168
  makes efforts to bolster border defences in the wake of defeat, 160–161, 181, 193–194
  shrewd redistribution of lands after Bannockburn, 174–175
  third invasion of Scotland (1319), 17, 31, 40, 70, 169
  fourth invasion of Scotland (1322), 31, 40, 90, 169
  thirteen-year truce with the Scots (1323), 174
Edward III, King of England (r.1327–77), 57, 69, 70, 98, 177
Elias, abbot of Holyrood, 111
Ely, 80, 82–83
English army:
  size, 126–127
  make-up, 127–129
  route to Bannockburn, 126, 129–132
  attitude on evening of 23rd June, 148–149
  losses, 165
Ettrick Forest, 30, 37, 39, 49
Eye, Matthew de, 21

Falkirk, 132, 135
Falkirk, Battle of (1298), 5, 25, 57, 91, 95, 101, 114, 121, 154, 160, 194
Farndon (Hampshire), 125
Fauconberg, Sir Walter, 66–68, 124
Faughart, Battle of (Dundalk, 1318), 109
Ferour, Master Walter le, 57
Fiennes, Sir William, constable of Roxburgh Castle, 20, 24, 45, 51, 62
Fieschi, Luca, cardinal, 197
Fife, Duncan, earl of (d.1353), 200, 201
Fimmer, Richard de, merchant, 77
Fitz Gilbert, Sir Walter, 30, 166–167, 199–200
Fitzpayne, Sir Robert, 31
Fitzwilliam, Ralph, keeper of Berwick, 20, 22, 24, 83, 125
Flanders, Count Robert of, 78
*Flores Historiarum*, English chronicle, 119
Fordun, John of, Scottish chronicler, 63, 103, 161, 213 n9
Francis, William, 64, 65
Friendship, noble, 144

*Gàidhealtachd* (Gaelic-speaking Scotland), 3, 9, 76, 105, 108–109, 136, 157
Gaveston, Piers, earl of Cornwall (d.1312), 10, 12, 24, 29, 31, 32, 41, 67, 71, 74, 85, 92, 119, 124, 191–192
Giffard, Sir John, 129
Gillies Hill, 146, 147
Glasgow, 30
Glencarnie, Sir Gilbert, 190
Gloucester, Gilbert de Clare, earl of (d.1314), 29, 31, 32, 41, 59, 73, 117, 119–120, 124, 136, 139, 140, 154–155, 163, 165, 166, 174
Goldyngham, Juliana de, spy, 194
Gordon, Sir Adam, 22–24
Graham, Sir David, 76
Graham, Sir John, 124
Graham, Patrick, 76
Gray, Sir Andrew, 199
Gray, Sir Richard, 127
Gray, Sir Thomas (d.c.1344), 128, 139, 140, 149
Gray, Sir Thomas (d.1369), English chronicler, author of the *Scalacronica*, 21, 34, 43, 50, 51, 62, 64–65, 98, 102, 110, 135, 138, 139–140, 148, 149–150, 153, 158, 171, 219 n14
Great Yarmouth, 81
Gretham, William de, prior of Coldingham, 111
Grey, John, 192
Guerrilla warfare, 10–12, 24, 30, 31, 32–33, 33–40, 74, 84–85, 202
Guisborough, Walter of, English chronicler, 53, 140–141

Hadleigh (Suffolk),
Håkon V, King of Norway (r.1299–1319), 13, 43

Halbert's Bog, 114
Haliburton, Walter, 110, 237 n75
Halidon Hill, Battle of (1333), 98, 110
Halton, John de, bishop of Carlisle, 170
Haltwhistle (Northumberland), 85
Hamilton (Cadzow), 167
Harclay, Sir Andrew, sheriff of Carlisle (d.1323), 141, 169–170, 179
Hartlepool, 45, 78, 86
Harwedon, Robert de, clerk, 91
Hastings, Sir Edmund, (d.1314), 199
Hay, Sir Gilbert of Errol (d.1333):
   replaced as lord constable (1312), 43
   attends assembly at Dundee (November 1313), 14
   present at Bannockburn? (June 1314), 107–108
   joins diplomatic mission to England (September 1314), 107, 183
   appointed hereditary constable of Scotland (November 1314), 193, 199
Hereford, earl of, Humphrey de Bohun (d.1322), 10, 29, 41, 73, 117, 118–120, 127, 136, 140, 154, 155, 160, 163, 166–167, 171, 184, 185
Hermitage Castle (Liddesdale)
Herries, Sir William, 21
Hexham, 86
Holland, Sir Robert, 193–194

Inchaffray Abbey (Perthshire), 46, 107
Inverkeithing, Battle of (1317), 111
Inverurie, Battle of (1308), 11
Ireland, 30, 70, 71–73, 103, 109, 117–118, 121–122, 186
Isabella of France, Queen of England (r.1308–27), 10, 70, 92, 118, 119, 168, 191
Islay, Donald of, 76

Jean II, King of France (r.1350–1364), 151
Joan 'of Acre', countess of Hertford and Gloucester, 43, 161
Joan of Bar, countess of Surrey, 41
John XXII, Pope (1316–1334), *see* Papacy

Keith, Sir Robert, lord marischal (d.1343/4):
  attends assembly at Dundee (November 1313), 14
  pre-Bannockburn career, 104–105
  leads 'improvised' Scottish cavalry division at Bannockburn (June 1314), 156
  joins diplomatic mission to England (September 1314), 107, 183
  rewarded for his service to King Robert, 199, 200
Kellaw, Richard, bishop of Durham (d.1316), 86, 116, 221 n28
Kendale, Jordan de, 21
Kildrum (Lanarkshire), 30
Kildrummy Castle (Mar), 9, 187–188, 190
King's Langley (Hertfordshire), 80
King's Park (Stirling), 135
King's Stanley (Gloucestershire), 129
Kingston, Sir Nicholas, 195–196
Kingston-upon-Hull, 77, 78
Kininmund, John of, bishop of Brechin, 14
Kirkintilloch Castle, 30
Kirkoswald (Cumbria), 179
Kirkpatrick, Sir Roger, 21, 107, 183
Kirkstead (Lincolnshire), 66, 90

Lamberton, William, bishop of St Andrews (d.1328), 8, 14, 29, 49, 218 n18, 219 n35
Lanark, 128

Lancaster, Thomas, earl of (d.1322), 12, 29, 41, 42, 67, 117, 129, 147, 169, 176, 191–192, 194
Landale, Sir John, 22
*Lanercost Chronicle*, 32, 33, 50, 64, 80, 85, 87, 89, 92, 93, 124, 135, 139, 141, 153–154, 156–157, 160, 166, 169, 175, 178–179, 181, 219 n14
Larkedaunce, Robert de, 21
Lebaud, Piers, 62
Ledhouse, Simon, 50, 51–52
Lennox, Malcolm earl of (d.1333), 14, 108
Leslie, Sir Norman, 109
Letham, Sir Edward, 22
Lincoln, 90
Lindsay, Sir Alexander (d.1309) of Barnweill, Crawford and the Byres, 190 Linlithgow, 30, 62, 225 n105
Lindsay, Alexander, 189
Lindsay, Sir David of Barnweill, 189–190
Lindsay, Reginald, 189
Loch Doon Castle, 187
Lochmaben Castle (Annandale), 21
London, 84
Long Bennington (Lincolnshire), 172
Loudoun Hill, Battle of (1307), 10, 74, 218 n21
Lovel, Sir Richard, 174
Lucy, Sir Anthony, 118, 120, 166
Lyle, Sir Ranulph, 109

Macdonald, Angus Óg, of Islay (d.1314x18), 105, 107
Macdougall, Alexander of Argyll, 29
Macdougall, John of Argyll (d.c.1316), 9, 29, 75–76, 82, 120, 121–122, 127, 131, 184
Macdowell, Dougal, 169–170, 231 n120
Macduff, Isabella, Countess of Buchan, 9
Macnakild, John, 76

MacRuairi, Christina 'of the Isles', 108–109
MacRuairi, Lachlan (d.c.1307), 109
MacRuairi, Ruairi, *rí Innse Gall?* (d.1318?), 108–109
MacRuairi, Ruairi (Christina's son), 109
Man, Isle of, 13, 31, 70, 75, 184
Mar, Donald earl of (d.1332), 171–172, 185, 186, 187
Mar, Gartnait earl of (d.c.1302), 186
Mar, Isabella of (King Robert's first wife, d.c.1296), 42, 171, 186
Margaret, Maid of Norway (d.1290), 3–4, 16
Mauleverer, John, 176
Mauley, Sir Edmund (d.1314), 95, 158
Maurice, abbot of Inchaffray, 46, 111, 151
Melrose, 31, 111
  abbey/abbot, 94, 95
Menteith, Sir John, of Arran and Knapdale (d.c.1323), 14, 108
Menzies, Sir Alexander, 14
Methven, Battle of (1306), 9, 74, 105, 107, 108, 110, 129, 131, 187
Middleton, Sir Gilbert de, 23, 24, 177
Milton Bog, 114
Montague, Sir William, keeper of Berwick, 195
Monthermer, Sir Ralph, 43, 161, 168
Moravia, David de, bishop of Moray (d.1326), 14
Morham, Sir Thomas, 189
Morpeth (Northumberland), 178
Mountforth, Sir Piers, 138, 242 n18
Mowbray, Sir Alexander, 42, 106
Mowbray, Sir Geoffrey, 76
Mowbray, Sir John, 43, 127
Mowbray, Sir Philip (d.1318/20?), 30, 76, 98, 106, 135, 139, 161, 165
Mowbray, Sir Roger (d.1320), 42, 76, 149

Multon, Thomas de, 85
Murray, Sir Andrew (d.1297), 5, 110
Murray, Sir Andrew (d.1338), 110, 187, 189–190, 201
Muschamp, Sir Mornus de, 110
Muster orders, 40–42, 56–57, 71–74, 78, 90–91, 93–94, 116–117

Neville's Cross, Battle of (1346), 95
New Park (Stirling), 114, 132, 135–139, 140, 142, 146, 147, 148, 149, 152, 154, 157
Newbigging, John de, 124–125
Newcastle-upon-Tyne, 45, 73, 95, 96, 128, 169, 171, 176–177
Newminster (Northumberland), 71, 115, 117, 180, 181
Norfolk, Thomas of Brotherton, earl of (1300–1338), 41, 69–70, 117
Northburgh, Roger, keeper English privy seal, 158
Northwell, William de, clerk, 77
Nottingham, sheriff of, 42

Ordainers/Ordinances, 12, 29, 32, 59, 68
Osgodby, Adam, keeper of the English Great Seal, 118, 120

Papacy, 7
  Clement V (1305–1314), 8, 11, 26
  John XXII (1316–1334), 72
parliament (English)
  general, 32
  September 1314 (York), 175–176, 180, 183–184
  April 1315 (Westminster), 96
parliament/assemblies (Scottish)
  general, 15, 19
  council October 1308 (Auldearn), 19, 105–106

March 1309 (St Andrews), 11, 19, 29, 190
council October 1313 (Dundee), 14–20, 188, 198
war council June 1314 (New Park?), 150
November 1314 (Cambuskenneth), 18, 19, 101, 104, 105, 106, 107, 108, 109, 110, 111, 130, 190, 197–202
April 1315 (Ayr), 15, 104, 188, 252 n18
December 1318 (Scone), 15–16, 111
July 1326 (Cambuskenneth), 16
Pass of Brander, Battle of (1308/9), 11, 76
Pelstream, 144, 135, 147, 148, 152, 153, 161, 162
Pelstream Burn, 115
Pencaitland, Sir Thomas of, 23, 24
Penrith (Cumbria), 96, 179
Percy, Sir Henry (d.1314), 5, 12
Percy, Sir Henry 'Hotspur' (d.1403), 69
Perriers, Sir James de, 175
Perth, 13, 32, 37–38, 43, 70, 109, 128, 199
Pessagno, Antonio, Genoese merchant and financier, 54, 68
Peterborough, 83
Philippe IV, King of France (r.1285–1314), 6, 10, 11, 26, 190, 191
Piracy, 77–78
Poitiers, Battle of (1356), 151
Prisoners, English, 165–167, 171, 172, 175, 189–191
Prudhoe, 85

'Ragman' rolls (1296), 106, 109, 193
Ramsey (Cambridgeshire), 83, 189
Randolph, John, earl of Moray, lord of Annandale and Man (d.1346), 201
Randolph, Thomas, earl of Moray, lord of Annandale and Man (d.1333):
generous patronage from King Robert, 11, 44, 63, 103, 106
captured at Methven (1306), 23
attends assembly at Dundee (November 1313), 14
possible reaction to King Robert's ill-health, 47
captures Edinburgh Castle (March 1314), 38, 62–66
leading role at Bannockburn (June 1314), 102–103, 153, 155, 178
forfeited lands regranted by Edward II (June 1314), 124
drives off English cavalry on 23$^{rd}$ June, 140–142
raids northern England? (August 1314), 177–180
makes truce with community at Durham (October 1314), 194–195
raids northern England (1319), 17
Barbour's critical approval of, 63, 142–146
Relics, 46, 82–83, 92–93, 94–95, 123, 130, 131–132
Renfrew, 30
Reynolds, Walter, archbishop of Canterbury (d.1327), 20, 22, 93, 129
Richmond (North Yorkshire), 178–179
Richmond, John of Brittany, earl of, 29
Robert I, King of Scots (r.1306–1329):
multi-lingual upbringing, 3
claim to the kingship, 4
receives earldom of Carrick (1292), 4
opposes English alongside Bishop Wishart and the Steward (1297), 5 joint guardianship of Scotland (1298–1300), 5–6
'defects' into English allegiance (1302–6), 6–7
kills John Comyn (February 1306), 8, 120, 128, 176, 182, 183, 186, 217–218 n16

inauguration (March 1306), 8–9 'exile' (1306–7), 9–10
tackles domestic opposition to his authority (1307–1309), 10–11
illness, 11, 17–18, 47, 52, 64, 138
diplomatic correspondence with Edward II (1310), 30–31
holds assembly at Dundee (October 1313), 14–20, 188, 198
'ultimatum' to his domestic opponents, 18–20
visits Ayr (December 1313), 28
visits Scotlandwell (February 1314), 46–47
response to the deal made with Stirling garrison (May 1314), 99–100
kills Sir Henry de Bohun, 136–139
address(es) to the troops at Bannockburn (June 1314), 151–152
leads reserve into battle, 157–158
treatment of English prisoners, 166
diplomatic activities after Bannockburn, 182–184, 191, 194–195
Forfeits domestic opponents in parliament (November 1314), 197–202
expresses intention to be buried at Dunferminline Abbey (November 1314), 130
rebukes papal legates (1317), 196–197
makes final peace deal with England (1328), 197
itinerant kingship, 84–85
literary culture at court, 34–35
raiding strategy, 85–89, 179–180
supported by Scottish clergy, 7–8, 110–111
Roger, son of Finlay, 28
Ros, Sir Robert de, 53
Rose Castle, 89

Ross, Hugh, earl of (d.1333), 105
Ross, Isabella, 44
Ross, John, 105
Ross, Thomas, 106
Ross, Walter, 105, 106
Ross, William, earl of (d.1323), 11, 19, 44, 105–106, 149
Rothesay Castle, 104
Roxburgh Castle, 20, 24, 30, 38, 45–46, 47, 49–52, 53, 61, 62, 63, 66, 74, 95, 96, 98, 103, 118, 196
Roxburgh, William of, burgess, 195
Rybille, Isolde de, widow of John, 118

Saints,
St Aidan, 94
St Alban, 80, 82–83
St Albans (Hertfordshire), 80–81, 92
St Andrew, 151
St Andrews (Fife), 11, 19, 29
St Bede (the Venerable Bede), 92
St Bride's Kirk (Lanarkshire), 144
St Columba, 123
St Cuthbert, 94–95
St Fillan, 46, 131–132
St John the Baptist, 82, 98, 151
St John of Beverley, 92–93
St Margaret (Queen of Scots 1069/70-1093), 65, 129–131
St Ninians (Stirlingshire), 140
St Serf, 47
St Thomas Becket, 47, 48–49, 151–152, 168–169
Salkeld (Cumbria), 179
Sanser, Thomas, 76
*Scalacronica*, chronicle, *see* Gray, Sir Thomas (d.1369)
Scalby, Thomas de, merchant, 78
Scarborough (North Yorkshire), 77, 78

'Schiltrons', Scottish spear formations, 114–115, 140–141, 154, 155–156, 238 n93, 242 n32
*Scotichronicon, see* Bower, Walter,
Scotlandwell (Kinross-shire), 46
Scottish army:
  size, 100–101
  make-up, 101–112
  experience and discipline of leaders, 102
  preparations, 112–115
  attitude on evening of 23rd June, 149
  losses, 164–165
Seagrave, Sir John, 128, 166, 189
Seger, John le, pirate, 77–78
Selkirk, 30
Seton, Sir Alexander, 107, 110, 121, 129, 149–150
Seton, Sir Christopher (d.1306), 187
Seton, John of, 28
Sinclair, Sir Henry, 14, 110
Sinclair, John of Herdmanston, 110
Sinclair, William, bishop of Dunkeld, 111
Sixhills (Lincolnshire), 171, 187
Skinburness (Cumbria), 79, 82
Slengesby, Richard de, merchant, 77
'Small folk', 157–158
Sneton, Richard de, merchant, 78
Somerville, Sir Thomas, 22
'Soules conspiracy' (1320), 200–201
Soules, Sir John, 174, 178
Soules, Muriella, 174
Soules, Sir William, lord of Liddesdale (d.1322?), 22, 178
Soutra (Scottish Borders), 129
Stainmore, 179
Stapledon, Walter, bishop of Exeter (d.1326), 125–126
Stapleton, Sir Miles, 66–68, 124, 192

Stewart, Sir Alexander of Bonkyl (d.1319), 22, 95
Stewart, Sir James (Steward) (d.1309), 5, 104
Stewart, Sir John of Kyle (Robert III, King of Scotland, r.1390–1406), 15
Stewart, Robert (King Robert's grandson) (Steward), Robert II, King of Scotland (r.1371–90), 35, 144, 145, 189, 201–202
Stewart, Robert, earl of Fife and Menteith, duke of Albany (d.1420), 145
Stewart, Sir Walter (Steward) (King Robert's future son-in-law, d.1327), 17, 104, 110, 151, 188–189, 252 n18
Stirling, 31, 128, 132, 148, 196
Stirling Bridge, Battle of (1297), 5, 128, 151, 160
Stirling Castle
  falls to the English (1304), 7, 112, 128, 140
  isolated after fall of Edinburgh (March 1314), 66
  deal between the garrison and the Scots, 69, 76–77, 90, 97–100, 115, 122, 126
  attempt to reach the castle on 23rd June? 139
  English soldiers flee to the castle, 159
  Edward II refused entry, 161
  slighted by the Scots, 164
  fate of the garrison, 165
Strathbogie, David, earl of Atholl (d.1326):
  attends assembly at Dundee (November 1313), 14
  makes contact with English royal administration (January 1314), 42–45, 116, 129

frustration with Bruce settlement in the Highlands, 44–45, 105
possible feud with Gilbert Hay, 108
attacks Scottish supply camp (23rd June), 149, 192
rewarded for shifting allegiance, 175, 192–193
Strathbogie, David, earl of Atholl (d.1335), 187–188, 193
Strathbogie, Isabella, 44, 149
Strathearn, Malise, earl of (d.c.1325), 108
Supplies, 54, 55–56, 58–59, 60, 68, 76, 77, 78–79, 81

Tickhill, Nicholas of, 58
Thirsk (North Yorkshire), 93
Threave Castle, 145
Tong, Andrew of, clerk, 193
Torskey (Lincolnshire), 91
Torthorwald, Sir Thomas de, 21
Torwood, 112, 114, 115, 116, 123, 130, 132, 135, 155
Tournaments, 42, 56
Treason, 125
Trivet, Nicholas, English chronicler, 168, 243 n109
Trokelowe, John of (d.c.1330), English chronicler, 115
Turnberry Castle (Ayrshire), 6, 104
Tweng, Sir Marmaduke, 66–68, 124, 128, 160–161
Tyndrum, Battle of (1306, 'Dalrigh'), 9, 76, 105, 107, 131

Ulster, Richard de Burgh, earl of (d.1326), 6, 71–72, 117–118, 121–122
Umfraville, family, 85, 120, 172
Umfraville, Sir Ingram, 29, 120, 129, 154, 166, 172–174, 200, 201
Umfraville, Robert, earl of Angus (d.1325), 120, 129, 166

Valence, Aymer de, earl of Pembroke (d.1324), 9, 10, 29, 41, 71, 74–75, 87, 93, 99, 127, 160, 176, 180, 182, 247 n122
Valence, Joan de, 182
Vaux, William de, 120–121, 129
Veer, Dionisia de, wife of Hugh, 93
Verneuil, Battle of (1424), 98
Vescy, Isabella de, 71, 226 n97
Vescy, William de (d.1314), 71
Vipont, Sir William, 106
*Vita Edwardi Secundi*, English chronicle, 30, 32, 33, 50, 58, 62, 103, 112, 127, 135, 137, 138, 142, 148, 153, 155, 158, 160, 162, 165, 171, 184

Wales, 70, 73, 116, 119, 137, 160
Wallace, Duncan of Auchincruive, 110
Wallace, Sir William (d.1305), 5, 49, 95, 101, 108, 110, 115, 128
Wallingford, Alan of, sergeant-at-arms, 189
Walsingham, Thomas (d.c.1422), English chronicler, 82, 162, 165, 166
Walwayn, John, clerk and possible author of the *Vita*, 184, 217 n24
Wark-on-Tweed, 53–54, 126
Warenne, John de, earl of Surrey, 29, 32, 41, 42, 151
Watton (Norfolk), 188
Westminster, 14, 20, 22–23, 24, 40, 69, 84, 122
Weston, John of, English chamberlain of Scotland, 24, 182, 195
Whitby, 78
Windsor Castle, 42
Wishart, Robert (d.1316), bishop of Glasgow, 5, 8, 171, 185–186
Wyntoun, Andrew of, prior of Loch Leven, chronicler (d.c.1422), 202

York, 93, 169, 170, 171, 174, 175, 176, 180, 194, 195